APPLIED NETWORKING LABS

A HANDS-ON GUIDE TO NETWORKING
AND SERVER MANAGEMENT

First Edition

RANDALL BOYLE Ph.D.

University of Utah

Prentice Hall

Boston   Columbus   Indianapolis   New York   San Francisco   Upper Saddle River

Amsterdam   Cape Town   Dubai   London   Madrid   Milan   Munich   Paris   Montreal   Toronto

Delhi   Mexico City   Sao Paulo   Sydney   Hong Kong   Seoul   Singapore   Taipei   Tokyo

Editorial Director: Sally Yagan
Editor in Chief: Eric Svendsen
Executive Editor: Bob Horan
Editorial Project Manager: Kelly Loftus
Director of Marketing: Patrice Lumumba Jones
Senior Marketing Manager: Anne Fahlgren
Marketing Assistant: Melinda Jensen
Senior Managing Editor: Judy Leale
Project Manager: Debbie Ryan

Senior Operations Supervisor: Arnold Vila
Operations Specialist: Ilene Kahn
Senior Art Director: Jayne Conte
Cover Designer: Suzanne Behnke
Manager, Cover Visual Research & Permissions:
  Hessa Albader
Cover Art: cybrain / Shutterstock Images
Printer/Binder: Edwards Brothers Malloy
Cover Printer: Edwards Brothers Malloy

Credits and acknowledgments borrowed from other sources and reproduced, with permission, in this textbook appear on appropriate page within text.

Microsoft® and Windows® are registered trademarks of the Microsoft Corporation in the U.S.A. and other countries. Screen shots and icons reprinted with permission from the Microsoft Corporation. This book is not sponsored or endorsed by or affiliated with the Microsoft Corporation.

Library of Congress Cataloging-in-Publication Data
Boyle, Randall.
  Applied networking labs : a hands-on guide to networking and server management / Randall Boyle. -- 1st ed.
    p. cm.
  Includes bibliographical references and index.
  ISBN 0-13-231034-1 (alk. paper)
  1. Computer networks--Management. 2. Web servers--Management. I. Title.
  TK5105.5.B72 2010
  004.6--dc22

                                        2010023323

Prentice Hall
is an imprint of

www.pearsonhighered.com

10 9 8 7 6 5

ISBN 10: 0-13-231034-1
ISBN 13: 978-0-13-231034-5

ABOUT THE AUTHOR

 Dr. Randall Boyle received his Ph.D. in Management Information Systems from Florida State University. His research areas include deception detection in computer-mediated environments, the effects of IT on cognitive biases, the effects of IT on knowledge workers, and e-commerce. He has published in journals such as *Journal of Management Information Systems*, *International Journal of E-Collaboration*, and *Journal of International Technology and Information Management*. He is the author of *Applied Information Security*.

Dr. Boyle has received the college teaching award at the University of Alabama in Huntsville, the Marvin J. Ashton Excellence in Teaching Award, and the Excellence in Education Award at the University of Utah. He has taught a variety of classes including Information Security, Network Defense, Telecommunications, Systems Analysis and Design, Decision Support Systems, Web Servers, and Introductory MIS courses. Dr. Boyle is currently a professor in the Operations and Information Systems department in the David Eccles School of Business, at the University of Utah.

DEDICATION

Courtney, thank you for your support and encouragement.

Jim and DeAnn, thank you for teaching me the value of hard work.

Contents

ABOUT THE AUTHOR..III
Dedication IV

INTRODUCTION VIII
Description VIII
Intended Audience..VIII
For the Instructor IX

GETTING STARTED X
Taking Screenshots X
Free Windows-based Software X
Software, Supplements, and Updates XI
Remote Class Machines...XI
Software Installation and Un-installation XI
Compressed (Zip) files XII

CHAPTER 1: DOS COMMANDS 1
1.1   DOS Basics..1
1.2   IPconfig 5
1.3   Ping 8
1.4   Tracert & Pathping 10
1.5   Netstat 12
1.6   Nslookup 15
1.7   Arp 16
1.8   Net 17
1.9   FTP 21
1.10 Create A Batch File 26
1.11 Windows PowerShell...29

CHAPTER 2: WINDOWS UTILITIES 37
2.1   Windows Task Manager 37
2.2   Windows Remote Desktop 39
2.3   MSINFO32 43
2.4   BGInfo...45
2.5   Perfmon 46
2.6   Windows Event Viewer 49
2.7   Process Explorer 51
2.8   Process Monitor 53
2.9   Text Editor (Notepad) 57
2.10 Backup & Recovery..61
2.11 Hardware Driver Updates 64
2.12 MSConfig 66
2.13 IExpress 68

CHAPTER 3: WEB TOOLS 73
3.1   Bandwidth Speed Test 73
3.2   Visual Trace Route 75
3.3   WHOIS Lookup...77
3.4   Using A Web Proxy 78
3.5   Web Hosting Statistics..80

3.6   ONLINE VIRUS SCAN 82
3.7   EMAIL TRACE 84

CHAPTER 4: VIRTUALIZATION 86

4.1   VMWARE PLAYER 87
4.2   VMWARE MARKETPLACE 91
4.3   SUN VIRTUALBOX 94
4.4   MICROSOFT VIRTUAL PC & XP MODE 99
4.5   MICROSOFT SERVER 2003 AND SERVER 2008 109
4.6   COMPUTER ON A USB 114
4.7   PORTABLE APPLICATIONS 117
4.8   BOOTABLE USB 121

CHAPTER 5: PACKET ANALYSIS 127

5.1   WIRESHARK INSTALLATION 127
5.2   CAPTURE TRAFFIC 129
5.3   PACKET INSPECTION 134
5.4   CONTENTS OF A PACKET (CAPTURE AN EMAIL) 140
5.5   PACKET FILTERING (DISPLAY FILTER) 142
5.6   PACKET ANALYSIS AND REPORTING 145

CHAPTER 6: NETWORK DESIGN 148

6.1   IP ADDRESSING 148
6.2   NETWORK MEDIA 152
6.3   SIMPLE LAN DESIGN (OPNET) 154
6.4   NETWORK EXPANSION AND TESTING 162
6.5   CONFIGURATION SCENARIO 165
6.6   CABLING SCENARIOS 171
6.7   SWITCH, ROUTER, HUB SCENARIOS 173

CHAPTER 7: WIRELESS 180

7.1   INSSIDER 180
7.2   EKAHAU HEATMAPPER 182
7.3   WIGLE.NET 184

CHAPTER 8: INTERNET INFORMATION SERVER (IIS) 187

8.1   INTERNET INFORMATION SERVER (IIS) INSTALLATION 187
8.2   BASIC HTML TUTORIAL 191
8.3   CREATE SITE AND HOST PAGES 202
8.4   MULTIPLE WEB SITES AND HOSTS FILE 207
8.5   AUTHENTICATION, DIRECTORY BROWSING, & LIMITS 214

CHAPTER 9: APACHE 218

9.1   INSTALLATION AND SETUP 218
9.2   APACHE COMMAND-LINE & BENCHMARKING 221
9.3   CONFIGURATION FILE (HTTPD.CONF) 229
9.4   HOST MULTIPLE WEB SITES (VIRTUAL HOSTS) 235

CHAPTER 10: WINDOWS SERVER 2008 241

10.1   SERVER MANANGER 241
10.2   ACTIVE DIRECTORY 247
10.3   GROUP POLICIES 252
10.4   SECURITY POLICIES AND AUDITING 256
10.5   FTP SERVER 259

CHAPTER 11: LINUX 263

11.1 INSTALLATION (FEDORA) 263
11.2 COMMAND-LINE PRIMER 272
11.3 SOFTWARE (UBUNTU) 280
11.4 NET-TOOLS AND NETWORKING COMMANDS 285
11.5 SYSTEM TOOLS AND CONFIGURATION 292
11.6 USER AND GROUP MANAGEMENT 298

CHAPTER 12: CAREERS IN NETWORKING 304

12.1 OCCUPATIONAL STATISTICS 304
12.2 IT CERTIFICATIONS 307
12.3 JOB SEARCH 309

APPENDIX 311

A.1 LINKS TO SOFTWARE 311

INTRODUCTION

DESCRIPTION

Applied Networking Labs guides students through the installation and basic operation of software used in the field of Networking. The primary audience is upper-division BS majors in Information Systems, Computer Science, and Computer Information Systems. This book is also intended for graduate students in MSIS, MBA, MACC, or other MS programs that are seeking a broader knowledge of Networking. This book can also be used in executive training programs or by anyone interested in learning the practical side of Networking.

Networking and Telecommunications are a core part of the information systems landscape. All students seeking a degree in Information Systems will take a Networking course. This book gives them hands-on experience with some of the tools they may have heard about. A book covering the breadth of Networking software presented in this book has not been produced before.

INTENDED AUDIENCE

This book was written for students with limited computer experience. Typically, students have already taken an introductory course about information systems or computer science. College-aged juniors enrolled in a Networking or Telecommunication class will use this book along with a traditional Networking textbook like one of the following:

Panko's *Business Data Networks and Telecommunications*
Stallings' *Business Data Communications*
Goldman & Rawles' *Applied Data Communications: A Business-Oriented Approach*
White's *Data Communications and Computer Networks: A Business User's Approach*
Fitzgerald and Dennis's *Business Data Communications and Networking*
Peterson and Davie's *Computer Networks: A Systems Approach*

Below is a table mapping chapters from *Applied Networking Labs* to chapters from these popular networking textbooks. This table allows instructors and students to see which projects correlate to content being presented in class. This book gives students real-world experience using actual software that may not be presented in a traditional textbook. Both practical and theoretical books are necessary to adequately train a student to be able to add value to an organization.

Applied Networking Labs		Panko	Stallings	Goldman & Rawles	White	Fitzgerald & Dennis	Peterson & Davie
Ch. 1	DOS Commands	2, 8, 10	4, 5, 8	2, 7, 8	1, 6, 11	2, 5, 10	1, 4
Ch. 2	Windows Utilities	8, 9, 10	5, 8, 18	7, 9, 11, 12	1, 13	5, 13	
Ch. 3	Web Tools	1, 2, 10	1, 5, 18	4, 8	1, 10, 11	2, 5, 8, 10	1, 3, 4
Ch. 4	Virtualization		3		9	8	
Ch. 5	Packet Analysis	1, 2, 8	5, 8	2, 6, 7, 8	10, 11, 14	1, 2, 4, 5, 10, 13	1, 2, 4, 5
Ch. 6	Network Design	1, 3, 4, 10	3, 4, 8, 9, 10, 21	3, 4, 6, 10	1, 7, 8, 10, 12, 14	2, 3, 6, 8, 9, 12	1, 2, 6
Ch. 7	Wireless	1, 5, 9, 10	11	3, 4	3, 9	3, 7, 10	2, 8

Applied Networking Labs		Panko	Stallings	Goldman & Rawles	White	Fitzgerald & Dennis	Peterson & Davie
Ch. 8	IIS	8, 9, 11	6, 7	2, 12	11	2, 11	9
Ch. 9	Apache	11	6, 7		9, 11	2	1, 6, 9
Ch. 10	Windows Server 2008	9, 10, 11	6, 7, 18, 19, 20	9, 11, 12	11, 13	2, 11, 13	8, 9
Ch. 11	Linux	1, 8, 10, 11	6, 8, 20	9, 11	9, 11	5, 12	4
Ch. 12	Careers in Networking						

FOR THE INSTRUCTOR

Applied Networking Labs reduces the amount of preparation an instructor has to do because it provides him/her with approximately 80 homework assignments ready to give to their students. These projects have been tested in both undergraduate and graduate classes across several semesters. Many students say that doing hands-on projects are the best part of the class.

Students learn how to use the tools they will need when they start working in the real world. Subsequently, they get more excited about the class. Throughout this book, students learn to use software in a building-block fashion that introduces them to progressively more complicated projects. Later chapters refer to skills learned in earlier chapters.

One of the main criticisms of Networking courses is that they are "too theoretical." Students hear "Networking" and they think it's going to be a really fun class. Sometimes, however, they are disappointed when they are presented with a class that deals exclusively with theoretical concepts. A healthy dose of real-world projects that support in-class lectures can change a student's attitude right away.

Each project contains instructions to take a screenshot by pressing Alt-PrtScn or Ctrl-PrtScn at specific points in the project to show that students have completed the project. These screenshots are then pasted into a document and emailed to the instructor. Grading an entire semester of projects can be done in a few minutes. Screenshots will be unique due to who is taking it and when it is taken. For example, a student will likely have a unique IP address, a unique file name, or a timestamp when they complete each project. Any sharing or cheating will be obvious.

Using this book in addition to a regular Networking textbook will greatly reduce the time and effort required to prepare a course. It will also get students excited about the course and give them hands-on experience using real-world tools.

GETTING STARTED

It takes a lot of time and effort to understand the fundamentals of Networking and servers. It requires an in-depth understanding of telecommunications, media, signaling, databases, operating systems, IT hardware, and some programming. You also need plenty of curiosity, a strong desire to learn, and the ability to learn on your own. There isn't a single person on the planet that knows everything about Networking. You don't need to know everything. It just takes time and hard work to become skilled in a few areas.

HANDS-ON EXPERIENCE

This book was designed to give you experience using a broad array of Networking and server tools. It will help give you an idea of the type of tools networking experts might use on a daily basis. It will also equip you with a repertoire of useful tools that you could use on your first job. Too many students graduate with a degree in IS from well-know colleges and only know what they were taught—theory. This book will introduce you to a broad array of practical tools and how to use them.

There is a lot more to learn about each tool presented in this book. Entire books could be written about the tools you will use. Please feel free to take time to become more familiar with each tool. This book will only introduce each tool and show you the basic functionality. You won't become an expert by completing these projects.

TAKING SCREENSHOTS

To show that you have completed your projects you will be required to take screenshots of your work. You will take a screenshot at the end of each project to show you successfully completed the project. You will then paste these screenshots into a document. You will be required to enter your name or another unique identifier to show that you were the one that completed the project.

Screenshots can be taken by pressing Alt-PrtScn for the current window or Ctrl-PrtScn for the entire desktop. You can also get freeware like MWSnap® (http://www.mirekw.com) or Screenshot Pilot (http://www.colorpilot.com/screenshot.html) that come with additional screen capturing functionality. Windows 7 comes with a Snipping tool that can be used to manually select the screenshot area.

If you need a word-processing program, you can download a free copy of the OpenOffice® suite (http://www.openoffice.org/). You will then turn in your project screenshots to your instructor. Instructors can choose the quantity and variety of projects to assign depending on their specific program of study.

FREE WINDOWS-BASED SOFTWARE

The software in this book is free and will run on any computer with Windows 7 or Windows XP® SP3. If you have the Windows Vista® operating system, some of these programs may not work. This is not intended to be a comprehensive manual for all IT Networking software. There are a lot of other great pieces of software that were not included due to space limitations. Online help manuals for each piece of software in this book are available at the links listed throughout the book.

This manual focuses on helping beginners have a good first experience with a wide breadth of Networking software. This book will focus mostly on Microsoft and open-source software. Most large organizations use a combination of the two. More experienced users may find the introductory projects presented in this book simplistic. The projects are intended to give the beginning user a survey of the field, not advanced training.

SOFTWARE, SUPPLEMENTS, AND UPDATES

The software you are going to use in this book will be available for download on the Internet, or will be available on WebCT®/Blackboard® if your teacher chooses to upload them. If one of the links listed doesn't appear to be working, please check Google or WebCT/Blackboard for a current link. Almost all of the programs in this book can be found by searching Google.

All of the programs in this manual were tested on a Windows 7 computer. Most of them are also compatible with Windows XP but may require modified instructions to complete the project requirements. If your computer starts running slowly when you are using one of the virtual machines you may need to add more RAM to your computer.

The Web site for this book will contain a current listing of links to each of the pieces of software and a few files necessary to complete a couple of the projects. The Web site can be found at http://www.pearsonhighered.com/boyle.

We recommend you make a folder labeled "**networking**" on your C: drive to store all the software that you will download. Creating this folder will make software organization and operation easier. This book is written with the understanding that you did create a networking folder on your C: drive. All of the programs in this manual will match the directions in the book if you create the **C:\networking** folder on your C: drive.

You will also need a 4GB (or larger) USB drive to complete a couple of the projects. Updates to the projects and errata can be found at http://www.pearsonhighered.com/boyle. Links and software will change.

REMOTE CLASS MACHINES

If you do not want to load the software listed in this book on your own computer, your instructor can set up a standard Windows 7 or Windows XP SP3 box for you to use remotely as a test machine. You can use Remote Desktop® (part of Windows) to remote into the test machine and run the projects. Hopefully your network administrator already has several remote machines set up for your class to use. Instructions on how to use Remote Desktop are shown in a later project.

Having a safe environment where you, as a student, can test software is nice because you don't have to worry about causing problems on your own machine. You will also have fewer installation issues, downloading problems, and compatibility conflicts. Overall, it will save your instructor countless hours answering emails if he/she sets up a remote test machine.

SOFTWARE INSTALLATION AND UN-INSTALLATION

Some of the programs you will install/run will require administrator privileges. Most users are administrators on their own computers. If you are not, you'll have to ask the owner of the computer to make you an administrator account. It's probably easier for you to use a remote machine set up by your instructor.

Once you have completed a project please feel free to uninstall or delete the software. Most of the software can be automatically uninstalled. You can also go to Control Panel, Add/Remove Software, and then select the software you want to uninstall.

COMPRESSED (ZIP) FILES

Many of the files you will open, and subsequently install, will be compressed (zipped). Windows 7/XP comes with a standard zip/unzip application. There are a variety of compression programs including WinZip® (http://www.winzip.com/index.htm), 7-Zip® (http://www.7-zip.org/), WinRAR® (http://www.rarlab.com/), etc. We recommend 7-Zip or the built in Windows zip program. Both will be used in this book.

CHAPTER 1: DOS COMMANDS

Below are a few DOS commands that are widely used by networking professionals on a daily basis. Although DOS commands may seem archaic to those that grew up on Windows, many useful programs still use a command-line interface. Learning command-line will become easier with practice. Knowing how to use a command prompt will make the transition from Windows to Linux much easier.

These projects cover just a few of the commands available. A larger list is available by typing "help" at the DOS prompt. One of the main advantages of using DOS commands is that they will work on all current versions of Windows in a command prompt. A network administrator can run DOS commands on any Windows machine without installing additional software. This will save him/her time and money.

All versions of Windows will have a command prompt where you can run DOS commands. Windows 7 includes PowerShell which has extended capabilities including being able to run many Linux/Unix/Mac commands. To pull up a command prompt you can go through the start menu by clicking Start, All Programs, Accessories, Command Prompt. Alternatively, you can click Start, Run and then type cmd.

For this book we will use CMD.exe because it is included in both Windows XP and Windows 7. When Windows 7 becomes more widely adopted users will be able to take advantage of the additional functionality in PowerShell. A short PowerShell primer is included at the end of this chapter.

1.1   DOS BASICS

This project will cover a few basic DOS commands. For later projects in this book you will need to create directories (folders), move between directories, create files, edit files, move/copy/delete files, etc. You are going to run through a couple of quick commands that you might already know. For beginning users these may be entirely new. Repetition is the key to knowing when and how to use these commands.

The dir command gives you a listing of the files, programs, and subdirectories in the current directory. Directories (called folders in Windows) are shown with a <DIR> before the name of the directory. Files and programs (executables) are shown with their file size. For example, notice in the screenshots below that Adobe is a directory and Fport.exe is a program. You can also see the identical listing of directories, programs, and files in both DOS and Windows Explorer (See Figure 1-1 and Figure 1-2.).

1. Click Start and Run.
2. Type **cmd**
3. Press Enter. (This will open a command prompt.)
4. Type **dir**
5. Press Enter. (This will show a listing of the files and directories.)
6. Type **time**
7. Press Enter twice. (This will display the current time and provide a time stamp for your project.)
8. Take a screenshot. (See Figure 1-1.)

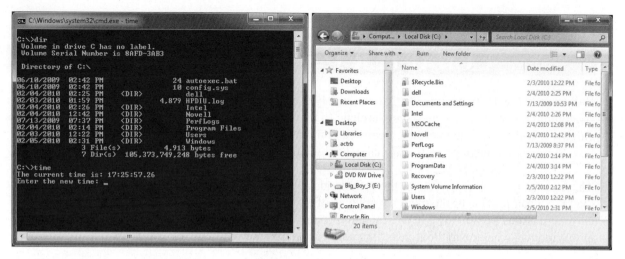

Figure 1-1: Contents of C:\ in a DOS prompt.   Figure 1-2: Contents of C:\ in Windows Explorer.

9. Type **dir /?**
10. Press Enter. (This will show the help listing for the **dir** command.)
11. Type **dir /w**
12. Press Enter. (This will show a listing of the directories and files with no other information.)
13. Type **dir /ad**
14. Press Enter. (This will show a listing of just directories. See Figure 1-3.)
15. Type **time**
16. Press Enter twice. (This will add a time stamp.)
17. Take a screenshot.

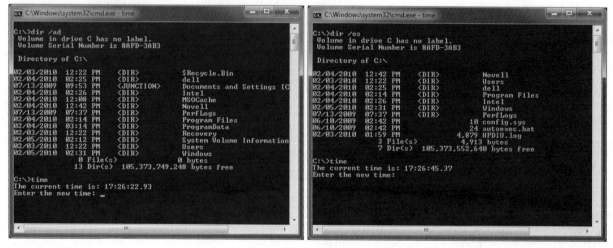

Figure 1-3: Output from the dir /ad command.   Figure 1-4: Output from the dir /os command.

18. Type **dir /oe**
19. Press Enter. (This will sort by file type.)
20. Type **dir /o-s**
21. Press Enter. (This will sort by file size largest first.)
22. Type **dir /os**
23. Press Enter. (This will sort by file size smallest first. See Figure 1-4.)
24. Type **time**
25. Press Enter twice. (This will add a time stamp.)
26. Take a screenshot.

27. Type **help**
28. Press Enter. (This will get a listing of DOS commands.)
29. Type **help time**
30. Press Enter. (To see the help for the **time** command.)
31. Type **time**
32. Press Enter twice. (This will add a time stamp.)
33. Take a screenshot. (See Figure 1-5.)

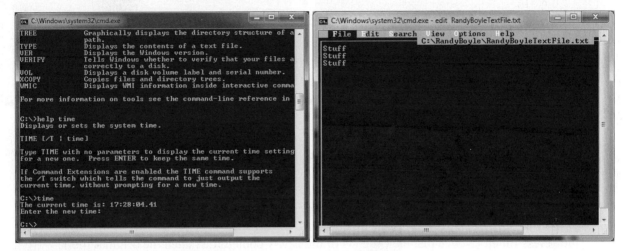

Figure 1-5: Output from the help command.   Figure 1-6: Editing a text file.

34. Type **cls**
35. Press Enter. (This will clear the screen.)

In the next command you will replace YourName with your first name and last name. In the screenshots it will show RandyBoyle (the author's name). Many examples throughout this book will use the YourName example; any time you see YourName please type your first and last name as a combined word.

36. Type **mkdir YourName**
37. Press Enter. (This will create a directory (folder) labeled YourName.)
38. Type **cd YourName**
39. Press Enter. (This will change to the newly created directory which should be C:\YourName\.)
40. Type **dir**
41. Press Enter.
42. Type **edit YourNameTextFile.txt**
43. Press Enter. (This will create a new text file and open it for editing.)
44. Type the word "Stuff" and press Enter three times.
45. Take a screenshot. (See Figure 1-6.)
46. Press Alt-F-S.
47. Press Alt-F-X.
48. Type **dir**
49. Press Enter. (The newly created file YourNameTextFile.txt should be showing.)
50. Take a screenshot. (See Figure 1-7.)

Figure 1-7: Output after creating a text file.

Figure 1-8: Copying and deleting a text file.

51. Type **copy YourNameTextFile.txt YourNameCopy.txt**
52. Press Enter. (This will create a copy of the text file.)
53. Type **dir**
54. Press Enter. (This will confirm that the copy was successful.)
55. Type **type YourNameCopy.txt**
56. Press Enter. (Notice that the contents of the newly copied file match the original file.)
57. Type **del YourNameCopy.txt**
58. Press Enter. (This will delete the copy.)
59. Type **dir**
60. Press Enter. (This will confirm the deletion.)
61. Take a screenshot. (See Figure 1-8.)

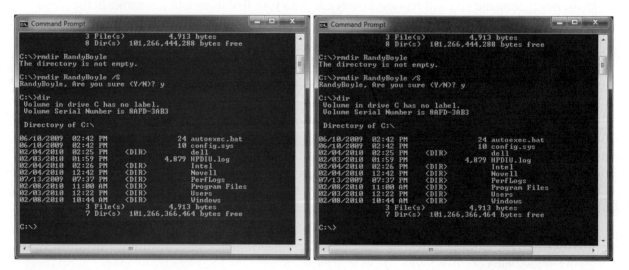

Figure 1-9: Deleting a directory.

Figure 1-10: Selecting a previously used command.

62. Type **cd ..**
63. Press Enter. (This will move back one level to C:\.)
64. Type **dir**
65. Press Enter. (This will confirm you are at C:\.)
66. Type **rmdir YourName**
67. Press Enter. (This will try to delete the directory labeled YourName but fail to do so.)

68. Type **rmdir YourName /S**
69. Press Enter. (This will force the deletion of the directory labeled YourName.)
70. Type **Y**
71. Press Enter.
72. Type **dir**
73. Take a screenshot. (See Figure 1-9.)
74. Press F7. (You can also keep pressing the up arrow key.)
75. Arrow up until you get to the command labeled **mkdir YourName**
76. Take a screenshot. (See Figure 1-10.)
77. Press Enter.

THOUGHT QUESTIONS

1. Can you use the DIR command to show only executables? How?
2. What happens if you start typing part of an existing file name and then press the Tab key?
3. Can you start programs from the command prompt? How?
4. What happens if you drag-and-drop a file from Windows Explorer onto the DOS window?

1.2 IPCONFIG

This command will give you a listing of your basic IP information for the computer you are using. You will get your IP address, subnet mask, and default gateway (the computer that connects you to the Internet). You will use your IP address for scanning, remote administration, penetration testing, etc. Ipconfig will also allow you to manage your DNS resolver cache and renew your IP address with the DHCP server. You will learn more about DNS and DHCP in later exercises.

1. Click Start and Run.
2. Type **cmd**
3. Press Enter.
4. Type **ipconfig**
5. Press Enter. (This will display basic network configuration information for adapters on your computer. See Figure 1-11.)
6. Type **ipconfig /all**
7. Press Enter. (This will display extended network configuration information for all adapters on your computer.)
8. Take a screenshot. (You can press Alt-PrtScn for the current window or Ctrl-PrtScn for the entire computer screen. See Figure 1-12.)

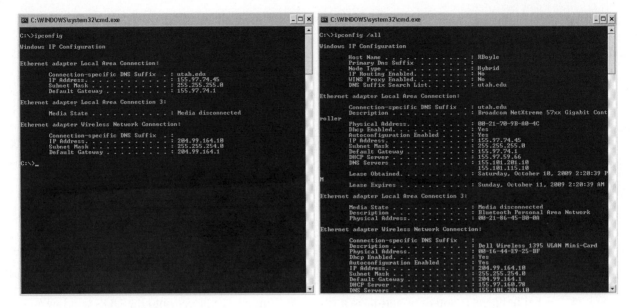

Figure 1-11: Output from the ipconfig command.   Figure 1-12: Output from the ipconfig /all command.

In the second command you used the /all option to get more information about each adapter. Note that this computer has three ways of connecting to different networks. There is a regular NIC to connect to the LAN, a wireless card, and a Bluetooth adapter. You now know the following about this LAN card:

The IP address for this computer is: **155.97.75.45**

The MAC address for this computer is: **00-21-70-9B-A0-4C**

The computer that connects to the Internet (Default Gateway) is: **155.97.74.1**

9. Type **ipconfig /flushdns**
10. Press Enter. (This will flush all DNS entries.)
11. Type **ping www.google.com**
12. Press Enter.
13. Type **ipconfig /displaydns**
14. Press Enter. (See Figure 1-13.)
15. Scroll down until you see the entry for www.Google.com.
16. Take a screenshot. (See Figure 1-14.)

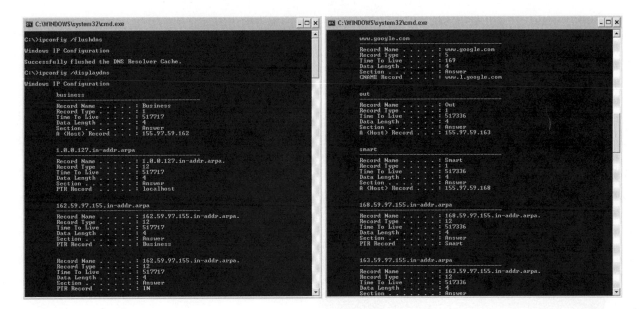

Figure 1-13: Output from the displaydns command.

Figure 1-14: Output showing the entry for www.Google.com.

17. Type **ipconfig /all**
18. Press Enter.
19. Take a screenshot. (See Figure 1-15.)
20. Type **ipconfig /renew**
21. Press Enter. (This will renew all network adapters on your computer.)
22. Take a screenshot. (See Figure 1-16.)

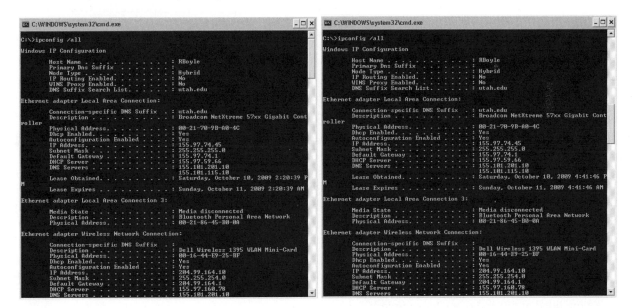

Figure 1-15: Showing lease time before renewal.

Figure 1-16: Showing lease time after renewal.

The DHCP server loaned you an IP address for a given amount of time. (In this case it was one day.) By renewing your IP address you can reserve this same IP address for a longer amount of time. The information provided by the ipconfig command will come in handy when you do the rest of the projects. If you want a listing of all the possible options available for a given DOS command (ipconfig) you can just type the name of the command followed by a question mark.

23. Type `ipconfig /?`
24. Type `time`
25. Press Enter twice.
26. Take a screenshot. (See Figure 1-17.)

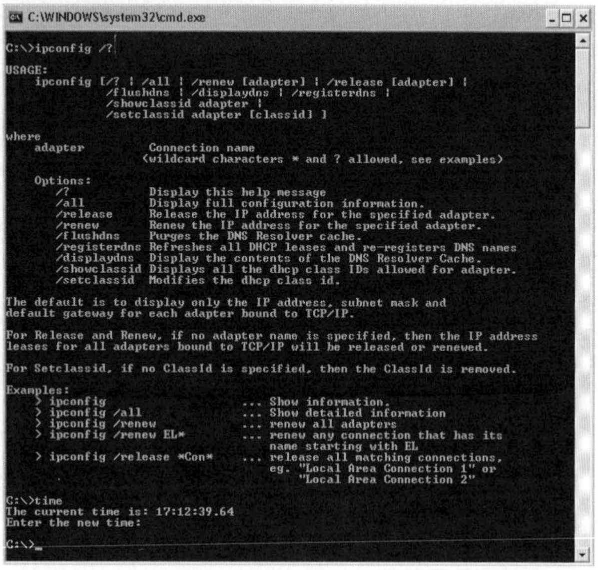

Figure 1-17: Displaying help for ipconfig.

THOUGHT QUESTIONS

1. What is the practical difference between an IP address and a physical (MAC) address?
2. What is the Default Gateway?
3. What do DNS servers do?
4. What is a subnet mask?

1.3 PING

Ping is a command that will tell you if a host is reachable and alive. It works just like pings in submarines (think back to the movie *The Hunt for Red October*). It sends out a packet that asks the target computer to send it back a message saying it's actually there. It also tells you how long it took to get back and if any of the packets were lost. This is very useful if you need to see if a server/computer is running. You can also diagnose latency and/or packet loss issues.

This example pings www.utah.edu repeatedly. Feel free to ping your own university or Web site of your choice. Instead of using "www.utah.edu" please use "www.YourUniversity.edu." Timestamps will also be included at the end of each example.

1. Click Start and Run.
2. Type `cmd`
3. Press Enter.
4. Type `ping www.utah.edu`
5. Press Enter. (This will ping www.utah.edu with four packets.)
6. Type `time`
7. Press Enter twice.

8. Take a screenshot. (See Figure 1-18.)

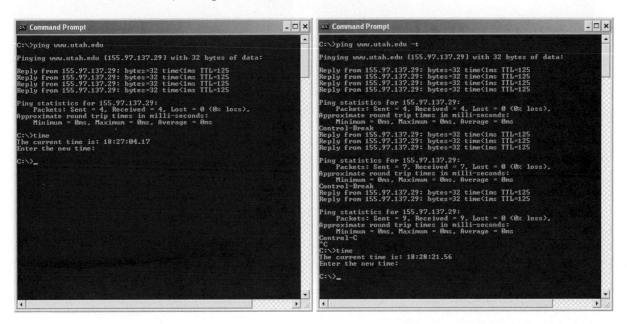

Figure 1-18: Output from ping command.   Figure 1-19: Output from ping -t command.

9. Type **ping www.utah.edu -t**
10. Press Enter.
11. Press Ctrl-Break after about 5 replies.
12. Press Ctrl-Break again after about 5 replies.
13. Press Ctrl-C to stop sending packets.
14. Type **time**
15. Press Enter twice.
16. Take a screenshot. (See Figure 1-19.)
17. Type **cls**
18. Press Enter. (This clears the screen.)
19. Type **ping www.utah.edu –n 6**
20. Press Enter.
21. Type **ping www.utah.edu –l 50**
22. Press Enter.
23. Type **time**
24. Press Enter twice.
25. Take a screenshot. (See Figure 1-20.)

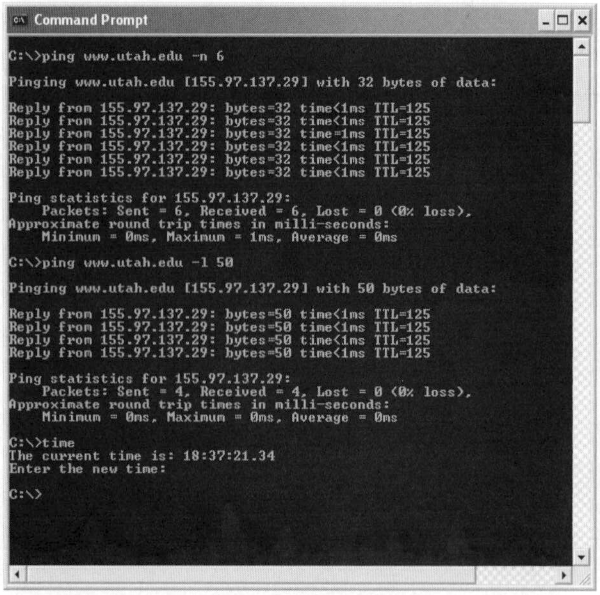

Figure 1-20: Output from ping -n command.

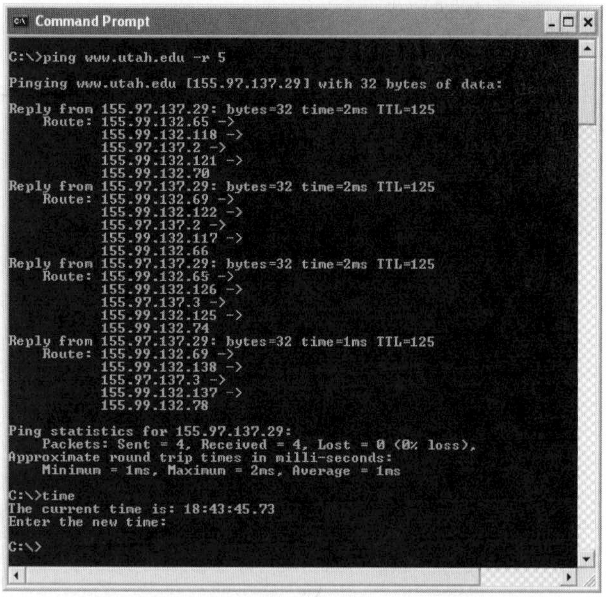

Figure 1-21: Output from ping -r command.

26. Type **cls**
27. Press Enter.
28. Type **ping www.utah.edu −r 5**
29. Press Enter.
30. Type **time**
31. Press Enter twice.
32. Take a screenshot. (See Figure 1-21.)

THOUGHT QUESTIONS

1. Can you adjust the number of packets that are sent? How?
2. What did the -t, -n, -l, -r options do?
3. Why would you experience packet loss?
4. Why would you want to send larger packets?

1.4   TRACERT & PATHPING

Trace route (tracert in Windows and traceroute in Linux) is a command that allows you to see every computer (including routers) between your computer and a target host of your choosing. You can type in the name of the computer (e.g. www.utah.edu) or the IP address of the computer (155.97.137.29). Tracert can be used to diagnose routing problems, latency issues, or network bottlenecks. Pathping combines the statistics from ping and the route tracing function from tracert.

Tracert can also provide you with information about the route packets are taking over a network. It can be surprising how many hops there are between you and a Web site that you visit. Oftentimes the route a packet takes is not the shortest geographical distance. This example uses www.utah.edu repeatedly. Feel free to use the hostname of your own university or any other Web site. Instead of using "www.utah.edu" please use "www.YourUniversity.edu."

1. Click Start and Run.

2. Type **cmd**
3. Press Enter.
4. Type **tracert www.utah.edu**
5. Press Enter. (This will list every computer on the route between your computer and www.utah.edu.)
6. Type **tracert www.google.com**
7. Press Enter. (This will list every computer on the route between your computer and www.Google.com.)
8. Type **time**
9. Press Enter twice.
10. Take a screenshot. (See Figure 1-22.)

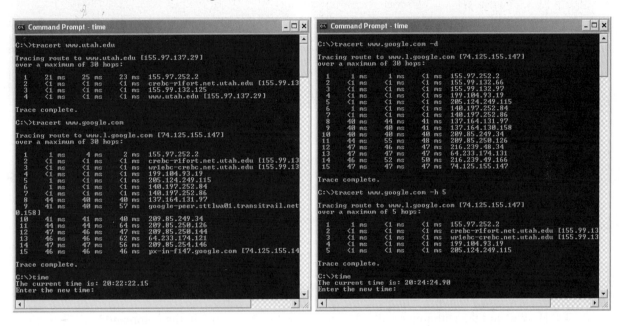

Figure 1-22: Output from tracert command.   Figure 1-23: Output from tracert -d and tracert -h commands.

11. Type **tracert www.google.com -d**
12. Press Enter.
13. Type **tracert www.google.com -h 5**
14. Press Enter.
15. Type **time**
16. Press Enter twice.
17. Take a screenshot. (See Figure 1-23.)
18. Type **pathping www.utah.edu -q 5 -w 5**
19. Press Enter.
20. Type **time**
21. Press Enter twice.
22. Take a screenshot. (See Figure 1-24.)
23. Type **pathping www.google.com -q 5 -w 5**
24. Press Enter.
25. Type **time**
26. Press Enter twice.
27. Take a screenshot. (See Figure 1-25.)

Figure 1-24: Output from pathping -q -w command.

Figure 1-25: Output from pathping -q -w command to Google.com.

At the time the route was traced there were 14 computers or routers between this host and www.Google.com. None of the nodes along the way timed out and most of the packets took less than 50 ms to come back.

THOUGHT QUESTIONS

1. Why would you use the -d option?
2. If you had several nodes "time out" how would the -w option help?
3. Why would a network administrator only want to see part of the route?
4. How would the pathping results change if you didn't use -q 5 in the command?

1.5 NETSTAT

Netstat is the command that lists all current network connections, connection statistics, and routing tables on your computer. The default netstat command will give you a listing of all of the ports open on your computer as well as the foreign address of the computer you're connected to.

Ports are like doors on your house. Information packets are addressed to a specific IP address (location) and port number (point of entry). Your house works the same way. It has an address (location) and door (point of entry) where packages are delivered. Netstat can tell you which programs are sending/receiving information to/from your computer.

1. Click Start and Run.
2. Type **cmd**
3. Press Enter.
4. Type **netstat**
5. Press Enter.
6. Type **time**
7. Press Enter twice.
8. Take a screenshot. (See Figure 1-26.)

Figure 1-26: Output from netstat command.   Figure 1-27: Output from netstat -b command.

In this example you can see multiple ports open with the www.umail.utah.edu:https server (Microsoft Outlook is open). The only problem is you don't know which program is opening all of those ports. You can use the -b option to get information about which program is opening each port.

The -a option will show all of the ports (including UDP ports) that may be open on your machine. The -n option will show the local and foreign addresses for each connection. The -e option will display statistics about the number of packets sent/received, errors, and packets that were discarded.

9. Type **cls**
10. Press Enter.
11. Type **netstat -b**
12. Press Enter.
13. Take a screenshot. (See Figure 1-27.)
14. Type **netstat -a**
15. Press Enter.
16. Take a screenshot. (See Figure 1-28.)

Now you know that Outlook.exe is opening a lot of ports to send/receive email. Using the -b option you can find out if a rogue program is opening a port. This is useful when you want to identify programs that are sending/receiving information. You don't want rogue programs sending/receiving information.

17. Type **cls**
18. Press Enter.
19. Type **netstat -n**
20. Press Enter.
21. Take a screenshot.
22. Type **netstat -e**
23. Press Enter.
24. Take a screenshot. (See Figure 1-29.)

Using the -n option you can see which external computers are connected to your computer and which port(s) they are using. Knowing which foreign address your computer is connecting to can be helpful if you want to be sure where your data is going to or coming from. The -e option is a quick way to tell if you are sending/receiving packets and if you are getting a large number of errors. This will help you identify a bad network card, cable, or configuration issue.

Figure 1-28: Output from netstat -a command.　　　　Figure 1-29: Output from netstat -n and netstat -e commands.

25. Type **cls**
26. Press Enter.
27. Type **netstat -e 5**
28. Press Enter.
29. Let it run for about 15 seconds.
30. Press Ctrl-C to stop sending packets.
31. Type **time**
32. Press Enter twice.
33. Take a screenshot. (See Figure 1-30.)
34. Type **netstat -s**
35. Press Enter.
36. Take a screenshot. (See Figure 1-31.)

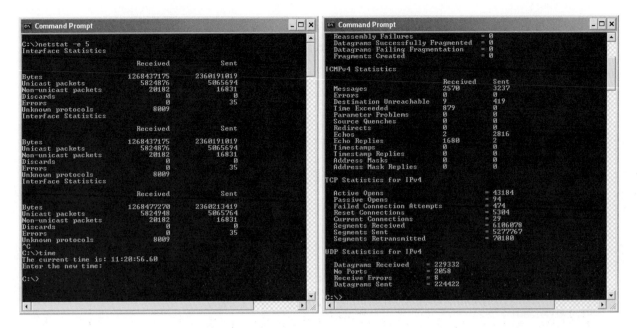

Figure 1-30: Output from netstat -e command.   Figure 1-31: Output from netstat -s command.

THOUGHT QUESTIONS

1. How can netstat help you track the information coming in and out of your computer?
2. How can netstat help you diagnose network problems?
3. How would the routing table (`netstat -r`) be useful?
4. Why would someone need different statistics for IP, IPv6, ICMP, TCP, UDP, etc.?

1.6   NSLOOKUP

Nslookup is a command that will give you all of the IP addresses that are associated with a given domain name from the local DNS server (it's like an Internet phone book). For example, if you wanted to find the IP addresses of www.CNN.com you could use nslookup to identify them. Nslookup is also useful for solving DNS problems.

There are two modes when you use nslookup (non-interactive and interactive). You will use the non-interactive mode for this exercise and can learn more about the interactive mode here: http://support.microsoft.com/kb/200525.

1. Click Start and Run.
2. Type **cmd**
3. Press Enter.
4. Type **nslookup www.utah.edu**
5. Press Enter.
6. Type **nslookup www.cnn.com**
7. Press Enter.
8. Type **nslookup www.google.com**
9. Press Enter.
10. Type **time**
11. Press Enter twice.
12. Take a screenshot. (See Figure 1-32.)

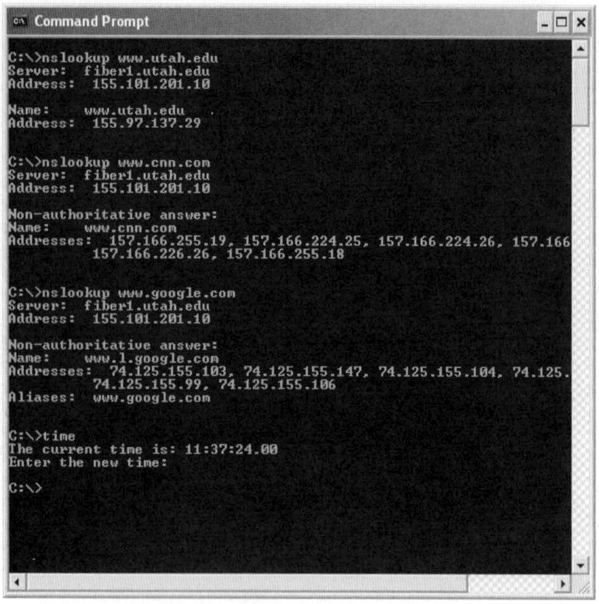

Figure 1-32: Output from nslookup command.

THOUGHT QUESTIONS

1. Why are there multiple IP addresses associated with a single domain name (e.g. www.cnn.com and www.Google.com)?
2. Why did Nslookup query fiber1.utah.edu instead of querying www.cnn.com directly?
3. Why does www.Google.com use an alias?
4. How do domain names and IP addresses get registered?

1.7   ARP

Address Resolution Protocol (ARP) is a protocol used to resolve IP addresses into MAC (Ethernet) addresses. Computers (and routers) use ARP requests to determine the MAC address of the next hop when sending packets from one computer to another. MAC addresses are used to send packets from hop to hop until they reach their final destination.

In this example, you will learn how to display your ARP table and all of the current entries. You will also add a new entry to that table and subsequently delete it. This will give you practice manipulating an ARP table. This is important to know if you are managing a router or a multi-homed host. ARP is also an easy way to check and make sure your IP address is correctly matched with your MAC address.

1. Click Start and Run.
2. Type **cmd**
3. Press Enter.
4. Type **arp -a**
5. Press Enter.
6. Type **time**
7. Press Enter twice.
8. Take a screenshot. (See Figure 1-33.)

Command Prompt - time

```
C:\>arp -a

Interface: 155.97.243.202 --- 0x4
  Internet Address      Physical Address      Type
  155.97.243.193        00-1e-c9-ab-6d-51     dynamic

C:\>time
The current time is: 12:25:58.10
Enter the new time:
```

Command Prompt

```
C:\>arp -a

Interface: 155.97.243.202 --- 0x4
  Internet Address      Physical Address      Type
  155.97.243.193        00-1e-c9-ab-6d-51     dynamic

C:\>time
The current time is: 12:37:01.75
Enter the new time:

C:\>arp -s 127.0.0.2 11-22-33-44-55-66

C:\>arp -a

Interface: 155.97.243.202 --- 0x4
  Internet Address      Physical Address      Type
  127.0.0.2             11-22-33-44-55-66     static
  155.97.243.193        00-1e-c9-ab-6d-51     dynamic

C:\>arp -d 127.0.0.2

C:\>arp -a

Interface: 155.97.243.202 --- 0x4
  Internet Address      Physical Address      Type
  155.97.243.193        00-1e-c9-ab-6d-51     dynamic

C:\>_
```

Figure 1-33: Output from arp -a command.

Figure 1-34: Output from arp -s and arp -d commands.

9. Type **arp –s 127.0.0.2 11-22-33-44-55-66**
10. Press Enter.
11. Type **arp -a**
12. Press Enter.
13. Take a screenshot.
14. Type **arp –d 127.0.0.2**
15. Press Enter.
16. Take a screenshot. (See Figure 1-34.)

THOUGHT QUESTIONS

1. Why do we need both MAC and IP addresses? Aren't IP addresses enough?
2. Where/when is your MAC address assigned?
3. Can you change your MAC address? How?
4. What notation are MAC addresses written in?

1.8   NET

The net command can do a lot of different tasks. You can get a full listing of the commands you can use with the net command by typing `net /?` at the command prompt. The net command can make a network administrator's life much easier by providing a common command set available on all Windows machines. He or she can then use a few common commands to solve a variety of problems.

Below you will use the net command to 1) see which users are on the network, 2) look at the configuration for this computer, 3) create a new user, and 4) create a network share. Please feel free to explore the other things you can do with the net command (i.e. solve printer problems).

For this project we will have to run the DOS prompt as an administrator. In prior projects you didn't need administrator-level permission to execute the commands. In this one you will. If you get an error message saying "access denied" then you probably didn't start the DOS prompt as an administrator.

1. Click Start, All Programs, and Accessories.
2. Right-click Command Prompt
3. Select Run as administrator. (You can skip this step if you are using Windows XP.)

4. Click Yes.
5. Type **net user**
6. Press Enter.
7. Type **net config workstation**
8. Press Enter.
9. Type **time**
10. Press Enter twice.
11. Take a screenshot. (See Figure 1-35.)

Figure 1-35: Output from net command.   Figure 1-36: Net command used to add user.

12. Type **net user /add "YourNameNewUser" "password"**
13. Press Enter. (In this case it was RandyBoyleNewUser.)
14. Type **net user**
15. Press Enter.
16. Take a screenshot. (See Figure 1-36.)
17. Click Start and Control Panel.
18. Click User Accounts and Family Safety and Add or remove user accounts.
19. Take a screenshot showing the newly created account. (See Figure 1-37.)

Note: At this point you can log out of your regular user account and log back in using your new user account to confirm that this is a real account. Return to your regular user account to complete the rest of this project.

20. Return to the DOS command prompt.
21. Type **net user /delete YourNameNewUser**
22. Press Enter. (In this case it was RandyBoyleNewUser.)
23. Type **net user**
24. Press Enter.
25. Take a screenshot. (See Figure 1-38.)

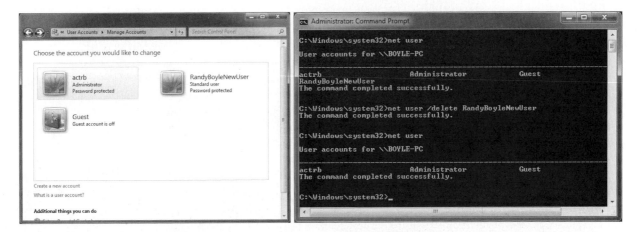

Figure 1-37: New user account created.　　　　　　　Figure 1-38: New user account deleted.

26. Click Start and Run.
27. Type **explorer**
28. Press Enter.
29. Click on Network. (This is labeled "My Network Places" in Windows XP.)
30. Take a screenshot. (See Figure 1-39.)
31. Click Start and Run.
32. Type **cmd**
33. Press Enter.
34. Type **cd ..**
35. Press Enter. (Repeat the **cd ..** command multiple times until you get to C:\. See Figure 1-40.)
36. Type **mkdir YourNameNetworkFolder**

In this case a folder (directory) labeled RandyBoyleNetworkFolder was created on the C: drive. You will replace YourName with *your* first name and last name as a combined word. Do not copy the example exactly as it is written above. The goal is to have a directory showing *your* name.

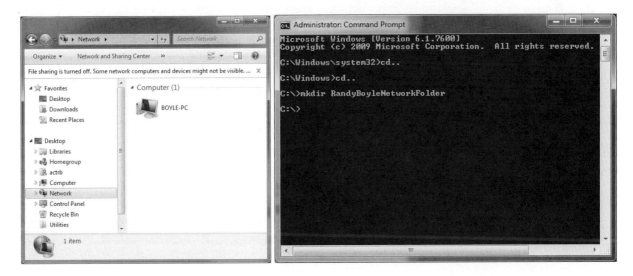

Figure 1-39: Network shares before creation of an additional share.　　　　　　　Figure 1-40: Making the directory that will be shared.

37. Press Enter.

38. Type **net share**

39. Press Enter.
40. Take a screenshot. (See Figure 1-41.)

Figure 1-41: Listing of network shares. Figure 1-42: Listing of network shares.

41. Type **net share YourNameShare=C:/YourNameNetworkFolder**
42. Press Enter. (See Figure 1-42.)
43. Type **net share**
44. Press Enter.
45. Type **time**
46. Press Enter twice.
47. Take a screenshot. (See Figure 1-43.)
48. Go back to Windows Explorer and select Network. (This is labeled "My Network Places" in Windows XP.)
49. Double-click your computer. (In Windows XP click View, Refresh.)
50. Take a screenshot showing your new network share. (See Figure 1-44.)

Figure 1-43: Creation of network share. Figure 1-44: New network share.

51. Type **net share C:/YourNameNetworkFolder /delete**
52. Press Enter.
53. Type **net share**
54. Press Enter.

55. Type **time**
56. Press Enter twice.
57. Take a screenshot. (See Figure 1-45.)
58. Return to the Windows Explorer window.
59. Press F5 to refresh the window.
60. Take a screenshot showing the network share removed. (See Figure 1-46.)

Figure 1-45: Deleting network share.   Figure 1-46: Network share is removed.

THOUGHT QUESTIONS

1. Could a network administrator reset an existing user's password using the `net user` command? How?
2. Why would a network administrator want to set up a network share?
3. What do the `net start` and `net stop` commands do?
4. When would a network administrator want to use the `net view` command?

1.9   FTP

File Transfer Protocol (FTP) is a way to transfer files from one computer to another. While it may be a little more convenient to use a modern FTP client, it's still valuable to learn command-line FTP. Some systems/servers use a command-line interface exclusively. This makes FTP is an important skill to have in your repertoire.

FTP has both interactive and non-interactive modes. You will look at the differences between the two in this exercise. In this project you will download some images from NASA. Some of the file names and/or directories on the NASA FTP server may change over time. You can download any images from any of the directories to complete this project. The important part is to learn how to use command-line FTP.

First, you are going to make a folder on C:\ to store the images. Then you will FTP into the server and practice transferring images to your local machine.

1. Click Start and Run.
2. Type **cmd**
3. Press Enter.

4. Type **cd ..**
5. Press Enter. (Repeat **cd ..** command multiple times until you get to C:\.)
6. Type **mkdir images**
7. Press Enter.
8. Type **time**
9. Press Enter twice.
10. Type **ftp nssdcftp.gsfc.nasa.gov**
11. Press Enter.
12. Type **anonymous**
13. Press Enter.
14. Press Enter again.
15. Type **ls**
16. Press Enter. (See Figure 1-47.)

Note: If you get a popup message about your Windows Firewall you can click Allow Access.

17. Type **cd photo_gallery**
18. Press Enter. (See Figure 1-48.)

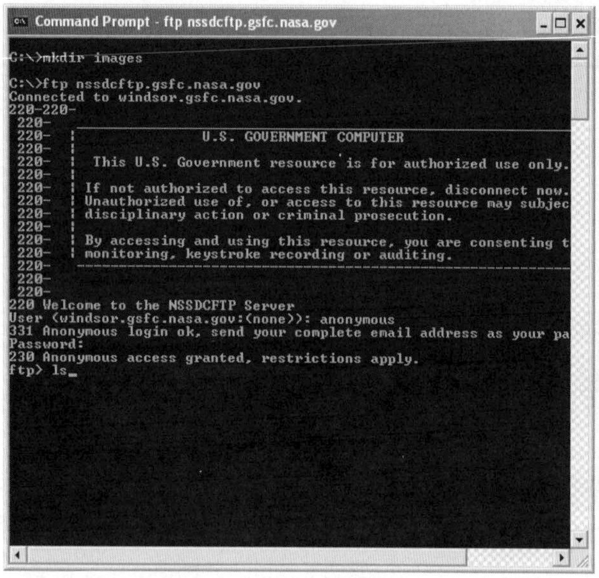

Figure 1-47: Accessing a FTP server.

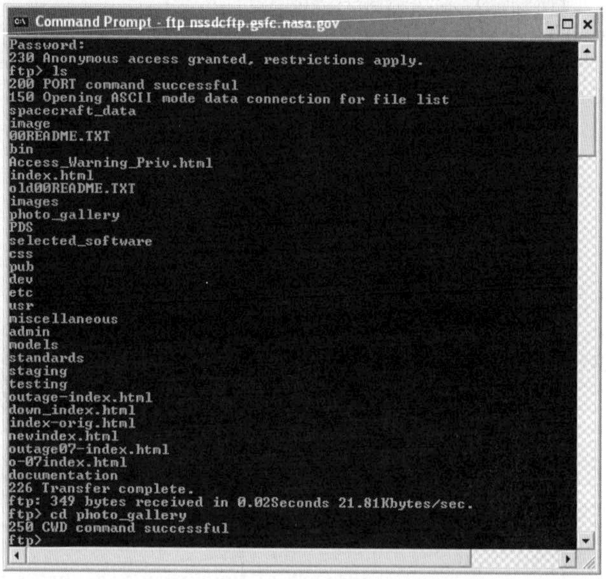

Figure 1-48: Listing directories on FTP server.

19. Type **ls**
20. Press Enter.
21. Type **cd image**
22. Press Enter.
23. Type **ls**
24. Press Enter.
25. Type **cd astro**
26. Press Enter.
27. Type **ls**
28. Press Enter. (See Figure 1-49.)
29. Type **binary**
30. Press Enter.

31. Type **lcd C:\images**
32. Press Enter.
33. Type **get hst_crab_nebula.jpg**
34. Press Enter. (You can get any image you want.)
35. Type **status**
36. Press Enter.
37. Take a screenshot. (See Figure 1-50.)

Figure 1-49: Listing files on FTP server.   Figure 1-50: Transferring file from FTP server.

38. Type **quit**
39. Press Enter.
40. Type **cd images**
41. Press Enter.
42. Type **dir**
43. Press Enter.
44. Type **hst_crab_nebula.jpg**
45. Press Enter. (See Figure 1-51.)
46. Take a screenshot of the Crab Nebula image. (See Figure 1-52.)

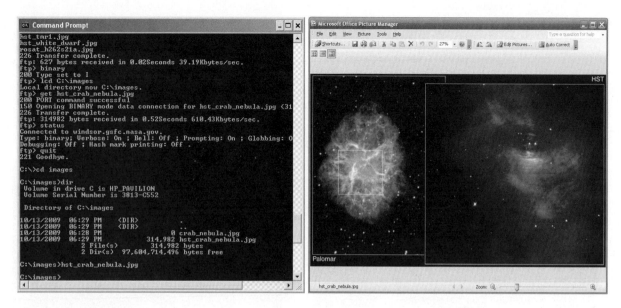

Figure 1-51: Quitting the FTP server. Figure 1-52: Image downloaded from FTP server.

47. Return to the DOS prompt.
48. Type **time**
49. Press Enter twice.
50. Press the up arrow key until you get to the following command:

ftp nssdcftp.gsfc.nasa.gov

51. Press Enter.
52. Type **anonymous**
53. Press Enter.
54. Press Enter again.
55. Take a screenshot.
56. Type **ls**
57. Press Enter.
58. Type **cd photo_gallery/image/astro**
59. Press Enter.
60. Type **ls**
61. Press Enter.
62. Type **binary**
63. Press Enter.
64. Type **prompt**
65. Press Enter. (See Figure 1-53.)
66. Type **mget ***
67. Press Enter.
68. Take a screenshot. (See Figure 1-54.)

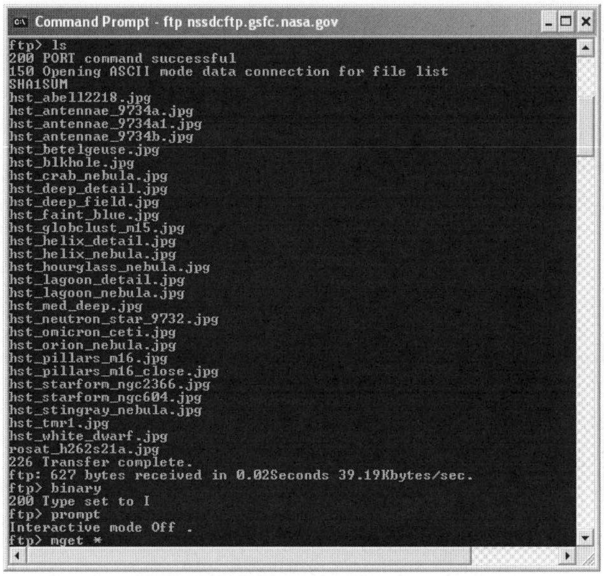

Figure 1-53: Transferring entire directory from FTP server.

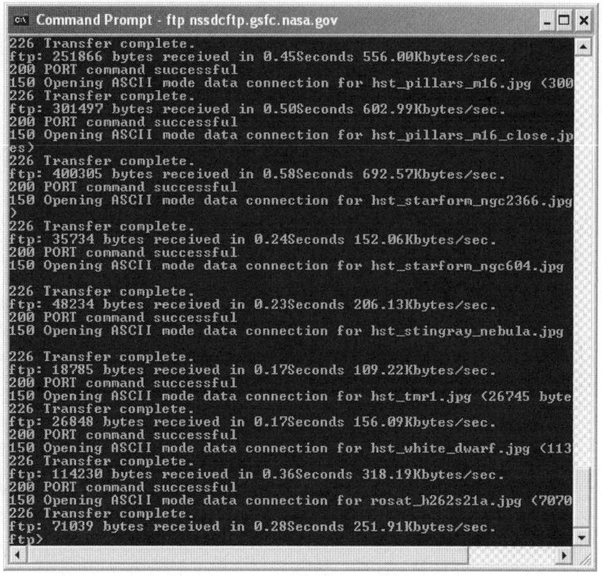

Figure 1-54: Files transferred.

69. Type **prompt**
70. Press Enter.
71. Type **quit**
72. Press Enter.
73. Type **dir**
74. Press Enter.
75. Type **time**
76. Press Enter twice.
77. Take a screenshot. (See Figure 1-55.)
78. Type **hst_pillars_m16.jpg**
79. Press Enter.
80. Take a screenshot. (See Figure 1-56.)

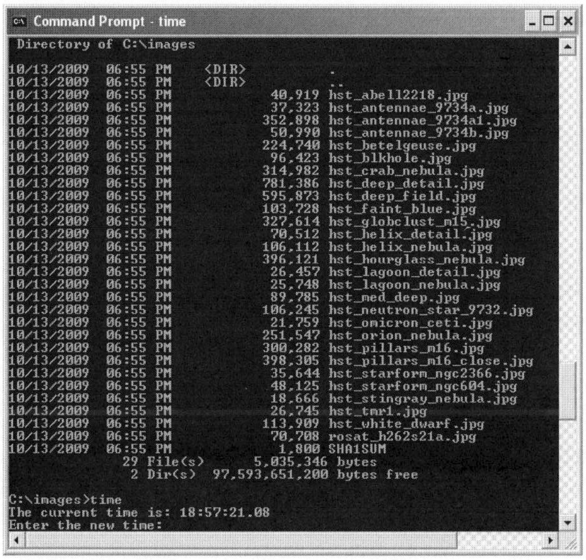

Figure 1-55: Displaying downloaded files on local host.

Figure 1-56: Downloaded image.

1. What would have happened if you had run the `mget *` command in interactive mode (i.e. without entering "prompt" first)?
2. Is transferring files with FTP faster than using HTTP?
3. What effect did the `binary` command have on the file transfer? Was it necessary?
4. Why did you use the `lcd` command?

1.10 CREATE A BATCH FILE

Network administrators create automated scripts in order to simplify and automate daily tasks. These scripts can quickly perform a long list of tasks that must be done every day. Administrators can also schedule these tasks to be run at specified intervals. For example, most people need to back up their data every day, week, or month.

This project will walk you through the creation of a very basic batch file (automated script). This batch file will 1) make a copy of the images you downloaded in the prior exercise, 2) start the card game called Freecell, 3) open Internet Explorer to a specific Web site, and 4) create a desktop shortcut to this batch file.

1. Click Start and Run.
2. Type **cmd**
3. Press Enter.
4. Type **cd ..**
5. Press Enter. (Repeat **cd ..** command multiple times until you get to C:\.)
6. Type **edit YourNameTimeSaver.bat**
7. Press Enter.
8. Type the following text into the window exactly as it is shown while replacing "YourName" with your first name and last name:

```
@echo off

REM YourName

REM This line performs the backup
xcopy "C:\images\*.*" "C:\images\backup\"

REM This line opens Microsoft Remote Desktop
start C:\windows\system32\mstsc.exe

REM This line opens Internet Explorer and goes to www.yahoo.com
start "C:\Program Files\Internet Explorer" iexplore.exe www.yahoo.com
```

9. Press Alt-F-S. (See Figure 1-57.)
10. Press Alt-F-X.
11. Type **copy YourNameTimeSaver.bat C:\images**
12. Press Enter.
13. Type **cd images**
14. Press Enter.
15. Type **dir**
16. Press Enter.

17. Take a screenshot. (See Figure 1-58.)

Figure 1-57: Creating a batch file.

Figure 1-58: Copying the batch file to another directory.

18. Type **YourNameTimeSaver.bat**
19. Press Enter. (You should see Remote Desktop and Internet Explorer open.)
20. Click on the DOS window showing the files copied.
21. Take a screenshot. (See Figure 1-59.)
22. Type **dir**
23. Press Enter. (This will show the new backup directory.)
24. Take a screenshot. (See Figure 1-60.)

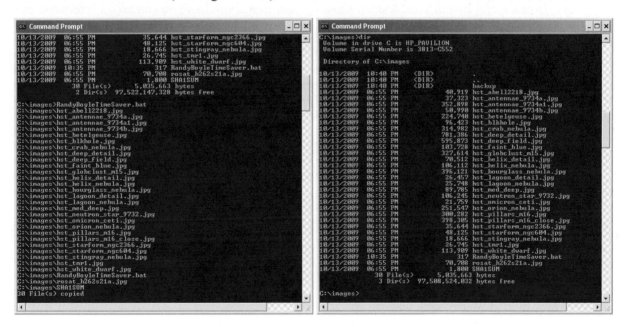

Figure 1-59: Running the batch file.

Figure 1-60: New "backup" directory after batch file was run.

25. Minimize all windows.
26. Right-click on your desktop.
27. Select New and Shortcut.
28. Click Browse.
29. Browse to C:\images\YourNameTimeSaver.bat. (See Figure 1-61.)
30. Click Next and Finish.
31. Right-click the new shortcut.
32. Select Properties.
33. Click Change Icon.

34. Select any icon from the list. (See Figure 1-62.)
35. Click OK and OK.

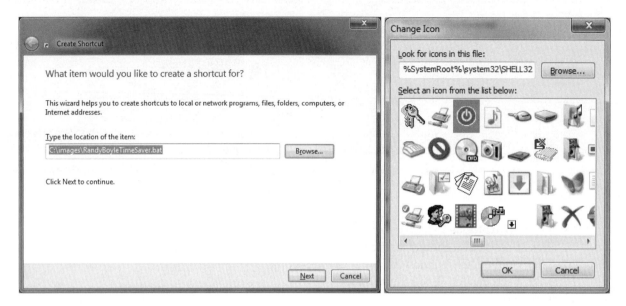

Figure 1-61: Creating a shortcut.   Figure 1-62: Selecting an icon.

36. Take a screenshot of your desktop showing your new shortcut. (You can take a screenshot of your entire desktop by pressing Ctrl+PrtScn. See Figure 1-63.)
37. Double-click the icon to make sure it works.

Figure 1-63: Icon to batch file created.

THOUGHT QUESTIONS

1. What tasks do you think network administrators automate the most? Why?
2. Could batch files be dangerous? How/Why?
3. What does "REM" in the batch file stand for and what does it do?
4. Could you rename this shortcut and change the icon to use the same icon as one of your other shortcuts (i.e. make it look exactly like one of the other shortcuts)? How could you have fun with this?

1.11 WINDOWS POWERSHELL

This project will provide you with a quick introduction to Windows PowerShell. PowerShell is a command-line interface similar to DOS but with expanded functionality. You can use all of the DOS commands (`dir`, `cd`, `ipconfig`, etc.), many Linux/Unix commands (`ls`, `cd`, `ifconfig`, etc.), and new cmdlets (pronounced command-lets). In fact, DOS and Linux/Unix commands are actually aliases for cmdlets. You will see an example of how to do this using just one of over 100+ cmdlets.

One of the key distinctions between DOS and PowerShell is that DOS is text-based whereas PowerShell uses cmdlets as objects. Using cmdlets, you can direct output from one object to another object. You will see how to do this later in this project. Powershell also provides .NET integration and a custom scripting environment. You can create your own custom cmdlets.

Powershell provides extensive help documentation via the Get-Help cmdlet. You will learn how to use the help pages (similar to man pages in Linux/Unix) to perform a variety of tasks. You will see that there is a lot to learn about PowerShell. This is a primer into the most basic functionality available through PowerShell.

STOP: If you are using Windows XP you will need to download and install PowerShell before you can start this project. Instructions on how to download and install PowerShell are given at the end of this project. After installing PowerShell you can proceed. If you have Windows 7 you don't have to install anything.

1. Click Start, All Programs, Accessories, Windows PowerShell, and Windows PowerShell. (You can also press ⊞+r and enter "powershell.")
2. Type **cd C:\images**
3. Press Enter. (This will take you to the C:\images\ directory you created earlier in the FTP project. If you don't have a directory labeled "images" you can create one and put a copy of any text file in the directory.)
4. Type **del *.jpg**
5. Press Enter. (This will delete all of the .JPG images and leave the batch file.)
6. Type **dir**
7. Press Enter. (This will list all of the files and subdirectories. This is a Windows/DOS command listed as an alias. You should see a backup directory and a batch file with your name on it. You created these in an earlier project. See Figure 1-64.)
8. Type **ls**
9. Press Enter. (This will list all of the files and subdirectories. This is a Linux/Unix command listed as an alias for the Get-ChildItem cmdlet.)
10. Type **gci**
11. Press Enter. (This will list all of the files and subdirectories. This is a PowerShell alias for the Get-ChildItem cmdlet.)
12. Type **Get-ChildItem**
13. Press Enter. (This will list all of the files and subdirectories.)
14. Type **get-childitem**
15. Press Enter. (Note that cmdlets are NOT case-sensitive.)
16. Take a screenshot. (See Figure 1-65.)

Figure 1-64: Directory listing in PowerShell.   Figure 1-65: Aliases for Get-ChildItem.

Note: In PowerShell the commands `dir`, `ls` and `gci` are all aliases for the Get-ChildItem cmdlet. They all returned the same results. Next, you will see all the aliases for the `dir` command and create your own alias. This alias will last until you end the current PowerShell session. You can make your new alias permanent. However, you won't be shown how to do that in this tutorial.

17. Type **Get-Alias dir**
18. Press Enter. (This will show that the dir command is an alias for the Get-ChildItem cmdlet.)
19. Type **Get-Alias –definition Get-ChildItem**
20. Press Enter. (This will get all of the aliases for the Get-ChildItem cmdlet.)
21. Type **Set-Alias YourNameList Get-ChildItem**
22. Press Enter. (This will create a custom alias called "YourNameList" for the Get-ChildItem cmdlet. This alias will only last until you close the PowerShell window. In this case the alias was RandyBoyleList. See Figure 1-66.)
23. Type **YourNameList**
24. Press Enter. (This will list all of the files and subdirectories using your custom alias. In this case it was RandyBoyleList.)
25. Take a screenshot. (See Figure 1-67.)

Figure 1-66: Listing aliases for Get-ChildItem.   Figure 1-67: Creating a custom alias.

Note: Below is Table 1-1 showing a few of the aliases from DOS/Windows, Linux/Unix, and PowerShell. You will learn more about the Linux/Unix commands in a later project. You can use the Get-Alias cmdlet to get aliases for individual commands.

DOS, Windows	Linux, Unix, Mac	PowerShell - Cmdlet	PowerShell - Aliases
Dir	ls	Get-ChildItem	dir, ls, gci
Help	Man	Get-Help	help, man
tasklist	ps	Get-Process	ps, gps

Table 1-1: Aliases for cmdlets in PowerShell.

In the next part of this project you are going to explore the Get-Help cmdlet. This will show you how to learn what each cmdlet can do and give you examples of how to use them. You will also learn how to list all PowerShell cmdlets and sort them by function.

PowerShell cmdlets are named using the "verb-noun" convention. In other words, nouns (Process, Help, ChildItem, etc.) are preceded by verbs (Get, Set, Stop, etc.). You will sort all PowerShell cmdlets by specific verbs/nouns to narrow your search. Later you will see how to list all the methods and functions associated with a cmdlet.

26. Type **Get-help Get-ChildItem**
27. Press Enter. (This will display the help file for the Get-ChildItem cmdlet. You can also use the help and man commands.)
28. Press the space bar to page through the help file.
29. Type **Get-help Get-ChildItem -examples**
30. Press Enter. (This will display examples for Get-ChildItem.)
31. Type **help dir –examples | more**
32. Press Enter. (This will also display examples for Get-ChildItem. This displays the same result as the previous command. The commands help and dir are aliases for Get-Help and Get-ChildItem respectively. See Figure 1-68.)

Note: The " | more" addition makes the output come page by page. That is NOT the lower-case letter L or the number 1. It is the vertical bar "|" (a.k.a. pipe). It may appear as "¦" on your keyboard. Piping sends the results from one cmdlet to another cmdlet. You can press the space bar to page through to the end or press q to quit.)

33. Type **Get-Command**
34. Press Enter. (This will display a list of all of the cmdlets, aliases, and functions. There are a lot of cmdlets. That's why it's called PowerShell. You can use " | more" if you want to page through the entire list.)
35. Type **Get-Command –verb Get**
36. Press Enter. (This will display a list of all of the cmdlets starting with "Get.")
37. Type **Get-Command –verb Set**
38. Press Enter. (This will display a list of all of the cmdlets starting with "Set.")
39. Type **Get-Command –noun Process**
40. Press Enter. (This will display a list of all of the cmdlets ending with "Process.")
41. Type **Get-Command –noun Service**
42. Press Enter. (This will display a list of all of the cmdlets ending with "Service.")
43. Type **Get-Date**
44. Press Enter. (This will display the date and time.)

45. Take a screenshot. (See Figure 1-69.)

Figure 1-68: Contents of a help file.   Figure 1-69: Listing of Process and Service cmdlets.

Note: In the next part of this project you will look more closely at one cmdlet (Get-Process). You will look at the methods and properties associated with this cmdlet (object). You will pipe the output from one cmdlet to another cmdlet and then to an html document. The concept of "objects" can be confusing if you haven't done a lot of programming.

The following example may help. Think of an object (cmdlet) like an IPod®. Your IPod has properties associated with it (i.e. color, size, capacity, etc.) and things it can do (i.e. play, stop, turn on, turn off, etc.). The things your IPod can do are called methods. Output (music) from your IPod can be "piped" through other objects (car, stereo, computer, etc.).

This modularity is advantageous because you can use a single IPod rather than having multiple players in your car, computer, etc. Piping output from cmdlets works the same way. Add custom scripting into the equation and you have a very powerful tool.

46. Type **Get-Process | Get-Member**
47. Press Enter. (This will display a listing of all of the properties and methods associated with the Get-Process cmdlet. The Get-Member cmdlet is helpful when you want to know what you can do with a specific cmdlet.)
48. Type **Get-Process | Get-Member –membertype method**
49. Press Enter. (This will display all of the methods associated with the Get-Process cmdlet. In other words, these are things the Get-Process object can do. See Figure 1-70.)
50. Type **Get-Process | Get-Member –membertype properties**
51. Press Enter. (This will display all of the properties associated with the Get-Process cmdlet. In other words, these are the attributes about the Get-Process object.)
52. Type **Get-Process | Get-Member –membertype AliasProperty**
53. Press Enter. (This will display all of the alias properties associated with the Get-Process cmdlet. In other words, these are the aliases to the properties.)
54. Take a screenshot. (See Figure 1-71.)

Figure 1-70: Listing of the methods associated with Get-Process.

Figure 1-71: Listing of the alias properties for Get-Process.

Note: In this part of the project you will use the Get-Process cmdlet to list and sort all of the processes currently running on your computer. You will open the Windows Task Manager to see the GUI equivalent of Get-Process. You may realize that the Get-Process cmdlet offers a great deal more functionality than is available in Windows Task Manager.

55. Type **Get-Process**
56. Press Enter. (This will display all of the processes currently running on your computer. See Figure 1-72.)
57. Right-click the task bar.
58. Select Start Task Manager. (In Windows XP you will select Task Manager.)
59. Click on the Processes tab. (This will also display all processes running on your computer. See Figure 1-73.)

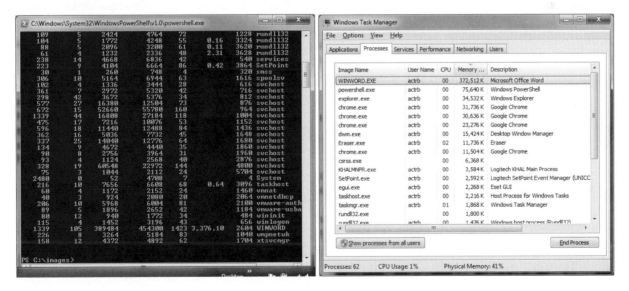

Figure 1-72: List of processes.

Figure 1-73: Running processes displayed in Windows Task Manager.

60. Return to your PowerShell window.
61. Type **Invoke-Item C:\windows\system32\notepad.exe**

62. Press Enter. (This will start Notepad.)
63. Type **Get-Process notepad -FileVersionInfo**
64. Press Enter. (This will display all of the information available about the notepad process. This is helpful in identifying a process you may not immediately recognize.)
65. Type **Get-Process | Group-Object Name**
66. Press Enter. (This will display processes grouped by name. Note that "Name" is listed as one of the alias properties for the Get-Process cmdlet. Also note that there were four Chrome processes grouped together in this example. Grouping and sorting are different. You will see the effects of sorting next. See Figure 1-74.)
67. Type **Get-Process | sort WS**
68. Press Enter. (This will sort the processes by the amount of memory (Working Set) they are using.)
69. Type **Get-Process | sort CPU**
70. Press Enter. (This will sort the processes by the amount of processor time they have used.)
71. Take a screenshot. (See Figure 1-75.)

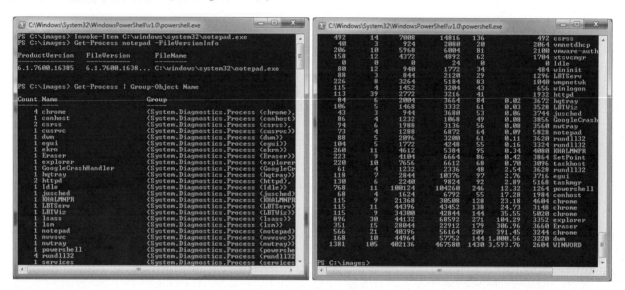

Figure 1-74: Grouping processes by process name.   Figure 1-75: Sorting processes by CPU usage.

72. Type **Get-Process | ConvertTo-Html | out-file "LNameProcess.html"**
73. Press Enter. (This will convert a list of currently running processes to an HTML file. Replace LName with your last name. In this case it was BoyleProcess.html.)
74. Type **Get-Process | ConvertTo-CSV | out-file "LNameProcess.csv"**
75. Press Enter. (This will convert a list of currently running processes to a CSV file. Replace LName with your last name. In this case it was BoyleProcess.csv.)
76. Type **dir**
77. Press Enter. (This will confirm that the files were created. See Figure 1-76.)
78. Type **Invoke-Item LNameProcess.html**
79. Press Enter. (This will open the HTML file showing all of the currently running processes. Replace LName with your last name. In this case it was BoyleProcess.html.)
80. Take a screenshot. (See Figure 1-77.)

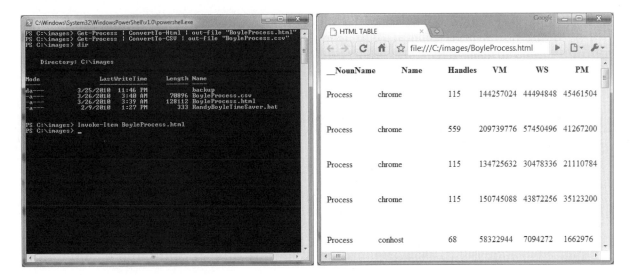

Figure 1-76: Piping process information to HTML and CSV files.   Figure 1-77: HTML page showing process information.

81. Type **Get-Process *n**
82. Press Enter. (This will display all of the processes starting with the letter n.)
83. Type **Stop-Process -name notepad.exe**
84. Press Enter. (This will stop the notepad process.)
85. Type **Get-Process *n**
86. Press Enter. (This will confirm that notepad was stopped. See Figure 1-78.)
87. Take a screenshot.
88. Type **Get-History**
89. Press Enter. (This will list a history of the most recent commands you entered.)
90. Take a screenshot. (See Figure 1-79.)

Figure 1-78: Stopping a process.   Figure 1-79: History of commands entered.

Note: Windows XP and Windows Vista users will have to download and install PowerShell (instructions below) before they can start this project. Windows 7 comes with PowerShell preinstalled. If you are using Windows 7 you do not have to download or install PowerShell.

1. Download Microsoft PowerShell from: http://www.microsoft.com/powershell.

2. Click Downloads tab at the top of the page. (See Figure 1-80.)
3. Click the link labeled Download Windows PowerShell 2.0.
4. Click on the link labeled "Download the Windows Management Framework Core for Windows XP and Windows Embedded package now." (See Figure 1-81.)
5. Click Download.

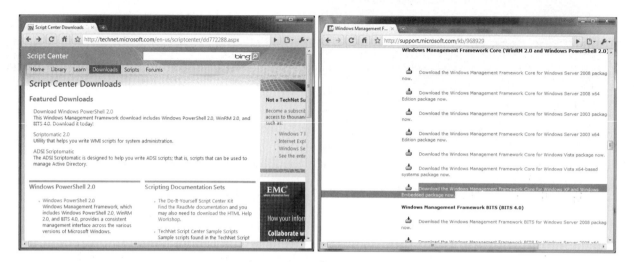

Figure 1-80: Microsoft Script Center.   Figure 1-81: Download for PowerShell.

6. Click Save.
7. Select the C:\networking\ folder (If you haven't already created the "networking" folder on your C:\ you will have to do so now.)
8. If the program doesn't automatically open, browse to C:\networking\.
9. Right-click WindowsXP-KB968930-x86-ENG.exe.
10. Complete the installation process.
11. Return to the start of this project.

THOUGHT QUESTIONS

1. Could you use the Invoke-Command to start a process on a remote computer?
2. What would you use the Measure-Object cmdlet for?
3. Which cmdlet would you use to stop a service?
4. Pwd is an alias for which cmdlet?

CHAPTER 2: WINDOWS UTILITIES

This chapter will go over some fundamental Windows-based utilities that every network administrator uses. It will cover concepts such as monitoring and managing processes, remote administration, monitoring system performance, backup, and hardware configuration. The focus of this chapter is to give you practical experience using the tools that network administrators commonly use.

This chapter focuses on the operation of basic utilities that come built into Windows (with two exceptions). These are simple tools that most network administrators simply assume are widely known and used by everyone. It turns out that many people have not used these utilities. The goal of this chapter is to give the most inexperienced reader exposure to these applications.

2.1   WINDOWS TASK MANAGER

One of the most commonly used utilities in Windows is Windows Task Manager. Computers have a variety of problems including running slow, locking up, running out of available memory, etc. Network administrators use Windows Task Manager as a tool to quickly access the current state of a host.

Network administrators can see which applications and/or process are running in order to identify a potential cause of a system failure. They can then shut down offending applications and/or processes. They can also see how much memory and/or networking resources are being used. Windows Task Manager ends up being a commonly used tool for technical support. It's important that you know how to use it.

1. Open Windows Task Manager by pressing Ctrl-Alt-Delete.
2. Click Start Task Manager.
3. Click on the Performance tab.
4. Take a screenshot. (Notice how little of your CPU's capacity is being used. See Figure 2-1.)
5. Click on the Networking tab.
6. Open a Web browser (Internet Explorer, Firefox, Chrome, etc.).
7. Go to http://www.vmware.com/download/player/download.html.
8. Click on the download link for VMware Player 2.5.3 for Windows (or the latest version).
9. Click Save. (This step will vary depending on your Web browser.)
10. Return to Windows Task Manager with the Networking tab showing.
11. Take a screenshot showing an increase in network usage. (See Figure 2-2.)

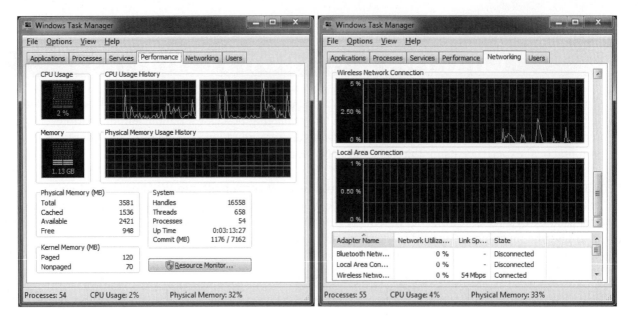

Figure 2-1: Performance tab.   Figure 2-2: Networking tab.

12. Click on the Processes tab.
13. Click on the column heading labeled "Image Name" to sort the processes alphabetically.
14. Click on the process that is responsible for the Web browser you just opened. (In this case it was Chrome.)
15. Take a screenshot. (See Figure 2-3.)
16. Click on the column heading labeled Memory (Mem Usage in Windows XP) to sort the processes by overall memory usage.
17. Take a screenshot. (See Figure 2-4.)

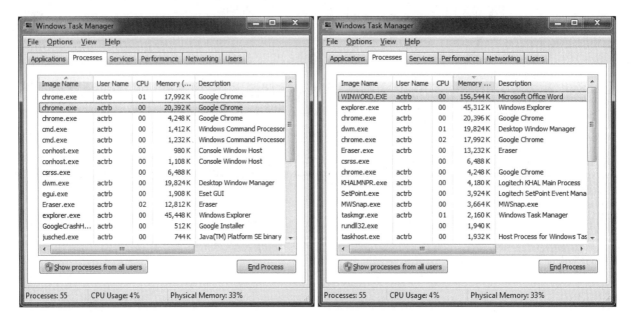

Figure 2-3: Processes tab.   Figure 2-4: Sorting by Memory Usage.

18. Click the button labeled "Show processes from all users."
19. Click on the column heading labeled "CPU" to sort the processes by CPU usage.
20. Take a screenshot. (See Figure 2-5.)

21. Click on the Applications tab.
22. Click on the row showing the Web browser you just opened. (In this case it was Chrome.)
23. Click End Task.
24. Take a screenshot. (See Figure 2-6.)

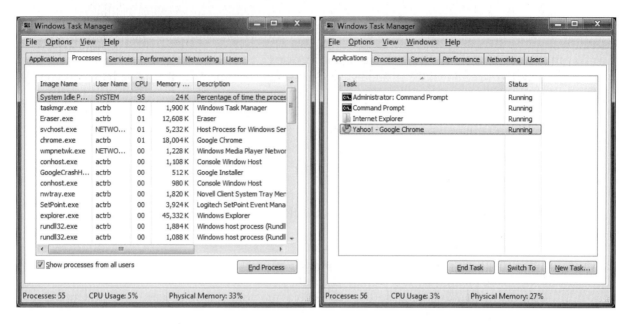

Figure 2-5: Sorting by CPU usage.   Figure 2-6: Running applications.

THOUGHT QUESTIONS

1. Can you send messages to other people on the same computer through Windows Task Manager?
2. What key sequence allows you to switch users?
3. Why are there so few applications running yet so many processes running?
4. What happens if you press Ctrl-Alt-Del twice?

2.2   WINDOWS REMOTE DESKTOP

Remote Desktop is an extremely useful tool for IT professionals. It allows you to log in to a remote computer and use it as if it were the local machine. You have access to all of the drives and printers on both the local and remote machines. Remote Desktop comes preloaded on all Windows-based computers that have Windows XP (or newer).

The ability to remotely administer a computer/system is advantageous because a network administrator could remote into multiple machines at a single time that are all in different locations. Many employees and employers are taking advantage of the ability to work on their office computers from home. The cost savings are tremendous. Remote Desktop is compatible with most of the newer Linux distributions.

In order for Remote Desktop to work correctly make sure you check the following:

(1) Have the remote computer turned on.

(2) Have it configured with a password-protected user account.

(3) Enable Remote Desktop connections.

(4) Allow Remote Desktop connections through the firewall (port 3389).

(5) Do NOT have Windows XP Home Edition or Windows Vista Home Edition

You can remote into any computer anywhere as long as you know the IP address (written in dotted-decimal notation). You can work on computers that are literally thousands of miles away as if you were sitting right in front of them. You just need to know the IP address. The example below uses the IP address of a server at the University of Utah (155.97.61.141).

You can see what your IP address is by using the **ipconfig** command you learned in an earlier project. It's a good idea to write down the IP addresses of the computers you want to remote into until you have them memorized.

If your instructor doesn't give you the IP address of a test machine you may have to complete the second half of this project when you are at another computer (so you can remote into your own computer). Once you see how it is done in the example below you will likely be able to remote into your own home computer with minor changes.

1. Open an Internet Explorer Web browser by clicking Start, All Programs, Accessories, and Internet Explorer.
2. In the address bar enter "www.Google.com".
3. In the Google search box enter "my IP address".
4. Click on the link for the first displayed result.
5. Write down your IP address so you can remote into your computer later. (In this example it was 155.97.61.141 but your IP address will be different.)
6. Take a screenshot.
7. Click Start and Run.
8. Type **cmd**
9. Press Enter.
10. Type **ipconfig**
11. Press Enter.
12. Take a screenshot.

You just used the Web and the **ipconfig** command to confirm your IP address. If they are not the same you will use the IP address provided by the **ipconfig** command to remote into another computer on your local network.

It may appear as if you have two different IP addresses. This is due to your router using one real IP address to send/receive packets for the entire internal network (Network Address Translation – NAT). All computers on the internal network will have non-routable IP addresses (typically starting with 10.X.X.X or 192.168.X.X or 127.X.X.X). This is a common on home networks.

If you are remoting into your instructor's machine then NAT is irrelevant in this situation. You can configure port forwarding on your router to send all Remote Desktop connections (port 3389) to a specific internal computer. This will allow you to remote into your home machine even though it's using NAT. Search www.Google.com for instructions on "port forwarding remote desktop" and you'll see plenty of help.

Note: At this point you will have to move to another computer so you can remote into your own computer.

13. Go to another computer. (This can be a computer belonging to a friend, classmate, or your school. You are going to remote into your own computer.)
14. Click Start, All Programs, Accessories, and Remote Desktop Connection. (See Figure 2-7.)

Figure 2-7: Remote Desktop.

15. Click Options.
16. Click Local Resources.
17. Select Printers and Clipboard. (See Figure 2-8.)
18. Click More.
19. Select all options for Local Devices and Resources. (See Figure 2-9.)
20. Click OK.

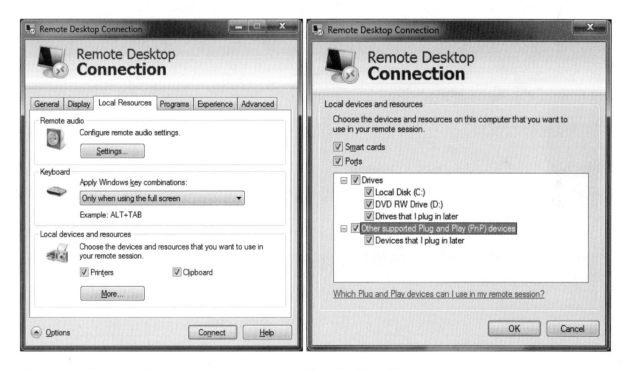

Figure 2-8: Local resource options.   Figure 2-9: Select all drives to share.

21. Click on the General tab.
22. On the Remote Desktop Window enter your IP address. (Do NOT enter the IP address you see in the screenshots in this book. See Figure 2-10.)
23. Click Connect.
24. Click Connect again if prompted.
25. Click Yes if prompted to verify the remote computer.

26. Enter your username and password just as if you were logging into your home computer. (See Figure 2-11.)

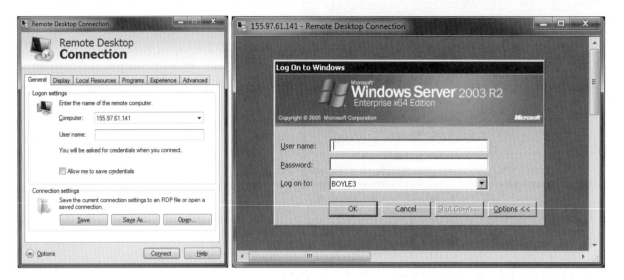

Figure 2-10: Enter your IP address.   Figure 2-11: Enter your username and password.

27. Click the Restore Down button in the top right-hand corner of the window so the remote desktop will be a smaller window (so you can take a screenshot of the whole window).
28. Take a screenshot of your whole local desktop with the Remote Desktop window in the middle. (See Figure 2-12.)

Figure 2-12: Remote Desktop session.

THOUGHT QUESTIONS

1. Can you remote into more than one computer at a time?
2. Can you remote through a chain of multiple computers?
3. Can you copy files from a remote desktop and paste them to the local desktop?
4. What is the DOS command to start Remote Desktop (hint: Terminal Services)?

2.3   MSINFO32

MSINFO32 is a utility that summarizes information about hardware and software for the system you are currently using. This becomes a useful utility when troubleshooting configuration issues. MSINFO32 will give you detailed information about all of your hardware components including printers, displays, network cards, drives/disks, etc.

It can also show you listings of changes that were made over a given time frame. This can be important if you need to reload a driver for a specific piece of hardware. MSINFO32 can also be helpful if you need a snapshot showing the configuration of a particular host at a given time. Performing an inventory of all hosts and how they are configured can go a lot smoother using MSINFO32.

1. Click Start and Run.
2. Type **cmd**
3. Press Enter.
4. Type **msinfo32**
5. Press Enter.
6. Take a screenshot. (See Figure 2-13.)
7. Click Components, Network, and Adapter.
8. Take a screenshot. (See Figure 2-14.)

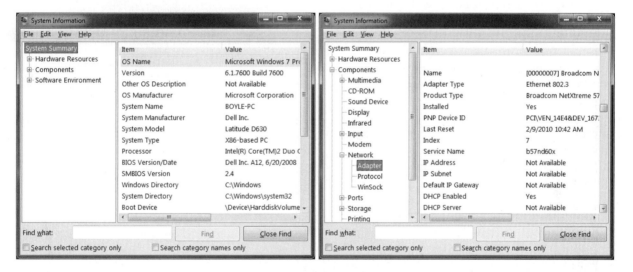

Figure 2-13: System Summary.   Figure 2-14: Network adapter information.

9. Click Printing.
10. Take a screenshot. (See Figure 2-15.)
11. Click Software Environment and Services.
12. Take a screenshot. (See Figure 2-16.)

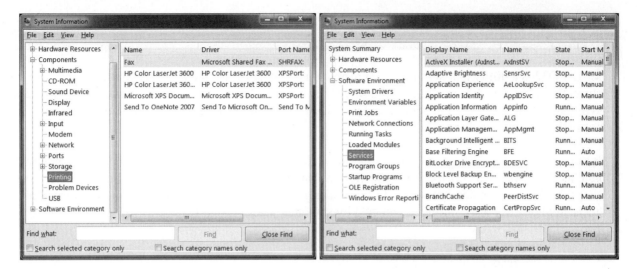

Figure 2-15: Printer information.   Figure 2-16: Services currently running.

13. Click Loaded Modules. (This shows programs that were installed on your computer.)
14. Take a screenshot. (See Figure 2-17.)
15. Click Startup Programs. (This lists programs that will automatically start when your computer boots up.)
16. Take a screenshot. (See Figure 2-18.)

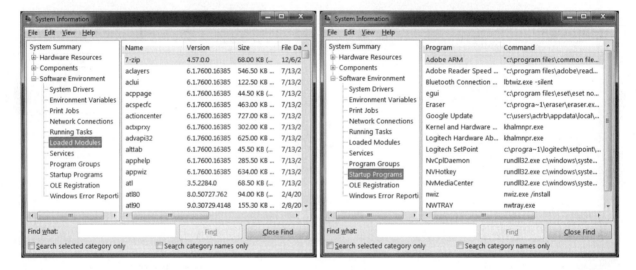

Figure 2-17: Refreshing system information.   Figure 2-18: System changes.

17. Click on System Summary.
18. Click File and Export.
19. Browse to your desktop.
20. Enter "YourNameConfiguration.txt" in the File Name box (replacing YourName with your first name and last name as a single word).
21. Click Save.
22. Go to your Desktop.
23. Open the file named YourNameConfiguration.txt.
24. Take a screenshot. (See Figure 2-19.)

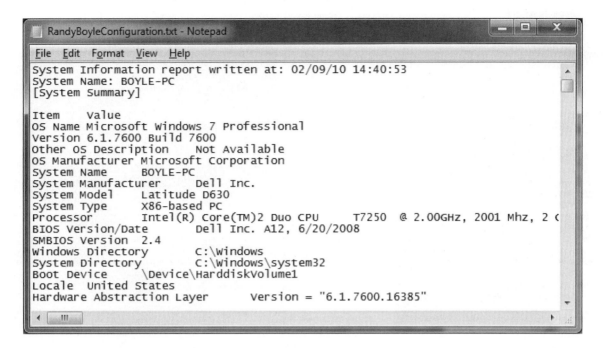

Figure 2-19: Configuration file.

THOUGHT QUESTIONS

1. Can MSINFO32 tell you the model number of your network card?
2. Why would you want to know IRQs?
3. Can you tell if your hard disks are formatted with FAT32 or NTFS? Does it matter?
4. What are environmental variables and why are they important?

2.4 BGINFO

In general, computer forensics gathers information (artifacts) from a computer system while trying to explain what information is present and its origin. When people first hear the word "forensics" they put up mental road blocks and just assume that they won't understand what is going on. You are going to start slowly with basic software that gathers general information from a computer. Then you will move on to applications with more functionality.

BgInfo® was developed at Sysinternals® by Bryce Cogswell. It shows basic system information on the computer background. Systems administrators are always running multiple DOS commands or clicking through a series of windows to get basic information that they need about the local computer. Having it displayed in the background saves administrators time and effort.

1. Download BgInfo from http://technet.microsoft.com/en-us/sysinternals/bb897557.aspx.
2. Click Download BgInfo at the bottom of the page.
3. Click Save.
4. Select the C:\networking\ folder.
5. If the program doesn't automatically open, browse to C:\networking\.
6. Right-click Bginfo.zip.
7. Select Extract All, Next, Next, and Finish.
8. Browse to C:\networking\BgInfo.
9. Double-click Bginfo.exe.

10. Click anywhere on the text to stop the ten-second timer. (If you don't it will close the program.)

Figure 2-20: BgInfo configuration screen.   Figure 2-21: Desktop showing system details.

11. Remove any fields you don't want to see by editing the text directly (i.e., select and delete lines).
12. Take a screenshot. (See Figure 2-20.)
13. Click OK.
14. Take a screenshot of your computer background with the system information showing. (See Figure 2-21.)

THOUGHT QUESTIONS

1. What DOS commands would you have to enter to get the information shown by BgInfo?
2. Why would an administrator need to know the IP and MAC addresses for a given computer?
3. Why does this computer have three IP addresses and three MAC addresses?
4. Can you change your MAC address?

2.5 PERFMON

Network administrators need to be able to correctly understand what is happening on a particular box (computer). They need to know how much memory is being used, how much disk space is used up, how much CPU power is being expended, etc. They also need to be able to set alerts if they run out of memory, disk space, etc.

System monitors can be practical and useful. Imagine that your online business is growing rapidly and one day you get a warning that you are low on disk space. Having a thorough understanding of what is happening on each of your boxes may affect the survival of your company.

Performance Monitor® (perfmon) is a tool that will introduce you to the concept of monitoring system activity. There are better tools available to monitor system performance but Performance Monitor is a simple tool that comes built into Windows.

1. Click Start and Run.

2. Type **perfmon**
3. Press Enter.
4. Click on Performance Monitor in the left-hand pane. (This will automatically be open in Windows XP.)
5. Let it run for about 30 seconds.
6. Take a screenshot. (See Figure 2-22.)
7. Click the + button (or press Ctrl-I).
8. Double-click Network Interface under available counters.
9. Select Bytes Total/sec.
10. Select your network card. (If you don't know which network card is correct you can just select "all instances" See Figure 2-23.)
11. Click Add.
12. Take a screenshot.
13. Click OK.

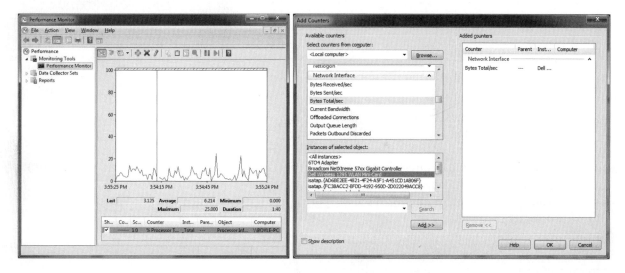

Figure 2-22: Performance Monitor.   Figure 2-23: Highlighting processor usage.

14. Open a Web browser and browse to several pages. (This will make the bytes/second graph clearer.)
15. Take a screenshot. (See Figure 2-24.)
16. Right-click the new row labeled Bytes Total/sec.
17. Select Properties.
18. Click on the Data tab.
19. Change the color to purple. (See Figure 2-25.)
20. Click OK.
21. Take a screenshot.

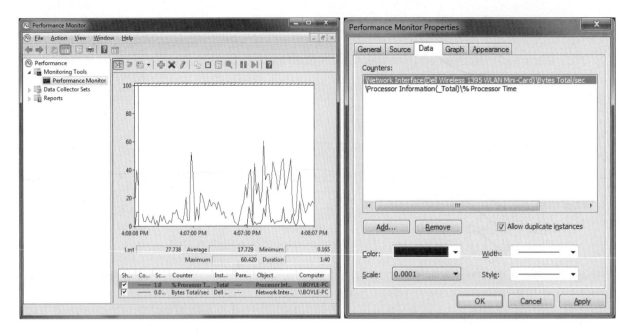

Figure 2-24: Adding counter.   Figure 2-25: Changing color of counter.

22. Click the Clear Display button (or press Ctrl-D).
23. Take a screenshot. (See Figure 2-26.)
24. Open a Web browser (e.g. Internet Explorer, Chrome, Firefox, etc.).
25. Repeatedly click the refresh button or press F5. (Do this about 25 times in rapid succession.)
26. Return to Performance Monitor.
27. Take a screenshot. (You should see the purple line increase when you reloaded your Web browser. See Figure 2-27.)

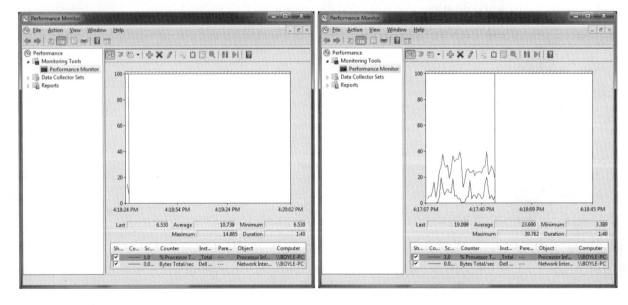

Figure 2-26: Cleared graph.   Figure 2-27: Showing new counter.

1. Can Performance Monitor look at past log files? How?
2. Could you create a custom log to measure specific counters during a given period of time?
3. Why would a network administrator be interested in Pages/sec on a host?
4. Can you set Performance Monitor to alert you if one of the counters passes a certain threshold?

2.6 WINDOWS EVENT VIEWER

Good network administrators check their logs as soon as they get to work. They need to know what went on when they were away. They need to look for intruders, successful backups, changes in log files, network usage, etc. The list of things to look for can be long depending on your role in the organization.

Windows Event Viewer® is a simple program that organizes these logs in a way that makes them easy to view. Learning how Event Viewer works is a great training platform for beginners. You need to understand how all the pieces fit together and how important it is to look at your logs every day. It's also a great way to diagnose problems on your machines. This project will look at an example where you enable logging of security events, log in and out of your machine, and then look up the event in Event Viewer.

1. Click Start and Control Panel.
2. Double-click System and Security and Administrative tools.
3. Double-click Local Security Policy. (See Figure 2-28.)
4. Click on Local Policies and Audit Policy.
5. Double-click on the policy labeled "Audit account logon events." (See Figure 2-29.)
6. Select both Success and Failure.
7. Click OK.
8. Double-click on the policy labeled "Audit logon events."
9. Select both Success and Failure.
10. Click OK.
11. Take a screenshot.

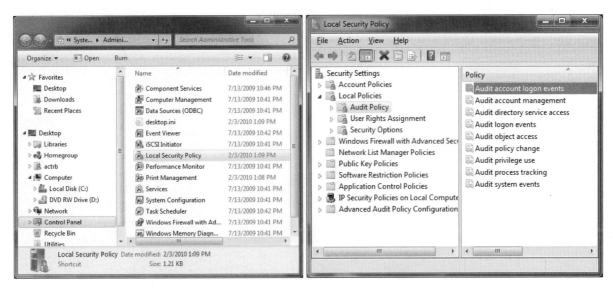

Figure 2-28: Windows administrative tools.   Figure 2-29: Local security settings.

12. In the Control Panel double-click Administrative tools.
13. Click Event Viewer. (Under Computer Management in Windows XP.)
14. Double-click Windows logs.
15. Click Security.
16. Take a screenshot. (The most recent entry should show the change in security policy you just made. See Figure 2-30.)
17. Log off your computer (you don't need to shutdown) by clicking Start, Log Off, and Log Off.
18. Log onto your computer by clicking your username and entering your password.
19. In the Control Panel double-click Administrative tools.
20. Double-click Computer Management.
21. Click Event Viewer.
22. Click Security.
23. Take a screenshot. (See Figure 2-31.)

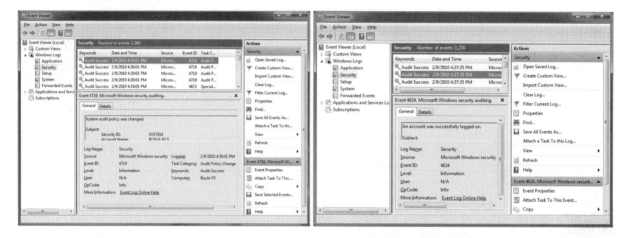

Figure 2-30: Security logs.   Figure 2-31: Details for logged security event.

24. Click on Microsoft Office Sessions.
25. Take a screenshot. (See Figure 2-32.)
26. Click on Event Properties for that event.
27. Take a screenshot. (See Figure 2-33.)

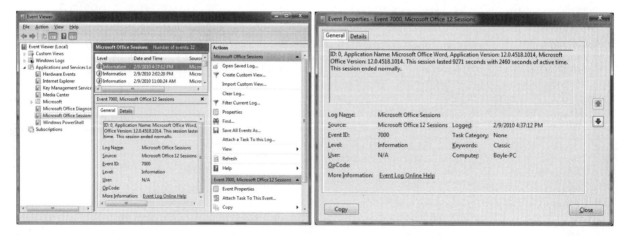

Figure 2-32: Log for Microsoft Office sessions.   Figure 2-33: Details for a specific event.

1. Will these security logs track failed logon attempts? From remote machines?
2. Will it track security events other than just logon/logoff events?
3. Can you use Event Viewer to view other logs?
4. Why is there a log that tracks which Microsoft office programs you use and how long you use them?

2.7 PROCESS EXPLORER

Even though you may only be running two programs (i.e., MS Word, Firefox, etc.) you will likely have a couple dozen processes running behind the scenes. Your operating system can run many processes without the user even knowing they are loaded into memory. Other programs can also take up large amounts of physical memory or CPU speed. It's critical to have the ability to identify the offending program and/or process and kill it.

Network administrators use Process Explorer® (or a program similar to it) all the time. They need to know exactly which programs and processes are running. They also need to know which DLLs are being used, the location of the process, what the process does, who made it, if it's sending or receiving information, etc. Process Explorer is an invaluable diagnostic tool.

1. Download Process Explorer from: http://technet.microsoft.com/en-us/sysinternals/bb896653.aspx.
2. Click Download Process Explorer.
3. Click Save.
4. Select the C:\networking\ folder. (If you haven't already created the "networking" folder on your C:\ you will have to do so now.)
5. If the program doesn't automatically open, browse to C:\networking\.
6. Right-click ProcessExplorer.zip.
7. Select Extract All.
8. Click Next.
9. Browse to C:\networking\.
10. Click Next and Finish.
11. Double-click procexp.exe. (If you find this to be a useful tool you might want to make it a shortcut on your desktop.)
12. Open a Web browser. (In this case it was Firefox.)
13. Scroll down the list of processes open until you find your Web browser.
14. Select your Web browser.
15. Take a screenshot. (See Figure 2-34.)
16. Double-click the line with your Web browser highlighted.
17. Take a screenshot. (See Figure 2-35.)
18. Click Kill Process to close your browser.
19. Click OK to close the properties window for that process.

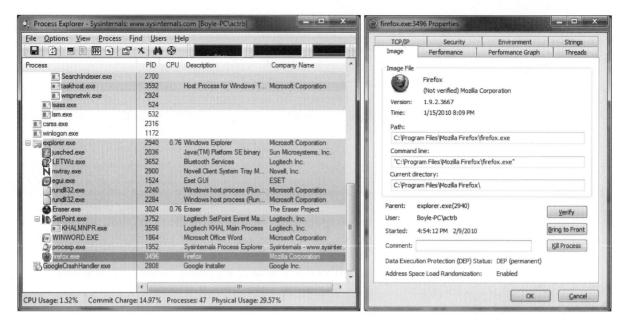

Figure 2-34: Processes shown with firefox.exe highlighted.

Figure 2-35: Details for firefox.exe.

20. In Process Explorer click View and System Information.
21. Take a screenshot. (See Figure 2-36.)
22. Click View, Lower Pane View, and DLLs.
23. Take a screenshot. (See Figure 2-37.)

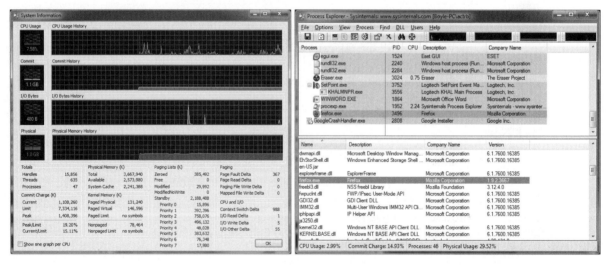

Figure 2-36: System information.

Figure 2-37: Detailed DLL information.

THOUGHT QUESTIONS

1. Why are all of these processes started?
2. Can you keep these processes from starting? How?
3. Are there any processes you recognize or don't recognize?
4. What do DLLs do and why are they associated with a specific process?

2.8 PROCESS MONITOR

Process Monitor® is a collection of tools available from Microsoft (developed by Sysinternals) that give you real-time monitoring capabilities for your local machine. It will show you any changes made to files, the registry, network activities, and/or process activity. This is a useful tool for understanding the types and quantity of traffic each program is sending/receiving on a given host. It can also be useful in tracking down malicious programs that may be lurking on your computer.

This program can be overwhelming for many users due to the number of events shown. You will start with the component that tracks file changes (Filemon).

1. Download Process Monitor from: http://technet.microsoft.com/en-us/sysinternals/bb896645.aspx.
2. Click Download Process Monitor.
3. Click Save.
4. Select the C:\networking\ folder.
5. Browse to C:\networking\.
6. Right-click ProcessMonitor.zip.
7. Select Extract All, Next, Next, and Finish.
8. Browse to C:\networking\ProcessMonitor\.
9. Double-click the procmon.exe program.
10. As it opens, click Cancel to close the smaller window.

Note: Process Monitor will start collecting large amounts of data immediately. It's collecting a variety of changes including changes to or by the registry, processes, and files. You need to stop all these log entries and only collect information about changes in files. You will see that there are a large number of entries. Knowing how to use filters will be a useful skill at this point.

11. In Process Monitor click File and Capture Events. (This should stop Process Monitor from capturing events.)
12. Click Edit and Clear Display. (You can use the icons if you can decipher their symbolic meaning.)
13. Click Filter and Reset Filter. (This will show all captured events.)
14. Click File and Capture Events. (This will start capturing MANY events. See Figure 2-38.)

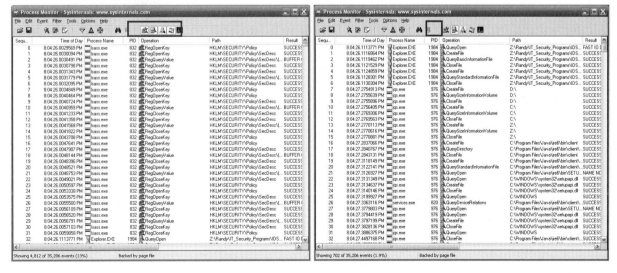

Figure 2-38: Process Monitor.   Figure 2-39: Filter only file system activity.

15. After about 10 seconds click File and Capture Events to stop capturing events.
16. Deselect all of the depressed buttons in the middle of the Process Monitor Screen that act as basic filters. (This should make your screen blank.)
17. Press the icon labeled Show File System Activity. (It looks like a file cabinet with a magnifying glass. See Figure 2-39.)
18. Take a screenshot.
19. Open a Web browser (Internet Explorer, Firefox, Chrome, etc.) behind Process Monitor.
20. Make sure Process Monitor is reduced and your Web browser is maximized in the background as shown in the screenshot. (See Figure 2-40.)

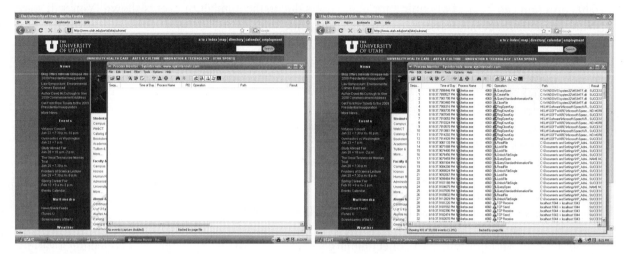

Figure 2-40: Process Monitor and Web browser.   Figure 2-41: Events recorded for Web browser activity.

21. Click Edit and Clear Display.
22. Click-and-drag the icon labeled Include Process From Window (it looks like a cross-hair) from the Process Monitor window onto the Web browser window.
23. Click File and Capture Events (to start capturing events).
24. In your Web browser click on any link or reload the page.
25. In Process Monitor click File and Capture Events (to stop capturing events). (See Figure 2-41.)
26. Take a screenshot.

In the first part of this project you captured events and filtered out all events happening on your computer except those that dealt with file system activity. In the second example you directed Process Monitor to capture events but only show those events that were associated with your Web browser (e.g. Firefox.exe). In the next part of this project you will look at the network traffic coming in/out of your computer.

27. Deselect all of the depressed buttons in the middle of the Process Monitor Screen that act as basic filters.
28. Press the icon labeled Show Network Activity.
29. Take a screenshot. (See Figure 2-42.)
30. Deselect all of the depressed buttons in the middle of the Process Monitor Screen that act as basic filters.
31. Press the icon labeled Show Registry Activity.
32. Take a screenshot. (See Figure 2-43.)

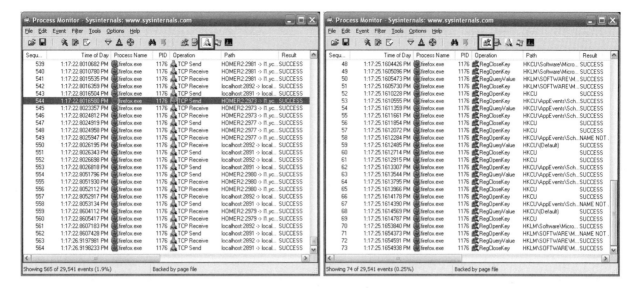

Figure 2-42: TCP activity.   Figure 2-43: Registry activity.

33. Select all of the depressed buttons in the middle of the Process Monitor Screen that act as basic filters. (This should show a lot of captured events.)
34. Click Tools and Process Activity Summary. (See Figure 2-44.)
35. Select the row associated with your Web browser. (In this case it was Firefox.)
36. Take a screenshot. (See Figure 2-45.)
37. Click Detail.
38. Click Close to exit out of the Process Timeline for your Web browser.
39. Click Close again to exit out of the Process Activity Summary.

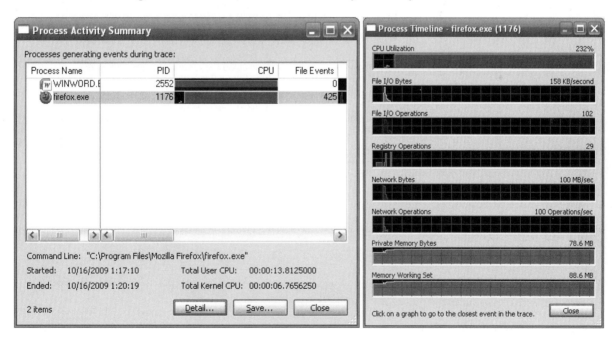

Figure 2-44: Process activity summary.   Figure 2-45: Graphs for Firefox.exe.

40. Click Tools and File Summary.
41. Take a screenshot. (See Figure 2-46.)
42. Click OK.

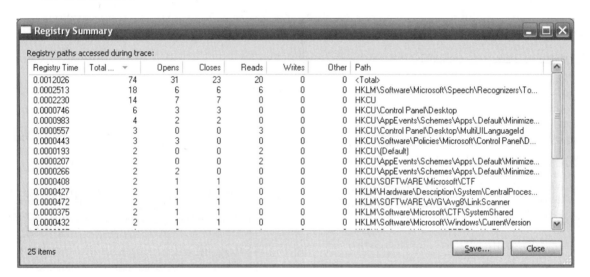

File Time	Total ... ▼	Opens	Closes	Reads	Writes	Get ACL	Set ACL	Other	Path
0.1475533	425	75	40	21	175	0	0	107	<Total>
0.0037342	75	0	0	11	64	0	0	0	C:\Documents and Settings\HP_Ac
0.0021985	48	0	0	0	48	0	0	0	C:\Documents and Settings\HP_Ac
0.0009177	28	7	7	0	0	0	0	14	C:\WINDOWS\system32\MSIMTF.
0.0009222	24	0	0	0	24	0	0	0	C:\Documents and Settings\HP_Ac
0.0004556	17	4	4	0	0	0	0	9	C:\Program Files\Mozilla Firefox\fire
0.0506988	16	0	0	1	11	0	0	4	C:\Documents and Settings\HP_Ac
0.0006763	16	3	3	0	0	4	1	5	C:\Documents and Settings\HP_Ac
0.0001586	12	6	3	0	0	2	0	1	C:\Documents and Settings\HP_Ac
0.0177751	12	3	2	0	1	0	0	6	C:\Documents and Settings\HP_Ac
0.0000912	12	2	2	0	0	0	0	8	C:\WINDOWS\Fonts\tahomabd.ttf
0.0000890	12	2	2	0	0	0	0	8	C:\WINDOWS\Fonts\trebucbd.ttf
0.0047543	9	1	1	6	0	0	0	1	C:\Documents and Settings\HP_Ac
0.0010476	9	3	3	0	1	0	0	2	C:\Documents and Settings\HP_Ac

64 items

Figure 2-46: File summary.

43. Click Tools and Registry Summary.
44. Take a screenshot. (See Figure 2-47.)
45. Click Close.

Registry Time	Total ... ▼	Opens	Closes	Reads	Writes	Other	Path
0.0012026	74	31	23	20	0	0	<Total>
0.0002513	18	6	6	6	0	0	HKLM\Software\Microsoft\Speech\Recognizers\To...
0.0002230	14	7	7	0	0	0	HKCU
0.0000746	6	3	3	0	0	0	HKCU\Control Panel\Desktop
0.0000983	4	2	2	0	0	0	HKCU\AppEvents\Schemes\Apps\.Default\Minimize...
0.0000557	3	0	0	3	0	0	HKCU\Control Panel\Desktop\MultiUILanguageId
0.0000443	3	3	0	0	0	0	HKCU\Software\Policies\Microsoft\Control Panel\D...
0.0000193	2	0	0	2	0	0	HKCU\(Default)
0.0000207	2	0	0	2	0	0	HKCU\AppEvents\Schemes\Apps\.Default\Minimize...
0.0000266	2	2	0	0	0	0	HKCU\AppEvents\Schemes\Apps\.Default\Minimize...
0.0000408	2	1	1	0	0	0	HKCU\SOFTWARE\Microsoft\CTF
0.0000427	2	1	1	0	0	0	HKLM\Hardware\Description\System\CentralProces...
0.0000472	2	1	1	0	0	0	HKLM\SOFTWARE\AVG\Avg8\LinkScanner
0.0000375	2	1	1	0	0	0	HKLM\Software\Microsoft\CTF\SystemShared
0.0000432	2	1	1	0	0	0	HKLM\Software\Microsoft\Windows\CurrentVersion

25 items

Figure 2-47: Registry summary.

46. Click Tools and Network Summary.
47. Take a screenshot. (See Figure 2-48.)
48. Click Close.

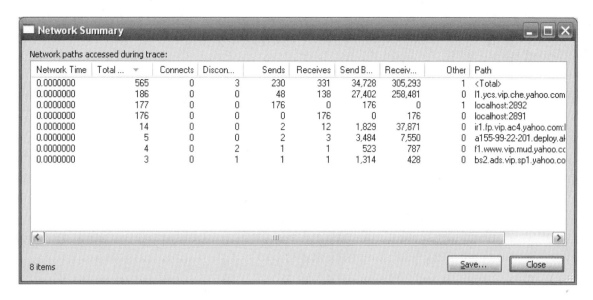

Figure 2-48: Network summary.

Process Monitor is an excellent piece of software that can help you identify the effect an application or process is having on a system. It can give you insight as to the applications interactions with the registry, read/writes, sending/receiving information, etc. It can also give a network administrator a detailed look at what an application does and if it may or may not be harmful.

THOUGHT QUESTIONS

1. Why do programs make so many read/writes to the hard drive?
2. Can you stop programs from running or starting up?
3. Why are there so many entries for the registry? What is the registry?
4. What is the difference between a process and a thread?

2.9 TEXT EDITOR (NOTEPAD)

It may seem a tad simplistic to be learning how to use Notepad. Beginning users could likely learn it in a couple of minutes. What beginning users don't realize is how often network administrators use Notepad (or another basic text editor). Network Administrators use it all the time to modify configuration files, read manuals, look at basic logs, etc. It's a tool that is used many times a day. Anyone that has loaded or configured Apache (the most commonly used Web server) has spent plenty of time in the httpd.conf text file.

In this example you will see why you must use a basic text editor and NOT Microsoft Word to edit certain files. You will also see how you can create files in Notepad and save them as a different type of file. In later projects you will use Notepad to modify a configuration file (httpd.conf).

1. Click Start and Run.
2. Type **notepad**
3. Press Enter.
4. Type your first and last name three times on three separate lines. (In this case it was Randy Boyle, Randy Boyle, and Randy Boyle.)
5. Take a screenshot. (See Figure 2-49.)
6. Click File and Save As.

7. Browse to C:\networking\.
8. Enter the file name "YourNameNotepad.txt". (See Figure 2-50.)
9. Click Save.

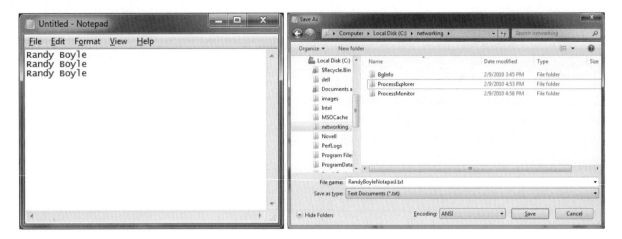

Figure 2-49: Creating Notepad text file.   Figure 2-50: Saving text file.

10. Click Start and Run.
11. Type **write**
12. Press Enter. (This will open WordPad.)
13. Type your first and last name three times on three separate lines. (In this case it was Randy Boyle, Randy Boyle, and Randy Boyle.)
14. Take a screenshot. (See Figure 2-51.)
15. Click File and Save As.
16. Browse to C:\networking\.
17. Enter the file name "YourNameWrite.rtf". (See Figure 2-52.)
18. Click Save.

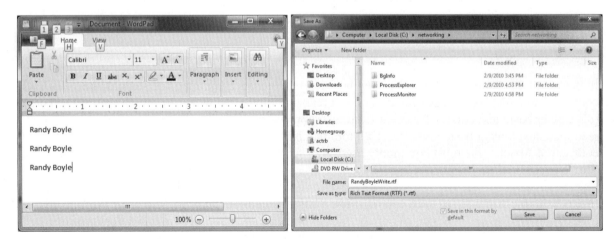

Figure 2-51: Text file in WordPad.   Figure 2-52: Saving in rich text format.

19. Click Start and Run.
20. Type **winword**
21. Press Enter. (This will open Microsoft Word if you have it installed.)
22. Type your first and last name three times on three separate lines. (In this case it was Randy Boyle, Randy Boyle, and Randy Boyle.)
23. Take a screenshot. (See Figure 2-53.)

24. Click File and Save As.
25. Browse to C:\networking\.
26. Enter the file name "YourNameWord.doc". (You can also save it as YourNameWord.docx. See Figure 2-54.)
27. Click Save.

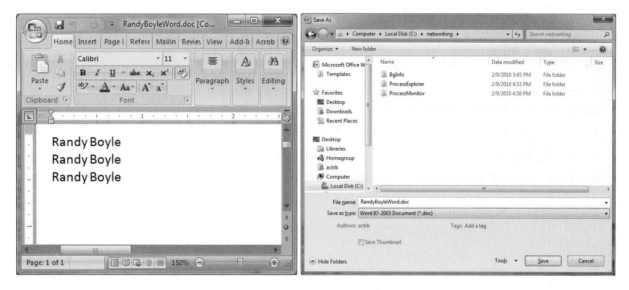

Figure 2-53: Saving Word document.   Figure 2-54: Saving in .doc format.

28. Click Start and Run.
29. Type **explorer**
30. Press Enter. (This will open Windows Explorer.)
31. Browse to C:\networking\.
32. Right-click YourNameWrite.rtf.
33. Select Open With, Choose default program, and Other Programs.
34. Deselect the option labeled "Always use the selected program to open this kind of file."
35. Select Notepad.
36. Click OK.
37. Highlight your name in the text.
38. Take a screenshot. (See Figure 2-55.)

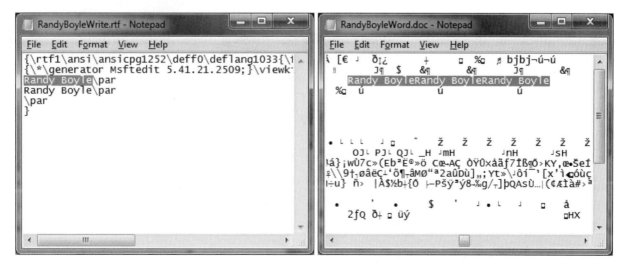

Figure 2-55: RTF document open with Notepad.   Figure 2-56: Word document open with Notepad.

39. Browse to C:\networking\.
40. Right-click YourNameWord.doc (or YourNameWord.docx).
41. Select Open With, Choose default program, and Other Programs.
42. Deselect the option labeled "Always use the selected program to open this kind of file."
43. Select Notepad.
44. Click OK.
45. Highlight your name in the text.
46. Take a screenshot. (See Figure 2-56.)

In the next part of this project you are going to make a basic Web page using Notepad and save it as an html page. You will then open it and view it in your Web browser.

47. Browse to C:\networking\.
48. Double-click YourNameNotepad.txt.
49. Modify the text to match the HTML code below replacing YourName with your first and last name.
50. Take a screenshot. (See Figure 2-57.)

```
<html>
<body>

This is YourName's first Web site!!

<p>YourName</p>
<p>YourName</p>
<p>YourName</p>

</body>
</html>
```

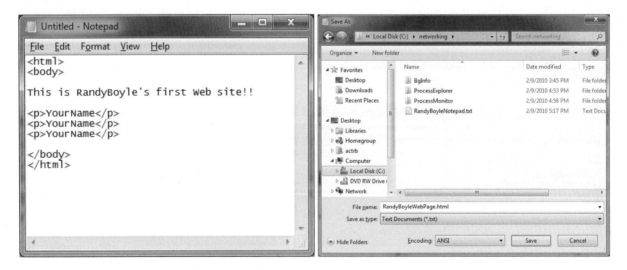

Figure 2-57: Basic HTML code.   Figure 2-58: Saving a text file as a Web page.

51. Click File and Save As.
52. For the File name enter "YourNameWebPage.html". (See Figure 2-58.)
53. For the file type select All Files.
54. Click Save.

55. In Windows Explorer browse to C:\networking\.
56. Double-click YourNameWebPage.html.
57. Take a screenshot. (See Figure 2-59.)

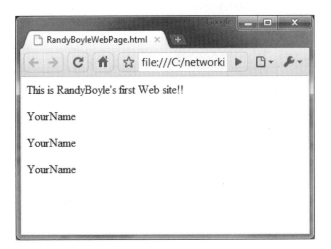

Figure 2-59: Web page opened in a Web browser.

THOUGHT QUESTIONS

1. Why did the three different files (.txt, .rtf, and .doc) all look different when opened in Notepad?
2. Could a configuration file be affected if it were saved with a .doc extension?
3. Can you open any file (including images) with Notepad?
4. Why do so many programs still have help files and configuration files written with the .txt extension?

2.10 BACKUP & RECOVERY

One of a network administrator's primary duties is to backup the organization's data. Hard drives will fail. It's just a matter of time. It's a good idea to set up a full back up of all your data and then practice recovering it. You will be glad you took the time to protect yourself against a future disaster.

In this project you will use the backup functionality built into Windows. If you are backing up an entire network you will use better tools with more functionality than this simple tool. It is likely you will also be backing up data to an off-site storage facility if you are working in a corporate environment.

Since this may be your first time performing a backup it is good to start with a simple tool. It might surprise you to know how many organizations/individuals don't back up their data every week to an off-site storage facility. It only takes one case of catastrophic data loss to become a true believer in secure off-site data backup and storage.

Note: If your computer is running Windows XP you will want to enter "NTBACKUP.exe" instead of "SDCLT.exe". There are minor differences in the instructions but the interface is fairly intuitive.

1. Attach a USB drive or external hard drive.
2. Click Start and Run.
3. Type **sdclt.exe**

4. Press Enter. (In Windows XP the command is NTBACKUP.exe. This backup utility can also be found in the Control Panel in Windows 7. See Figure 2-60.)
5. Click Set up Backup.
6. Select your USB or external hard drive. (See Figure 2-61.)
7. Click Next.

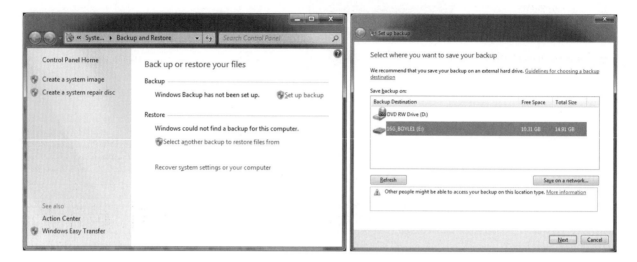

Figure 2-60: Backup wizard in Windows.   Figure 2-61: Backup of My Documents folder and settings.

8. Select Let me choose. (See Figure 2-62.)
9. Click Next.
10. Deselect all of the check boxes except the Documents library under your username.
11. Take a screenshot. (See Figure 2-63.)
12. Click Next.

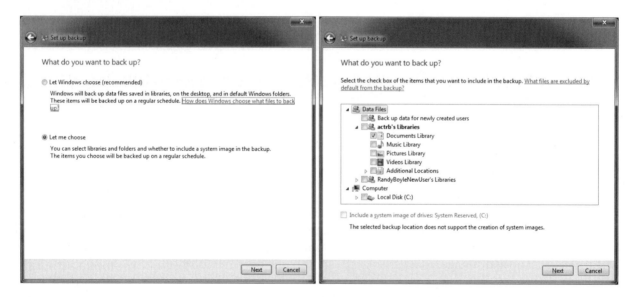

Figure 2-62: Choose a location and a name backup.   Figure 2-63: Enter job name.

13. Click Change schedule.
14. Select Weekly from the drop-down.
15. Set the start time to a time in the early morning (e.g. 3:00AM).
16. Make sure the only day selected is Saturday. (See Figure 2-64.)
17. Click OK.

18. Take a screenshot. (See Figure 2-65.)
19. Click Save settings and run backup.

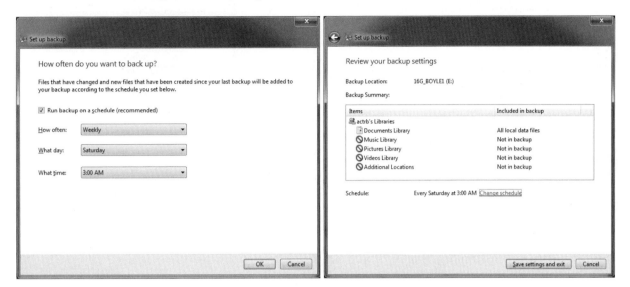

Figure 2-64: Set schedule for backup.   Figure 2-65: Set forced stop time.

20. Click Start and Control Panel.
21. Double-click System and Security, Administrative Tools, and Schedule tasks.
22. Expand the directory tree under Task Schedule Library, Microsoft, Windows, and Windows Backup.
23. Take a screenshot. (See Figure 2-66.)
24. Double-click the Automatic Backup you just created from the list in the middle column.
25. Click on the Settings tab.
26. Change the stop time to four hours.
27. Take a screenshot. (See Figure 2-67.)
28. Click OK.

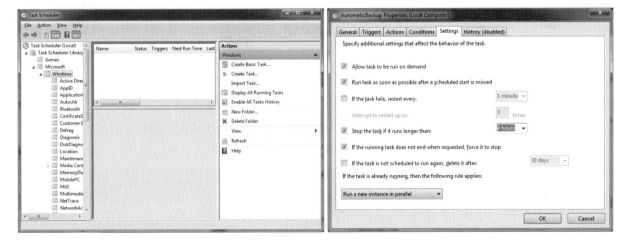

Figure 2-66: Open Scheduled Tasks.   Figure 2-67: Manually start backup.

29. Take a screenshot after the backup starts. (See Figure 2-68.)
30. Press Enter.
31. Take a screenshot. (See Figure 2-69.)

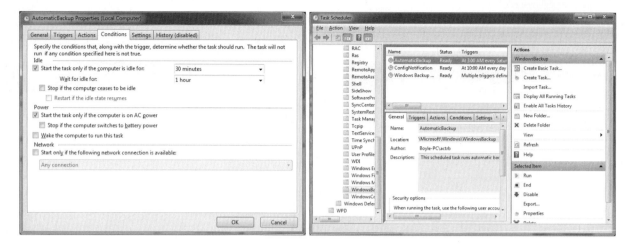

Figure 2-68: Backup running.　　　　　　　Figure 2-69: List of scheduled tasks in DOS.

THOUGHT QUESTIONS

1. Can you start/stop tasks from the DOS prompt? How?
2. What utility would you use to restore a prior backup?
3. Could you back up your computer to an external hard drive attached to another computer?
4. Could you automate the backup of an entire network to an off-site location?

2.11 HARDWARE DRIVER UPDATES

Drivers help your operating system know how to operate the hardware they were written for. Your operating system will interact with a printer in a completely different way than it would with a digital camera. Drivers tell your operating system how your hardware works. If you have the wrong driver installed you can experience a variety of problems.

Sometimes hardware manufacturers issue new drivers (updates) for a piece of hardware. This may be due to an improvement in the driver or it could modify the driver to work with a new version of the operating system. You can typically download the latest drivers for all your hardware from the manufacturer's Web site.

It's a good idea to burn a disk containing the drivers for your computer. If you have to reinstall your operating system you may need them. In this project, you will see where to go to install a new driver or update an existing driver. If you have a piece of hardware that is not working correctly it might be due to a faulty driver.

1. Click Start and Control Panel.
2. Double-click Hardware and Sound. (See Figure 2-70.)
3. Click the link labeled Device Manager. (See Figure 2-71.)

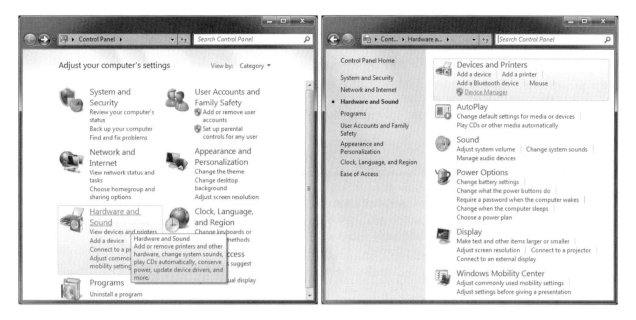

Figure 2-70: Control Panel.

Figure 2-71: Hardware tab in system properties.

4. Double-click Network Adapters.
5. Select your network adapter (wired or wireless). (See Figure 2-72.)
6. Click Action and Properties.
7. Click the Driver tab.
8. Take a screenshot. (See Figure 2-73.)

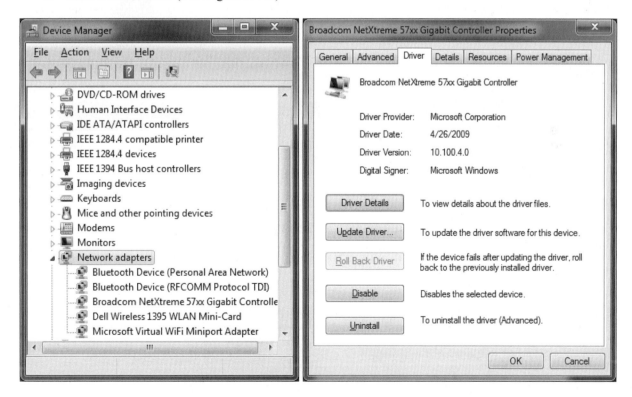

Figure 2-72: Network cards.

Figure 2-73: Driver details for a network card.

1. Is it possible to get your hardware working with a generic driver?
2. Do hardware manufacturers have to write different drivers for different operating systems? Why?
3. Why wouldn't your operating system come with all drivers for all hardware by default?
4. Could a piece of hardware automatically install its own driver?

2.12 MSCONFIG

Users tend to find that their computers run more slowly the longer they own them. Their computers are still processing data just as fast as the day they bought them. However, users experience a general slowing because they have given their computers more work to do.

Users load dozens of different programs on their computers in addition to the litany of software that came preloaded on their machines from the manufacturer. Oftentimes, the software they load will configure itself to start up each time the computer is booted. This uses memory and CPU power. They stay loaded in memory even if they are not used. Users are rarely aware that these processes are even running.

This project will show you how to identify which applications are set to start when you boot your machine. You will also see how to set a program to automatically start. This can save you time if you repeatedly open the same programs every time you log in (i.e. start a Web browser, open Outlook, check certain logs, etc.).

1. Click Start and Run.
2. Type **msconfig**
3. Press Enter.
4. Click on the Startup tab.
5. Take a screenshot. (See Figure 2-74.)

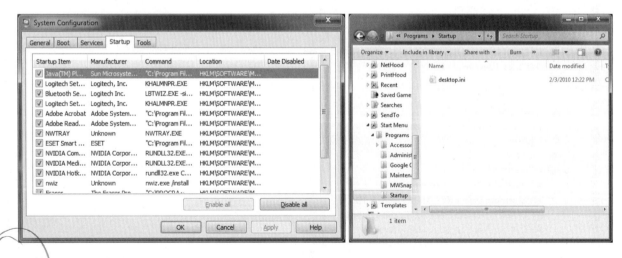

Figure 2-74: Startup tab in the system configuration utility.   Figure 2-75: Startup folder.

6. Click Start and Run.
7. Type **explorer**
8. Press Enter.

9. Browse to YourUserName\StartMenu\Programs\Startup. (In Windows XP it will be C:\Documents and Settings\YourUserName\Start Menu\Programs\Startup where YourUserName is your login user name. If you get an error see the note below.)

Note: Some users get an "access denied" error message and see a padlock on the folder. If you get this error message you need to take "ownership" of the folder. You can take ownership of the folder by right-clicking the folder (the one you can't access) and select Properties, Security tab, Advanced, Owner, Edit, select your username, check the box labeled "Replace owner on Subcontainers and objects," OK, Yes, OK, OK, and OK. This should give you permission to access the folder.

10. Take a screenshot. (See Figure 2-75.)
11. Right-click in the Startup directory.
12. Select New, Shortcut.
13. Browse to C:\Program Files\Internet Explorer\.
14. Select iexplore.exe. (See Figure 2-76.)
15. Click Next.
16. Type **YourNameInternetExplore.exe** for the name of the shortcut. (In this case it was RandyBoyleInternetExplore.exe. See Figure 2-77.)
17. Click Finish.
18. Take a screenshot of the Explorer window showing the new shortcut with your name in the title. (See Figure 2-78.)

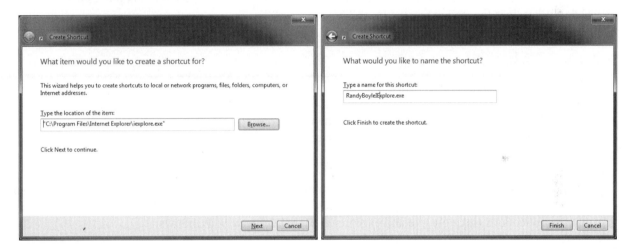

Figure 2-76: Creating a shortcut to Freecell.exe.   Figure 2-77: Naming the shortcut.

19. Click Start and Run.
20. Type **msconfig**
21. Press Enter.
22. Click on the Startup tab.
23. Scroll down until you see the shortcut you just created (Internet Explorer).
24. Take a screenshot. (See Figure 2-79.)

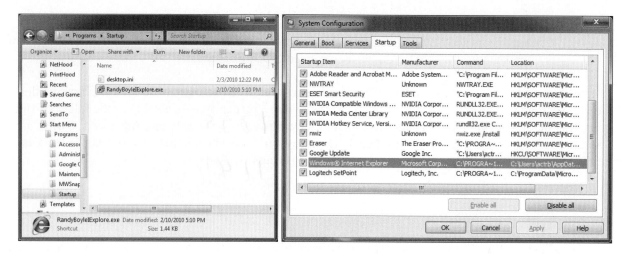

Figure 2-78: New shortcut in the startup folder.   Figure 2-79: New shortcut set to start when computer is booted.

THOUGHT QUESTIONS

1. Why do all of those processes have to be running at startup?
2. If you uninstalled some of those programs would your computer seem to run faster? Why?
3. What programs do you start each time you log in? Could you automate this process?
4. What does the .INI extension mean?

2.13 IEXPRESS

Correctly installing software can be tricky. If you are working with a group of users that are relatively inexperienced the installation process can become more complicated. Hopefully the installation package runs perfectly every time. If it doesn't install perfectly or you need a custom installation you can create your own self-extracting installation program.

Creating your own installation program gives you more control over the installation process. It can also force your users to reboot their computers if necessary. This project will create a simple installer that will run two applications (iexplore.exe and explorer.exe) that come with Windows.

1. Click Start and Run.
2. Type **iexpress**
3. Press Enter.
4. Make sure "Create new Self Extracting Directive file" is selected. (See Figure 2-80.)
5. Click Next.
6. Make sure "Extract files and run an installation command" is selected.
7. Click Next.
8. Enter "YourNameInstaller" for the package title. (In this case it was RandyBoyleInstaller.)
9. Take a screenshot. (See Figure 2-81.)

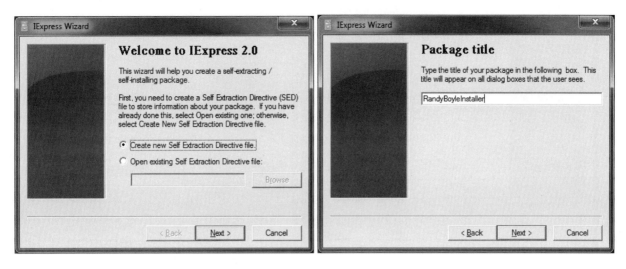

Figure 2-80: Creating the SED.   Figure 2-81: Naming the package.

10. Make sure "No prompt" is selected.
11. Click Next.
12. Make sure "Do not display a license" is selected.
13. Click Next.
14. Click Add.
15. Browse to C:\Program Files\Internet Explorer.
16. Select iexplore.exe. (See Figure 2-82.)
17. Click Open.
18. Click Add (again).
19. Browse to C:\WINDOWS\.
20. Select explorer.exe. (See Figure 2-83.)
21. Click Open.

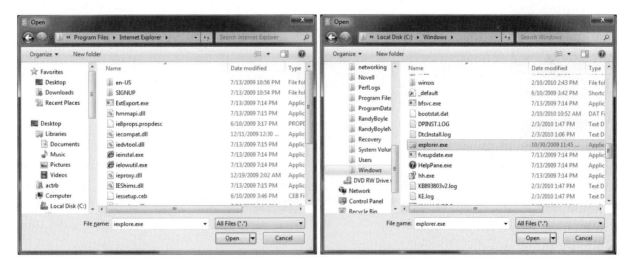

Figure 2-82: Selecting iexplore.exe.   Figure 2-83: Selecting explorer.exe.

22. Click Next.
23. Click Add. (See Figure 2-84.)
24. Select iexplore.exe as the install program selection.
25. Select explorer.exe as the post install command. (See Figure 2-85.)
26. Click Next and Next.

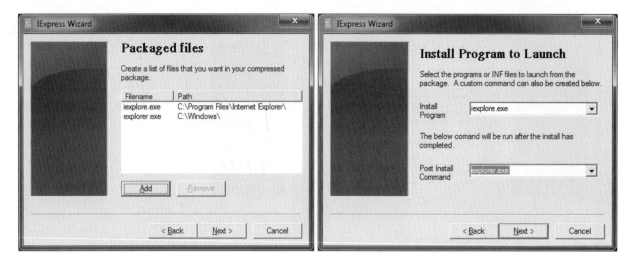

Figure 2-84: List of files in the SED.   Figure 2-85: Designating the program to run at launch.

27. Select Display message.
28. Enter "YourName created a self-extracting file!" for the message (replacing YourName with your first and last name). (See Figure 2-86.)
29. Take a screenshot.
30. Click Next.
31. Click Browse.
32. Browse to C:\networking\.
33. Name the file YournameInstaller.exe. (See Figure 2-87.)
34. Click Save.

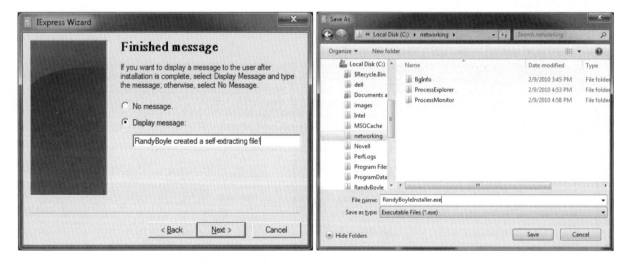

Figure 2-86: Message to display after installation.   Figure 2-87: Naming the executable.

35. Click Next. (See Figure 2-88.)
36. Select No Restart. (See Figure 2-89.)
37. Click Next, Next, Next, and Finish. (See Figure 2-90.)

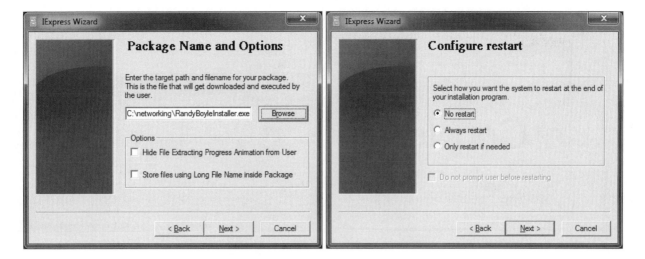

Figure 2-88: Package options.   Figure 2-89: Options for restarting.

38. Browse to C:\networking\.
39. Double-click the file named YournameInstaller.exe. (See Figure 2-91.)

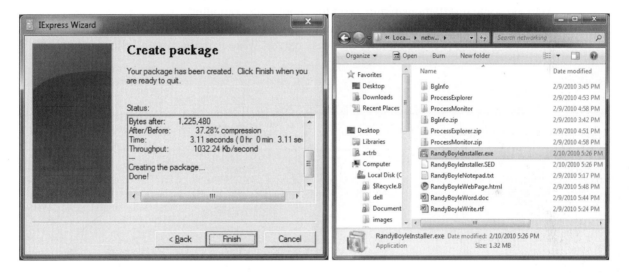

Figure 2-90: Package created.   Figure 2-91: New executable created.

40. Close iexplore.exe after it opens. (See Figure 2-92.)
41. Close explorer.exe after it opens.
42. Take a screenshot showing the message with your name. (See Figure 2-93.)

Figure 2-92: Internet Explorer.   Figure 2-93: Confirmation that file was created.

THOUGHT QUESTIONS

1. Can you add more than just .exe files to the list of installation files?
2. Why do some installations require you to reboot your computer?
3. Give an example of when a network administrator might use this tool.
4. In addition to the .exe file another file was created. What is in this second file?

CHAPTER 3: WEB TOOLS

There are a large number of useful tools available on the Web. Your Internet Web browser could very well be your future operating system. Many of the tools presented in the prior two chapters are also available on the Web. This chapter goes over Web tools that do not come built into Windows but are widely used by network administrators.

In this chapter you will test the speed of your network connection, geographically trace the route of packets, use a Web proxy, examine some Web hosting statistics, trace an email, and perform an online virus scan. This is just a small number of the networking tools you can find on the Web. Bookmark the tools you like so you can use them again.

3.1   BANDWIDTH SPEED TEST

Substantial increases in bandwidth have dramatically changed the way people use the Internet. This trend will likely continue for many years. Most people know they like a fast Internet connection because they can do more things with a faster connection. However, most people do not know how fast their connection is or if they are getting what they are paying for each month.

Testing your bandwidth will enable you to compare different internet service providers (ISP) to see which one is best for you. Cable and DSL throughput rates vary widely. Before you sign up for an ISP it's a good idea to test the speed of the connection at your neighbor's house. It's even more important if you are a business buying a dedicated T3. Drive it before you buy it. You might be surprised.

1. Go to the bandwidth tool hosted by SpeedTest.net at http://www.speedtest.net/.
2. Click on the star icon that is closest to you. (In this case it was XMission in Salt Lake City, Utah. See Figure 3-1.)
3. Click Begin Test.
4. Take a screenshot while the test is going. (See Figure 3-2.)

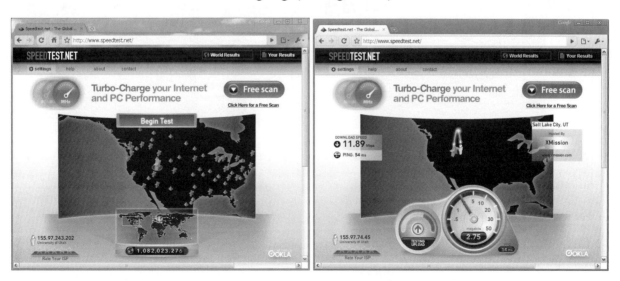

Figure 3-1: Select the closest server.   Figure 3-2: Testing download speed.

5. Take another screenshot when the test is finished. (See Figure 3-3.)
6. Click on the small link labeled "View Upload Speed."
7. Take a screenshot. (See Figure 3-4.)

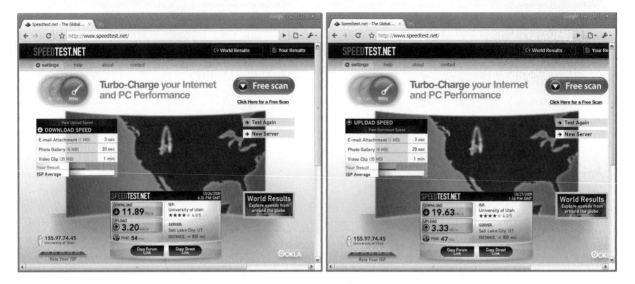

Figure 3-3: Download speed.   Figure 3-4: Upload speed.

8. Click New Server.
9. Click-and-drag the map to the left until you see Europe.
10. Randomly select a server located in Europe. (In this case it was Warsaw, Poland.)
11. Click Begin test.
12. Take a screenshot while it is going. (See Figure 3-5.)
13. Take another screenshot when it is finished. (See Figure 3-6.)

Figure 3-5: Testing international connection speed.   Figure 3-6: International download speed.

THOUGHT QUESTIONS

1. In general, is uploading or downloading faster? Why?
2. Does it make a difference if the speed is measured in bits or bytes? Why?
3. Was the download speed from Europe slower or faster? Why?

4. What could slow down your Internet connection?

3.2 VISUAL TRACE ROUTE

The Internet is an extremely large connection of networks. It's not a magical blue box sitting in a room somewhere. Seeing the geographic route a packet takes as it crosses the Internet helps emphasize the fact that information is crossing many different networks before it gets to your computer.

Students are typically surprised at the number of hops a packet takes when it travels from one host to another. They are also surprised to learn that packets don't always take the shortest geographic route. There is a great online trace route tool that maps the physical location of every computer between you and the IP address you enter.

YouGetSignal.com© has several useful tools that are worth looking at. Having them online is also nice because the tools are not operating system dependent. You just need to make sure your Internet connection doesn't go down. Let's trace an IP address to another university.

1. Go to the host name resolution tool hosted by You Get Signal at http://www.yougetsignal.com/tools/network-location/.
2. Enter the URL of a university you know. (In this case it was www.FSU.edu.)
3. Click Locate.
4. Take a screenshot. (See Figure 3-7.)
5. Write down the IP address shown on the screen.
6. Go to the tracing tool hosted by You Get Signal at http://www.yougetsignal.com/tools/visual-tracert/.
7. Enter the IP address of the university you searched for in the Remote Address text box. (In this case it was 128.186.6.14 for www.fsu.edu. See Figure 3-8.)
8. Click Host Trace (from yougetsignal.com to your target). (See Figure 3-9.)
9. Take a screenshot.

IP 128.186.6.14

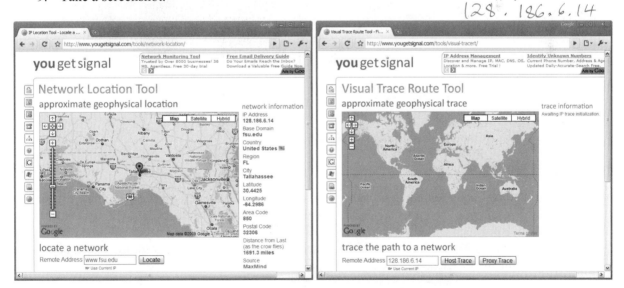

Figure 3-7: Locating a Web site.   Figure 3-8: Entering the IP address.

10. Click Proxy Trace. (From you to yougetsignal.com to your target. See Figure 3-10.)
11. Take a screenshot.

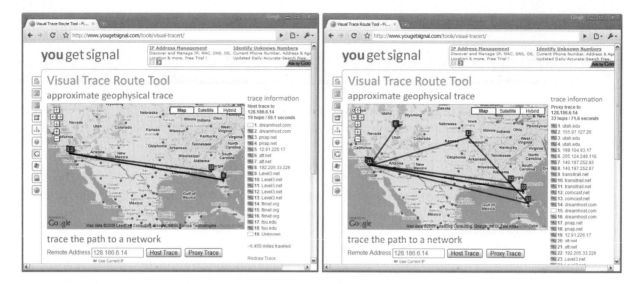

Figure 3-9: Host trace.   Figure 3-10: Proxy trace.

12. Enter "www.toyota.jp" in the Remote Access box.
13. Click Host Trace. (See Figure 3-11.)
14. Zoom in until you see the city in Japan where the server is located.
15. Take a screenshot.

Figure 3-11: International trace.

Not only did you learn the actual physical location of the remote computer, (Florida State University in Tallahassee, FL) but you can also see that information doesn't always take a straight line between hosts. The information between these two computers took what appears to be a wildly inefficient path from the University of Utah to Florida State University. This was likely the "best" path for the information to take depending on the metric used.

Information traveling through the Internet moves quickly and passes through many different computers. Trace route programs are also useful in diagnosing network problems (i.e., determining slow points in a network). It is worth the time and effort to become well acquainted with a trace route program. Network administrators use them every day.

1. Could any person along the route look at your information? How?
2. How could you keep someone from looking at your information as it is passed along the Internet?
3. Who owns the routers that forward your information?
4. How does the program map the IP addresses of the routers to their physical location?

3.3 WHOIS LOOKUP

Network administrators need to know where network traffic is coming from. They may experience a denial of service (DoS) attack, see some strange traffic patterns, or see a list of entries on their intrusion detection system (IDS). They need to be able to find contact information for the person in charge of that range of IP addresses to solve the problem.

Using a WHOIS lookup you can tell who the network administrator is (the person in charge of managing that range of IP addresses) and get his/her contact information. In this project you will see how to find out who is in charge of a specific IP address range.

1. Go to the WHOIS Lookup Tool hosted by You Get Signal at http://www.yougetsignal.com/tools/whois-lookup/.
2. Enter your IP address in the Remote Address text box.
3. Click Check. (See Figure 3-12.)
4. Take a screenshot.
5. Enter the domain name for your university. (In this case it was www.utah.edu.)
6. Click Check.
7. Take a screenshot. (See Figure 3-13.)

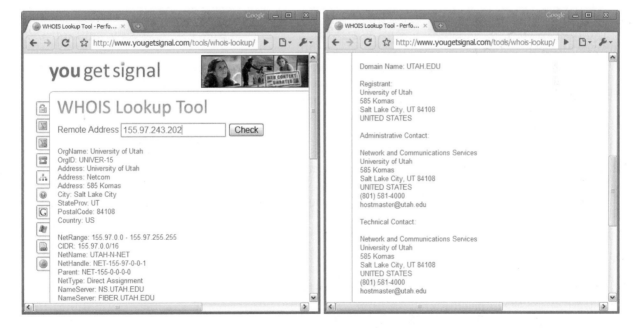

Figure 3-12: Enter your IP address.   Figure 3-13: Contact information for your network administrator.

8. Enter "www.YourNameWebsite.com". (In this case it was www.RandyBoyleWebsite.com.)
9. Click Check.
10. Take a screenshot. (See Figure 3-14.)

Figure 3-14: Web site availability.

1. Approximately how many IP addresses are there using IPv4? IPv6?
2. Which organization registers IP addresses with domain names?
3. Who decides ownership over a given IP address range?
4. Can you run multiple Web sites off a single IP address? How?

3.4 USING A WEB PROXY

A proxy is a person that can act on your behalf. For example, you can give someone your proxy if you can't make it to a meeting but still want to cast your vote. Another example would be giving a lawyer your power of attorney. Computers can also have proxies. Essentially one computer has another computer do tasks for it. Proxies have their good and bad uses.

In this project you will use a Web proxy. You will see that your IP address will appear different if you surf the Web through a Web proxy. Privacy advocates argue that proxies protect them from undue government monitoring. Employers tend to dislike Web proxies because employees can abuse Internet access and make it difficult to monitor their behavior. However, employers can use proxies to mask much of the information about their internal networks.

1. Open a Web browser.
2. Go to www.Google.com.
3. Search for "my IP address." (See Figure 3-15.)
4. Press Enter.
5. Click on the first result. (See Figure 3-16.)
6. Take a screenshot showing your IP address.

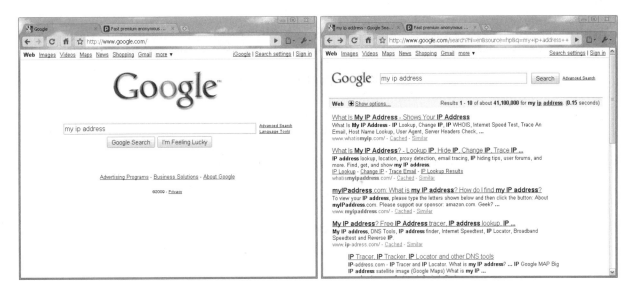

Figure 3-15: Search for your IP address.　　　　　Figure 3-16: Results for "my IP address" search.

7. Go to the Web proxy at http://www.proxylicious.net/.
8. Enter "www.Google.com" as the Web address you'd like to visit. (See Figure 3-17.)
9. Search for "my IP address". (See Figure 3-18.)
10. Press Enter.
11. Click on the first result.
12. Take a screenshot showing the IP address as it shows through the proxy (it should be different).

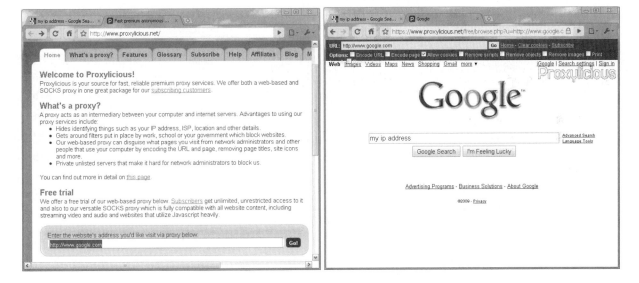

Figure 3-17: Web proxy.　　　　　　　　Figure 3-18: Google search through Web proxy.

THOUGHT QUESTIONS

1. Can a proxy server really hide your identity?
2. Could a company block any/all traffic to/from a proxy server?
3. Could your company use a proxy server to hide confidential information about an internal network from hackers? How?
4. Would your employer become suspicious if you were using a proxy server?

3.5   WEB HOSTING STATISTICS

Netcraft[©] is a Web site that provides statistics about Web servers, operating systems running Web servers, hosting providers, etc. This information can be useful because it can save you time and money. For example, Netcraft may tell you that Apache is the most popular Web server in use today. This may mean it is more stable, robust, scalable, and easier to support. If true, this would save you time and money.

Network administrators also have to decide if they want to run their own servers or have them hosted with a professional hosting company (e.g. GoDaddy.com[©]). A hosting provider might be the best answer if they lack the hardware, technical knowledge, infrastructure, etc. to maintain the appropriate level of availability. Some Web sites can't be down for more than a minute per year. Netcraft will give you statistics on hosting providers and tell you what OS/Web server they are running.

1. Open a Web browser.
2. Go to www.netcraft.com.
3. Scroll down until you see the graph labeled "Market Share for Top Servers Across All Domains."
4. Take a screenshot. (See Figure 3-19.)
5. Scroll to the top of the page.
6. Enter "Micrsoft.com" into the box labeled "What is that site running." (See Figure 3-20.)
7. Press Enter.
8. Take a screenshot. (See Figure 3-21.)

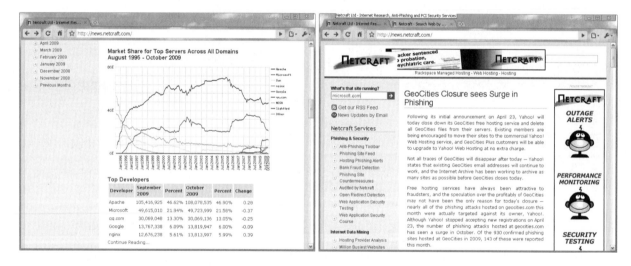

Figure 3-19: Top Web server statistics.   Figure 3-20: Search for Microsoft.com.

9. Click back in your Web browser to return to www.netcraft.com.
10. Enter "Google.com" into the box labeled "What is that site running."
11. Press Enter.
12. Take a screenshot. (See Figure 3-22.)

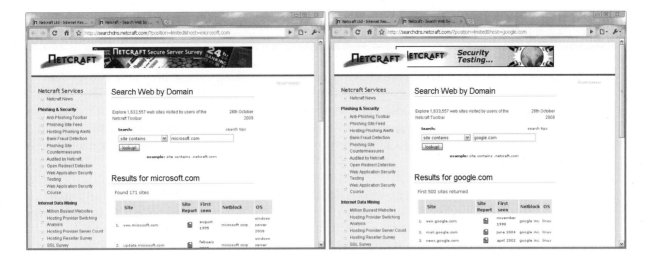

Figure 3-21: Results for Microsoft.com.   Figure 3-22: Results for Google.com.

13. Click back in your Web browser to return to www.netcraft.com.
14. Click on the link on the left-hand side labeled "Hosting Providers Network Performance."
15. Take a screenshot. (See Figure 3-23.)
16. In the top-left menu click on Today's changes.
17. Click on the NUMBER (NOT the company name!) of new sites for one of the top 10 sites. (On this day Go Daddy was #10 with 125 new sites.)
18. Take a screenshot showing the new Web sites from that hosting provider. (See Figure 3-24.)

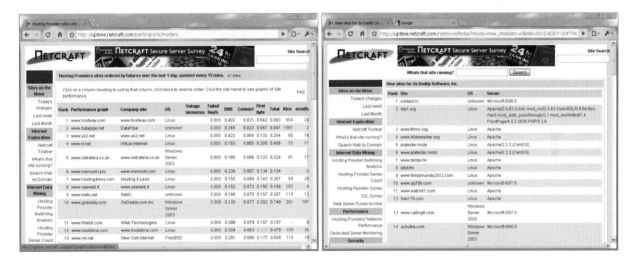

Figure 3-23: Hosting provider statistics.   Figure 3-24: New sites through Go Daddy.

THOUGHT QUESTIONS

1. What operating system is most popular at Google? Why?
2. Does Netcraft offer statistics on the general number of Web sites worldwide? Approximately how many are there?
3. What is the most popular Web server in use today? Why do you think this is so?
4. What operating system(s) show up when you enter your universities domain name?

New viruses come out every day. Some antivirus companies are better at catching new viruses than others. An antivirus company's ability to catch viruses may vary from year to year depending on its business goals. A company may choose to focus resources on expanding their offerings or making their existing product(s) faster. Shifting resources toward other areas may reduce their ability to catch viruses. The net effect is that the effectiveness of antivirus products change from year to year. It's good to have a variety of options at your disposal.

One antivirus company may catch a new virus and another may take a while to find it. Most major antivirus companies offer a free online version of their antivirus scanner. You have to have an Internet connection for it to run and you have to manually start it. If you are considering buying an antivirus product you should try them all out. If you catch a virus that shuts down your regular antivirus client you need to be able to access an online antivirus scanner.

In the following example you will run an online antivirus scan. This project uses ESET© but could have just as easily used another major antivirus scanner. There are several options available. If you keep a list of the major online antivirus scanners you can send it to users that request help removing a virus and save yourself valuable time. Make sure you are using Internet Explorer for this exercise.

1.   Click Start and Run.
2.   Type **iexplore**
3.   Press Enter.
4.   Go to http://www.eset.com/onlinescan/.
5.   Click on the button labeled ESET Online Scanner. (See Figure 3-25.)
6.   Select YES. (See Figure 3-26.)
7.   Click Start.

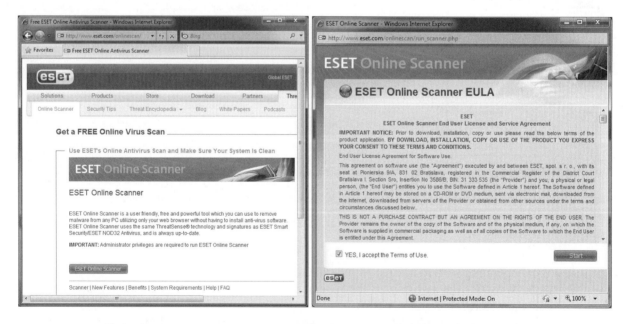

Figure 3-25: ESET online virus scan.   Figure 3-26: EULA for ESET online virus scanner.

8.   Click the notification bar at the top of the screen to install the add-on component if necessary. (See Figure 3-27.)
9.   Click Yes/Install if asked to install the add-on. (See Figure 3-28.)

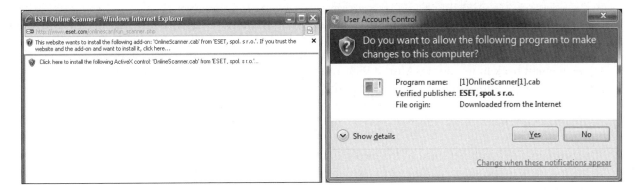

Figure 3-27: Add-on is necessary to run ESET.   Figure 3-28: Install add-on.

10. Deselect the option labeled "Remove found threats." (You can leave it selected if you want it to remove any viruses it finds. See Figure 3-29.)
11. Click Start.
12. Click Yes if prompted.
13. Wait for the virus signature database to download.
14. Take a screenshot after the scan has run for a couple of minutes. (See Figure 3-30.)

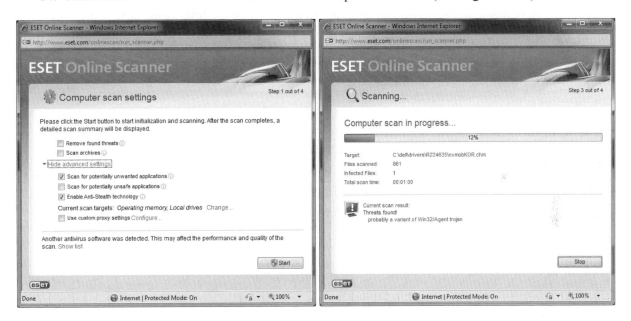

Figure 3-29: Scan settings.   Figure 3-30: Virus scan in progress.

Note: You can let the virus scan run to completion or stop it before it finishes. Take an additional screenshot if you find any viruses.

THOUGHT QUESTIONS

1. When would you need an online antivirus scanner?
2. Why would you need an antivirus scanning client if you could just use an online scanner?
3. Could a virus block access to your antivirus scanner and/or online scanners?
4. Who writes these viruses and why?

3.7 EMAIL TRACE

Occasionally a network administrator will have an individual come to them and ask if it is possible to trace an email back to its source. Almost 99% of the time they have gotten a nasty email from someone that was unhappy with them and they want to find out who it was. Whether or not they deserved it is another story. There are other reasons for wanting to track down the source of an email but this is a fairly common occurrence.

It's surprisingly easy to get most of the information. Let's look at an example that uses the email's header to trace it back to the source. The header, which is typically hidden, contains all of the routing information for that specific email. Finding the header information will be the hardest part. Most people are unaware that emails even have headers. Below is a really good tool by Butterfat.net®. There are other Web sites that have similar tools.

1. Open Outlook. (Hotmail and Gmail also have header information.)
2. Open any email message (preferably from someone that lives in another state/country). (See Figure 3-31.)
3. Click on Message Options.

Note: If you're using the MS ribbon feature you need to click on the little arrow next to the word "Options." Yes, this can be confusing. Before Office 2007 it was easier to view an email header. If you are using another email program you may have to look around for some option that allows you to view the email header. Most online email accounts like Hotmail and Gmail have this option.

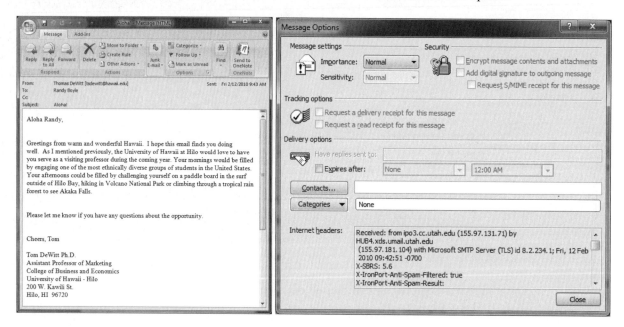

Figure 3-31: Any email.   Figure 3-32: Email header information.

4. Select ALL of the header information in the bottom text box (Ctrl-A). (See Figure 3-32.)
5. Copy all of the information you just selected (Ctrl-C).
6. Go to the Email Trace tool hosted by Butterfat.net at http://map.butterfat.net/emailroutemap/. (You can also go to http://www.ip-adress.com/trace_email/.)
7. Paste all of the information you just copied from Outlook into the text box at the bottom of the page. (See Figure 3-33.)

8. Take a screenshot.
9. Click "Do it". (See Figure 3-34.)
10. Take a screenshot.

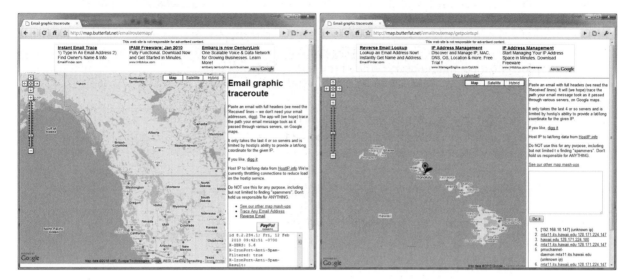

Figure 3-33: Pasted header information.   Figure 3-34: Traced email to source.

This email came from Dr. Tom DeWitt on Hawai'i. Even if you didn't know the actual name of the person sending the email, you would still have their IP address. Knowing a person's IP address can be better than knowing their name. As you've seen from prior examples once you have one piece of information you can gather any additional information quickly.

The moral of this story is simple. Don't send "flaming" emails. Most people don't really have a strong grasp of the IP addressing system, how routers work, how mail servers work, or how email works. These are unknowns that can get you into trouble. Nowadays almost all electronic messages are copied, logged, and tracked. This includes the emails YOU send to other people.

There are many information gathering tools that could be demonstrated but it is best to stop here. It might shock you to learn the types and quantities of information available on the Internet.

THOUGHT QUESTIONS

1. Do all emails have headers?
2. Why do emails have headers?
3. How does the email trace program convert the header information to a physical address?
4. Can you modify and/or fake header information?

CHAPTER 4: VIRTUALIZATION

Virtualization is a new concept to most people. It has become much easier to make, run, and modify virtual machines in the last few years. Virtualization has a variety of advantages depending on what you are using it for. Most beginning users will experience virtualization by downloading a virtual machine to try out a different operating system.

Larger companies will run numerous servers in a virtual environment to increase fault tolerance and availability while lowering setup costs, utility expenses, administrative overhead, etc. Systems administrators that use enterprise-level virtualization love it.

Below is a short primer on the concept of virtualization. It's necessary to understand the basics of virtualization before doing the projects. If you don't understand the basics you'll end up just pushing buttons and won't learn anything from these projects.

VIRTUALIZATION

To explain virtualization we will compare physical computers to buildings and operating systems (OS) to people. Think of a person as an operating system (e.g. Windows XP, Mac, Ubuntu, Fedora, etc.) and think of a building as a computer (e.g. Dell Latitude 630, HP Blade server, IBM mainframe, etc.). Below are a couple of examples of how virtualization might work.

BACHELOR PAD

This is the situation where you have one person living in a building. It may have a lot of room (RAM) or a little. This is the equivalent of one physical machine with one operating system. This is the most common configuration when you buy a personal computer.

SINGLE FAMILY HOME

This is the situation where you have multiple people living in a single building. You'll need more room (RAM) to house more people. This is the equivalent of having one computer running two (or more) operating systems. Sometimes it's beneficial to have two operating systems (i.e. Mac and Windows) on a single physical computer so you can run software that may be proprietary to each OS.

While this does give you more functionality it may also use up more resources (RAM) if they are both running on the same computer at the same time. You'll need plenty of RAM to run multiple operating systems at the same time.

HOTEL

This is the situation where you combine multiple dwellings into a single structure. You have a lot of rooms and can house many people. If one room becomes flooded you can close that room down and move the occupants to another room. If you don't have a lot of demand you can shut down some rooms and only use part of the hotel. It's also easy to add more capacity to the hotel without disturbing the guests. Hotels are nice but expensive.

This is the equivalent of having a group (cluster) of servers acting as one. You can put multiple operating systems (virtual machines) on multiple servers. If one of the physical servers fails you can instantly move the virtual machine to a different physical server. If your servers are experiencing low demand you can move multiple virtual machines to a single physical server and shut down the other physical servers (this saves a lot of money).

If your servers are being pushed really hard you can add additional physical hardware to increase your capacity. You never have to shut down your virtual machines (operating systems) to do a hardware upgrade. Server clusters, like hotels, are really nice but can be expensive.

4.1 VMWARE PLAYER

VMware© is the industry leader in virtualization software. VMware Player is a piece of software that allows users to download preinstalled and configured "virtual machines" that can be used on a local machine. This means that you could be using a Windows XP computer with a "virtual" Linux computer running in a window.

The Linux computer would share all the hardware that your Windows XP computer is using and still have the full functionality that you would see if you loaded it on your computer. Not only could you run Windows and Linux at the same time, but you could run a variety of preloaded systems. You can download a wide variety of preloaded virtual machines and choose which one you want to use.

VMware Player is great for training new users and testing new software/systems. Another advantage of using virtual machines is that you can just delete the virtual machine if you don't like it. You don't have to deal with the litany of installation issues that unavoidably arise when you set up a new system. Once you see how easy VMware is to use you'll probably download several images.

Note: Some of the images in the following exercises will be large. You can save time downloading the images if your instructor has already placed them on a local server like Blackboard or WebCT. Downloading them from your school's LAN will be much faster. Also, don't uninstall this software. You'll need it for later projects.

1. Download VMware Player from one of the following sites:
   http://www.filehippo.com/download_vmware_player/
   http://www.vmware.com/download/player/download.html
   http://www.softpedia.com/get/System/OS-Enhancements/VMware-Player.shtml
2. Click Start Download Manager for VMware Player for Windows.
3. Click Save.
4. Select the C:\networking\ folder.
5. Click Run, Next, Next, Next, Install, Next, and Finish.
6. Save all of your work and close all other programs.
7. Click Yes to restart your computer.
8. Click Yes to accept the licensing agreement.
9. Double-click the VMware icon on your desktop.
10. Click Download and a Web browser window will open.
11. Type "OpenSUSE" in the search box labeled Search Virtual Appliances.
12. Click Search.
13. Click on the link labeled "OpenSUSE 11.0 RC KDE." (Feel free to try another image if you want to.)

14. Write down the primary account information. (In this case it was Username: **vmplanet** and Password: **vmplanet.net**. With newer virtual machines becoming available it's likely that the usernames and passwords will have changed.)

Note: If you download a different virtual image of OpenSUSE (or any other appliance) the primary username and password will be different. It will be difficult to log in if you don't have the correct username and password. Some students have reported having trouble downloading using Google Chrome. Firefox and Internet Explorer seem to work fine.

15. Click Download this Appliance. (If your instructor hosts a copy of this download on a local file server you can save a lot of time by downloading it on your local area network (LAN).)
16. Click on the link that reads, "OpenSUSE VMware image" to download the image.
17. Click Save.
18. Select the C:\networking\ folder.

Note: These images are large and may take a while. Now that you have the VMware player installed and the image downloaded you need to unzip the image and start the virtual machine. The VM images are zipped because they are very large. Some of the virtual machines you will download will use the .7z file compression format. The .7z compression format does a great job. You will now download the 7-Zip program and unzip the VM image you just downloaded.

19. Download 7-Zip from: http://www.7-zip.org/download.html.
20. Click Download for 7-Zip 4.65. (Select Windows, 32-bit, .exe or .msi, and the version will likely be more current than 4.65. See Figure 4-1.)
21. Click Save.
22. Select the C:\networking\ folder. (See Figure 4-2.)

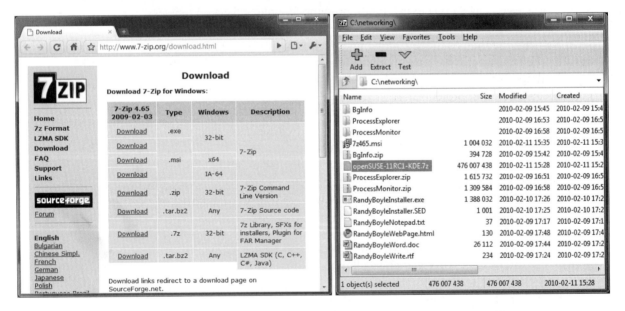

Figure 4-1: 7-Zip download page.   Figure 4-2: Using 7-Zip to decompress image.

23. Double-click the executable file you just downloaded (7z457.msi or 7z457.exe) to install the 7-Zip program.
24. Click Run, Next, I Accept, Next, Next, Install, and Finish.
25. If 7-Zip File Manager doesn't automatically open you can click Start, All Programs, 7-Zip, and 7-Zip File Manager.

26. Browse to C:\networking\ and locate the VM image you downloaded from the Web (openSUSE-11.0-KDE.7z).
27. Select openSuse-11.0-KDE.7z.
28. Click the button labeled Extract.
29. Click OK to extract the openSUSE image. (See Figure 4-3.)
30. Wait for the extraction to complete. (This may take a couple minutes. See Figure 4-4.)

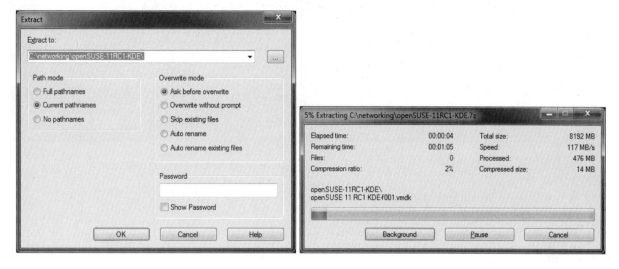

Figure 4-3: Designate directory.   Figure 4-4: Extracting the virtual machine.

31. Return to the VMware Player screen.
32. Click Open.
33. Browse to C:\networking\openSUSE-11.0-KDE\openSUSE-11.0-KDE\.
34. Select the image named openSUSE 11.0 KDE.vmx.
35. Click Open.
36. If you see a window telling you that the machine is in use click "Take Ownership."
37. If you see a window asking you if you moved/copied the virtual machine click "I moved it."
38. Click OK and wait for the OS to load for the first time. (Subsequent boot sequences will be faster.)

Note: Your desktop may not start for some reason. This may be due to a screen resolution issue. Most users don't experience this problem. If the virtual machine starts at the command line you can type startx and it should start the desktop environment.

39. Click on the virtual machine screen.
40. Click on the SUSE icon on the bottom left-hand of the screen to open the SUSE menu.
41. Click on Word Processor to open the OpenOffice Writer program (like Microsoft Word).
42. Type your first and last name in the document as well as the date. (In this case it was Randy Boyle and 10/31/09.)
43. Leave the virtual machine and click on your desktop. (You may have to press Ctrl-Alt to leave the virtual machine.)
44. Take a screenshot of the OpenSUSE virtual machine showing your name in the document. (See Figure 4-5.)

Note: If you have problems taking the screenshot using Ctrl-Alt you can use MWSnap®. If you didn't install MWSnap earlier you can download it at: http://www.mirekw.com/winfreeware/mwsnap.html. You can take the screenshot with MWSnap and then copy/paste it into your word document.

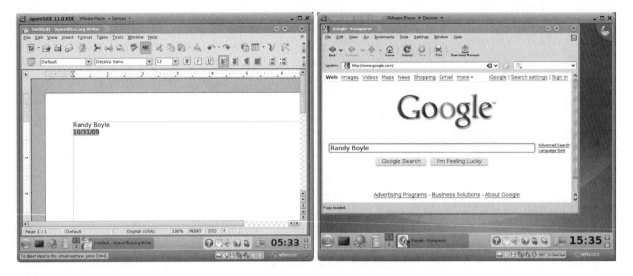

Figure 4-5: Document in openSUSE.   Figure 4-6: Browsing the Web in a virtual machine.

45. Return to the virtual machine.
46. Minimize the document.
47. Click the Firefox icon on the desktop.
48. Enter "www.Google.com" as the URL.

Note: Some students have been unable to access the Internet from their virtual machine because of an IPv6 conflict. To solve this click the OpenSUSE icon, Computer tab, YaST, enter your password (vmplanet.net), Network Devices, Network Settings, Global Options tab, deselect "Enable IPv6", Finish. Then you need to restart the virtual machine by clicking the OpenSUSE icon, Leave, Restart, Restart, and then wait for the virtual machine to reboot. This should solve the IPv6 conflict.

49. Enter "YourName" in the search box.
50. Leave the virtual machine
51. Click on your desktop. (You may have to press Ctrl-Alt to leave the virtual machine if you have an older version of VMware Player.)
52. Take a screenshot of the OpenSUSE virtual machine showing your name Google search box. (See Figure 4-6.)

You can run any version of Linux, FreeBSD, UNIX, or any other virtual machine without having to install them on a dedicated machine. The time savings from using virtual machines is immense. Take some time and explore this Linux desktop.

For many people this will be the first time they have seen Linux. If you want to see the differences between Linux "flavors" feel free to download desktop versions of Ubuntu, Debian, Fedora, Mandriva, etc. After you're done you can just delete them without affecting your computer.

THOUGHT QUESTIONS

1. Can you transfer files from your local host to the virtual machine? How?
2. Does your virtual machine have its own IP address or does it share one with the local host?
3. How many virtual machines can you run at once?
4. If you liked one of the virtual Linux machines could you load it on your computer as the main operating system? How?

4.2   VMWARE MARKETPLACE

In the prior project you installed VMware Player and downloaded a virtual machine. VMware also provides other virtual machines that you can download at VMware Marketplace. This project will explore some of the other virtual machines that you could download. These are preloaded and preconfigured virtual machines that you can download and test drive. This can be a valuable learning resource.

You will also download a virtual machine directly from another Web site that has hosted its own download. Companies like to offer virtual machines of their products because it's an easy way for network administrators to test new software. Network administrators like virtual machines because they don't have to worry about installation or configuration issues.

1. Double-click the VMware icon on your desktop.
2. Click Download and a Web browser window will open.
3. Click on the link labeled Networking.
4. Select Rating in the Sort By drop-down box.
5. Take a screenshot.
6. Click on a virtual machine that interests you. (In this case it was CensorNet.)
7. Take a screenshot.
8. Click Back in your Web browser until you return to the main VMware Marketplace.
9. Click on the link labeled IT Management.
10. Click on a virtual machine that interests you. (In this case it was SpamSniper.)
11. Take a screenshot.
12. Open a new Web browser.
13. Go to http://www.backtrack-linux.org/downloads/. (See Figure 4-7.)
14. Scroll down to the section labeled BackTrack 4 Final Release VMware Image.
15. Click Download. (This is a big download (2GB) that will take awhile unless you get it from your instructor or classmate. If you want a smaller download you can download the Beta version of BackTrack 4 which is half the size (1GB). (See Figure 4-8.)

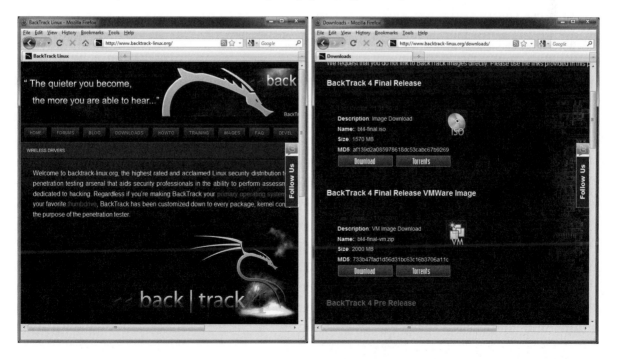

Figure 4-7: BackTrack download page.   Figure 4-8: BackTrack virtual machine.

16. Click Save.
17. Select the C:\networking\ folder.
18. Browse to C:\networking\ and locate the VM image you downloaded from the Web. (See Figure 4-9.)
19. Right-click bt4-final-vm.zip.
20. Select 7-Zip and Extract to "bt4-final-vm \." (You should already have 7-Zip installed from a prior project.)
21. Wait for the extraction to complete. (This may take a minute. See Figure 4-10.)

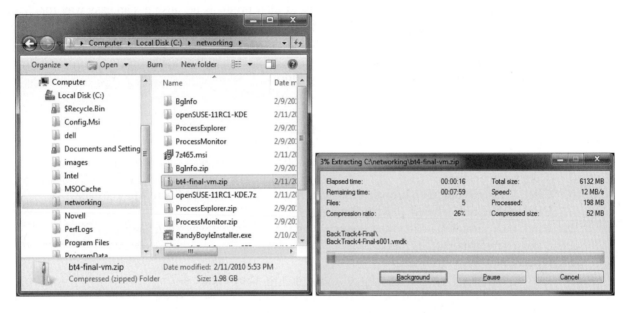

Figure 4-9: Downloaded virtual machine.   Figure 4-10: Extracting BackTrack virtual machine.

22. Double-click the VMware icon on your desktop.
23. Click Open.
24. Browse to C:\networking\bt4-final-vm\BackTrack4-Final.
25. Select the image named BackTrack4-Final.vmx.
26. Click Open.
27. If you see a window asking you if you moved/copied the virtual machine just click "I moved it."
28. At the login enter "root" for the username and "toor" for the password.
29. Type **startx** to start the BackTrack desktop. (See Figure 4-11.)

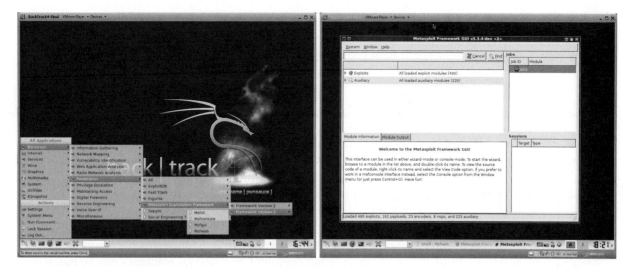

Figure 4-11: BackTrack virtual machine desktop.   Figure 4-12: Metasploit within BackTrack.

30. Click on the virtual machine screen.
31. Click on the BackTrack icon on the bottom left-hand of the screen to open the menu.
32. Click BackTrack, Penetration, Framework Version 3, Framework3-Msfgui. (See Figure 4-12.)
33. Click on Exploits, Windows, Games.
34. Select one of the exploits to read about.
35. Enter your first and last name in the search box at the top.
36. Leave the virtual machine and click on your desktop. (You may have to press Ctrl-Alt to leave the virtual machine.)
37. Take a screenshot of the virtual machine showing your name in the search bar. (See Figure 4-13.)

Figure 4-13: Vulnerability listed in Metasploit.

Note: Several students have noted that there is a DHCP configuration issue with early versions of BackTrack 4. If you can't get on the Internet you can open a command prompt in the virtual machine and enter `dhclient eth0`. This will reconfigure your network connection.

THOUGHT QUESTIONS

1. Are there programs that will allow you to manage multiple virtual machines at once?

2. Can you adjust the amount of RAM a virtual machine uses? How?
3. Will the virtual machine keep all the changes you make to it? Why?
4. How do companies benefit from providing virtual machines for administrators to test drive?

4.3   SUN VIRTUALBOX

There are some distributions that do not come as a preinstalled virtual machine. In this project you will create a virtual machine. When you create your own virtual machine you can create a custom virtual hard drive, set the amount of RAM you want allocated, and set additional installation parameters. If you are running short on RAM or hard disk space it's better to create your own virtual machine.

Sun VirtualBox® is a free product that allows you to create custom virtual machines. VMware's Workstation is the rough equivalent of VirtualBox but costs $189 at the time this book was written. Microsoft gives users Virtual PC 2007® for free but creating Linux virtual machines can be much more difficult because they are not supported. You will use Virtual PC 2007 in a later project. Let's create a virtual machine and load a Linux distribution called Ubuntu.

1. Download Ubuntu from: http://www.ubuntu.com/.
2. Click Download Ubuntu. (This project uses Ubuntu 9.10 but any later version will also work. See Figure 4-14.)
3. Select a location that is close to you.
4. Click Begin Download. (See Figure 4-15.)
5. Click Save.
6. Select the C:\networking\ folder. (This is a big download that will take awhile unless you get it from your instructor or classmate. It should be about 700 MB.)

Figure 4-14: Ubuntu main page.   Figure 4-15: Ubuntu download page.

7. Download VirtualBox from http://www.virtualbox.org/wiki/Downloads.
8. Click on the "x86" link next to VirtualBox 3.1.4 for Windows hosts.
9. Click Save.
10. Select the C:\networking\ folder.
11. Browse to the C:\networking\ folder.

12. Double-click VirtualBox-3.1.4-57640-Win.exe.
13. Click Next, I Accept, Next, Next, Next, Yes, Install, and Finish. (Click Yes if you see any other popup windows.)
14. Click Cancel on the registration window.

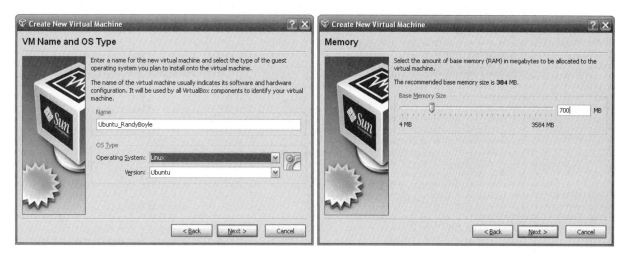

Figure 4-16: Naming a virtual machine.   Figure 4-17: Amount of RAM for the virtual machine.

15. Click Start, All Programs, Sun VirtualBox, and VirtualBox.
16. Click New and Next.
17. Enter "Ubuntu_YourName" for the Name. (In this case it was Ubuntu_RandyBoyle. See Figure 4-16.)
18. Select Linux for the Operating System.
19. Select Ubuntu for the Version.
20. Click Next.
21. Increase the amount of memory to 700 MB+. (See Figure 4-17.)
22. Click Next, Next, Next and Next.

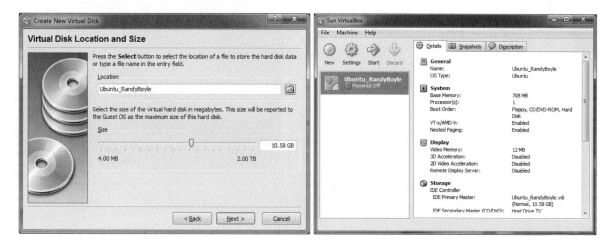

Figure 4-18: Naming your virtual disk.   Figure 4-19: Ubuntu virtual machine was created.

23. Increase the hard drive space to 10GB (or more). (See Figure 4-18.)
24. Click Next, Finish, and Finish.
25. Select the Virtual machine labeled Ubuntu_YourName. (See Figure 4-19.)
26. In the right-hand pane click Storage.
27. Click on the IDE Controller labeled "Empty."

28. Click the browse button on the right-hand side of the screen next to CD/DVD Device. (You are going to browse to the Ubuntu ISO image you downloaded earlier and mount it.)
29. Click Add.
30. Browse to C:\networking\.
31. Select the Ubuntu image you downloaded. (See Figure 4-20.)
32. Click OK and Select. (See Figure 4-21.)
33. Click OK.

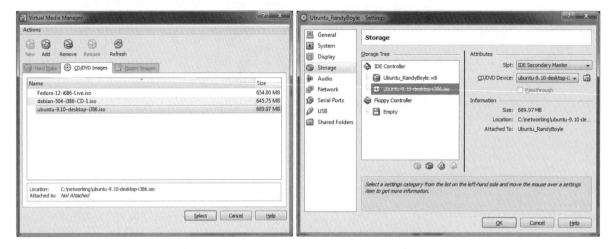

Figure 4-20: Capturing the downloaded .ISO image.   Figure 4-21: ISO image is mounted.

34. Take a screenshot showing the new virtual machine. (See Figure 4-22.)
35. Click Start.

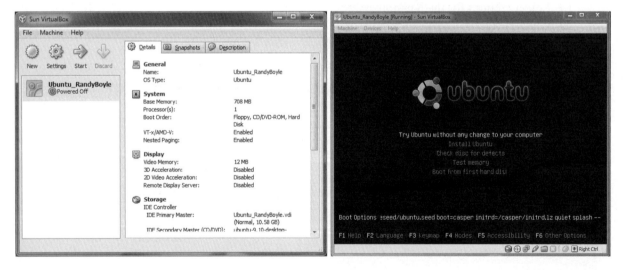

Figure 4-22: Ubuntu .ISO image is captured and ready to boot.   Figure 4-23: Ubuntu installation screen.

36. Press Enter to select English as the language. (You must select a language before the timer expires or you won't be able to go through the installation process. See Figure 4-23.)
37. Arrow down to the menu option labeled Install Ubuntu.
38. Press Enter. (You can leave the virtual machine by holding down the right Ctrl key.)
39. Click Forward.
40. Select your time zone.
41. Click Forward, Forward, and Forward.
42. Enter your first name and last name.

43. Enter a password (twice) that you can remember. (It's also a good idea to write down both the username and password if you have a bad memory. You'll need it to log in.)

Note: You may have to press the right Ctrl key to exit the virtual machine and then use MWSnap to take screenshots in VirtualBox. If you didn't install MWSnap earlier you can download it at: http://www.mirekw.com/winfreeware/mwsnap.html.

44. Take a screenshot. (See Figure 4-24.)
45. Click Forward and Install.
46. Wait for the installation to complete. (This may take awhile. You may want to take a break and come back when it's finished. See Figure 4-25.)

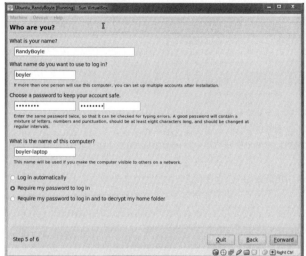

Figure 4-24: Entering login information.

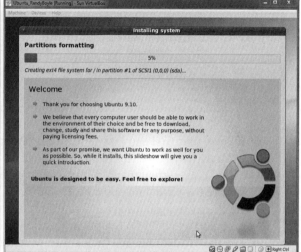

Figure 4-25: Installing Ubuntu.

47. Press the right Ctrl key to exit the virtual machine.
48. In the VirtualBox menu click Devices and CD-DVD ROM. (If you don't unmount the CD ROM drive it will start the installation process again.)
49. Deselect the Ubuntu CD.
50. Click force unmount and OK.
51. Return to the virtual machine.
52. Click Restart Now.
53. Press Enter. (This will restart your virtual machine. You can also manually restart the virtual machine through the VirtualBox menu, Machine, Restart.)
54. Click on your username.
55. Enter your password.
56. Click Log In. (See Figure 4-26.)

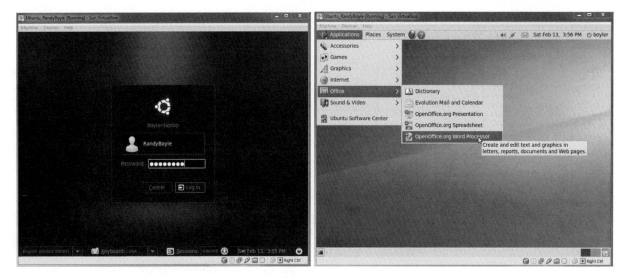

Figure 4-26: Ubuntu login screen.   Figure 4-27: Ubuntu menu system.

57. Click on the Ubuntu icon on the top left-hand of the screen to open the Ubuntu menu.
58. Click Office and OpenOffice.org Word Processor. (See Figure 4-27.)
59. Type your first and last name in the document as well as the date and time. (In this case it was Randy Boyle, 02/13/10, 03:59:24 PM.)
60. Leave the virtual machine and click on your desktop. (You may have to press the right Ctrl key to leave the virtual machine.)
61. Take a screenshot of the Ubuntu virtual machine showing your name in the document. (You may have to use the MWSnap tool mentioned earlier. See Figure 4-28.)
62. In the virtual machine menu click Machine and Close.
63. Select Save State. (See Figure 4-29.)
64. Click OK.

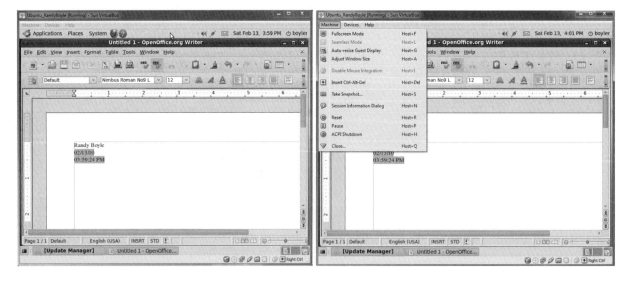

Figure 4-28: Editing a document in Ubuntu.   Figure 4-29: Shutting down a virtual machine.

THOUGHT QUESTIONS

1. Why would application testers like virtual machines?
2. Could you remote into a virtual machine?

3. What advantage would come from being able to adjust the disk size or amount of RAM available to a virtual machine?
4. Could you access a USB drive from within this virtual machine? How?

4.4 MICROSOFT VIRTUAL PC & XP MODE

Windows Virtual PC (free) is a competing product for Sun VirtualBox (free) and VMware Workstation ($189). You can create your own virtual machines in Virtual PC. However, creating virtual machines for some of the open source distributions (i.e. Linux distributions) can sometimes be problematic. Virtual PC 2007 does work well with virtual machines running Microsoft operating systems.

Within Windows 7, you can use Virtual PC to run programs in Windows XP Mode. Basically it is a Windows XP virtual machine within your Windows 7 host. This allows you to run legacy Windows XP programs that may not work with Windows 7. Files, drives, and most hardware are fully integrated. In this project you will download both Virtual PC and the files necessary for Windows XP Mode.

You will also load a copy of Ubuntu as a virtual machine similar to the prior project. You will use the same ISO file. Virtual PC cannot open virtual machines created by VirtualBox. Creating another Linux virtual machine will give you additional practice and make you familiar with creating virtual machines on different platforms.

You can still complete this project if you are running Windows XP as your host operating system. Alternate instructions for installing Virtual PC and getting the appropriate Windows XP image are given at the end of this project. You will download Virtual PC and an XP virtual machine from separate links.

WARNING: There are large downloads for this project. It will save you time if you can get them from your instructor, a classmate, or from a computer with a high-speed connection.

1. Download Microsoft Windows XP Mode and Virtual PC 2007 from the following link: http://www.microsoft.com/windows/virtual-pc/download.aspx
2. Select your version of Windows 7 and your hardware platform. (In this case it was Professional 32-bit in English.)
3. Click Download for the Windows XP Mode (WindowsXPMode_en-us.exe). (See Figure 4-30.)
4. Click Save.
5. Select the C:\networking\ folder.
6. Click Download for the Windows Virtual PC (Windows6.1-KB958559-x86.msu). (See Figure 4-31.)
7. Click Save.
8. Select the C:\networking\ folder.
9. Browse to the C:\networking\ folder.
10. Double-click WindowsXPMode_en-us.exe.
11. Click Run, Next, Next, Yes, and Finish.

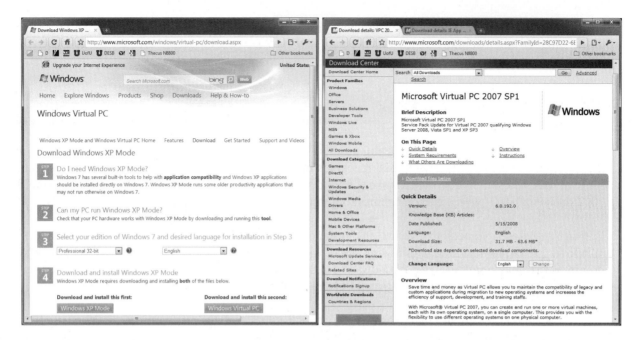

Figure 4-30: Download for Windows XP Mode and Virtual PC.   Figure 4-31: Download for Windows Virtual PC SP1.

12. Browse to the C:\networking\ folder.
13. Double-click Windows6.1-KB958559-x86.msu.
14. Click Yes and I Accept.
15. Save all of your work because you will have to restart your machine in the next step.
16. Click Restart now.

Note: You may see an error message when you try to run Virtual PC (Figure 4-32). If you see this error message you may need to adjust your BIOS (Basic Input/Output System) settings to allow virtualization (Figure 4-33). If you don't know how to adjust your BIOS settings please see a classmate, TA, or your instructor.

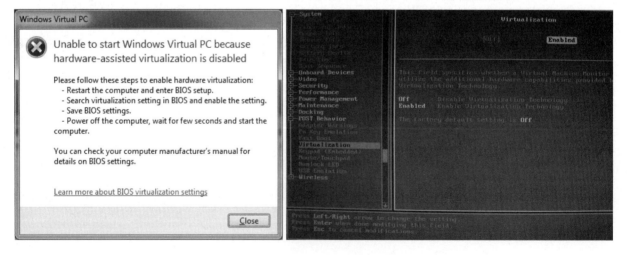

Figure 4-32: Virtualization error message.   Figure 4-33: Change BIOS settings to allow virtualization.

17. Click Start, All Programs, Windows Virtual PC, and Windows XP Mode.
18. Click I Accept and Next.
19. Enter a password that you can remember.
20. Click Next, Turn on automatic updates, Next, and Start Setup. (This may take several minutes.)

21. Take a screenshot of your Windows XP virtual machine within your Windows 7 desktop. (You can use Ctrl-Print Screen to capture the entire desktop. See Figure 4-34.)
22. Within the Windows XP virtual machine click Start, All Programs, Accessories, and Command Prompt.
23. Type `ipconfig /all`
24. Press Enter. (Note that you have a non-routable IP address.)
25. Take a screenshot of your entire desktop. (See Figure 4-35.)

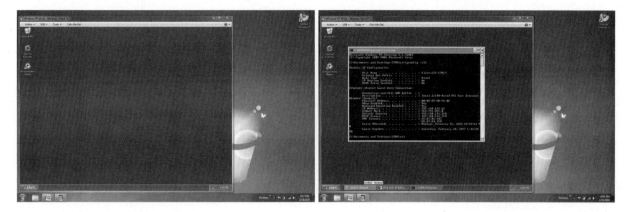

Figure 4-34: Windows XP Mode within Windows 7.   Figure 4-35: Displaying IP address of the virtual machine.

26. Within your Windows XP virtual machine double-click the Internet Explorer icon on your virtual desktop.
27. Go to www.Google.com.
28. Search for "my IP address."
29. Click on any of the first few links provided. (You want to see what outsiders think the IP address is of your virtual machine.)
30. Take a screenshot showing this IP address as it is viewed by external hosts. (Note that it shows the IP address of your host computer.)

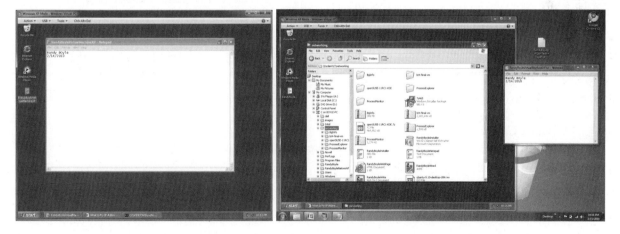

Figure 4-36: Windows XP Mode and Virtual PC.   Figure 4-37: Local host disk access and copy/past functionality.

31. Within the Windows XP virtual machine click Start, All Programs, Accessories, and Windows Explorer.
32. Browse to \\tsclient\C\networking. (This is the C: drive on your Windows 7 Host machine.)
33. Take a screenshot.
34. Within the Windows XP virtual machine right-click the desktop.
35. Select New and Text Document.

36. Type your name and today's date. (See Figure 4-36.)
37. Click File and Save.
38. Enter "YourNameVirtualMachineXP.txt" as the file name and save it on your Windows XP desktop.
39. Copy and then paste the newly saved text file from your Windows XP desktop to your Windows 7 Desktop.
40. Open the new text file.
41. Take a screenshot. (See Figure 4-37.)
42. Close your Windows XP virtual machine.

Note: You are now going to create an Ubuntu virtual machine using Virtual PC. You will use the same ISO image you downloaded and used in a prior project.

43. Double-click the Virtual Machines icon on your desktop.
44. Click Create Virtual Machine.
45. Enter "YourName_Ubuntu2" as the name of the virtual machine. (In this case it was RandyBoyle_Ubuntu2. See Figure 4-38.)
46. Click Next.
47. Change the amount of memory allocated to 700 MB. (See Figure 4-39.)
48. Click Next.

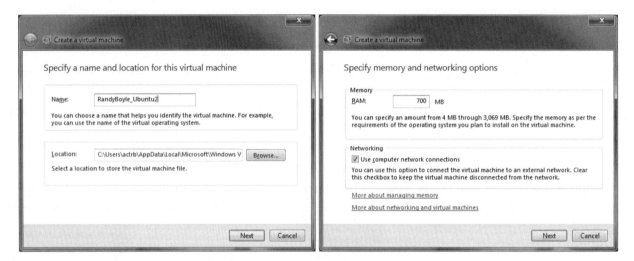

Figure 4-38: Naming a new virtual machine.   Figure 4-39: Allocating memory for the virtual machine.

49. Click Create. (See Figure 4-40.)
50. Select the new virtual machine you just created. (See Figure 4-41.)
51. Click Settings in the File menu.

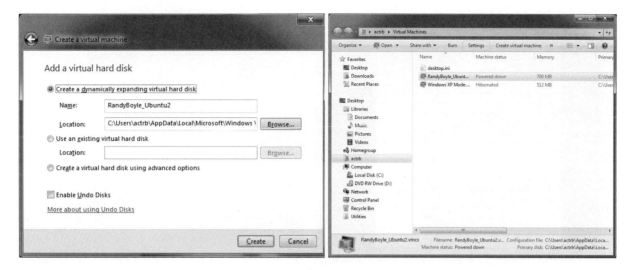

Figure 4-40: Name virtual machine.   Figure 4-41: Virtual machine created.

52. Click on the DVD Drive link in the left-hand pane.
53. Click Open ISO image in the right-hand pane. (See Figure 4-42.)
54. Browse to C:\networking\. (You may have stored the Ubuntu ISO image in another directory. Browse to the directory where you stored the image and select the image.)
55. Click Open. (See Figure 4-43.)
56. Click OK.

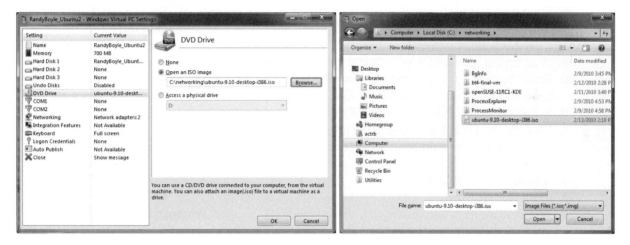

Figure 4-42: Mount Ubuntu ISO image.   Figure 4-43: Select Ubuntu ISO image.

57. Double-click the new virtual machine you just created.
58. Wait a minute or two for the virtual machine to boot up the Ubuntu ISO image.
59. When you see the installation menu click English (or the language of your choice). (See Figure 4-44.)

Note: If you don't select a language BEFORE the time expires it will bypass the installation process and load Ubuntu temporarily in memory. This won't be a permanent installation and you won't be able to make lasting changes to the virtual machine.

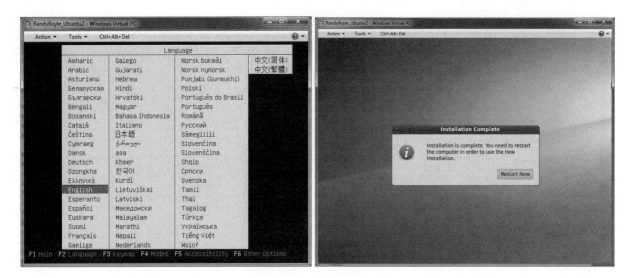

Figure 4-44: Start Ubuntu installation.

Figure 4-45: Ubuntu installation complete.

60. Arrow down to the menu option labeled Install Ubuntu.
61. Press Enter. (You can leave the virtual machine by holding down the right Alt key.)
62. Click Forward.
63. Select your time zone.
64. Click Forward, Forward, and Forward.
65. Enter your first name and last name.
66. Enter a password (twice) that you can remember. (It's also a good idea to write down both the username and password if you have a bad memory. You'll need it to log in.)
67. Click Forward and Install.
68. Wait for the installation to complete. (This may take awhile. See Figure 4-45.)
69. Press the right Alt key to exit the virtual machine. (You can also press Alt-Tab to switch to another window in your Windows 7 machine.)
70. In the Virtual PC File menu select Tools and Settings.
71. Click on the DVD Drive link in the left-hand pane.
72. Click None in the right-hand pane. (See Figure 4-46.)
73. Click OK.
74. Return to the virtual machine.
75. Click Restart Now.
76. Press Enter. (This will restart your virtual machine. You can also manually restart the virtual machine through the Virtual PC menu, Action, Close, Shutdown, OK.)
77. Wait for the virtual machine to restart.
78. Take a screenshot with your username showing. (In this case it was RandyBoyle. See Figure 4-47.)

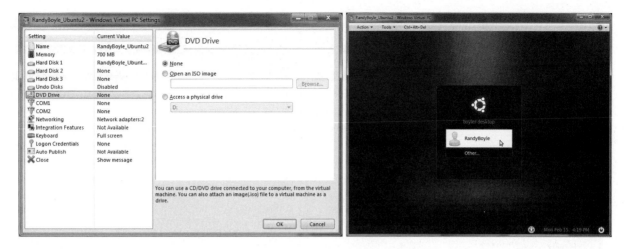

Figure 4-46: Unmounting the Ubuntu ISO.   Figure 4-47: Ubuntu virtual machine in Virtual PC.

ALTERNATIVE INSTRUCTIONS FOR WINDOWS XP USERS

Windows XP users can follow these instructions to install Windows Virtual PC and configure a Windows XP virtual machine. You will install Virtual PC and create the Windows XP virtual hard drive. Then you will be ready to finish the rest of the project. You can continue the rest of the project starting at Step 22 above.

You do not have to go through these instructions if you have already completed this project using Windows 7.

1. Download Microsoft Virtual PC 2007 from the following link: http://www.microsoft.com/downloads/details.aspx?FamilyId=28C97D22-6EB8-4A09-A7F7-F6C7A1F000B5&displaylang=en. (You can also search the Web for "Virtual PC SP1 download.")
2. Click Download for the 32 BIT\setup.exe. (See Figure 4-48.)
3. Click Save.
4. Select the C:\networking\ folder.
5. Click Run and OK.
6. If your download doesn't automatically unzip and run you should run the file labeled setup.exe.
7. Click Run, Next, I accept, Next, Next, Next, and Finish.

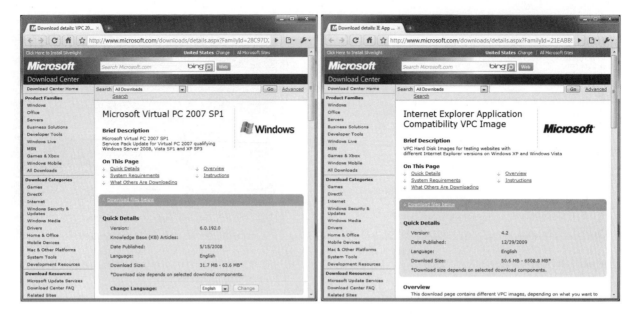

Figure 4-48: Download for Virtual PC 2007.   Figure 4-49: Download for Windows XP virtual machine.

8. Download a Windows XP virtual machine from
    http://www.microsoft.com/downloads/details.aspx?FamilyId=21EABB90-958F-4B64-B5F1-
    73D0A413C8EF&displaylang=en. (You can also do a Web search for "Internet Explorer
    Application Compatibility VPC Image.")
9. Click on the Download button for IE7-XPSP3.exe (or later version if you want to). (See Figure 4-
    49.)
10. Click Save.
11. Select the C:\networking\ folder.
12. After the download completes double-click IE7-XPSP3.exe. (This will create a virtual hard drive
    in the C:\networking\ folder.)
13. Click Run, Accept, and Install. (See Figure 4-50.)

Figure 4-50: Extracting to the networking folder.   Figure 4-51: Creating a new virtual machine.

14. Double-click the Virtual PC icon on your desktop.
15. Click New. (The Virtual Machine Wizard may automatically start. See Figure 4-51.)
16. Click Next.
17. Select "Create a virtual machine." (See Figure 4-52.)

18. Click Next and Browse.

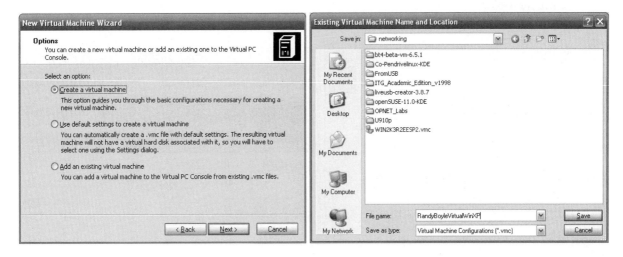

Figure 4-52: Add an existing virtual machine.   Figure 4-53: Naming the new virtual machine.

19. Navigate to the C:\networking\ folder.
20. Name the file YourNameVirtualWinXP. (In this case it was RandyBoyleVirtualWinXP. See Figure 4-53.)
21. Click Save and Next.
22. Check to make sure the operating system is Windows XP. (See Figure 4-54.)
23. Click Next.
24. Select Adjusting the RAM.
25. Adjust the RAM to 700 MB+. (See Figure 4-55.)
26. Click Next.

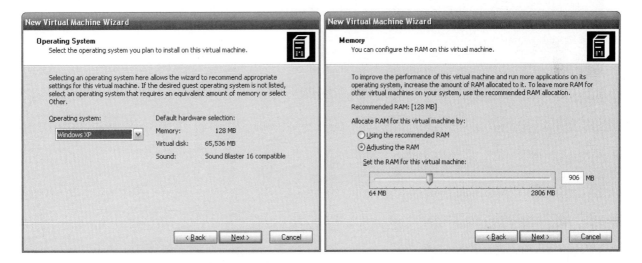

Figure 4-54: Select operating system for the virtual machine.   Figure 4-55: Allocated amount of RAM for the virtual machine.

27. Select the option labeled "An existing hard drive."
28. Click Next and Browse.
29. Browse to your C:\networking\ folder.
30. Select IE7 on XP SP3.vhd. (See Figure 4-56.)
31. Click Open, Next, and Finish.
32. If a small window appears notifying you of some hardware changes just click OK.
33. Double-click the Virtual PC icon on your desktop if Virtual PC isn't open.

34. At the main Virtual PC Console select the Windows XP virtual machine you just created. (See Figure 4-57.)
35. Click Start.

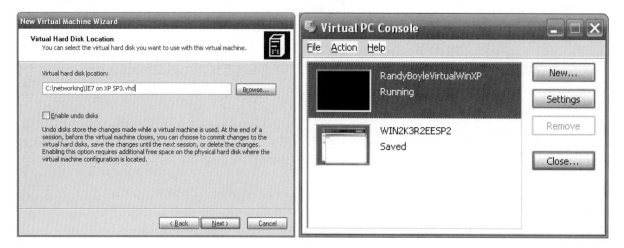

Figure 4-56: Loading the virtual hard disk.   Figure 4-57: Starting a virtual machine.

36. Take a screenshot of your Windows XP virtual machine with your name at the top. (See Figure 4-58.)
37. Go to Step 22 near the start of this project and complete the rest of the project requirements.

Figure 4-58: Windows XP virtual machine.

THOUGHT QUESTIONS

1. Why does the virtual machine show a different IP address using ipconfig than is shown when searching on the Web?
2. Does the virtual machine use the same MAC address as the host or does it get a new MAC address?
3. What would happen if you started 3 or more virtual machines at the same time on the same host?
4. Why would Windows 7 come with Windows XP mode? Are all programs backward compatible?

One of the leading server operating systems in use today is Microsoft Windows Server 2003. The latest iteration is Microsoft Windows Server 2008. It's important to be familiar with what Windows Server 2003/2008 can do because it is used by a large number of companies on a day-to-day basis. In this project you will download copies of Windows Server 2003 and Windows Server 2008. You will use the virtual machines from this project as part of later projects.

Running these virtual machines will allow you to becoming more familiar with them and not have to worry about damaging a critical system. Because it's an image you won't have to worry about "crashing" it or improperly configuring it. If you run into a problem you can just delete the image and open a fresh copy from the zipped archive you downloaded. Virtual machines are excellent training tools.

VMWARE ESX, HYPER-V, AND XENSERVER

As organizations grow they also get more servers. The more servers you have the harder they are to manage. You could load a couple of virtual machines each on bunch of old PCs but the management costs would be enormous and reliability would be horrible. It's much better to buy a few powerful servers and run many different virtual machines on them as a combined physical machine.

There are systems that enable you to remotely administer virtual machines through a single interface, delegate control, allocate RAM /CPUs, run multiple processors, and handle multi-threading. All of these are substantial advantages over Virtual PC/VMware Player/VirtualBox.

Larger companies have stacks of servers with multi-core 64-bit architecture. Better hardware enables you to run VMware ESX, Hyper-V, XenServer, etc. They allow network administrators to easily manage all of their servers from a single console. They also ensure a high degree of availability, scalability, and reliability.

Due to the fact that you must have 64-bit hardware to run these systems, some students wouldn't be able to complete projects using these virtual machine managers. At this stage in the development of computing, about 50% of students still have 32-bit systems (and not enough RAM). Most newer computers will be 64-bit and have enough resources to run these systems. The next edition of this book likely include these projects. This edition will focus on 32-bit virtual machine clients.

WARNING: There are large downloads for this project. It will save you time if you can get them from your instructor, a classmate, or from a computer with a high-speed connection. Additional virtual machines from Microsoft can be downloaded from: http://technet.microsoft.com/en-us/bb738372.aspx.

1. Download the virtual machine for Microsoft Windows Server 2003 from the following link: http://www.microsoft.com/DOWNLOADS/details.aspx?familyid=77F24C9D-B4B8-4F73-99E3-C66F80E415B6&displaylang=en. (You can also search the Web for "Server 2003 VHD." See Figure 4-59.)
2. Click Download for parts 1-3 including the following:
   WIN2K3R2EESP2.part1.exe (700 MB)
   WIN2K3R2EESP2.part2.rar (700 MB)
   WIN2K3R2EESP2.part3.rar (495 MB)
3. Click Save.
4. Select the C:\networking\ folder.
5. Download the virtual machine for Microsoft Windows Server 2008 from the following link: http://www.microsoft.com/downloads/details.aspx?FamilyID=764b531e-4526-4329-80b5-

921fd3297883&displaylang=en. (You can also search the Web for "Server 2008 VHD." See Figure 4-60.)

6. Click Download for parts 1-3 including the following:
   Windows2008Fullx86Ent.part01.exe (700 MB)
   Windows2008Fullx86Ent.part02.rar (700 MB)
   Windows2008Fullx86Ent.part03.rar (473 MB)
7. Click Save.
8. Select the C:\networking\ folder.

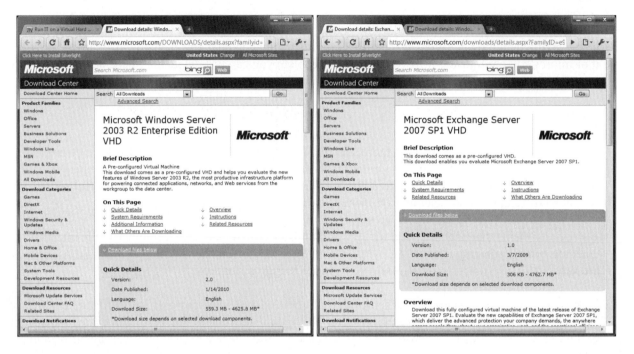

Figure 4-59: Add virtual machine.   Figure 4-60: Virtual machines running.

9. Browse to the C:\networking\ folder.
10. Double-click WIN2K3R2EESP2.part1.exe to unzip the compressed image and create the virtual machine.
11. Click Run, Accept, and Install.
12. Wait until the compressed files create the .vmc file in the C:\networking\ folder. (The two main files you need are WIN2K3R2EESP2.vhd and WIN2K3R2EESP2.vmc.)
13. Double-click the file labeled WIN2K3R2EESP2.vmc. (This will start the virtual machine.)
14. Click the Ctrl+Alt+Del button in the VMware Player File menu.
15. Enter "Evaluation1" as your password. (You can find this password in the ReadMe.txt file that was created when you ran WIN2K3R2EESP2.part1.exe. See Figure 4-61.)
16. Minimize any windows that may be open.
17. Right-click the desktop and select New, Text Document.
18. Type your name, "Virtual Server," and the current date in the new text document (e.g. Randy Boyle, Virtual Server, 11/3/2009).
19. Leave the Windows Server 2003 virtual machine and click on your host desktop.
20. Click on the desktop and press Ctrl-PrtScn to take a screenshot with your name showing. (You can also use MWSnap to take the screenshot. See Figure 4-62.)

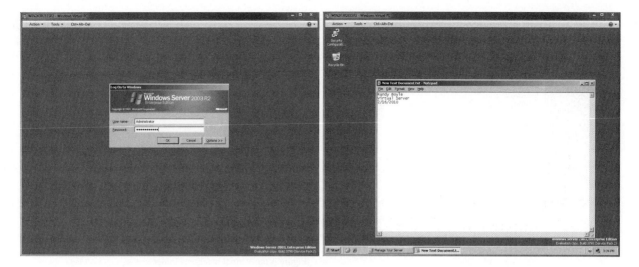

Figure 4-61: Virtual machine log on for Server 2003.   Figure 4-62: Working in a Server 2003 virtual machine.

Note: The virtual machines in these exercises will expire after 60-90 days. If you register them they will not expire (Figure 4-63). If you are a college student you should have access to an MSDNAA account through your department. You can get product keys through your online MSDNAA account. Please ask your instructor about how to register for these product keys. Once they are registered you can use them indefinitely (Figure 4-64).

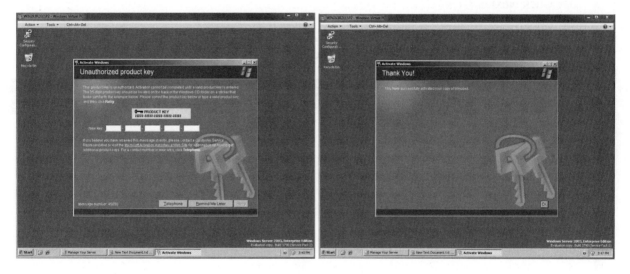

Figure 4-63: Registering Server 2003.   Figure 4-64: Registration of Server 2003 successful.

21. Browse to the C:\networking\ folder.
22. Double-click Windows2008Fullx86Ent.part01.exe to unzip the compressed image and create the virtual machine.
23. Click Run, Accept, Install. (It may take awhile for the virtual machine to be assembled in the C:\networking\ folder. See Figure 4-65.)
24. Double-click the Virtual Machines icon on your desktop. (You can also reach this shortcut by clicking Start, All Programs, Windows Virtual PC, and Virtual Machines.)
25. Click Create Virtual Machine. (See Figure 4-66.)

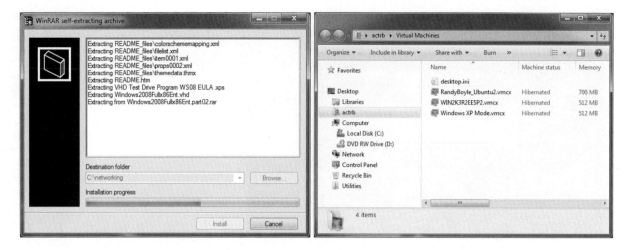

Figure 4-65: Unpacking Server 2008.   Figure 4-66: Virtual machines folder.

26. Enter "YourNameServer2008" for the name of the virtual machine. (In this case it was RandyBoyleServer2008.)
27. Click Browse.
28. Set the location to store the virtual machine to the C:\networking\ folder. (See Figure 4-67.)
29. Click OK and Next.
30. Set the amount of RAM to 700+ MB.
31. Click Next.
32. Select "Use an existing hard disk."
33. Browse to C:\networking\.
34. Select the file labeled Windows2008Fullx86Ent.vhd. (See Figure 4-68.)

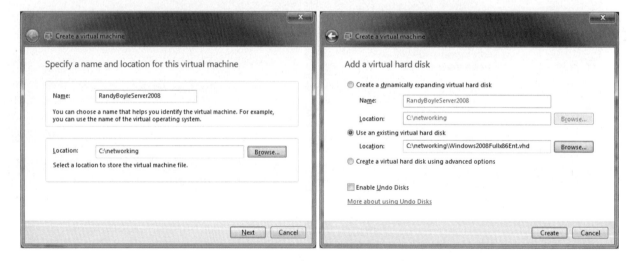

Figure 4-67: Naming your Server 2008 virtual machine.   Figure 4-68: Selecting the Server 2008 virtual disk.

35. Click Create.
36. Return to the window showing all of your virtual machines. (You can get here by double-clicking on the Virtual Machines icon on your desktop.)
37. Double-click YourNameServer2008.vmcx. (See Figure 4-69.)
38. Wait for the virtual machine to boot.
39. Click in the virtual machine. (To leave the virtual machine you can press Alt-Tab.)
40. Click Next. (See Figure 4-70.)

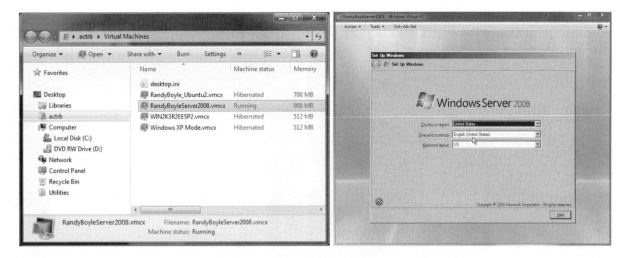

Figure 4-69: Server 2008 virtual machine was created.   Figure 4-70: Server 2008 setup screen.

41. Leave the product key blank.
42. Uncheck the check box labeled "Automatically activate Windows when I'm online." (See Figure 4-71.)
43. Click Next, I Accept, and Next.
44. Enter "YourName" as the computer name. (In this case it was RandyBoyle. See Figure 4-72.)
45. Click Start and OK.

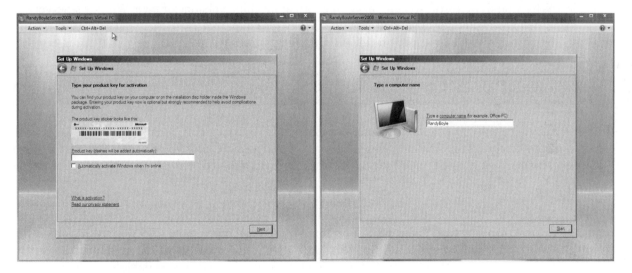

Figure 4-71: Registering Server 2008.   Figure 4-72: Naming your computer.

46. Enter "Evaluation1" as your password in both the New password and Confirm password boxes. (You can enter any password you want but it might be easier to remember if you use the same password for both Windows Server virtual machines. See Figure 4-73.)
47. Click OK.
48. Minimize any windows that may be open.
49. Right-click the desktop and select New and Text Document.
50. Type your name, "Virtual Server 2008," and the current date in the new text document (e.g. Randy Boyle, Virtual Server 2008, 11/3/2009).
51. Leave the Windows Server 2008 virtual machine and click on your host desktop.
52. Click on the desktop and press Ctrl-PrtScn to take a screenshot with your name showing. (You can also use MWSnap to take the screenshot. See Figure 4-74.)

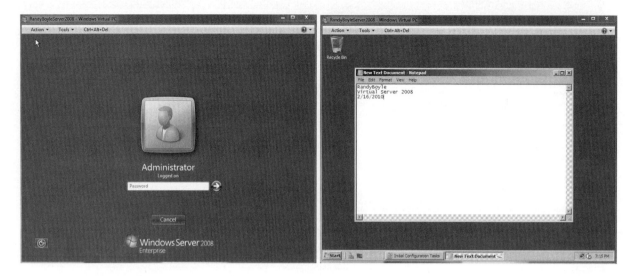

Figure 4-73: Server 2008 log on screen.　　　　Figure 4-74: Server 2008 desktop.

THOUGHT QUESTIONS

1. Name a new functionality in Windows Server 2008 that is not in Windows Server 2003.
2. What is one difference between "enterprise" and "standard" versions of Windows Server?
3. Why would Microsoft want to make free virtual machine versions of their Windows Server product available for download? Wouldn't they lose money?
4. Why would virtual machines be ideal for training purposes?

4.6   COMPUTER ON A USB

Imagine having a fully-functional computer the size of a USB drive. You'll make one in this project. It will run completely off the USB and will maintain a persistent state after you close it. The next time you need a computer you can just run a short script from the USB and your virtual machine will start on the local host.

Having a bootable USB is a great backup computer and is easily transported. It's also much harder for thieves to steal than a laptop. You can run a custom virtual machine without affecting the local host and you can boot it from almost any computer. This project will require a USB with a minimum capacity of 3.75 GB. You may have to borrow one from a friend if you don't have one available.

1. Download Pendrivelinux from: http://www.pendrivelinux.com/run-pendrivelinux-2009-in-windows/. (It can also be reached from the main page at http://www.pendrivelinux.com/.)
2. Click Download Pendrivelinux.
3. Click Save.
4. Select the C:\networking\ folder.
5. Double-click Co-Pendrivelinux-KDE.exe.
6. Click Run.
7. Click Extract. (This will take a couple of minutes.)
8. Open Windows Explorer.
9. Right-Click your inserted USB drive.
10. Select Properties. (This is to make sure you have a minimum of 3.75 GB.)
11. Click OK.

12. Copy the entire folder labeled Co-Pendrivelinux-KDE from the C:\networking\ folder to your USB drive. (This will take several minutes. See Figure 4-75.)

13. Once the download completes double-click on the file labeled Start-Pendrivelinlux.bat.

14. Press the spacebar to let the batch program complete running. (This will take about a minute. See Figure 4-76.)

Note: If you see popup windows asking you to allow several programs to access your network click allow. If you don't you may get several error messages.

Figure 4-75: Directory for Pendrivelinux.

Figure 4-76: Pendrivelinux disclaimer.

Note: Some students have noticed that DHCP is not working correctly and they can't access the Internet through this virtual machine. You can fix this error by clicking the tray.exe icon on your taskbar. This should open a command prompt like the one shown below. Then type `dhclient eth0` (Figure 4-77). This should solve the Internet connectivity problem (Figure 4-78).

Figure 4-77: Solution (`dhclient eth0`) to DHCP error.

Figure 4-78: DHCP error is fixed.

15. Take a full screen capture (Ctrl-PrtScrn) with the Linux panel running on your desktop. (See Figure 4-79.)

16. Click the Pendrivelinux menu icon.

17. Click Utilities, Editors, and KWrite.

18. Type your name, "Pendrivelinux," and the date. (In this case it was Randy Boyle, Pendrivelinux, and 2/22/2010.)

19. Take a full screen capture (Ctrl-PrtScrn) of your desktop showing the KWrite window. (See Figure 4-80.)

Figure 4-79: Pendrivelinux main menu.   Figure 4-80: Running Linux application in Windows.

20. Click the Pendrivelinux menu icon.
21. Click Internet and Konqueror.
22. Enter "www.Google.com" into the location bar.
23. Press Enter.
24. Type your name into the Google search box.
25. Take a full screen capture (Ctrl-PrtScrn) of your desktop showing the Konqueror window. (See Figure 4-81.)

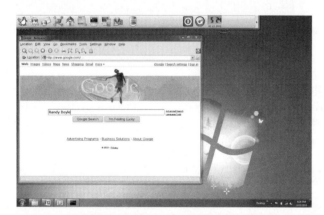

Figure 4-81: Konqueror window.

THOUGHT QUESTIONS

1. Can you install additional software on the USB computer?
2. Can you move files between the host machine and your USB computer? How?
3. Would a computer run off a USB have faster I/O than one run off a regular hard drive? Why?
4. Could you run applications on the USB computer that would be restricted on the local host? Why?

Network administrators spend quite a bit of time troubleshooting and solving a variety of issues. Sometimes they cannot reach the server, or user, remotely. In this project you will download several portable applications that can be used to enhance your troubleshooting ability. We will only look at a small number of applications. Please feel free to browse the entire list of portable applications at http://www.pendriveapps.com/.

Viruses are one of the many reasons you would need portable applications. Some of the more recent virus variants prevent users from receiving antivirus updates, visiting antivirus Websites, and installing antivirus software on their computers. Portable applications solve all of these issues.

Most applications need to be installed on your computer to be run. Portable applications run from your USB. They do NOT need to be installed on the local host. Some software writers release portable versions of their software and others don't. Portable applications are great if you don't have network access or can't install software on the local host. Also, they don't use up additional RAM needed for a full virtual operating system.

Let's look at a couple of examples. You are going to create a document using OpenOffice Portable®, delete it, and then use Recuva® to recover the document. All of this will be run off of your USB drive.

1. Open Windows Explorer by clicking Start, All Programs, Accessories, Windows Explorer. (Alternatively you can press ⊞+E.)
2. Create a new folder in the C:\networking\ folder named YourNamePortableApps.
3. Download the following applications from their respective links or navigate from the main page at http://www.pendriveapps.com/.
4. For each download click on the link near the bottom of the page labeled Download Here.
5. Click Save.
6. Select the C:\networking\YourNamePortableApps\ folder. (See Figure 4-82.)

    a) Recuva: http://www.pendriveapps.com/recuva-portable-file-recovery-tool/
    b) Kapersky Virus Removal Tool: http://www.pendriveapps.com/kaspersky-virus-removal-tool/
    c) Glary Utilities: http://www.pendriveapps.com/glary-utilities-pc-maintenance/
    d) Google Chrome Portable: http://www.pendriveapps.com/google-chrome-portable/
    e) OpenOffice: http://www.pendriveapps.com/openoffice-portable-free-office-suite/

7. Insert a USB drive with at least 2 GB of free space. (In this example it was 8GB of free space.)
8. Copy the folder from C:\networking\YourNamePortableApps\ folder to your USB drive.
9. Take a screenshot showing these five applications in a folder (showing your name) on your USB drive. (See Figure 4-83.)

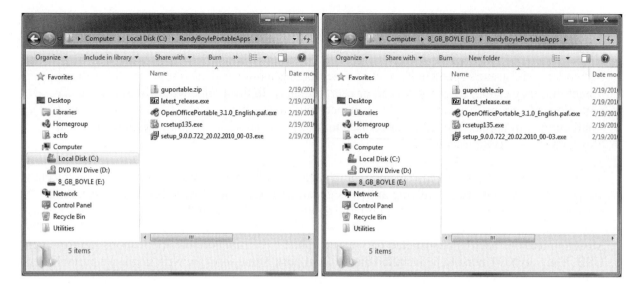

Figure 4-82: Downloaded portable applications.   Figure 4-83: Portable applications on a USB drive.

10. Double-click the file labeled OpenOfficePortable_3.1.0_English.paf.exe. (The version number will undoubtedly be different when you download your version of OpenOffice.)
11. Click Next and Browse.
12. Select your USB drive. (See Figure 4-84.)
13. Click OK and Install.
14. Wait for the installer to finish installing OpenOffice on your USB drive. (See Figure 4-85.)
15. Click Finish.

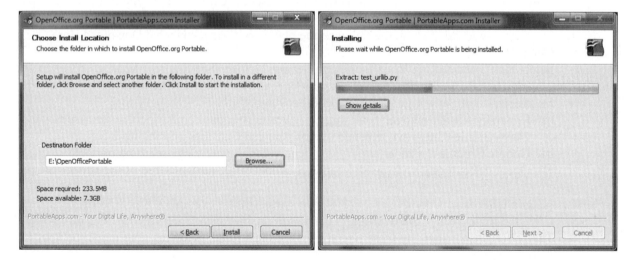

Figure 4-84: Choosing installation location.   Figure 4-85: Installing OpenOffice Portable.

16. Browse to your USB drive and the OpenOfficePortable directory. (In this case it was the E:\OpenOfficePortable.)
17. Double-click OpenOfficeWriterPortable.exe. (See Figure 4-86.)
18. Click Next.
19. Enter your first and last name.
20. Click Next, I do not want to register, Next, and Finish.
21. Type your name, "OpenOffice Portable," and the date. (In this case it was Randy Boyle, OpenOffice Portable, and 2/19/2010.)
22. Take a screenshot with your name showing. (See Figure 4-87.)

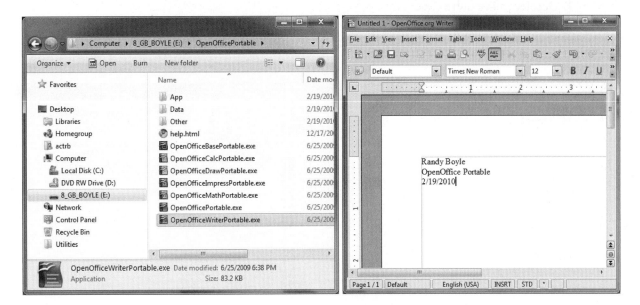

Figure 4-86: Portable OpenOffice executables.　　　　　　Figure 4-87: OpenOffice document.

23. Click File and SaveAs.
24. Select your USB drive as the location. (In this case it was the E: drive.)
25. Name the file YourName. (In this case it was RandyBoyle.)
26. Set the file type to Microsoft Word 6.0 (.doc). (See Figure 4-88.)
27. Click Save. (You are going to delete and recover this file later in this project.)
28. Close the OpenOffice window.

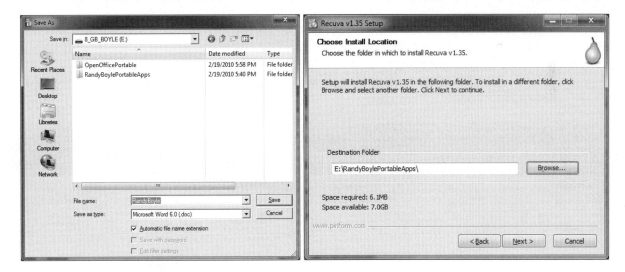

Figure 4-88: Naming the document.　　　　　　Figure 4-89: Recuva installation.

29. In Windows Explorer browse to your USB drive and the OpenOfficePortable directory. (In this case it was the E:\OpenOfficePortable.)
30. Double-click the file labeled rcsetup135.exe. (The version number will undoubtedly be different when you download your version of Recuva.)
31. Click Yes, OK, Next, and I Agree.
32. Select your USB drive and YourNamePortableApps as the Destination folder. (In this case it was E:\RandyBoylePortableApps\. See Figure 4-89.)
33. Click OK and Next.

34. Deselect all options. (See Figure 4-90.)
35. Click Install.
36. Wait for the installer to finish installing Recuva on your USB drive.
37. Click Finish.

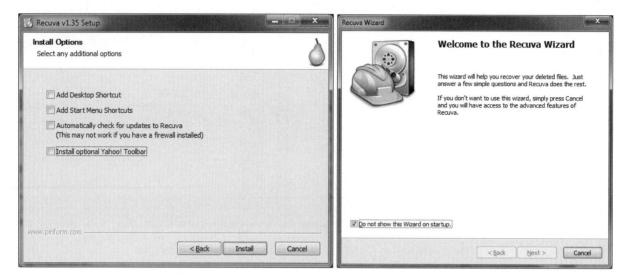

Figure 4-90: Recuva options.

Figure 4-91: Recuva Wizard.

38. Select the "Do not show this Wizard on startup" option. (See Figure 4-91.)
39. Click Cancel.
40. Return to Windows Explorer.
41. Delete the file you just saved in OpenOffice. (In this case it was RandyBoyle.txt.)
42. Return to Recuva.
43. Select your USB as the target drive. (In this case it was E:\.)
44. Click Scan. (See Figure 4-92.)
45. Select the file you just deleted.
46. Take a screenshot of the Recuva window with your deleted document showing. (See Figure 4-93.)

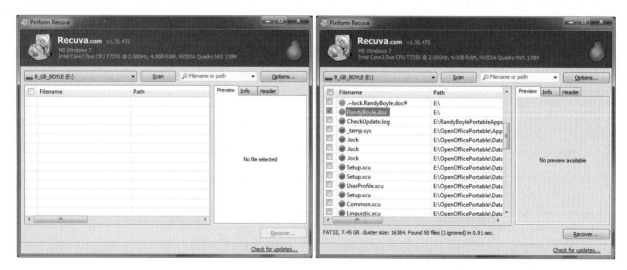

Figure 4-92: Recuva main screen.

Figure 4-93: Recovering files on a USB drive.

47. Click Recover.

48. Select your USB drive.
49. Click OK, Yes, and OK.
50. Take a screenshot of the recovered document in your USB drive. (See Figure 4-94.)

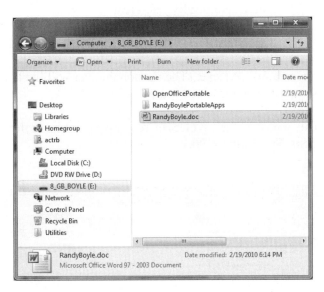

Figure 4-94: Recovered document.

THOUGHT QUESTIONS

1. What advantages would portable applications have over a virtual machine?
2. Describe a situation where you would want an application installed on a USB but not on a hard drive.
3. Could you run an antivirus scan from a portable USB application?
4. What other portable applications might be useful troubleshooting tools to a network administrator.

4.8 BOOTABLE USB

In a previous project you ran Linux as a virtual machine from within Windows. In this project you will create a bootable USB that will load a full Linux operating system (Fedora) without having to have Windows running at all. You will boot your computer from the USB instead of booting from your hard drive.

For some people the idea of booting a computer from anything other than a hard drive can be foreign. Your computer can boot from a hard drive, a USB, CD, etc. and it doesn't know the difference. In this example you will use a tool (LiveUSB Creator®) developed by Luke Macken and Kushal Das that will create a folder on your USB (using a Fedora image) to create the bootable USB.

This bootable USB won't harm your Windows OS or any of your files. You can also customize the Fedora distribution (add/remove software) and create files that will be saved on a dynamically sized virtual drive on your USB. This is a great way to have a fully customizable OS on a small USB. You won't need your Windows password to access any of the files on your hard drive.

There is a new universal USB installer available on Pendrivelinux.com that will automatically configure a variety of different Linux operating systems (http://www.pendrivelinux.com/universal-usb-installer-easy-

<u>as-1-2-3/</u>). This gives users more options and flexibility. However, for your first time creating a bootable USB it's probably best to use a simpler tool like the one below.

1. Download the LiveUSB Creator from: <u>https://fedorahosted.org/liveusb-creator/</u>.
2. Click on the Windows executable labeled liveusb-creator-3.9.1.exe.
3. Click Save.
4. Select the C:\networking\ folder.
5. Double-click the executable labeled liveusb-creator-3.9.1.exe. (The version number will likely be later than the one listed here. Use the most current version. See Figure 4-95.)
6. Click Install.
7. Click Yes to run the LiveUSB Creator. (This will start the LiveUSB Creator program but will not begin the actual creation of the bootable USB. See Figure 4-96.)
8. Close when it is finished.

Figure 4-95: Liveusb-creator.exe.   Figure 4-96: Fedora LiveUSB Creator.

9. Insert a USB with at least 1GB of free memory. (You can use another USB or delete the Pendrivelinux folder from the prior project and use the same USB.)
10. Start Windows Explorer.
11. Right-click your USB drive.
12. Select Properties.
13. Name the drive YourName. (In this case it was Boyle.)
14. Ensure that your USB is formatted with the FAT 32 file system.

Note: If your USB is formatted using NTFS the installation will not complete correctly (Figure 4-97). You will need to reformat your USB using FAT32. This will completely wipe your USB. Back up any files from your USB before you proceed.

The following instructions will explain how to format your USB with the FAT32 file system. Make sure you use the correct drive letter that corresponds with your USB drive. In this case the USB was the E: drive. Your drive letter may be different. Adjust the instructions below to match your correct drive letter.

1. Make sure your USB is inserted.
2. Click Start and Run.

3. Type **CMD**
4. Press Enter.
5. Type **format E: /FS:FAT32**
6. Press Enter. (See Figure 4-98.)
7. Press Enter again to confirm that your USB is inserted.
8. Wait for the format to complete. (This could take several minutes depending on the size of your USB.)
9. Proceed with the rest of the exercise.

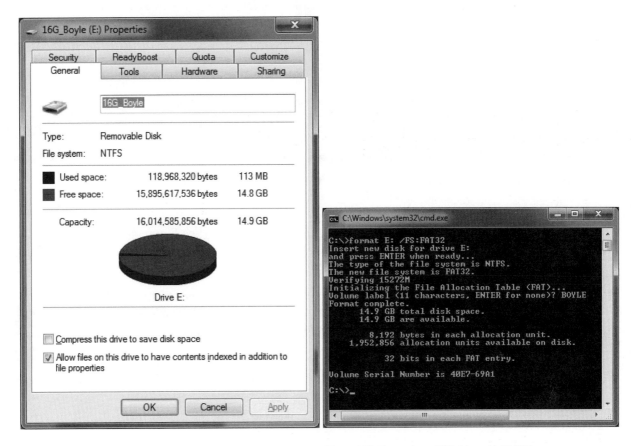

Figure 4-97: USB formatted with NTFS.   Figure 4-98: Formatting a USB drive with FAT32.

15. Return to the LiveUSB Creator window. (It should have started as part of the installation process. You can start it by clicking Start, All Programs, LiveUSB Creator, and LiveUSB Creator.)
16. Make sure you see your USB in the Target Device drop-down window with YourName showing. (In this case it was E: BOYLE.)
17. Set the Persistent Storage to about 1000 MB+. (See Figure 4-99.)
18. Change the download option to Fedora 12 KDE (i686). (If you have a 64-bit computer you can choose the option with the "_64" extension.)

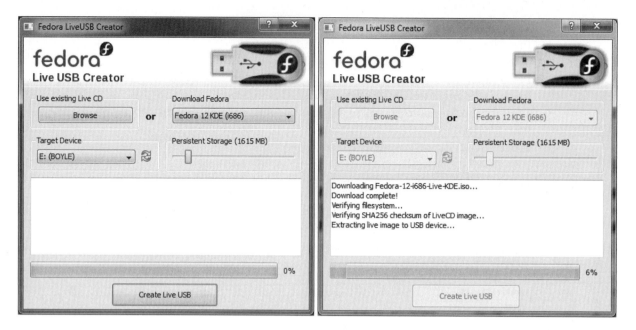

Figure 4-99: Select target device and persistent storage.

Figure 4-100: Creating the bootable USB.

19. Click Create Live USB.
20. Take a screenshot while it is downloading the Fedora image. (See Figure 4-100.)
21. Wait for the creation to complete. (This may take several minutes (about 5 minutes) depending on the speed of your Internet connection. See Figure 4-101.)

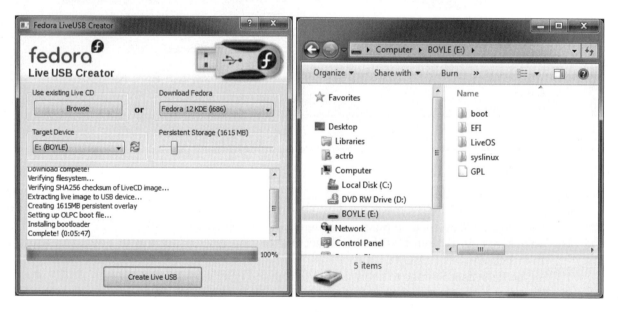

Figure 4-101: Creation of bootable USB is complete.

Figure 4-102: Contents of bootable USB.

Note: In the next part of this project you are going to shut down your computer and then boot it from your USB (Figure 4-102). Your computer is likely set to boot from your hard drive. You will need to enter your BIOS and change the boot order so it will try to boot from the USB first.

Your computer may have a different BIOS than the one used in this example. This means the instructions will be slightly different. This will require you to adapt these instructions to your specific BIOS. As your computer is booting you will press a key to enter the BIOS and/or change the boot order. In this example it was the ESC key. You will see a screen telling you which key to press. You may only get a couple of seconds to press the key.

Depending on your BIOS you may have to press one of the following keys to change the boot order: F2, DEL, ESC, CTRL+ALT+ESC, CTRL+ALT+S, etc. It will probably be ESC, F2, or DEL. After you press this key (or sequence of keys) you will need to navigate the BIOS menu and change the boot order. The computer used in this project was an HP Pavilion.

22. Save all documents and close all programs.
23. Shut down your computer.
24. Press the power button on your computer to start the boot process.
25. Press the ESC key (or the key shown on your screen) to enter the BIOS. (This must be done quickly before the boot process is allowed to complete. If you miss the setup screen you will have to restart your computer again.)
26. Select your USB to boot from. (You may have to save and exit your BIOS before the settings will take effect.)
27. Select Automatic Login. (You will see this at the Fedora login screen.)
28. Click Login.
29. Click Applications, Office, and AbiWord.
30. Type your name, "Bootable USB," and today's date. (In this case it was Randy Boyle, Bootable USB, and 11/18/2009.)
31. Click Applications, Accessories, and Take Screenshot.
32. Click Take Screenshot. (See Figure 4-103.)

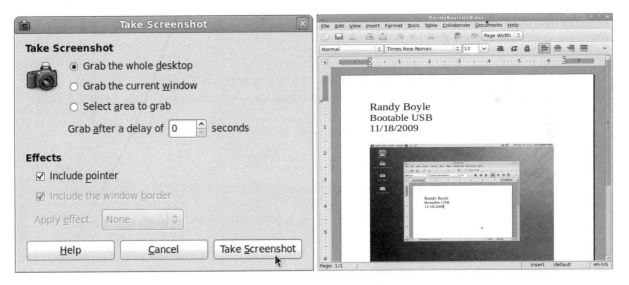

Figure 4-103: Taking a screenshot.   Figure 4-104: Pasting screenshot into AbiWord.

33. Click Copy to Clipboard.
34. Click Cancel.
35. Return to the AbiWord document.
36. Paste the screenshot by clicking Edit and Paste (or Ctrl-V). (See Figure 4-104.)
37. Click File and Save As.
38. Enter "YourNameUSB" in the Name text box. (In this case it was RandyBoyleUSB.)
39. Click Browse for other folders.
40. Select your computer in the left-hand pane. (In this case it was HP_Pavilion. It's very likely your computer will have a different name.)
41. Double-click the folder labeled "networking."

42. Change the drop-down labeled "Save file as type" to Microsoft Word (.doc). (See Figure 4-105.)

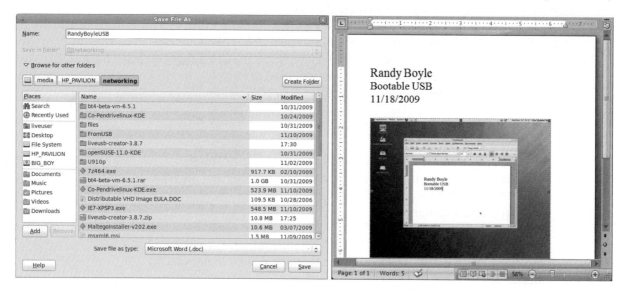

Figure 4-105: Saving the file.   Figure 4-106: Open file in Windows from Linux.

43. Click Save.
44. Close the document.
45. Click System, Shutdown, and Shutdown.
46. After your computer is shutdown remove the USB drive.
47. Restart your computer normally.
48. Open Windows Explorer.
49. Browse to the C:\networking\ folder.
50. Open the file named YourNameUSB.doc. (In this case it was RandyBoyleUSB.doc.)
51. Take a screenshot of this document. (The screenshot you took earlier of the Fedora desktop should be visible. See Figure 4-106.)

THOUGHT QUESTIONS

1. Could you access the files on your computer without entering your Windows username and password? How?
2. Could you recover files from your hard drive with this bootable USB if your Windows OS becomes corrupted?
3. Could you permanently install Fedora on your computer from this bootable distribution? How?
4. What advantage would a bootable USB have over a Live version of Linux?

CHAPTER 5: PACKET ANALYSIS

Packet sniffers are used to analyze network traffic as it is travels across a network. You can even pick up packets of information that may or may not be intended for your computer. Packet sniffers are an extremely valuable tool for network administrators. Network administrators use them to diagnose a wide array of everyday problems on both wired and wireless networks.

You will do a couple of basic exercises to learn how packet sniffers work on a fundamental level. Most people are shocked when they first see a packet sniffer because they didn't realize (1) that there were that many packets going across a network; (2) that a single packet had that much information in it; and (3) that someone else could look at their packets. Seeing a packet sniffer work for the first time can be overwhelming. The trick is to go slow and try to understand each part one at a time.

Packet sniffers are used by network administrators to gather information about traffic over a network, identify rouge machines/servers/services, get statistics about network usage, etc. It would be well worth your time to learn all the functionality that is built into Wireshark®.

There are several other packet sniffers available on the market today that you could learn how to use. Wireshark was chosen because it has excellent functionality and beginning students find it easy to use. Learning how to use a packet sniffer is a critical skill for anyone interested in a career in Networking.

5.1   WIRESHARK INSTALLATION

One of the most well-known packet sniffers is Wireshark (formerly named Ethereal®). This is a flexible and powerful tool. Any network administrator worth his/her salt will know how to run Wireshark. Most professionals use it often. Wireshark has been getting better and better with every release. It will likely be around for a long time as the industry standard.

You will install Wireshark and do a few examples to give you a small taste of what Wireshark can do. In addition to loading Wireshark you will also have to load WinPCap® in order to actually capture the packets being sent over your network.

1. Download Wireshark from http://www.wireshark.org/download.html.
2. Click Windows Installer 32-bit. (You can select the 64-bit version if you have 64-bit hardware.)
3. Click Save.
4. Select C:\networking\.
5. If the program doesn't automatically open, browse to C:\networking\.
6. Double-click Wireshark-win32-1.2.6.exe. (It's likely that a newer version will be available. Please download the latest version. The following directions should be very similar.)
7. Click Next, I Agree, and Next.
8. Select Desktop Icon.
9. Click Next, Next, and Install.
10. Click Next to install WinPCap.
11. Click Next, I Agree, and Finish.
12. Click Next and Finish.
13. Double-click the Wireshark icon on your desktop.
14. Click Capture and Options.
15. Take a screenshot. (See Figure 5-1.)

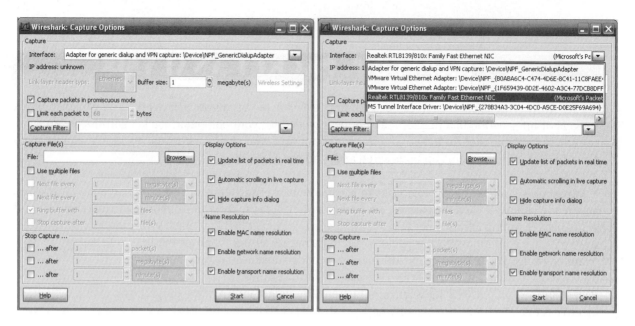

Figure 5-1: Wireshark configuration screen.   Figure 5-2: Select your network card.

16. Select your Network Interface Card (NIC) in the Interface drop-down menu at the top of the screen. (See Figure 5-2.)

Note: Your NIC will undoubtedly have a different name. If you don't know which NIC is your active network card, you should keep trying them all until one of them works. Then memorize the model name and number of your NIC. If you are still looking for a Realtek® NIC like the one shown in the screenshots above, please stop and ask your instructor for help.

17. Close ALL other programs you currently have open except your word processing program (e.g. MS Word or OpenOffice Writer).
18. Click Start.
19. Let it run for 30 seconds.
20. While you are waiting, open a Web browser and go to www.Google.com.
21. Click Capture and Stop.
22. Scroll up until you see a green and blue area. (These are the packets you captured when you requested Google's main page.)
23. Take a screenshot. (See Figure 5-3.)

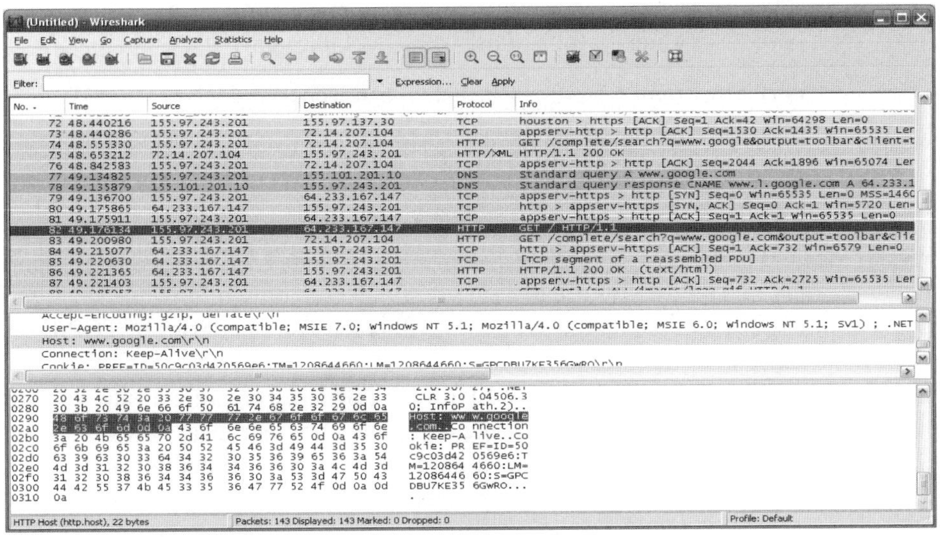

Figure 5-3: Captured packets.

24. Scroll down until you see a line that has "GET / HTTP/1.1" in the Info column. (You may have to try more than one until you get to the packet that shows "www.Google.com" in the bottom pane.)
25. Select that row.
26. In the bottom pane you will see a bunch of numbers to the left. (It's the packets contents in hexadecimal.) Just to the right you will see the content of the packet in a column.
27. Select the text: www.Google.com.
28. Take a screenshot.

Note: You just picked packets off your network and looked at their contents. There may have been a lot of traffic that you couldn't interpret. Don't worry about the information on your screen that is difficult to understand. In the next project you will use a filter to capture only Web traffic going over port 80.

THOUGHT QUESTIONS

1. What do the different colors mean?
2. Why does your computer get packets that are addressed to another machine?
3. How many packets does your computer send/receive in a single mouse click when you visit a Web site?
4. Could you organize or filter the traffic to make it easier to understand?

5.2   CAPTURE TRAFFIC

Now you are going to filter out all the "extra" packets you captured and just look at Web traffic. Too often you will capture much more information than you will ever want or need. Being able to filter out the traffic you don't want is an important skill. Before you can filter packets you need to understand a little bit about "ports."

Ports are like doors and windows on your house. Your house has several points of entry (including doors, windows, chimneys, etc.) through which people could enter your house. Computers work the same way. Each point of entry on a computer is called a port. Information comes into a computer through a port. Each port is given a specific number so it's easier to remember. Below are some of the more common port numbers that you'll need to know:

Port 80 - Web	Port 23 - Telnet	Port 143 - IMAP (email)
Port 20 - FTP (data)	Port 25 - Email	Port 443 - SSL (encrypted)
Port 21 - FTP (supervisory)	Port 110 - POP (email)	

Your house has an address to locate it and a front door for people to enter. Your computer works the same way. It has an IP address to locate it and a port to enter. You can filter packets by IP address or by port number. A thorough understanding of TCP/IP will greatly aid your understanding of how packet filtering works. There are many great tutorials available on the Web that will teach you the basics of TCP/IP.

Below are instructions on how to filter out all packets EXCEPT Web traffic by creating a filter for just port 80. This will capture all the Web traffic going to ALL the computers on your local network. Reread the last sentence. Yes, you read that correctly, it may even capture Web traffic intended for other computers on your network. This is one of the reasons why packet sniffers are important to learn.

1. With Wireshark open click Capture and Options.
2. If you haven't already done so, select your Network Interface Card (NIC) in the Interface drop-down menu at the top of the screen. (Your NIC will undoubtedly have a different name.)
3. Enter "tcp port 80" in the box next to Capture Filter. (See Figure 5-4.)

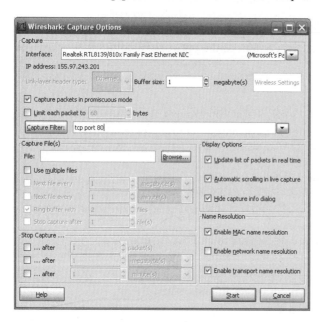

Figure 5-4: Configuring Wireshark to capture port 80 traffic.

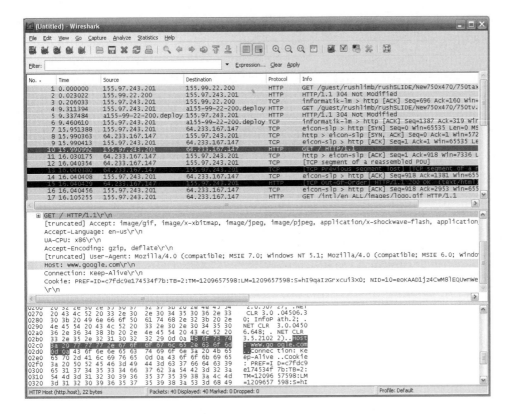

Figure 5-5: Viewing the contents of a packet.

4. Close ALL other programs you currently have open except your word processing program (Microsoft Word, OpenOffice Writer, etc.).
5. Click Start.
6. Open a Web browser and go to www.Google.com.
7. Click Capture and Stop.
8. Scroll down until you see a line that has GET / HTTP/1.1. (You may have to try more than one until you get to the www.Google.com packet.)
9. Select that row.
10. In the bottom pane you will see a bunch of numbers to the left. (It's the contents of the packet in hexadecimal.) Just to the right you will see the contents of the packet in a column.
11. Select the text www.Google.com.
12. Take a screenshot. (See Figure 5-5.)

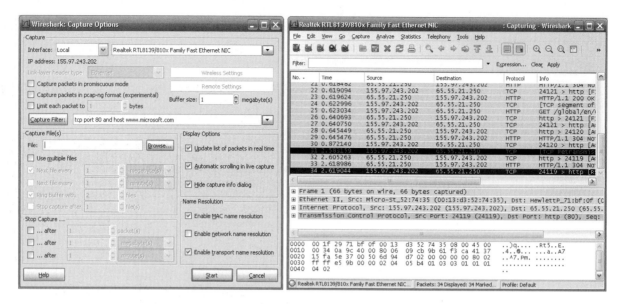

Figure 5-6: Capture filter to include www.microsoft.com.   Figure 5-7: Captured packets.

13. Click Capture and Options.
14. Enter "tcp port 80 and host www.microsoft.com" in the box next to Capture Filter. (See Figure 5-6.)
15. Click Start.
16. Open a Web browser and go to www.Google.com. (You shouldn't pick up any packets.)
17. Go to www.Microsoft.com in your Web browser. (You should pick up several packets.)
18. Click Capture and Stop.
19. Take a screenshot. (See Figure 5-7.)

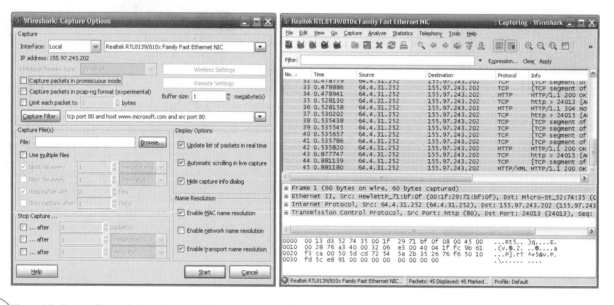

Figure 5-8: Capture filter to include "src port 80."   Figure 5-9: Captured packets from one source IP.

20. Click Capture and Options.
21. Enter "tcp port 80 and host www.microsoft.com and src port 80" in the box next to Capture Filter. (See Figure 5-8.)
22. Click Start.

23. Go to www.Microsoft.com in your Web browser. (You should pick up several packets with the same source IP.)
24. Click Capture and Stop.
25. Take a screenshot. (See Figure 5-9.)

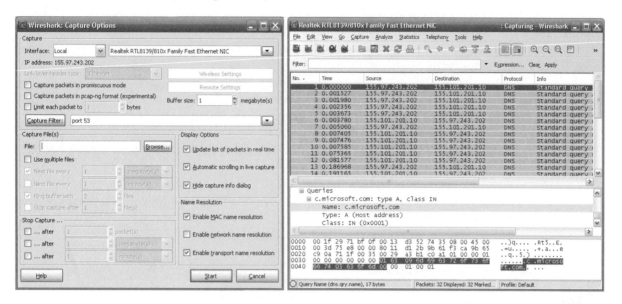

Figure 5-10: Capture filter for port 53.   Figure 5-11: Captured DNS packets.

26. Click Capture and Options.
27. Enter "port 53" in the box next to Capture Filter. (See Figure 5-10.)
28. Click Start.
29. Go to www.Microsoft.com in your Web browser. (You should pick up several packets colored blue by default. These are DNS requests.)
30. Click Capture and Stop.
31. Click on the first row.
32. Highlight the Microsoft entry in the Packet Contents pane.
33. Take a screenshot. (See Figure 5-11.)

In this project you learned how to 1) capture packets going to a specific port, 2) capture traffic addressed to a specific host (or IP address), 3) capture only the source/destination port, and 4) capture DNS traffic. For a list of the possible ports you can specify you can go to the following link: http://wiki.wireshark.org/PortReference.

By filtering only Web traffic (port 80) there was much less information to capture. There was even less traffic if you specified a particular Web site. You can even look at only one side of the conversation by specifying a source or destination port. Wireshark's wiki (http://wiki.wireshark.org/FrontPage) has a lot of information about how to capture specific kinds of traffic and even provides some sample captures.

THOUGHT QUESTIONS

1. Why does your computer send so many packets? Why not send just one really big packet?
2. What do SYN, ACK, FIN, GET mean?
3. Can you capture all of the packets for an entire network?
4. Can Wireshark automatically resolve the IP address into host names?

In the prior project you learned how to capture specific types of traffic. In this project you will look at the parts of a packet. Each packet comes with a lot of information that the end user never sees. Each packet has 1) both source and destination IP addresses, 2) both source and destination MAC addresses, 3) a TTL, and 4) both source and destination port numbers. In addition, they also have information about window size, IP version, timings, sequence numbers, etc.

Understanding the contents of a packet helps you understand how TCP/IP (and the Internet) works in the real world. Each field in a packet serves a purpose. There are also different types of packets (UDP, ICMP, etc.) that perform different functions. You will also walk through a TCP connection in this project. Understanding these fundamental components is critical to becoming a good network administrator.

1. With Wireshark open click Capture and Options.
2. If you haven't already done so, select your Network Interface Card (NIC) in the Interface drop-down menu at the top of the screen.
3. Enter "tcp port 80" in the box next to Capture Filter. (See Figure 5-12.)

Figure 5-12: Configuring Wireshark to capture port 80 packets. Figure 5-13: Captured packets for www.Google.com.

4. Close ALL other programs you currently have open except your word processing program.
5. Right-click anywhere on your desktop.
6. Select New and Shortcut.
7. Enter "www.Google.com". (See Figure 5-13.)
8. Click Next.
9. Enter "Google" for the name. (See Figure 5-14.)
10. Click Finish.

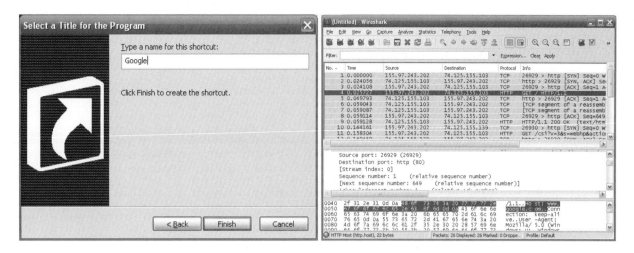

Figure 5-14: Naming the shortcut.

Figure 5-15: GET request showing Google's host name.

11. Close all other Web browsers. (This will reduce the number of packets you capture.)
12. Go back to Wireshark and click Start.
13. Double-click the Google shortcut on your desktop.
14. Wait for the page to load.
15. Close your Web browser.
16. Go back to Wireshark and click Stop.
17. Click on the line that has Get in the Info field. (In this example it was the 4th packet. See Figure 5-15.)
18. In the Packet Details pane (the middle pane) click on the line labeled "Ethernet II."
19. Click on the line labeled "Source."
20. Take a screenshot. (See Figure 5-16.)
21. Open a command prompt by clicking Start and Run.
22. Type **CMD**
23. Type **ipconfig /all**
24. Take a screenshot. (Notice that the MAC and IP addresses are the same as those shown in the Wireshark capture. In this case the MAC address was 00-13-D3-52-74-35. See Figure 5-17.)

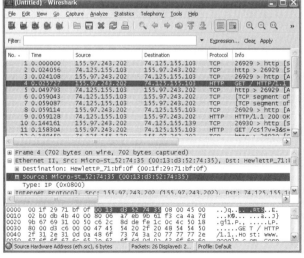

Figure 5-16: Source MAC address on a packet.

Figure 5-17: DOS prompt showing MAC addresses.

25. In the Packet Details pane (the middle pane) click on the line labeled "Hypertext Transfer Protocol."
26. Click on the line labeled "Cookie."
27. Take a screenshot. (See Figure 5-18.)
28. In the File menu click Analyze and Follow TCP Stream.
29. Take a screenshot. (See Figure 5-19.)

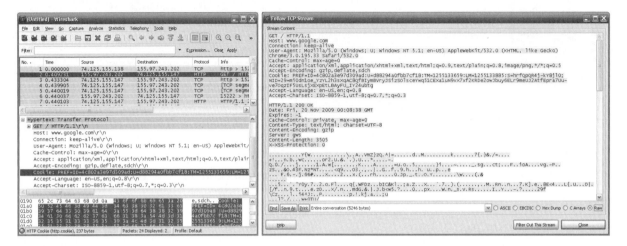

Figure 5-18: Cookie within a packet.   Figure 5-19: Contents of a TCP stream.

Note: In the next part of this project you are going to identify the three parts of a TCP transaction. You will identify 1) connection establishment, 2) data transfer and acknowledgement, and 3) connection termination. You will identify these parts of the TCP process by looking in the Info column of the capture you just performed.

30. In the File menu click View and Packet Details. (This should make the middle pane disappear.)
31. In the File menu click View and Packet Bytes. (This should make the bottom pane disappear.)
32. Maximize the Wireshark window so you can clearly see the column labeled Info.
33. Click on the row that has the first [SYN] occurrence in the Info column. (In this case it was row 1 in the list. It may be farther down in your list of captured packets.)
34. Take a screenshot. (See Figure 5-20.)

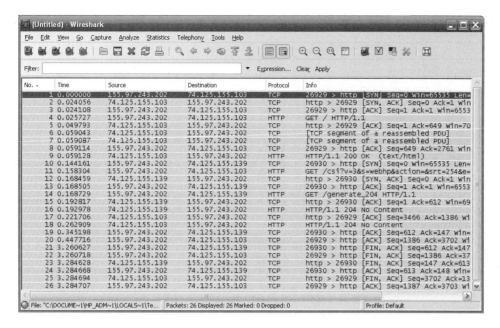

Figure 5-20: Captured SYN packet.

35. Double-click on the next row that has the first [SYN, ACK] occurrence in the Info column. (In this case it was row 2. See Figure 5-21.)
36. Expand the tree for Transmission Control Protocol.
37. Expand the tree for [SEQ/ACK analysis].
38. Highlight the row that indicates that this [SYN, ACK] packet is an acknowledgement to the prior packet.
39. Take a screenshot. (See Figure 5-22.)

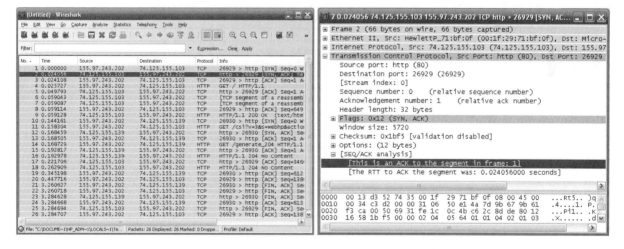

Figure 5-21: Captured SYN/ACK packet.

Figure 5-22: Noting the acknowledgement (ACK) to a segment.

40. Double-click on the next row that has an [ACK] occurrence after the [SYN, ACK] packet in the Info column. (In this case it was row 3. See Figure 5-23.)
41. Expand the tree for Transmission Control Protocol.
42. Expand the tree for [SEQ/ACK analysis].
43. Highlight the row that indicates that this [ACK] packet is an acknowledgement to the prior [SYN, ACK] packet you just looked at.
44. Take a screenshot. (This was the 3-way opening. See Figure 5-24.)

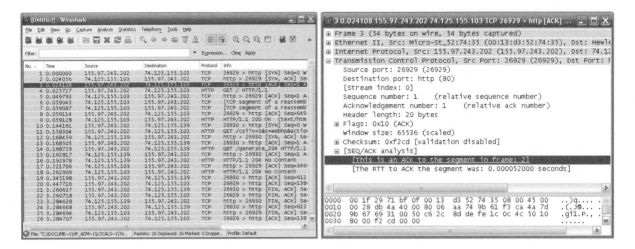

Figure 5-23: Captured ACK packet.   Figure 5-24: Acknowledgement (ACK) to the 3-way opening.

45. Double-click on the next row that has an [ACK] occurrence after the GET request in the Info column. (In this case it was row 5. See Figure 5-25.)
46. Expand the tree for Transmission Control Protocol.
47. Expand the tree for [SEQ/ACK analysis].
48. Highlight the row that indicates that this [ACK] packet is an acknowledgement to the prior GET request. (In this case it was frame 4.)
49. Take a screenshot. (This is an acknowledgement of a data transfer. See Figure 5-26.)

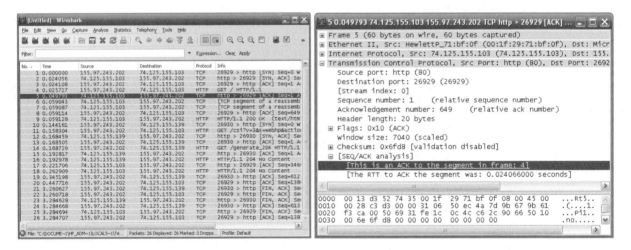

Figure 5-25: Captured ACK packet.   Figure 5-26: Acknowledgement (ACK) to the data transfer.

50. Double-click on the row that has the first [FIN/ACK] occurrence in the Info column with your IP address as the **source**. (In this case it was row 21. See Figure 5-27.)
51. Expand the tree for Transmission Control Protocol.
52. Expand the tree for [SEQ/ACK analysis].
53. Highlight the row that indicates that this is a [FIN, ACK] packet.
54. Take a screenshot. (This was the first part of the connection termination. See Figure 5-28.)

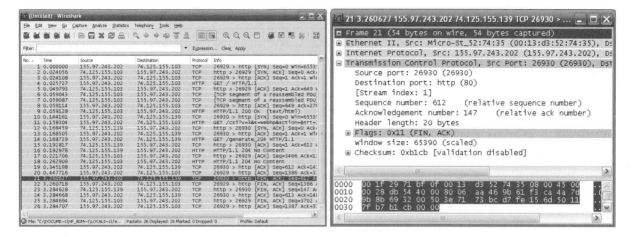

Figure 5-27: Captured FIN/ACK packet from your computer.   Figure 5-28: FIN/ACK segment from your computer.

55. Double-click on the row that has the first [FIN, ACK] occurrence in the Info column with your IP address as the **destination**. (In this case it was row 23. See Figure 5-29.)

56. Expand the tree for Transmission Control Protocol.

57. Expand the tree for [SEQ/ACK analysis].

58. Highlight the row that indicates that this is a [FIN, ACK] packet and an acknowledgement to the first [FIN, ACK].

59. Take a screenshot. (This was the second part of the connection termination. See Figure 5-30.)

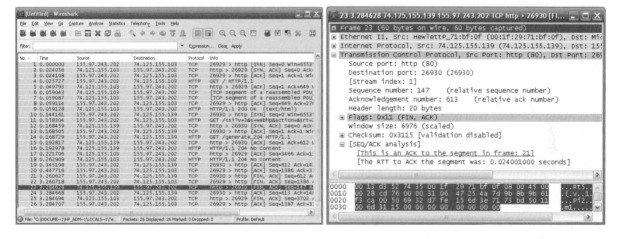

Figure 5-29: Captured FIN/ACK packet from the Web server.   Figure 5-30: FIN/ACK segment from the Web server.

THOUGHT QUESTIONS

1. Did the packets you captured have a TTL listed? Why?
2. Why do packets have both IP addresses and MAC addresses on them?
3. Which packet had the html code for Google's page (Hint: 200)?
4. What do all the letters and numbers in the bottom pane represent?

5.4 CONTENTS OF A PACKET (CAPTURE AN EMAIL)

In this project you will capture a packet and look at its contents. You will use Wireshark to capture packets containing an email message. You will send an email to a generic Hotmail.com account and capture it as it's going over the network. Then you will look at the contents of the email without opening it in an email client.

Most email traffic has traditionally not been encrypted. However, many providers are starting to make encrypted email an option for their users. A packet sniffer allows you to look at the contents of many different types of packets.

1. With Wireshark open click Capture and Options.
2. If you haven't already done so, select your Network Interface Card (NIC) in the Interface drop-down menu at the top of the screen. (Your NIC will undoubtedly have a different name.)
3. Enter "tcp port 80" in the box next to Capture Filter. (See Figure 5-31.)

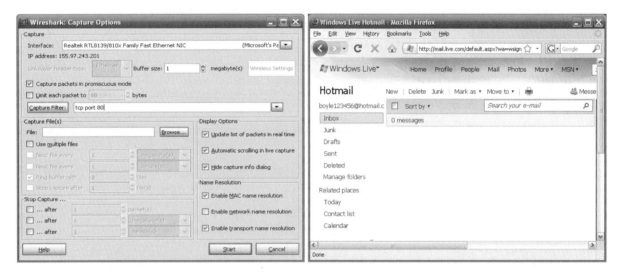

Figure 5-31: Configuring Wireshark to capture port 80 packets.   Figure 5-32: Hotmail.com inbox.

4. Close ALL other programs you currently have open except your word processing program (e.g. MS Word or OpenOffice Writer) and your Web browser.
5. Enter "www.hotmail.com" into your Web browser. (If you already have a hotmail account, skip to Step 11.)
6. Click Sign Up.
7. Click Get It (free).
8. Under the Create a Windows Live® ID enter a fake Windows Live ID and a hotmail.com extension. (Write down the information you enter. In this example it was boyle123456@hotmail.com.)
9. Enter information (fake or real) for all of the required fields marked with an asterisk. (In this case it was John Doe, from Utah, and born in 1980.)
10. Click "give me the classic version." (See Figure 5-32.)
11. Click New. (This will start a new email.)
12. In the "To:" field put your real email address. (You can also use the same email address you just created.)
13. In the Subject line put TEST.
14. In the body of the email put the words "EMAIL TEST" and copy/paste it until it fills up the body of the email message. (This will help you identify the packet when you see it. See Figure 5-33.)

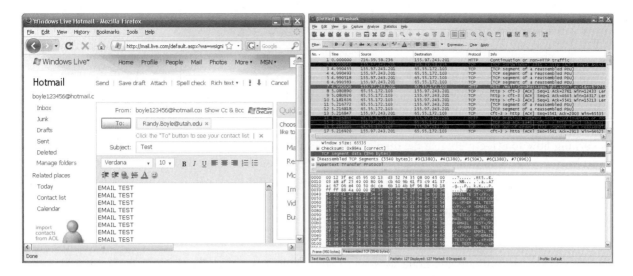

Figure 5-33: Sending a test email.　　　　　　Figure 5-34: Viewing the contents of the captured email.

15. Go back to Wireshark.
16. Click Start.
17. Go back to your hotmail account.
18. Click Send.
19. Go back to Wireshark.
20. Click Stop.
21. Click on the line that has Post /mail/sendmessage in the Info field. (In this example it was the seventh packet.)
22. Click on the bottom window pane where you see a column of words saying EMAIL TEST. (This is the body of the message you just sent.)
23. Take a screenshot. (See Figure 5-34.)

You just picked up your email off the network that was on its way to www.hotmail.com. Unless specified your emails are NOT encrypted. Most people are unaware of this and send confidential information on a regular basis over unencrypted email systems. Do NOT send sensitive information by email.

It's important to understand that Wireshark picked up your email from the network. It can just as easily pick up ALL email traffic going over your network. One of the main concepts you will learn by doing these projects is that you may not fully understand how computers (or information systems) work. Hopefully knowing more about computers, networks, and information systems will help protect you.

THOUGHT QUESTIONS

1. How many people do you think are unaware that their emails may be unencrypted?
2. Why wouldn't email be encrypted by default?
3. Can you look at Web content just as easily as Web traffic?
4. Can you look at information being sent to/from your bank?

In the prior projects you learned to use *capture* filters to reduce the number of packets you collected. You can also apply *display* filters after you have captured a large number of packets. Using display filters ensures that you capture all relevant data and reduces the processing load.

Learning how to effectively use the display filters in Wireshark will make your life much easier. By now you have noticed that there are a lot of packets flowing through a network. It takes a lot of mental energy to sift through all those packets to get the ones you are looking for. Luckily, Wireshark can help filter out some of the responses you are not interested in. These post-capture filtering functions help network administrators diagnose problems on their network.

1. With Wireshark open click Capture, Options.
2. If you haven't already done so, select your Network Interface Card (NIC) in the Interface drop-down menu at the top of the screen.
3. Leave the Capture Filter blank.
4. Click Start.
5. Open a Web browser.
6. Go to the following Web sites: www.CNN.com , www.Yahoo.com, and www.Google.com.
7. Click Stop Capture.
8. Take a screenshot. (See Figure 5-35.)
9. Notice that you likely have a lot of packets that may not be intended for you. (In this example a lot of extra traffic was picked up from another router.)
10. In the empty box next to Filter enter the following: `ip.src == [enter your IP address without the brackets]`
11. Press Enter after you finish typing the filter syntax.
12. The filter box will be green if you get the syntax correctly entered. (In this case it was `ip.src == 155.97.243.202`. Now you are only getting packets where the source IP address is your own.)
13. Take a screenshot. (See Figure 5-36.)

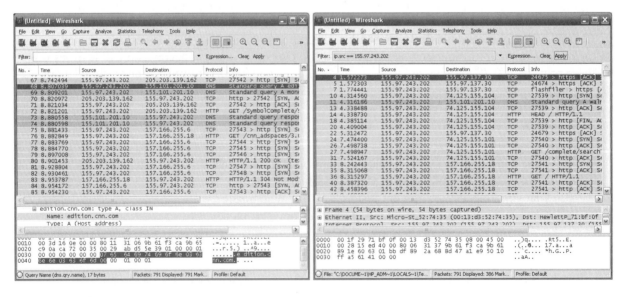

Figure 5-35: Captured packets.   Figure 5-36: Filtering packets based on IP address.

14. Click on the Expression button to the right of the filter box.

15. Click on TCP to get the tcp.port field name.
16. Click ==.
17. Enter "80" for the value (to view only Web traffic). (See Figure 5-37.)
18. Click OK.

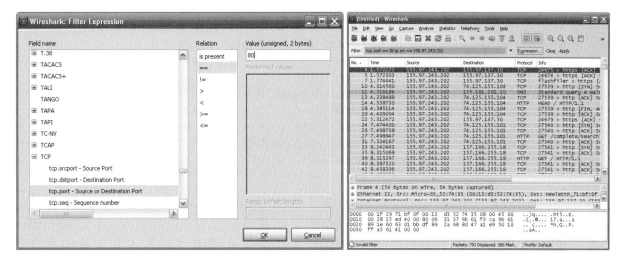

Figure 5-37: Creating a filter expression.　　　　　　　　　　Figure 5-38: Filter without "and" in the expression.

Note: The filter box will be *red* indicating *incorrect* syntax. After you fix the syntax in the next step the box will turn green. (See Figure 5-38.)

19. Add an "**and**" to the syntax so that both the new filtering rule and the prior rule are applied together. (The filter box will turn green when you have the syntax correctly entered.)
20. Re-enter the correct syntax if you didn't get it to work correctly (`tcp.port == 80 and ip.src == 155.97.243.201`) replacing this example IP address with your own.
21. Take a screenshot. (See Figure 5-39.)
22. Click on the column heading labeled Protocol to sort by protocol type.
23. Take a screenshot. (See Figure 5-40.)

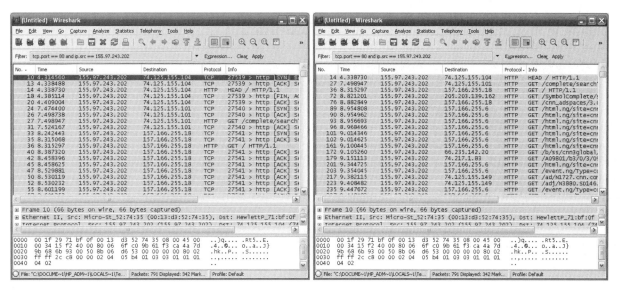

Figure 5-39: Filter packets by IP address and port 80.　　　　　Figure 5-40: Sort results by protocol.

24. Delete the current display filter.
25. Click Apply.
26. Click on the Expression button to the right of the filter box.
27. Click on DNS to get the dns.flags.response field name.
28. Click == .
29. Click "Message is a response." (This will display only DNS responses). (See Figure 5-41.)
30. Click OK.
31. Click Apply.
32. Take a screenshot. (See Figure 5-42.)

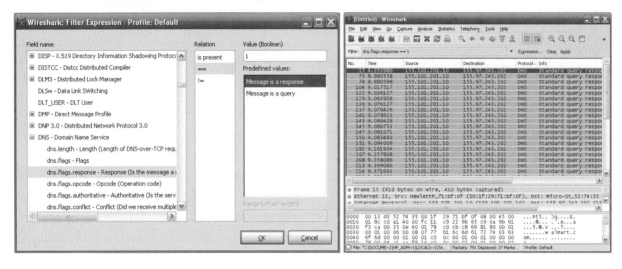

Figure 5-41: Creating DNS filter.   Figure 5-42: Filtered DNS packets.

33. Delete the current display filter.
34. Click Apply.
35. Type the following in the Filter text box: `!(ip.addr==[your IP address without brackets])`
36. Click Apply.
37. Take a screenshot. (See Figure 5-43.)

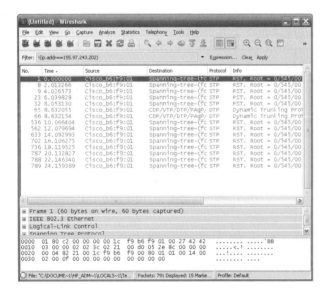

Figure 5-43: Packets not sent to/from your computer.

1. Could you filter the traffic based on IP address and packet type for a given person in your organization (e.g. John Doe's email)?
2. Why are there so many different field types to filter?
3. What protocols, other than TCP/IP, are used to manage traffic across networks?
4. What does a black row with red text indicate?

5.6 PACKET ANALYSIS AND REPORTING

In this project you will look at some of the statistics built into Wireshark. You can also calculate custom statistics using the same type of syntax you used for display filters. The statistic functions in Wireshark allow you to quickly see the types and volumes of traffic on your network.

Using these statistics you can easily identify network congestion, rogue servers/applications, and any packet loss that may be occurring. There is also a graphical tool that allows you to clearly see both sides of a communication between two hosts. You will look at a couple of simple examples in this project. Online tutorials about the statistics in Wireshark are available at http://wiki.wireshark.org/Statistics.

1. With Wireshark open click Capture and Options.
2. If you haven't already done so, select your Network Interface Card (NIC) in the Interface drop-down menu at the top of the screen.
3. Leave the Capture Filter blank.
4. Click Start.
5. Open a Web browser.
6. Go to the following Web sites: www.CNN.com , www.Yahoo.com, and www.Google.com.
7. Click Stop Capture.
8. Take a screenshot. (See Figure 5-44.)

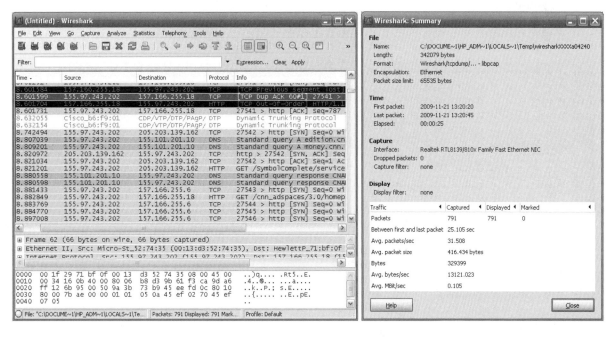

Figure 5-44: Captured packets.   Figure 5-45: Statistics on captured packets.

9. Click Statistics and Summary.
10. Take a screenshot. (See Figure 5-45.)
11. Click Close.
12. Click Statistics and Protocol Hierarchy.
13. Take a screenshot. (See Figure 5-46.)
14. Click Close.

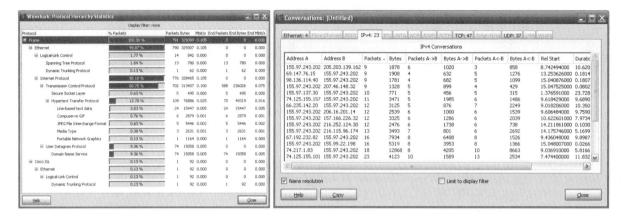

Figure 5-46: Protocol statistics.   Figure 5-47: IPv4 statistics.

15. Click Statistics and Conversations.
16. Click on the IPv4 tab.
17. Take a screenshot. (See Figure 5-47.)
18. Click Close.
19. Click View, Name Resolution, and Enable for Network Layer. (See Figure 5-48.)
20. Click Statistics and Conversations.
21. Click on the IPv4 tab.
22. Select the row where Address B is www.CNN.com. (This should have been one of the Web sites you visited.)
23. Take a screenshot. (See Figure 5-49.)
24. Click Close.

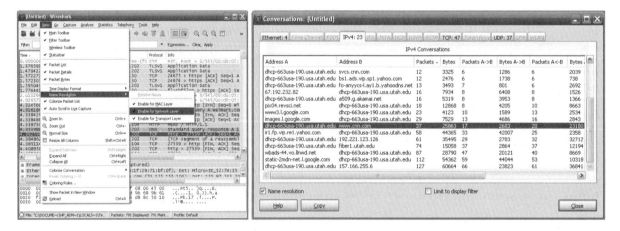

Figure 5-48: Enabling name resolution.   Figure 5-49: IP addresses are resolved into host names.

25. Click Statistics and Flow Graphs.
26. Click OK.
27. Take a screenshot. (You can see the TCP connections better in this graph. See Figure 5-50.)

28. Click Close.
29. Click Statistics and IP Addresses.
30. Enter `ip.addr == 155.97.243.202` as the filter.
31. Click Create Stat.
32. Expand the tree to show all IP addresses.
33. Take a screenshot. (See Figure 5-51.)

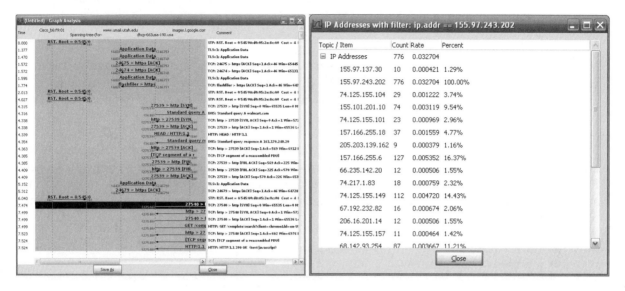

Figure 5-50: Graphical TCP connection diagram.   Figure 5-51: IP address filter.

THOUGHT QUESTIONS

1. Could you use Wireshark to determine if you have a computer infected with a virus? How?
2. Could you use the statistics in Wireshark to identify unauthorized behavior (e.g. using a proxy to browse the Web)?
3. How might Wireshark help you plan upgrades to your network?
4. How might Wireshark help load balance your servers?

CHAPTER 6: NETWORK DESIGN

It is difficult for students to get a lot of real-world networking experience. One reasons for this is that networking components themselves can be costly. Few students have the financial resources to purchase high-end routers, switches, load balancers, servers, etc. However, students can use simulators to design and test networks in a virtual environment.

In this chapter you will create several network simulations, gather data, and make changes to see their effect on network and/or server performance. OPNET provides students with an excellent network simulation tool called IT Guru. This is a free application with a staggering number of options, functionality, and possible networking configurations.

First, you are going to do a simple project to better understand how IP addresses are calculated. Next, you are going to search the Web for costs and specifications for a few widely-used networking components. Finally, you will proceed on to the network simulations. These simulations will include modeling 1) a small network, 2) a network expansion, 3) a change in the layout of a network, 4) a change in cabling, and 5) a change in the type of routing devices.

6.1   IP ADDRESSING

Understanding IP addresses is critical because as a network administrator you will likely be responsible for a range of IP addresses. You will need to know how they are calculated and allocated. As a network administrator you will likely assign these IP addresses to routers, servers, end users, etc. Each computer must have an IP address to send/receive packets over the Internet.

IPv4 addresses are 32 bits long. That means there are 32 ones/zeros that make up each IP address (Figure 6-1). Each IP address is broken up into 4 parts sometimes referred to as octets (8 bits). A unique combination of these four 8-bit parts makes up an IP address written in dotted-decimal notation (e.g. 155.97.243.202). Each of the four numbers is calculated using only 8 bits producing a number from 0 to 255.

The example below shows how a string of 1's and 0's can make an IP address. Using the second number set you can take any combination of 8 bits to create an octet value (ranging from 0 to 255). Figure 6-2 shows how alternating bits can be used to count from 1 to 16.

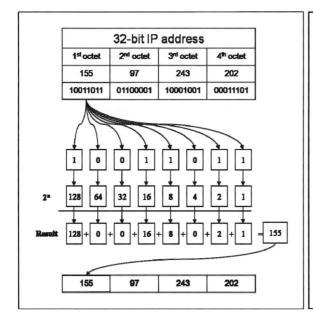

2ⁿ Number Set	
Decimal	Binary
0	0000 0000
1	0000 0001
2	0000 0010
4	0000 0100
8	0000 1000
16	0001 0000
32	0010 0000
64	0100 0000
128	1000 0000
255	1111 1111

Binary Counting	
Decimal	Binary
1	0000 0001
2	0000 0010
3	0000 0011
4	0000 0100
5	0000 0101
6	0000 0110
7	0000 0111
8	0000 1000
9	0000 1001
10	0000 1010
11	0000 1011
12	0000 1100
13	0000 1101
14	0000 1110
15	0000 1111
16	0001 0000

Figure 6-1: Dotted-decimal to binary conversion.   Figure 6-2: Decimal to binary conversions.

In the following exercises you will learn how to calculate the numbers in an IP address using the binary counting system. You will also learn how hostnames are converted to IP addresses and then to binary notation. Finally, you will learn the difference between counting in binary (used to calculate IP addresses) and the binary representation of a character set (e.g. ASCII). This difference can be confusing when you are initially introduced to the concept.

1. Click Start and Run.
2. Type **notepad**
3. Type your name and your birth date at the top of the screen.
4. Click Start and Run.
5. Type **calc**
6. Enter your birth month.
7. Click on the binary radial button to convert your birth month to its binary equivalent. (See Figure 6-3.)
8. Type your birth month (in binary) into the text document below your birthday shown in decimal.
9. Repeat this process to calculate your birth month/day/year in binary.
10. Type the binary equivalent of your birthday into the text document.
11. Take a screenshot. (See Figure 6-4.)

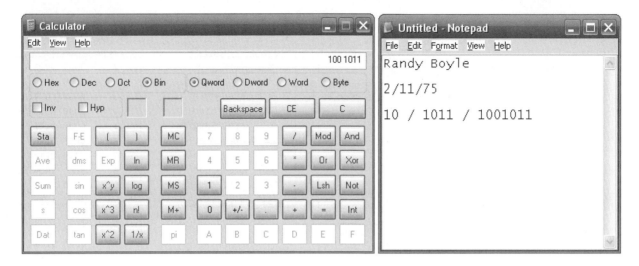

Figure 6-3: Binary conversion.

Figure 6-4: Date shown in binary notation.

Note: In the next part of this project you will convert your IP address (shown in dotted-decimal notation) into binary. This will be similar to the process shown in Figure 6-1.

12. Click Start and Run.
13. Type **cmd**
14. Type **ipconfig**
15. Take a screenshot. (See Figure 6-5.)
16. Enter your IP address in the text document with your name showing. (In this case it was 155.97.243.202.)
17. Click Start and Run.
18. Type **calc**
19. Enter each octet of your IP address and record the binary result in the text document with your name showing. (In this case it was 10011011.01100001.11110011.11001010.)
20. Take a screenshot. (See Figure 6-6.)

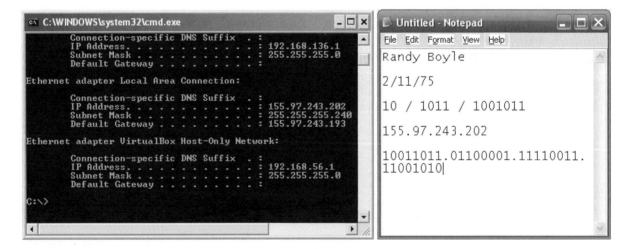

Figure 6-5: Results from ipconfig command.

Figure 6-6: IP address in binary notation.

21. Click Start and Run.
22. Type **cmd**
23. Type **ping www.YourSchool.edu**

24. Press Enter. (In this case it was www.Utah.edu.)
25. Take a screenshot. (See Figure 6-7.)
26. Enter your school's IP address in the text document with your name showing. (In this case it was 155.97.137.29.)
27. Click Start and Run.
28. Type **calc**
29. Enter each octet of your school's IP address and record the binary result in the text document with your name showing. (In this case it was 10011011.01100001.10001001.00011101.)
30. Take a screenshot. (See Figure 6-8.)

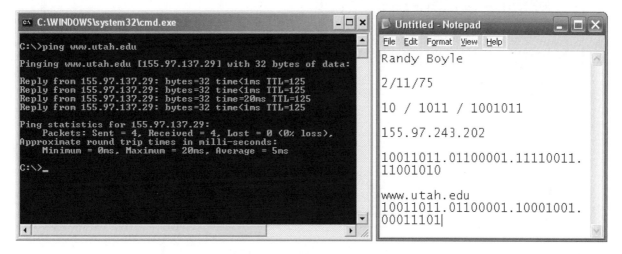

Figure 6-7: Results from ping command.   Figure 6-8: Web site's IP address in binary notation.

Note: In the next part of this project you will convert YourName into binary. Each number, letter, character, and key on your keyboard is represented by a specific binary sequence (Figure 6-9). Characters from foreign languages can also be represented by binary sequences. For this part of the project you will use an ASCII conversion to change your name into a binary sequence.

31. Type your name again in your text document.
32. Go to http://snarkles.net/scripts/binary/binary.php or use the condensed ASCII table below to convert your name to binary. (You can find a variety of text-to-binary converters on the Internet. Note that the ASCII table below uses only seven bits. Most online binary converters will display eight bits. The leading bit will be a zero.)
33. Paste the result into your text document.
34. Take a screenshot. (See Figure 6-10.)

Char	Binary	Char	Binary	Char	Binary
0	110000	A	1000001	a	1100001
1	110001	B	1000010	b	1100010
2	110010	C	1000011	c	1100011
3	110011	D	1000100	d	1100100
4	110100	E	1000101	e	1100101
5	110101	F	1000110	f	1100110
6	110110	G	1000111	g	1100111
7	110111	H	1001000	h	1101000
8	111000	I	1001001	i	1101001
9	111001	J	1001010	j	1101010
Space	100000	K	1001011	k	1101011
!	100001	L	1001100	l	1101100
"	100010	M	1001101	m	1101101
#	100011	N	1001110	n	1101110
$	100100	O	1001111	o	1101111
%	100101	P	1010000	p	1110000
&	100110	Q	1010001	q	1110001
'	100111	R	1010010	r	1110010
(	101000	S	1010011	s	1110011
)	101001	T	1010100	t	1110100
*	101010	U	1010101	u	1110101
		101011	V	1010110	v	1110110
,	101100	W	1010111	w	1110111
-	101101	X	1011000	x	1111000
.	101110	Y	1011001	y	1111001
/	101111	Z	1011010	z	1111010

Figure 6-9: ASCII to binary conversion.

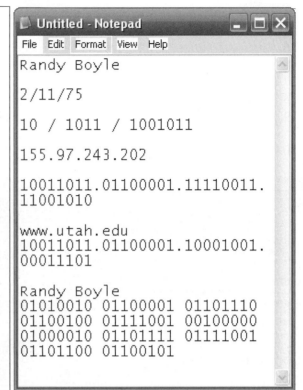

Figure 6-10: Name shown in binary notation.

THOUGHT QUESTIONS

1. Which standard is used to represent all characters including foreign language characters?
2. Which octet (1st, 2nd, 3rd, or 4th) is used to determine the IP address class? Why?
3. What is unique about the IP address 127.0.0.1?
4. What do IP addresses starting with 10.X.X.X and 192.168.X.X have in common?

6.2 NETWORK MEDIA

Part of being a network administrator is working with hardware. It's important to know the differences in media and devices as they relate to cost, performance, scalability, etc. Most network administrators work with limited budgets, a litany of user requests, and somewhat unrealistic expectations from upper management. They need to know what requests they can accommodate and at what cost.

In this project you will search the Web for certain pieces of commonly used hardware. Then you will copy the image you find, record the cost, and note the specification requested (e.g. speed rating). You may only need to visit a couple of sites to get the images and information. This project will give you an idea of the general costs associated with commonly used networking equipment.

1. Open a word processing program (e.g. Microsoft Word, OpenOffice Writer, etc.).
2. Create the following tables with the same media, image, price, and rated speed columns. (See Table 6-1.)
3. For each of the media listed below find the associated image, price, and speed rating by searching the Internet.
4. Complete the table below with images, prices, and speed ratings you obtained in your search.

5. Include this completed table with your screenshots.

	Media	Image	Price	Rated Speed
1	Cat 5e cable		$6.99	10/100 Mb/s
2	Cat 6 cable			
3	Cat 7 cable (hard to find)			
4	Multi-mode ST patch cable (fiber)			
5	Multi-mode SC patch cable (fiber)			
6	Single-mode patch cable (fiber)			
7	802.11g wireless router			
8	802.11n wireless router			

Table 6-1: Network media.

6. For each of the media listed below find the associated image and price by searching the Internet.
7. Complete the table below with images and prices you obtained in your search. (See Table 6-2.)
8. Include this completed table with your screenshots.

	Media	Image	Price
1	RJ45 connector		$0.99
2	SVGA cable		
3	UPS (Uninterruptable Power Supply)		
4	Cisco 24-port+ switch		
5	Cisco 24-port+ router		
6	Blade server (any)		
7	SAN (Storage Area Network)		
8	19'' Rack Enclosure (any)		
9	Wiring diagram for Cat5 cable		NA
10	Wiring diagram for Cat5 cross-over cable		NA

Table 6-2: Network equipment.

THOUGHT QUESTIONS

1. Which Web site had most of the media listed above?
2. Were there a variety of Cisco routers/switches for you to choose from? Why?
3. Do hardware purchases or salaries for IT workers demand a greater share of the total cost of ownership for an IT infrastructure at a typical medium-sized company? Why?
4. Is it less expensive for companies to install wired or wireless networks? Why?

6.3 SIMPLE LAN DESIGN (OPNET)

Designing networks can be complex. You need to account for users, applications, distance, security, cost, performance requirements, availability, expected growth, etc. These are just a few of the factors that go into a good network design. Being able to test the performance of your design before it is implemented can greatly reduce your overall costs. Even the best plans need to be changed and adjusted.

OPNET produces software that allows you to simulate a large variety of networks before you actually proceed to the implementation phase. They make a student version available for college students free of charge. This is an invaluable resource to students just starting out in the networking field. In this project you will install IT Guru® Academic Edition and go through a built-in tutorial.

OPNET IT Guru is a large product that can be intimidating when you first use it. This project utilizes an existing tutorial provided by IT Guru that has additional documentation. If this is your first exposure to network planning and simulation, this documentation will be very helpful. It is a good idea to have the PDF tutorial provided by OPNET open at the same time you are doing this project. The PDF provides more explanation than is included in this project.

More involved tutorials will follow but it is important for you to understand the basics of how IT Guru works. First you will install IT Guru and then you will build a simple network. The next project will cover an expansion of your network (also in the PDF help file).

1. Download IT Guru Academic Edition from: http://www.opnet.com/university_program/index.html. (See Figure 6-11.)
2. Click IT Guru Academic Edition in the left-hand navigation pane.
3. Click Register and Download.
4. Enter information in the required fields including a real email address. (Your username, password, and download link will be sent to this email address.)
5. Take a screenshot.
6. Enter your username as your first name and last name (e.g. RandyBoyle).
7. Click Submit. (See Figure 6-12.)

Figure 6-11: OPNET University Program.   Figure 6-12: OPNET IT Guru Academic Edition.

8. Retrieve the email OPNET sends you. (See Figure 6-13.)
9. Click on the link for the "IT Guru Academic Edition installer" within the email.
10. Enter the username and password provided in the email.
11. Click Log In. (See Figure 6-14.)
12. Click Download.
13. Click on the software agreement.
14. Save the compressed file to C:\networking\.

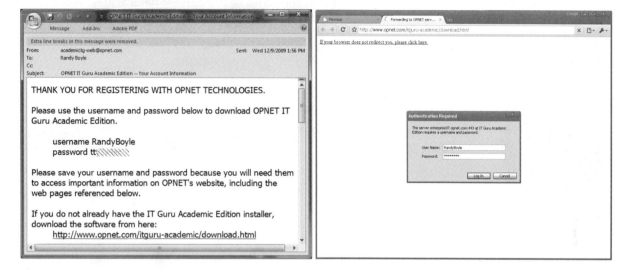

Figure 6-13: Email with username and password.   Figure 6-14: Login for download.

15. If the compressed file doesn't automatically open, browse to C:\networking\.
16. Right-click ITG_Academic_Edition_v1998.zip. (The version number might be different.)
17. Select 7-Zip, Extract to "ITG_Academic_Edition_v1998\." (You should already have 7-Zip installed from the previous project in Chapter 4.)
18. Wait for the extraction to complete.
19. Browse to C:\networking\ITG_Academic_Edition_v1998.
20. Double-click the setup.exe application. (It may take a few seconds to start depending on the speed of your computer. See Figure 6-15.)

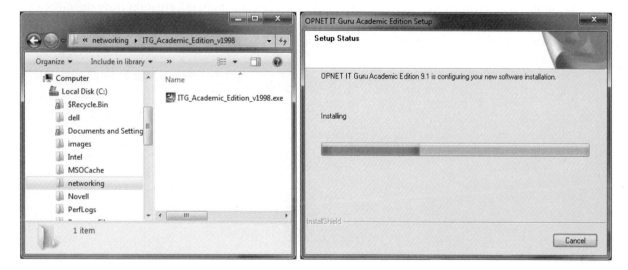

Figure 6-15: OPNET IT Guru setup.exe.   Figure 6-16: OPNET IT Guru installation.

21. Click Next, Next, and Next. (Wait for the installation to complete. See Figure 6-16.)
22. Click OK if you see a notice about Adobe Reader. (You should already have this installed http://get.adobe.com/reader/.)
23. Save all of your work and exit any programs you may have running.
24. Click Finish. (See Figure 6-17.)

Note: Windows XP users will see a window asking them to restart their computer. Windows 7 users may not. To make sure the installation process completed correctly, and to prevent other issues, you will restart at this point regardless of your operating system.

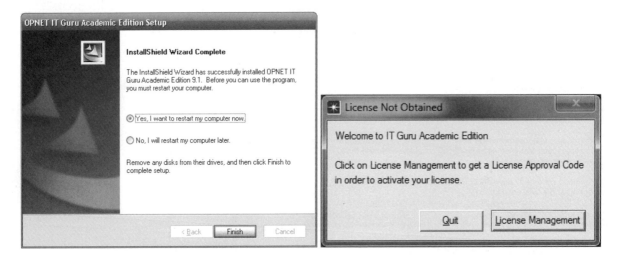

Figure 6-17: Computer restart required after installation.　　　Figure 6-18: Licensing for OPNET IT Guru.

25. Wait for your computer to reboot.
26. Click Start, All Programs, OPNET IT Guru Academic Edition 9.1, and OPNET IT Guru Academic Edition.
27. Click Allow Access or Unblock if you see a notice from Windows Firewall.
28. Click License Management and Next. (See Figure 6-18.)
29. Copy the License Request code from the OPNET Perform License Transaction window. (See Figure 6-19.)
30. In the Web browser that automatically opened enter your login information from the OPNET email you received. (It may take a couple of minutes for the email to be sent.)
31. Paste your License Request code into the License Activation Web browser window.
32. Click Submit.

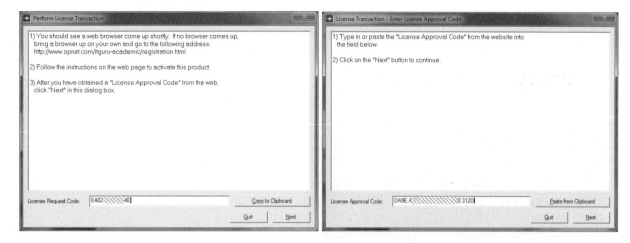

Figure 6-19: License request code.   Figure 6-20: License approval code.

33. Copy the License Activation code from the Web browser window.
34. Click Next on the OPNET Perform License Transaction window.
35. Paste your License Activation code into the License Transaction - Enter License Approval Code window.
36. Take a screenshot. (See Figure 6-20.)
37. Click Next and Close.
38. Click Start, All Programs, OPNET IT Guru Academic Edition 9.1, and OPNET IT Guru Academic Edition.
39. Click Accept on the Software Agreement. (See Figure 6-21.)

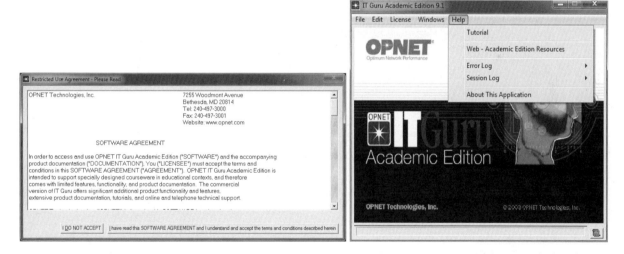

Figure 6-21: Software agreement.   Figure 6-22: OPNET IT Guru tutorial in the Help menu.

40. Click Help, Tutorial, and Small Networks. (This will open a PDF that has additional explanation and help for this basic tutorial. See Figure 6-22.)
41. Return to the IT Guru main window.
42. Click File, New, and OK. (Project should be showing in the window. See Figure 6-23.)
43. Name the project "YourNameOfficeProject". (In this case it was RandyBoyleOfficeProject.)
44. Enter "First_Floor" for the scenario name. (See Figure 6-24.)
45. Click OK and Next.

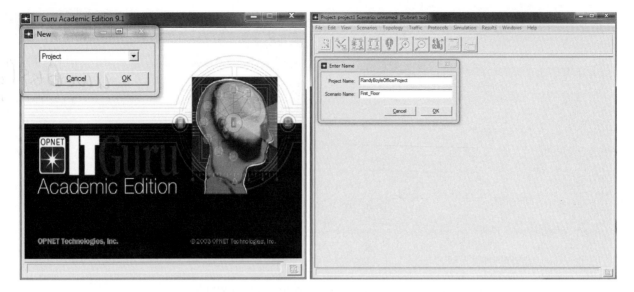

Figure 6-23: Creating a new project.   Figure 6-24: Naming your project and scenario.

46. Select Office. (See Figure 6-25.)
47. Click Next and Next.
48. Select Sm_Int_Model_List from the Model Family list. (See Figure 6-26.)
49. Click Next and OK.

Figure 6-25: Choosing the scale of your network.   Figure 6-26: Selecting technologies for your network design and simulation.

50. In the File menu click Topology and Rapid Configuration. (See Figure 6-27.)
51. Select Star from the drop-down menu.
52. Click OK.
53. Select 3C_SSII_1100_3300 for the Center Node Model. (This is a 3COM switch. See Figure 6-28.)
54. Select Sm_Int_wkstn for the Periphery Node Model. (This is a workstation that will be connected to the switch.)
55. Set the number of periphery nodes to 30.
56. Select 10BaseT as the Link Model. (This is the cable that will connect the workstations to the switch.)

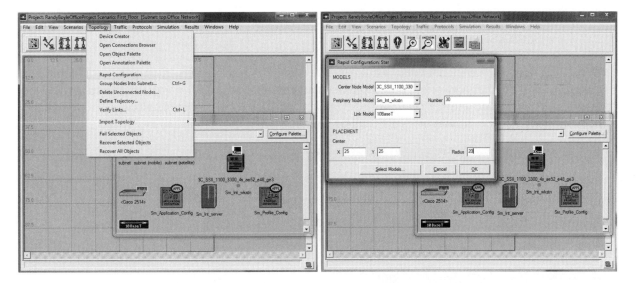

Figure 6-27: IT Guru File menu.

Figure 6-28: Settings for rapid configuration of a network.

57. Set the placement to X:25 and Y:25 with a radius of 20. (This sets the location and size of the network on the workspace. See Figure 6-28.)
58. Click OK.
59. Drag-and-drop the icon labeled Sm_Int_server from the palette to the workspace. (This is a small server. Click ESC or right-click the workspace to stop creating this object on the workspace. See Figure 6-29.)
60. Click on the 10BaseT link on the Object Palette. (This will be the cable that you will use to link the 3COM switch and the server together.)
61. Click on the 3COM switch and then the server. (This should create a link between the two. Click ESC to stop creating links. You should see a model similar to the one below. See Figure 6-30.)

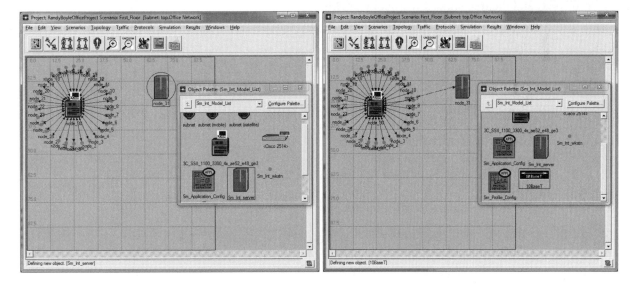

Figure 6-29: Adding a server to the workspace.

Figure 6-30: Connecting network to a server.

62. Drag-and-drop the icon labeled Sm_Application_Config from the palette to the workspace. (This will determine what applications your workstations are running. Click ESC to stop creating this object on the workspace.)
63. Drag-and-drop the icon labeled Sm_Profile_Config from the palette to the workspace. (This object will model light database access. Click ESC to stop creating this object on the workspace.)

64. Take a screenshot of your newly created network with your name showing at the top of the window. (See Figure 6-31.)

Note: Now that you have a network created you are going to see if the server (and network) could handle the addition of another network. You will gather statistics about the performance of the server and the network. You will add another network and compare the impact of the new network on the server and network performance. Adding networks and/or hosts is common when businesses grow.

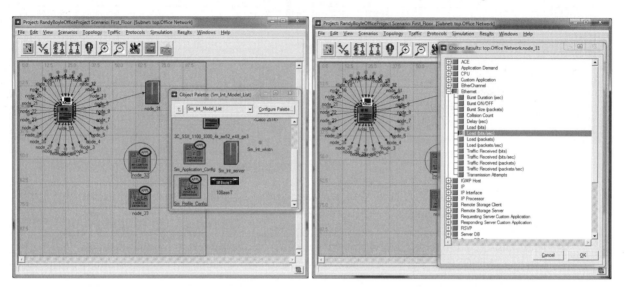

Figure 6-31: Adding application and profile objects.   Figure 6-32: Selecting server statistics.

65. Right-click your server node. (In this case it was node_31.)
66. Select Choose Individual Statistics.
67. Expand the tree under Ethernet by clicking +.
68. Select Load (bits/sec). (This will measure the load on the server from all of the workstations. See Figure 6-32.)
69. Click OK.
70. Right-click the workspace. (This is where you will select options to measure the overall performance of the network (global statistics). Make sure you right-click the workspace and not any of the objects.)
71. Select Choose Individual Statistics.
72. Expand the tree under Global Statistics.
73. Expand the tree under Ethernet.
74. Select Delay (bits/sec). (This will measure the delay on the network. See Figure 6-33.)
75. Click OK.
76. Click File, Save, and OK. (This will save your project.)

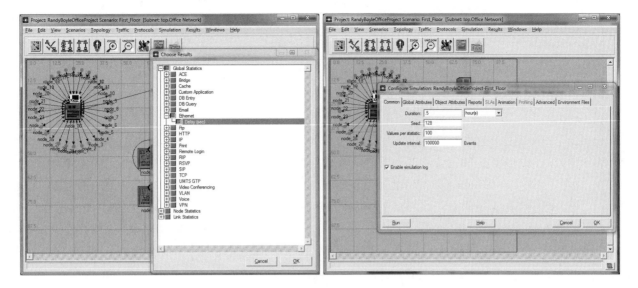

Figure 6-33: Selecting network statistics.   Figure 6-34: Simulation settings.

77. Click Simulation and Configure Discrete Event Simulation.
78. Change the duration to 0.5 hours. (See Figure 6-34.)
79. Click Run. (Notice that thirty minutes of simulation took about 1 second to complete.)
80. Click Close.
81. Right-click your server node. (In this case it was node_31.)
82. Select View Results.
83. Expand the tree under Ethernet.
84. Select Load (bits/sec). (Note the peak bits/sec.)
85. Take a screenshot. (See Figure 6-35.)
86. Click Close.
87. Right-click the workspace.
88. Select View Results.
89. Expand the Ethernet tree under Global Statistics.
90. Select Delay (sec). (Note that it is around .0004 seconds.)
91. Take a screenshot. (See Figure 6-36.)
92. Click Close. (Don't close your project if you are moving on to the next project. You will use these results in the next project.)
93. Click File, Save, and OK. (This will save your project.)

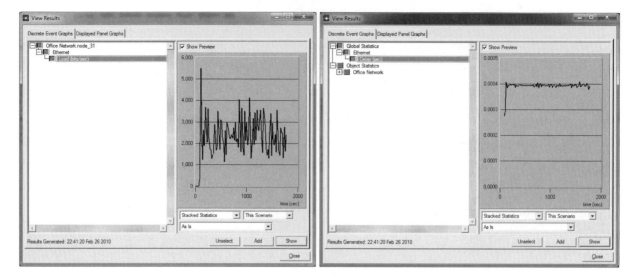

Figure 6-35: Server load statistics.   Figure 6-36: Delay statistics for network.

THOUGHT QUESTIONS

1. How would you change the application settings to increase the HTTP traffic on the network?
2. Can you get different types of switches, routers, etc. on the object palette? How?
3. Could you add a wireless network to this existing network? How?
4. Could you run a simulation to see what would happen if one of the nodes failed? How?

6.4   NETWORK EXPANSION AND TESTING

In the prior project you created a very simple network with a switch, a server, and several workstations. In this project you are going to expand your existing network by adding another network. It is very common for businesses to grow and need additional workstations, servers, routing equipment, etc. They need to know if the expansion will work with existing infrastructure or if new capital will need to be invested to make the expansion successful.

You will use baseline statistics gathered in the prior project (for your existing network) and compare them to statistics gathered after the new network is added. This comparison will show how the expansion would affect overall performance of your server and network. After adding the network you will run the same simulation and compare the statistics.

If you still have IT Guru open from the prior project you do not have to reopen the project. You can continue the project at Step 9.

1. Click Start, All Programs, OPNET IT Guru Academic Edition 9.1, and OPNET IT Guru Academic Edition.
2. Click Accept on the Software Agreement.
3. Click File and Open.
4. Select the project labeled YourNameOffice.
5. Click OK.
6. Click Simulation and Run Discrete Event Simulation.
7. Wait for the simulation to complete. (Notice that thirty minutes of simulation took about 1 second to complete.)
8. Click Close.

9. Click Scenario and Duplicate Scenario.
10. Enter "YourNameExpansion" as the name of the Scenario. (In this case it was RandyBoyleExpansion.)
11. Click OK.
12. In the File menu click Topology and Rapid Configuration.
13. Select Star from the drop-down menu.
14. Click OK.
15. Select 3C_SSII_1100_3300 for the Center Node Model. (This is a 3COM switch.)
16. Select Sm_Int_wkstn for the Periphery Node Model. (This is a workstation that will be connected to the switch.)
17. Set the number of periphery nodes to 15.
18. Select 10BaseT as the Link Model. (This is the cable that will connect the workstations to the switch.)
19. Set the placement to X:75 and Y:63 with a radius of 20. (This sets the location and size of the network on the screen. See Figure 6-37.)
20. Click OK. (This will create another network on your workspace. See Figure 6-38.)

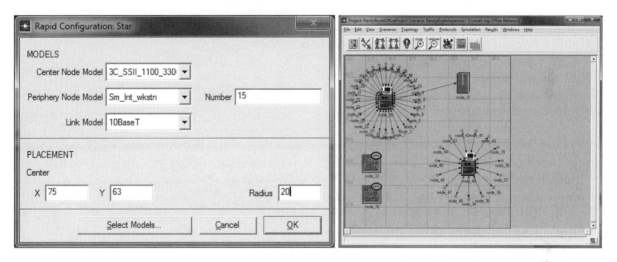

Figure 6-37: Settings for new network.   Figure 6-38: Network added for expansion.

21. Click on the Object Palette icon to open the object palette for this project. (You can also click Topology and Open Object Palette.)
22. Drag-and-drop the Cisco 2514 router icon from the palette to a position between the two networks. (See Figure 6-39.)
23. Click on the 10BaseT link on the Object Palette. (This will be the cable that you will use to link the two networks and Cisco router together.)
24. Click on one of the 3COM switches and then the Cisco router. (This should create a link between the two. Click ESC to stop creating links. Make sure the connection is made from the router to each switch and not accidentally connected to a workstation.)
25. Create another link between the other network and the Cisco router. (You should see a model similar to the one below.)
26. Click File, Save, and OK. (This will save your project.)
27. Take a screenshot showing the new expansion with your name showing in the top of the window. (See Figure 6-40.)

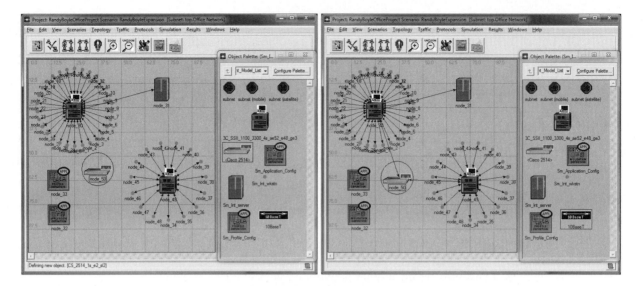

Figure 6-39: Added router to network.   Figure 6-40: Connecting networks through a router.

28. Click Simulation and Run Discrete Event Simulation.
29. Wait for the simulation to complete.
30. Click Close.
31. Right-click your server node. (In this case it was node_31.)
32. Select Compare Results.
33. Expand the tree under Ethernet.
34. Select Load (bits/sec). (Note the peak bits/sec is now over 9,000 whereas it was barely over 5,000 before.)
35. Click Show.
36. Take a screenshot. (See Figure 6-41.)
37. Click Close.
38. Right-click the workspace.
39. Select Compare Results.
40. Expand the Ethernet tree under Global Statistics.
41. Select Delay (sec). (Note that it stayed around .0004 seconds.)
42. Click Show.
43. Take a screenshot. (See Figure 6-42.)
44. Click Close.
45. Click File, Save, and OK. (This will save your project.)

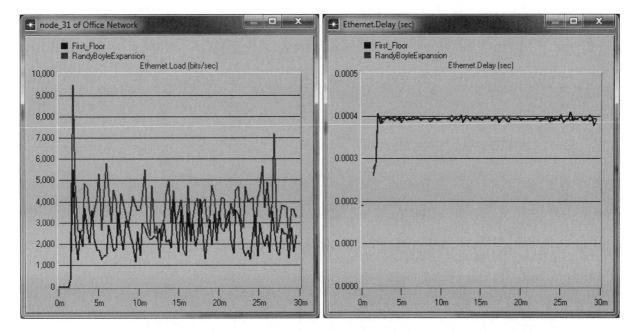

Figure 6-41: Comparison of server load after expansion.   Figure 6-42: Comparison of delay after expansion.

If you enjoy these network design and simulation exercises you can find additional tutorials and projects at the following link. They are much more detailed and go through real-world scenarios. They are all worth the time and effort.

http://www.opnet.com/university_program/teaching_with_opnet/textbooks_and_materials/index.html

THOUGHT QUESTIONS

1. Why was the sever load more affected than the delay on the network?
2. What other statistics might be of interest on the server?
3. What other statistics might be of interest on the network?
4. Are there different types of graphs available when you are comparing statistics? How might they be useful?

6.5   CONFIGURATION SCENARIO

In this project you will look at how the configuration of your network may affect the response times between workstations and your database. In the first part of this project you will notice that response times on the top floor of the 3-story building are longer than on the bottom floor. The network in this part will be connected in a daisy-chain topology.

In the second part of this project you will move the cables and see how a different configuration affects response time between the workstations and the database. This project will help you understand how differences in configuration or topology may affect application and network performance.

You will create a new IT Guru project for this network modeling project. Additional practice will help you become more familiar with this software and give you more confidence in your ability to create a variety of different networks.

1. Click Start, All Programs, OPNET IT Guru Academic Edition 9.1, and OPNET IT Guru Academic Edition.

2. Click Accept on the Software Agreement.
3. Click File, New, and OK.
4. Enter "YourNameOffice_Part2" for the project name. (In this case it was RandyBoyleOffice_Part2.)
5. Enter "YourName_LAN_Daisy_Switch_10MB" for the scenario name. (In this case it was Boyle_LAN_Daisy_Switch_10MB.)
6. Click OK and Next.
7. Select Office for the network scale.
8. Click Next.
9. Enter "200" for both the X Span and Y Span.
10. Click Next.
11. Select Sm_Int_Model_List.
12. Click Next and OK.
13. Drag-and-drop the following onto the workspace: Sm_Application_Config, Sm_Profile_Config, and Sm_Int_Server. (Right-click to stop creating objects on your workspace.)
14. In the File menu click Topology and Rapid Configuration.
15. Select Star from the drop-down menu.
16. Click OK.
17. Select 3C_SSII_1100_3300 for the Center Node Model. (This is a 3COM switch.)
18. Select Sm_Int_wkstn for the Periphery Node Model. (This is a workstation that will be connected to the switch.)
19. Set the number of periphery nodes to 25.
20. Select 10BaseT as the Link Model. (This is the cable that will connect the workstations to the switch.)
21. Set the placement to X:40 and Y:30 with a radius of 25. (This sets the location and size of the network on the screen.)
22. Click OK. (This will create another network on your workspace.)
23. Select the switch and all of the workstations you just created.
24. Press Ctrl-C. (This will copy them to the clipboard.)
25. Click on the workspace.
26. Press Ctrl-V. (This will paste the objects to the workspace.)
27. Click on a space below the first network. (This will create the network. Make sure there is a space between the networks. You are going to create links between the switches and you will need to be able to see them clearly.)
28. Repeat this (copy/paste) until you have three networks on the workspace. (See Figure 6-43.)
29. Add another 3COM switch to the workspace without any workstations. (This will give you a total of 4 switches on the workspace.)
30. Right-click each switch in the three new networks and select Set Name.
31. Name each of the three switches from top to bottom Marketing, Sales, and Finance respectively. (Naming the switches will make understanding the instructions and analysis easier.)
32. Set the name of the 4th switch (without workstations) to CoreSwitch.
33. Set the name of the server to Server. (In this case it was node_2.)
34. Connect each switch, CoreSwitch, and Server with 10BaseT cable in a daisy-chain (bus-like) topology. (The cables should be linked Marketing ->Sales->Finance->CoreSwitch->Server. Make sure you click on each switch and not any of the workstations. This is common in businesses that are housed in a multi-floor building.)
35. Take a screenshot. (You should have a network model similar to the one shown below. See Figure 6-44.)

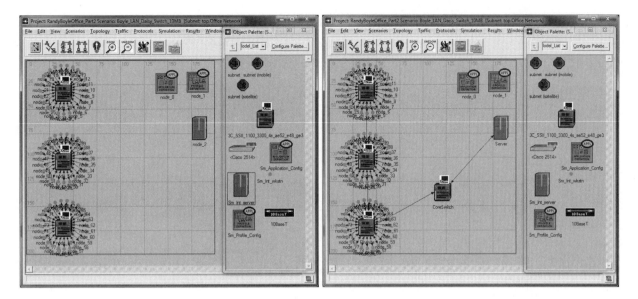

Figure 6-43: Reconfigured network.

Figure 6-44: Added links in daisy-chain topology.

36. Right-click your Server node.
37. Select Choose Individual Statistics.
38. Expand the tree under Ethernet by clicking +.
39. Select Load (bits/sec). (This will measure the load on the server by all of the workstations. See Figure 6-45.)
40. Click OK.
41. Right-click the workspace. (This is where you will select options to measure the overall network performance. Make sure you right-click the workspace and not any of the objects.)
42. Select Choose Individual Statistics.
43. Expand the tree under Global Statistics.
44. Expand the tree under Ethernet.
45. Select Delay (bits/sec). (This will measure the delay on the network.)
46. Click OK.
47. Right-click one of the workstation nodes in the Marketing network. (This is the top network.)
48. Select Choose Individual Statistics.
49. Expand the tree under Client DB Query.
50. Select Response Time (sec). (This will measure the response time relative to the server. See Figure 6-46.)
51. Click OK.
52. Repeat the last five steps (47-51) and select the Response Time (sec) statistic for a workstation node in both the Sales (middle) and Finance (bottom) networks. (In this example nodes 11, 37, and 62 were chosen. You must correctly select the Response Time statistic for a workstation in each of the three networks for this project to work correctly.)
53. Click File, Save, and OK. (This will save your project.)

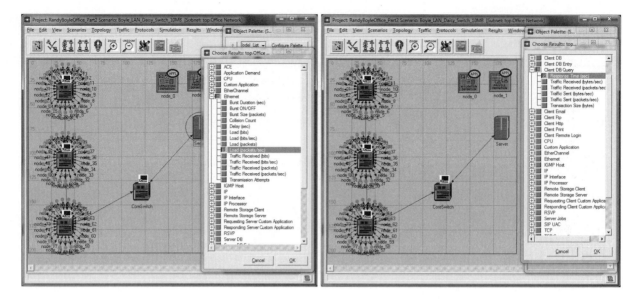

Figure 6-45: Select statistic for server load.   Figure 6-46: Select statistic for response time.

Note: You are now going to run a couple of different scenarios and compare the performance differences after making small changes to the network.

54. Click Simulation and Run Discrete Event Simulation.
55. Wait for the simulation to complete.
56. Click Close.
57. Click Scenario and Duplicate Scenario.
58. Enter "YourName_LAN_**STAR**_Switch_10MB" for the scenario name. (In this case it was Boyle_LAN_STAR_Switch_10MB.)
59. Click OK.
60. Delete the links between all of the switches.
61. Connect each network switch (Marketing, Sales, and Finance) directly to the CoreSwitch with 10BaseT cable in a star topology. (The cables should be linked Marketing ->CoreSwitch, Sales->CoreSwitch, Finance->CoreSwitch, and CoreSwitch->Server.)
62. Take a screenshot. (You should have a network model similar to the one shown below. See Figure 6-47.)
63. Click Simulation and Run Discrete Event Simulation.
64. Wait for the simulation to complete. (See Figure 6-48.)
65. Click Close.

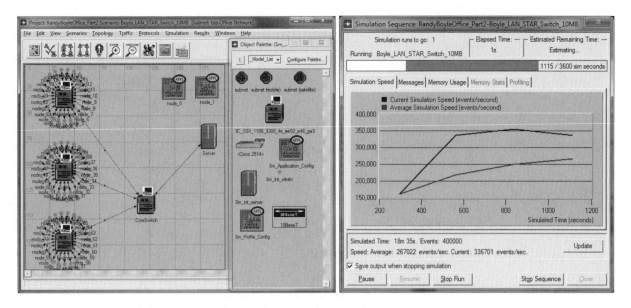

Figure 6-47: Reconfigured network with star topology.　　　　Figure 6-48: Running simulation.

66. Click Scenarios, Switch to Scenario, and YourName_LAN_Daisy_Switch_10MB. (This will take you back to the prior scenario. You can also press Ctrl+ up arrow.)
67. Click Results and Compare Results.
68. Change the bottom right-hand drop-down from All Scenarios to This Scenario. (The other drop-downs should be Overlaid statistics and As Is.)
69. Expand the tree under Office Network and each of the three nodes until you can see the Response Time option for each node.
70. Select the Response Time (sec) statistic for each of the three nodes.
71. Click Show.
72. Take a screenshot. (You should see higher response times for the nodes in the top network and lower response times for the nodes in the lower network. See Figure 6-49.)
73. Close the graph.
74. Close the Compare Results window.

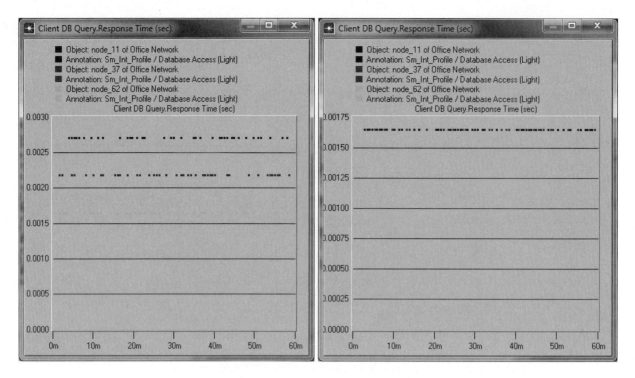

Figure 6-49: Response times for the daisy-chain configuration.　　　Figure 6-50: Response times for the star configuration.

75. Click Scenarios, Switch to Scenario, and YourName_LAN_STAR_Switch_10MB. (This will take you back to the second scenario. You can also press Ctrl- down arrow.)
76. Click Results and Compare Results.
77. Change the bottom right-hand drop-down from All Scenarios to This Scenario. (The other drop-downs should be Overlaid statistics and As Is.)
78. Expand the tree under Office Network and each of the three nodes until you can see the Response Time option for each node.
79. Select the Response Time (sec) statistic for each of the three nodes.
80. Click Show.
81. Take a screenshot. (Response times for all nodes should be the same. You should notice that response times for nodes in the top and middle networks were reduced. See Figure 6-50.)
82. Close the graph.
83. Close the Compare Results window.
84. Click File, Save, and OK. (This will save your project.)

Note: You will use this same model in the next project. Don't close your project if you are moving on to the next project.

THOUGHT QUESTIONS

1. Why were response times longer for the nodes in the top network than the bottom network?
2. Why did the response times improve with the new star configuration?
3. If you had a 20-story building could you connect the top floor with a core switch on the bottom floor or would it be too far away? If possible, how would you do this?
4. Did the new configuration affect network delay? (Hint: Look at the network delay statistic.)

6.6 CABLING SCENARIOS

You can get a really fast network but purchasing and installing the hardware can be expensive. It is important to understand how much bandwidth you actually need (including reasonable growth). It would be nice to have a TB/sec Internet connection to your house but it's unlikely that you could utilize it or even afford to pay for it. A better solution would be to pay for a connection speed that will eliminate (or minimize) any *noticeable* delay. Don't pay for excess bandwidth.

In this project you will change cables on your simple network to see what effect it will have on overall network delay. You will use three different cables including 10BaseT, 100BaseT, and 1000BaseX that will provide speeds of 10 Mbps, 100 Mbps, and 1000 Mbps respectively. In each scenario you will delete the prior cables and make connections with higher speed cables. After changing the cables you will run the same simulation and compare the statistics.

Notice the delay with each cable and see if the additional reduction in network delay could justify the cost of new hardware/cables. You will use baseline statistics gathered in the prior project and compare them to statistics gathered in the new scenarios. You will delete a couple of the prior scenarios to make the comparison easier. If you have your IT Guru project open from the prior project you can start this project at Step 6.

1. Click Start, All Programs, OPNET IT Guru Academic Edition 9.1, and OPNET IT Guru Academic Edition.
2. Click Accept on the Software Agreement.
3. Click File and Open.
4. Select "YourNameOffice_Part2". (In this case it was RandyBoyleOffice_Part2.)
5. Click OK.

Note: You should have the "star" scenario open. If your project doesn't open to the star scenario you can switch scenarios by clicking Scenarios, Switch to Scenario, and then select the scenario labeled YourName_LAN_STAR_Switch_10MB. This is shown in Figure 6-51.

6. Click Scenario and Duplicate Scenario.
7. Enter "YourName_LAN_STAR_Switch_**100MB**" as the name of the Scenario. (In this case it was Boyle_LAN_STAR_Switch_100MB.)
8. Click OK.
9. Delete all of the links between the switches and server.
10. Click the Palette button to show the Object Palette. (You can also click Topology, Open Object Palette.)
11. Change the drop-down to links. (You should see icons for a variety of connecting links.)
12. Connect the switches and server with **100BaseT** links. (You should have a network similar to the one shown below. See Figure 6-52.)
13. Click File, Save, and OK. (This will save your project.)

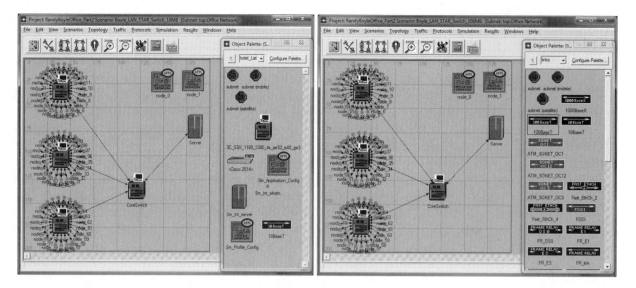

Figure 6-51: Model of 10BaseT scenario.   Figure 6-52: Model of 100BaseT scenario.

14. Click Simulation and Run Discrete Event Simulation.
15. Wait for the simulation to complete.
16. Click Close.
17. Click File, Save, and OK. (This will save your project.)
18. Click Scenario and Duplicate Scenario.
19. Enter "YourName_LAN_STAR_Switch_**1000MB**" as the name of the Scenario. (In this case it was Boyle_LAN_STAR_Switch_1000MB.)
20. Click OK.
21. Delete all of the links between the switches and server.
22. Click the Palette button to show the Object Palette. (You can also click Topology, Open Object Palette.)
23. Change the drop-down to links. (It should already be selected.)
24. Connect the switches and server with **1000BaseX** links. (You should have a network similar to the one shown below. See Figure 6-53.)
25. Click Simulation and Run Discrete Event Simulation.
26. Wait for the simulation to complete.
27. Click Close.

Note: Before you compare the three scenarios you just ran you will delete any prior scenarios. This will make the comparison easier to read. You should have a scenario named "YourName_LAN_Daisy_Switch_10MB" saved in this project. The instructions below will show you how to delete it.

28. Click Scenarios and Manage Scenarios.
29. Click on the row for the "YourName_LAN_Daisy_Switch_10MB" scenario.
30. Click Delete.
31. Click OK.

Note: You are now going to make the comparison between the scenarios you just created for this project. Make sure you only have the three cabling scenarios saved.

32. Click Results and Compare Results from the File menu.
33. Expand the Ethernet tree under Global Statistics.
34. Select Delay (sec). (You should see lines for each of the cabling scenarios.)

35. Click Show.
36. Take a screenshot. (Your name should appear on the graph. See Figure 6-54.)
37. Click Close.
38. Click File, Save, and OK.

Note: You will use this same model in the next project. Don't close your project if you are moving on to the next project.

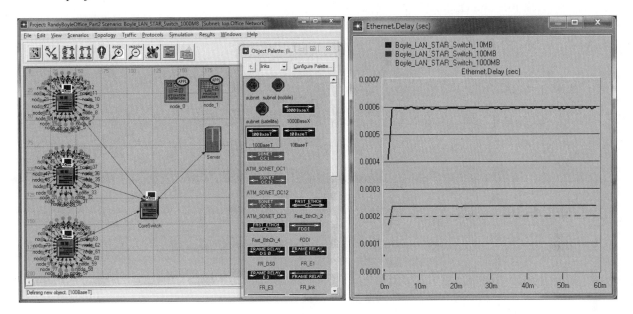

Figure 6-53: Model of 1000BaseX scenario.

Figure 6-54: Comparison of network delay with different media.

THOUGHT QUESTIONS

1. Which change in cable caused the greatest reduction in network delay?
2. What unit of measurement is network delay usually measured in?
3. Is 0.0003 seconds a lot of delay in a network? Is an upgrade necessary?
4. How many ms does it take a packet to get from www.Google.com to your computer? How much greater is the network delay in this example than the delay to/from Google?

6.7   SWITCH, ROUTER, HUB SCENARIOS

Students in introductory Networking courses sometimes express the notion that routers are better than switches and switches are better than hubs. By better they mean faster. However, this isn't always the case. Routers, switches, and hubs operate in different ways. Each device has its own benefits and advantages.

In this project you will change routing devices on your simple network to see what effect it will have on overall network delay. You will use three different devices including a router, a switch, and a hub. In each scenario you will delete the device and make connections with 10BaseT cables. After changing the devices you will run the simulation and compare the statistics.

You will use baseline statistics gathered in the prior project and compare them to statistics gathered in this project. You will delete a couple of prior scenarios to make the comparison easier. This comparison will show how each device may influence the performance of your network. If you still have IT Guru open from the prior project you do not have to reopen the project. You can continue the project at Step 6. You will need to complete the prior project before starting this project.

1. Click Start, All Programs, OPNET IT Guru Academic Edition 9.1, and OPNET IT Guru Academic Edition.
2. Click Accept on the Software Agreement.
3. Click File and Open.
4. Select the project labeled YourNameOffice_Part2.
5. Click OK.
6. Click Scenarios, Switch to Scenario, YourName_LAN_STAR_Switch_10MB. (In this case it was Boyle_LAN_STAR_Switch_10MB.)
7. Click Scenarios and Manage Scenarios. (See Figure 6-55.)
8. Delete all of the scenarios except YourName_LAN_STAR_Switch_10MB. (You delete a scenario by clicking the row and then the Delete button. (See Figure 6-56.)
9. Click OK.

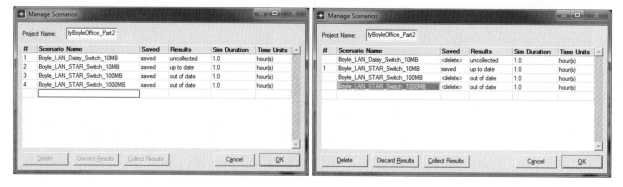

Figure 6-55: Managing scenarios.   Figure 6-56: Scenarios deleted.

10. Click Scenario and Duplicate Scenario.
11. Enter "YourName_LAN_STAR_**Router**_10MB" as the name of the Scenario. (In this case it was Boyle_LAN_STAR_**Router**_10MB.)
12. Click OK.
13. Click the Palette button to show the Object Palette.
14. Change the drop-down to Cisco.
15. Add the Cisco 7000 router to the workspace above the CoreSwitch.
16. Right-click the router and name it Router.
17. Change the drop-down on the Object Palette to Internet_toolbox.
18. Add the hub labeled Ethernet32_hub to the workspace above the router.
19. Right-click the hub and name it Hub. (See Figure 6-57.)
20. Delete the links connected to the CoreSwitch.
21. Connect links from the network switches and the server to the Router with **10BaseT** links. (You should have a network similar to the one shown below. See Figure 6-58.)
22. Take a screenshot.
23. Click Simulation and Run Discrete Event Simulation.
24. Wait for the simulation to complete.
25. Click Close.
26. Click File, Save, and OK. (This will save your project.)

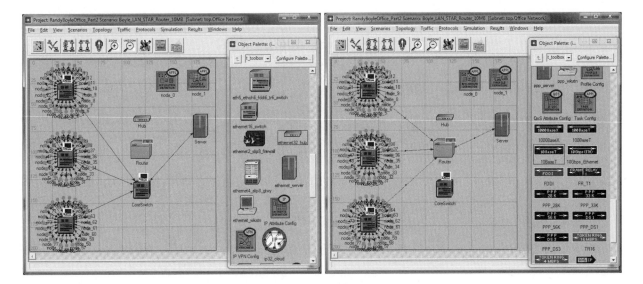

Figure 6-57: Router and hub are added to the workspace.　　　Figure 6-58: New "switch" simulation is completed.

27. Click Scenario and Duplicate Scenario.
28. Enter "YourName_LAN_STAR_**Hub**_10MB" as the name of the Scenario. (In this case it was Boyle_LAN_STAR_**Hub**_10MB.)
29. Click OK.
30. Delete the links connected to the Router.
31. Connect links from the network switches and the server to the Hub with **10BaseT** links. (You should have a network similar to the one shown below. See Figure 6-59.)
32. Take a screenshot.
33. Click the Verify Links button. (You can also click Topology, Verify Links, or press Ctrl-L. If you are not getting results when you run your simulations it might be due to failed link. Verifying the links after you create them is a good idea.)
34. Click OK.

Note: If you see a failed link (shown with a red X through it) you will need to delete that link and recreate it. In the past, there were a few instances where one of the links did not properly connect. If this happens you can delete the link and reconnect the objects.

35. Click Simulation and Run Discrete Event Simulation.
36. Wait for the simulation to complete. (See Figure 6-60.)
37. Click Close.
38. Click File, Save, and OK. (This will save your project.)

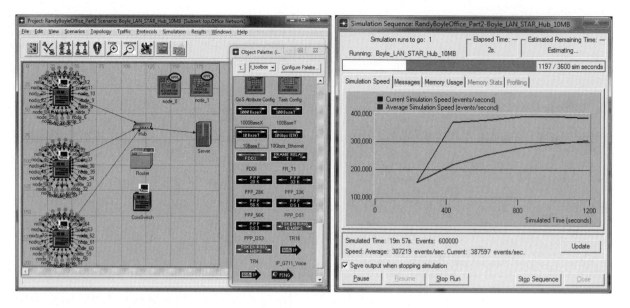

Figure 6-59: Switch is replaced with a hub.

Figure 6-60: Running the Hub simulation.

39. Click Results and Compare Results from the File menu.
40. Expand the Ethernet tree under Global Statistics.
41. Select Delay (sec). (You should see lines for each of the scenarios.)
42. Click Show.
43. Take a screenshot. (Your name should appear on the graph. See Figure 6-61.)
44. Expand the tree under Office Network and one of the workstation nodes until you can see the Response Time option for that node. (This is comparing the response time for one node in the three different scenarios.)
45. Select the Response Time (sec) statistic.
46. Click Show.
47. Take a screenshot. (You should see lower response times for the Hub scenario and higher times for the Switch and Router scenarios. See Figure 6-62.)
48. Close the graph.
49. Click Close.

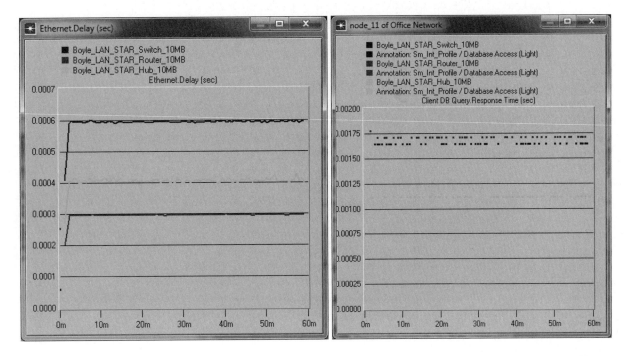

Figure 6-61: Comparison of network delay with different networking devices.

Figure 6-62: Comparison of server Response Time (sec) with a switch, router, and hub.

Note: You are now going to add additional servers to see if you can reduce the load on your main server.

50. Click Scenarios, Switch to Scenario, and YourName_LAN_STAR_Switch_10MB. (In this case it was Boyle _LAN_STAR_Switch_10MB.)
51. Click Scenario and Duplicate Scenario.
52. Enter "YourName_LAN_STAR_Switch_10MB _**4Servers**" as the name of the Scenario. (In this case it was Boyle_LAN_STAR_Switch_10MB _**4Servers**.)
53. Click OK.
54. Click the Palette button to show the Object Palette.
55. Change the drop-down to Sm_Int_Model_List.
56. Add 3 additional servers (Sm_Int_Server) to the workspace. (This will make a total of 4 servers on the workspace.)
57. Connect the servers with 10BaseT links. (You should have a network similar to the one shown below. See Figure 6-63.)
58. Click Simulation and Run Discrete Event Simulation.
59. Wait for the simulation to complete.
60. Click Close.
61. Click File, Save, and OK. (This will save your project.)

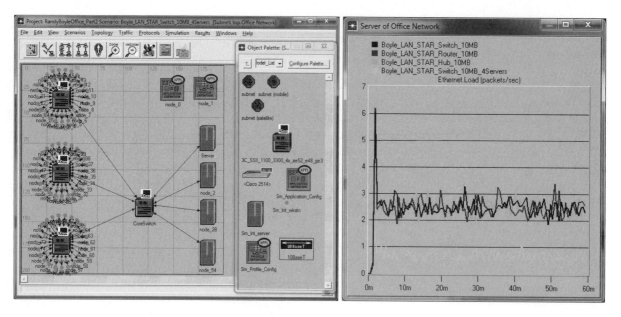

Figure 6-63: Additional servers added to the network.

Figure 6-64: Comparison of server load after adding additional servers to the network.

62. Click Results and Compare Results from the File menu.
63. Expand the tree under Object Statistics.
64. Select Load (bits/sec). (You should see lines for each of the scenarios.)
65. Click Show.
66. Take a screenshot. (Your name should appear on the graph. See Figure 6-64.)
67. Close that graph.
68. In the Compare Results window change the graphing option from "As Is" to "Average."
69. Click Show.
70. Take a screenshot. (Your name should appear on the graph. See Figure 6-65.)
71. Close the graph.
72. Click Close.
73. Click File, Save, and OK. (This will save your project)

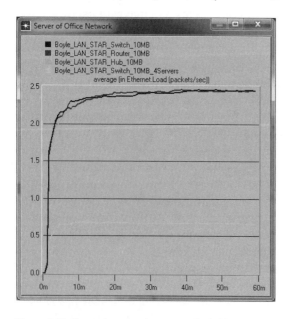

Figure 6-65: Comparison showing average load (bits/sec) on the server after the additional servers are added.

THOUGHT QUESTIONS

1. Why did the addition of more servers reduce the load on the first server?
2. Why did the hub have smaller network delay than the switch?
3. What would have happened to overall network delay if you had replaced both switches with hubs?
4. When do switches become more effective at reducing network delay than hubs?

CHAPTER 7: WIRELESS

Wireless networks are relatively new compared to wired networks. There are a few really good wireless networking tools that have been ported to the Windows operating system but most of the cutting-edge tools are developed for Linux. Small wireless networks can be setup quickly but larger networks require a great deal of planning.

Wireless networks have additional security concerns that traditional wired networks don't have. Wireless networks can be difficult to secure. Rogue access points are easy to set up. Users can easily set up unauthorized and unprotected wireless networks within a secure wired network. Potential intruders can quietly and unobtrusively chip away at wireless networks. Wired networks are much easier to protect. You can secure the wires and keep people from attaching to the network. Wireless is more difficult because radio waves can't be seen.

Administrators are now starting to worry about potential security issues with cell phones. Cell phones are starting to include almost all of the functionality you find in desktop computers. Corporations are now starting to ban cell phones in certain workplaces. Wireless devices have the potential to provide a way for information to "leak" out of an organization without anyone noticing.

In this chapter we will look at some of the basic wireless tools that are available for Windows machines. If you want some of the more advanced wireless tools you'll need to get a laptop and load a Linux distribution.

Warning: You are going to be walking around in a couple of these projects. It's a good idea to do these projects with a partner that can keep you from bumping into other objects.

7.1   INSSIDER

A useful program that network administrators can use to manage their wireless networks is inSSIDer®. It shows 1) the MAC (physical) address of the network, 2) its SSID, 3) the channel it is using, 4) a signal-to-noise ratio, 5) the type of security the network is using, 6) the type and speed of the network, and 7) the times the network appeared.

Another benefit of inSSIDer is that it displays the encryption type used on a specific network. This is important information if you are doing a penetration test or a security audit. If your company is using wired equivalent privacy (WEP), it would be wise to switch to Wi-Fi protected access (WPA) or WPA2 (even better). There are several tools available that can crack WEP keys.

Running a quick scan of your network using inSSIDer may help you determine if you need to make changes to your network. It can also tell you if your network has dead spots or rogue access points. Let's look at a simple example.

1. Download inSSIDer from: http://www.metageek.net/products/inssider.
2. Click Download inSSIDer.
3. Click Download.
4. Click Save.
5. Select the C:\networking\ folder.
6. If the program doesn't automatically start, browse to the C:\networking\ folder.

7. Double-click Inssider_Installer.msi.
8. Click Next, Next, Next, and Close.

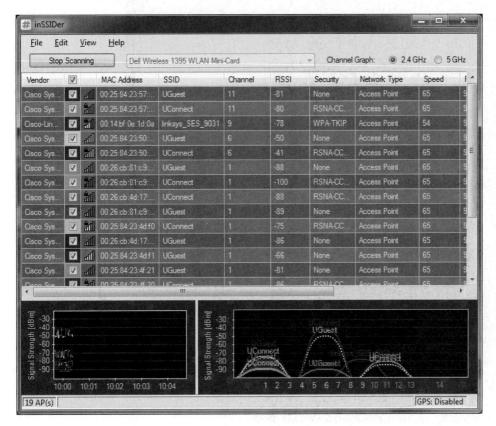

Figure 7-1: InSSIDer showing available wireless networks and their relative signal strengths.

9. Click Start, All Programs, MetaGeek, and inSSIDer.
10. Select your wireless network card from the drop-down menu.
11. Click Start Scanning.
12. Wait a few minutes for surrounding networks to show up on the list. (See Figure 7-1.)
13. Take a screenshot.
14. Walk 20-40 feet in one direction.
15. Wait a few minutes for surrounding networks to show up on the list.
16. Take another screenshot showing the changes in network strength. (See Figure 7-2.)

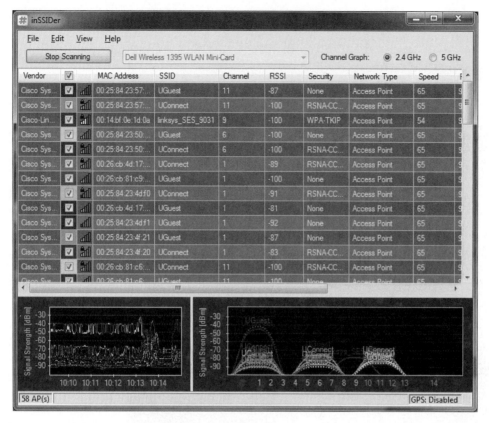

Figure 7-2: InSSIDer showing changes in wireless networks.

THOUGHT QUESTIONS

1. What are channels? Would one be better than another?
2. Why is WEP considered cryptographically weak?
3. What is the difference between WPA and WPA2?
4. Why do some networks run at 11 Mbps and others at 54 Mbps?

7.2 EKAHAU HEATMAPPER

Ekahau HeatMapper shows you the location of access points and relative signal strength of a wireless network on a map. This is a tremendous advantage to network administrators because they can identify dead zones, locate rogue access points, and map coverage areas.

Small wireless networks are easy to set up. Large wireless networks, on the other hand, are notoriously difficult to implement correctly. Placement of multiple access points to cover a specific geographic area can be difficult due to 1) variations in building materials in the walls/floors, 2) integrating different wireless standards (802.11b, 802.11g, or 802.11n), 3) the number of users in a given area, and 4) accounting for 3-dimensional buildings.

HeatMapper allows you to use your own custom map (building, campus, neighborhood, etc.) to pinpoint access points and wireless coverage. It's also free and easy to use.

1. Download Ekahau HeatMapper from:
   http://www.ekahau.com/products/heatmapper/overview.html.

2. Fill in any information in the required fields. (The download will start automatically so you do not have to put in your personal email address.)
3. Click Download.
4. Click Save.
5. Select the C:\networking\ folder.
6. If the program doesn't automatically start, browse to the C:\networking\ folder.
7. Double-click Ekahau_HeatMapper-Setup.exe.
8. Click Next, I Agree, and Install.
9. Click Install Driver Software if you are prompted.
10. Click Finish.
11. Click "I don't have a map."

Note: You are going to be walking around for this project. Be careful. You are going to be marking waypoints every few steps. It's important to keep your directions so the map is accurate. You can use the grid to help estimate your distance. You can use each block as five steps. You might get better results if you make a change in direction.

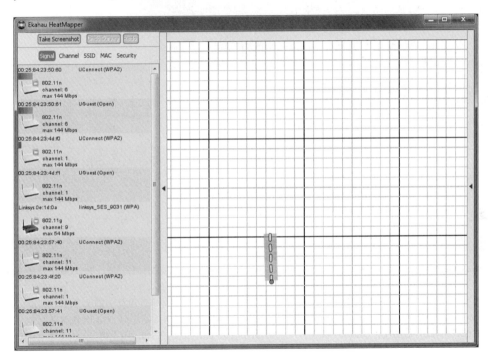

Figure 7-3: Setting waypoints using HeatMapper.

12. Click any point on the map as your first waypoint. (You are going to click several so it's a good idea to start at the bottom. See Figure 7-3.)
13. Walk 5-20 paces in one direction and stop.
14. Click another point on the grid. (In this example every square on the grid was five paces.)
15. Make at least three more waypoints including one change of direction. (Once enough data is collected HeatMapper will automatically map the access points (AP) and draw the map showing signal strength.)
16. Take a screenshot showing all access points and signal strength mapping. (See Figure 7-4.)

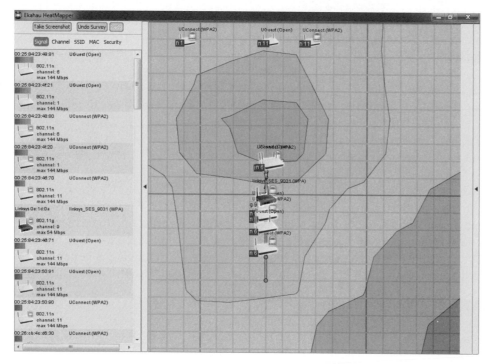

Figure 7-4: Mapped APs and relative signal strength using HeatMapper.

THOUGHT QUESTIONS

1. How does the program know where to place the icons representing other networks?
2. What do the colors represent on the map?
3. Would it be difficult to map an entire campus or corporate location?
4. Can you use your own existing map? Where would you get it?

7.3   WIGLE.NET

Wigle.net® is a Web site that gives you geographical maps with locations of wireless networks. It has recorded over 16 million networks from almost one billion observations since 2001. It has maps for almost every single street in the United States. It also has maps for Europe, Asia, and the Middle East.

Supporters of Wigle.net drive around and collect observations automatically. Then they upload these observations to Wigle.net to be included in the geographic map. They also collect general statistics about the network observations. This is a fun Web site to see the vast number of wireless networks that are in operation where you live.

1. Open a Web browser and go to http://www.wigle.net/.
2. Click on Web Maps at the top of the page.
3. Enter your zip code into the text box labeled Zip.
4. Click show address. (See Figure 7-5.)
5. Take a screenshot.

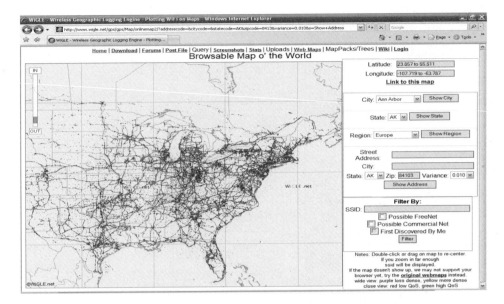

Figure 7-5: Wigle.net map of the United States.

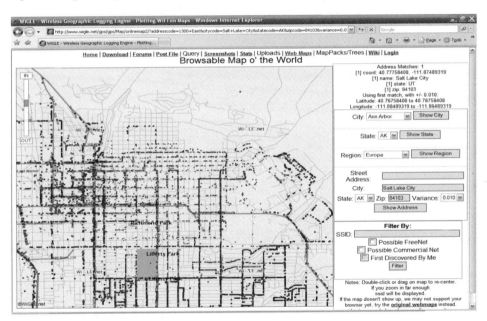

Figure 7-6: Showing wireless networks in Salt Lake City, Utah.

6. Drag the screen so it is approximately centered over your location.
7. Click the "In" button four or five times (so you can zoom in and see the SSIDs). (See Figure 7-6.)
8. Take a screenshot.
9. Zoom back out to the zip code level.
10. Select the filter labeled "Possible FreeNet."
11. Click Filter. (See Figure 7-7.)
12. Take a screenshot.
13. Choose a large city from the City drop-down menu.
14. Click Show City. (See Figure 7-8.)
15. Take a screenshot.

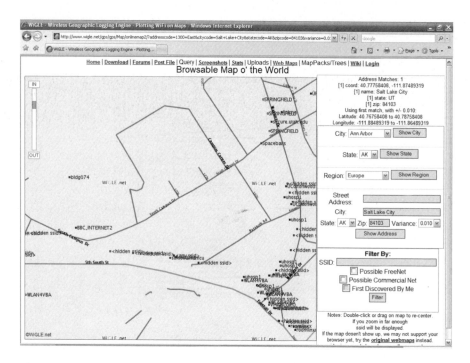

Figure 7-7: Street-view showing wireless networks.

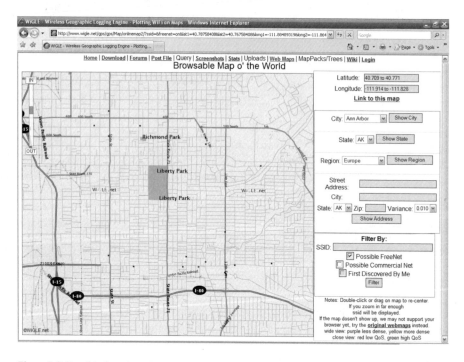

Figure 7-8: Possible free networks.

THOUGHT QUESTIONS

1. Who collects all these data points?
2. What equipment would you need to contribute to this Web site?
3. Does Wigle.net keep statistics on the number of networks with WEP, WPA, etc.?
4. Which manufacturer is listed most frequently in all submissions?

CHAPTER 8: INTERNET INFORMATION SERVER (IIS)

In these projects you will install and configure the second most popular Web server in use today (IIS). Netcraft (news.Netcraft.com) maintains current statistics about Web server usage. At the time this book was written Apache had 54% market share and Microsoft's IIS had 25% market share. Microsoft ships IIS with Windows XP (IIS 5.1), Vista (IIS 7.0), Windows 7 (IIS 7.5), Windows Server 2003(IIS 6.0) and Windows Server 2008 R2 (IIS 7.5).

Most people don't even know that they have the ability to run a Web server on their personal computer. Beginners find the IIS interface to be user friendly and intuitive. It makes learning how to manage a Web server less intimidating. Having a Web server on your own computer makes development and testing of new Web pages quick and convenient. You don't have to keep uploading changes to a remote server. You can test them right on your own machine.

IIS within Windows 7, Windows Server 2003, and Windows Server 2008 allows you to run as many Web sites as you would like. There are also no restrictions on the number of concurrent connections. The version of IIS for Windows XP is limited to one Web site. These examples will use IIS as it comes with Windows 7. If you are using Windows XP you can still complete these projects but the instructions will be slightly different.

These few projects barely scratch the surface when you consider all the functionality contained in IIS. Many books have been written about IIS. It's well worth your time to go through a more detailed resource and learn about every aspect of IIS. Many of the same concepts will translate across to Apache.

8.1 INTERNET INFORMATION SERVER (IIS) INSTALLATION

In this first project you will install the IIS and serve a simple Web page. Within the Windows Control Panel you can add additional Windows components. IIS is one of many additional components that don't come installed as part of a default Windows installation.

You will also create a simple Web page in this project from a text file. You will enter a few basic HTML tags into a text file and save it as a Web page. You will then open a Web browser and view it through your Web server.

1. Click Start and Control Panel.
2. Double-click Programs and Turn Windows features on or off.
3. Select Internet Information Services. (Make sure all subcomponents are selected. See Figure 8-1.)

Note: Make sure all subcomponents for Common HTTP Features, Health & Diagnostics, and Security are selected under World Wide Web Services. You will be using these subcomponents in later projects. These will be important for setting the authentication and logging features.

4. Click OK.
5. In the Control Panel double-click System and Security and Administrative Tools.
6. Double-click Internet Information Services (IIS) Manager. (See Figure 8-2.)

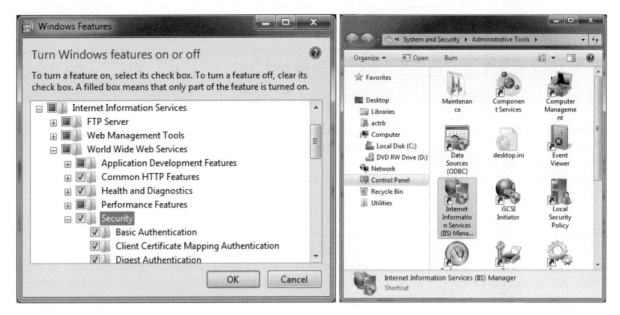

Figure 8-1: Selecting IIS components for installation.   Figure 8-2: IIS shortcut in the Control Panel.

7. Expand the file tree until you see the Default Web Site.
8. Click on the Default Web Site.
9. In the right-hand pane click Browse *:80 (http).
10. Take a screenshot of the default IIS page. (See Figure 8-3.)

Note: This will open a Web browser so you can see the default Web page being hosted on your computer. You can also manually open a Web browser and enter "localhost" or "127.0.0.1" to display this page. This step confirms that IIS is running correctly. If the default IIS page does not display in your Web browser you may want to try reinstalling IIS and/or using a different browser. If you are using Windows XP you may see a slightly different default page.

11. Return to IIS.
12. In the right-hand pane click Explore. (This will take you to the location (C:\inetpub\wwwroot) on your computer where the default Web page/site is stored. You are going to save your new Web page in this directory. See Figure 8-4.)

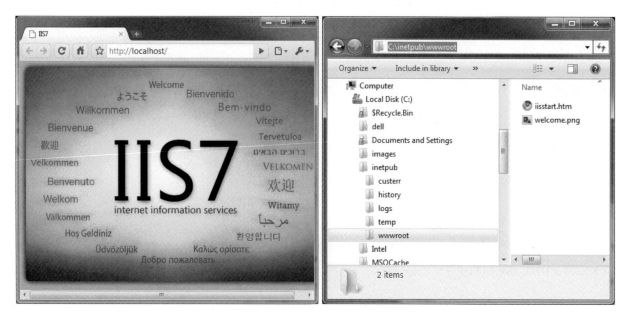

Figure 8-3: IIS 7 default Welcome page.

Figure 8-4: Default Web page (iisstart.htm) in the wwwroot directory.

13. Open Notepad by clicking Start, All Programs, and Accessories.
14. Right-click Notepad.
15. Select Run as administrator.
16. Type the following HTML code into the new text file. (Replace YourName with your first and last name. In this case it was RandyBoyle. Be careful to enter all of the tags correctly. See Figure 8-5.)

```
<html>

<head>
<title> Title for YourName's Web page </title>
</head>

<body>
The body is the main part of your Web page. You will put most of your
content here.
</body>

</html>
```

17. Click File and Save As.
18. Enter "yourname.html". (In this case it was "randyboyle.html" all in lowercase. You are NOT going to save this as a text file. You are going to save it as an .html file. If you get an error saying you don't have permission to write to this directory then you didn't start Notepad with administrator-level privileges. See Figure 8-6.)
19. Click Save.
20. Close Notepad.

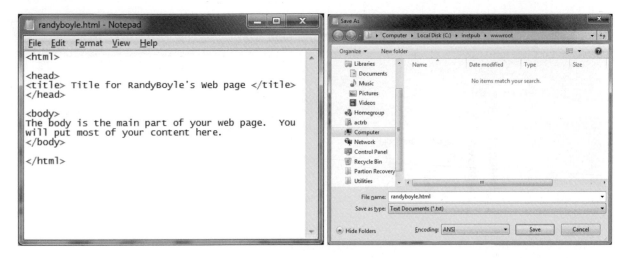

Figure 8-5: HTML code for a simple Web page.

Figure 8-6: Saving your simple Web page in the wwwroot directory.

21. Return to IIS.
22. Double-click Default Document.
23. Click Add.
24. Enter "yourname.html". (In this case it was randyboyle.html.)
25. Click OK. (You should see yourname.html at the top of the list. If you don't see it at the top of the list you can select yourname.html and click Move Up until it is at the top of the list. See Figure 8-7.)
26. Click on Default Web Site in the left-hand pane.
27. Click on Browse *:80 (http). (You can also open any Web browser and enter "localhost" or "127.0.0.1" in the address bar.)
28. Take a screenshot with your name showing in the title bar. (See Figure 8-8.)

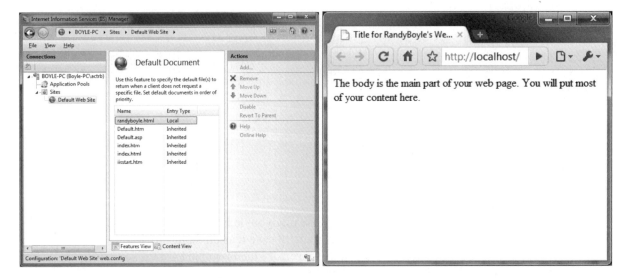

Figure 8-7: Adding yourname.html to the list of default documents in IIS.

Figure 8-8: Your simple Web page displayed in a Web browser.

29. Open any Web browser and enter "127.0.0.1" in the address bar.
30. Take a screenshot with 127.0.0.1 in the address bar and your name in the title. (See Figure 8-9.)
31. Change the address to "http://127.0.0.1/iisstart.htm".
32. Take a screenshot. (See Figure 8-10.)

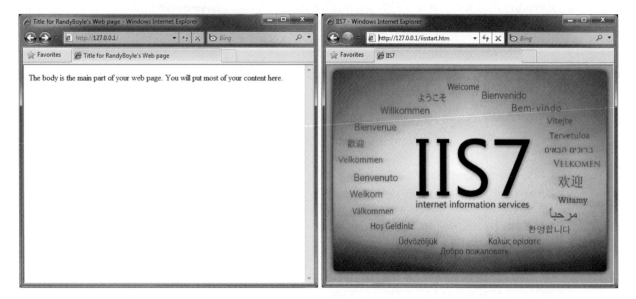

Figure 8-9: Accessing your Web page using the loopback adapter.   Figure 8-10: The IIS default Welcome page is still accessible.

Note: You have successfully installed and configured IIS. You also created a simple Web page and changed the IIS settings to have it load before iisstart.htm.

THOUGHT QUESTIONS

1. If you moved iisstart.htm above yourname.html as the Default Document, which Web site would show?
2. Could someone on another computer see your new Web page? How?
3. Can you run multiple Web sites with IIS 7.5?
4. Why do "localhost" and 127.0.0.1 both return the same page on your local machine?

8.2 BASIC HTML TUTORIAL

Below is a short HTML tutorial designed to give students an introductory experience to HTML coding. It is NOT comprehensive. It barely touches on all of the functionality available in HTML. It doesn't get into the advanced features of CSS, XHTML, or XML. These are all worth learning.

You are going to manually enter syntax into a text file, save it, and then view the changes in a Web browser. It's a good idea to have them both open at the same time. Be careful to enter all of the tags and syntax correctly. A small mistake can cause large problems.

Please feel free to use the Copy-Paste functionality to save yourself time. If you are interested in learning more about HTML, CSS, XHTML, or XML there are many well written tutorials on the Web at http://www.w3schools.com.

1. Open Notepad by clicking Start, All Programs, and Accessories.
2. Right-click Notepad.
3. Select Run as administrator.

4. Type the following DOCTYPE tag to text file. (You don't have to type this whole tag in by hand. You can copy this tag from: http://www.w3.org/TR/html401/struct/global.html#version-info. See Figure 8-11.)

Note: The DOCTYPE tag tells a Web browser what version of HTML the page was written in. For this exercise you are going to use HTML version 4.01 Transitional.

```
<!DOCTYPE HTML PUBLIC "-//W3C//DTD HTML 4.01 Transitional//EN"
"http://www.w3.org/TR/html4/loose.dtd">
```

5. Click File and Save As.
6. Browse to C:\inetpub\wwwroot.
7. Name the file yournametutorial.html. (Do not save it as a text file. You are going to save this text file as an HTML document. In this case it was randyboyletutorial.html.)
8. Click Save. (See Figure 8-12.)
9. Select Run as administrator. (If you don't start Notepad with administrator-level privileges you will not be able to save the changes you are going to make to this file. The rest of the project will not work if you don't save these changes.)

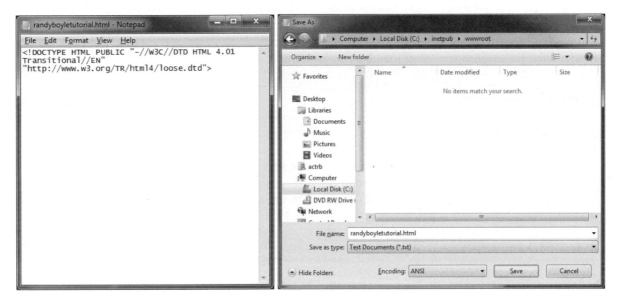

Figure 8-11: DOCTYPE tag.   Figure 8-12: Saving a text file as an HTML document.

10. Add the html opening and closing tags below the DOCTYPE tag. (The html tags indicate that the material between them is in HTML format. See Figure 8-13.)

```
<html>
</html>
```

11. Add the head and body tags between the html tags. (These are the tags that designate the two main sections (header and body) of a Web page. See Figure 8-14.)

```
<head>
</head>

<body>
</body>
```

Figure 8-13: The <html> tags are added.   Figure 8-14: The <head> and <body> tags are added.

12. Add the title tags and text shown below between the head tags. (These are the tags that indicate what will be shown in the title bar of your Web browser. Replace YourName with your first and last name.)

```
<title> Title for YourName's Web page </title>
```

13. Add the text shown below between the body tags. (Almost all of your html code will be placed between the body tags. The closing body tag (</body>) will stay near the bottom of the page as you add additional elements to your Web page. See Figure 8-15.)

```
The body is the main part of your Web page. You will put most of your
content here.
```

14. Click File and Save.
15. Browse to C:\inetpub\wwwroot.
16. Double-click the file labeled yournametutorial.html. (In this case it was randyboyletutorial.html. It should open the Web page you just created in a Web browser.)
17. Take a screenshot of your Web page. (See Figure 8-16.)

Note: For the rest of this project you will make changes to the text file, save it, and then refresh the Web browser you just opened. This will allow you to see how the changes in your html code affect how the page displays in a Web browser. It will save you time if you keep both the text file and the Web browser open at the same time.

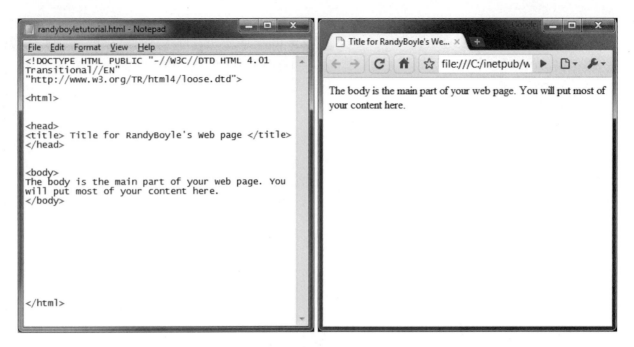

Figure 8-15: The <title> tags and text are added.　　　　Figure 8-16: The HTML code is displayed in a Web browser.

18. Add the paragraph tags (<p>) and text shown below after the text between the body tags. (The rest of the code in this project will be inserted between the body tags. **IMPORTANT**: Notice that the </body> tag is now at the bottom of the screen. See Figure 8-17.)

```
<p>This is a new paragraph. It doesn't have any line breaks so text
will flow onto the next line.</p>

This sentence <br />has many <br />line breaks.
<br />
<br />
```

19. Click File and Save. (You can also press Ctrl-S to save the file.)
20. Refresh your Web browser to display the changes. (You can also press F5 to refresh the screen.)
21. Take a screenshot. (See Figure 8-18.)

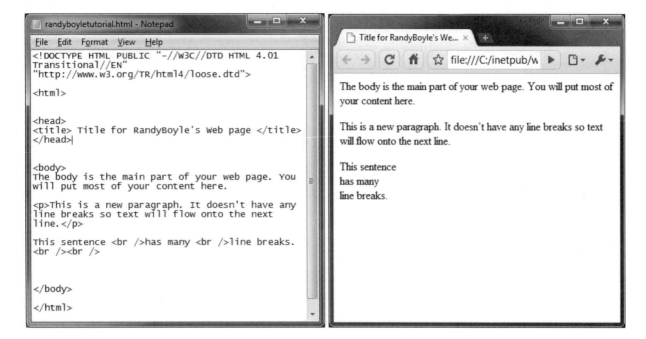

Figure 8-17: The <p> and <br /> tags are added.   Figure 8-18: HTML page showing a paragraph and line breaks.

22. Add the font style tags and text shown below. (These tags include bold, italic, underline, strike, superscript, subscript, and teletype. You can also see how to make changes in font color, size, and font face. See Figure 8-19.)

```
<b>YourName, </b>
<i>YourName, </i>
<u>YourName, </u>
<strike>YourName, </strike>
<sup>YourName, </sup>
<sub>YourName, </sub>
<tt>YourName, </tt>
<br />
<br />


<font color=blue face=fantasy size=3>Blue, fantasy, size 3.</font>
<br />

<font color=red face=arial size=5>Red, arial, size 5.</font>
<br />
<br />
```

23. Click File and Save. (You can also press Ctrl-S to save the file.)
24. Refresh your Web browser to display the changes. (You can also press F5 to refresh the screen.)
25. Take a screenshot. (See Figure 8-20.)

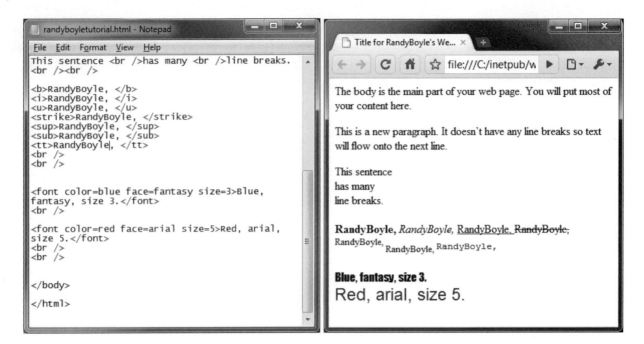

Figure 8-19: Formatting and <font> tags are added.   Figure 8-20: HTML page showing font and formatting effects.

26. Add the font tags and text shown below. (Notice that the <p> tag puts an extra line between the next text but the <div> tag does not add any extra spaces. See Figure 8-21.)

```
<p align=left>This paragraph is aligned left</p>
<p align=right>This paragraph is aligned right</p>
<p align=center>This paragraph is aligned center</p>

<div align=left>These words are aligned left</div>
<div align=right>These words are aligned right</div>
<div align=center>These words are aligned center</div>
<br />
<br />
```

27. Click File and Save. (You can also press Ctrl-S to save the file.)
28. Refresh your Web browser to display the changes. (You can also press F5 to refresh the screen.)
29. Take a screenshot. (See Figure 8-22.)

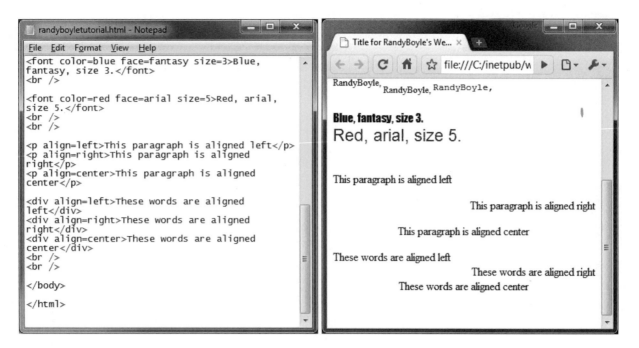

Figure 8-21: Paragraph and word alignment tags are added.

Figure 8-22: HTML page showing paragraph and word alignment effects.

30. Add the heading and horizontal line tags with the text shown below. (See Figure 8-23.)

```
<h1>Heading Level 1</h1>
<h2>Heading Level 2</h2>
<h3>Heading Level 3</h3>
<h4>Heading Level 4</h4>
<h5>Heading Level 5</h5>
<h6>Heading Level 6</h6>


<hr />
<hr size=8 />
<hr size=8 width=200 />
<hr size=8 width=200 align=left />
<hr size=8 width=200 align=left noshade />
<br />
<br />
```

31. Click File and Save. (You can also press Ctrl-S to save the file.)
32. Refresh your Web browser to display the changes. (You can also press F5 to refresh the screen.)
33. Take a screenshot. (See Figure 8-24.)

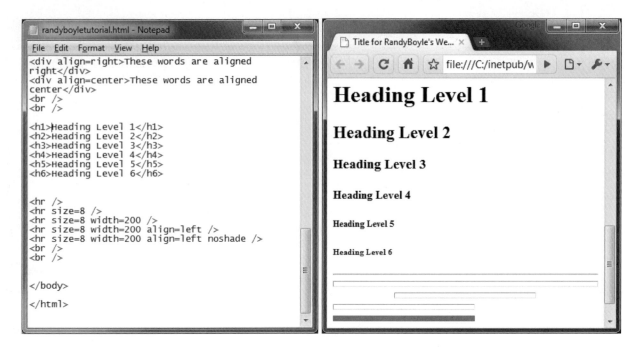

Figure 8-23: Heading and <hr> tags are added.

Figure 8-24: HTML page showing heading and horizontal line effects.

34. Add the ordered list tags with the text shown below. (Replace YourName with your first and last name. Notice that the <ol> tag starts/stops the list and the <li> tag designates a specific list item. See Figure 8-25.)

```
<h3>YourName's Favorite Classes</h3>
<ol>
 <li>Networking</li>
 <li>Database</li>
 <li>History</li>
</ol>


<h3>YourName's Outline</h3>
<ol type=I>
 <li>Introduction</li>
 <li>Beginning</li>
 <li>End</li>
</ol>
```

35. Click File and Save. (You can also press Ctrl-S to save the file.)
36. Refresh your Web browser to display the changes. (You can also press F5 to refresh the screen.)
37. Take a screenshot. (See Figure 8-26.)

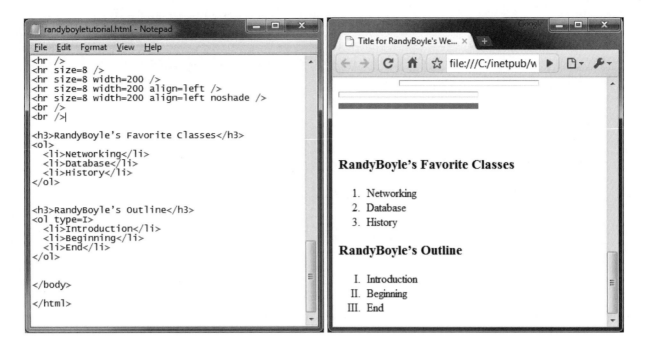

Figure 8-25: Ordered list tags are added.   Figure 8-26: HTML page showing ordered lists.

38. Add the hyperlink tags with the text shown below. (Replace YourEmailAddress@something.com with your email address. Some of the links have wrapped onto the next line. Type them in as if they were on a single line. The <br /> tag will be on a separate line. See Figure 8-27.)

```
Click <a href=http://www.google.com>Google</a> to go to Google's main
page.
<br />

Click <a href=iisstart.htm>here</a> to go to the local IIS default
page.
<br />

Click <a href=mailto:YourEmailAddress@something.com>
YourEmailAddress@something.com</a> to email me.
<br />
```

39. Click File and Save. (You can also press Ctrl-S to save the file.)
40. Refresh your Web browser to display the changes. (You can also press F5 to refresh the screen.)
41. Take a screenshot. (See Figure 8-28.)

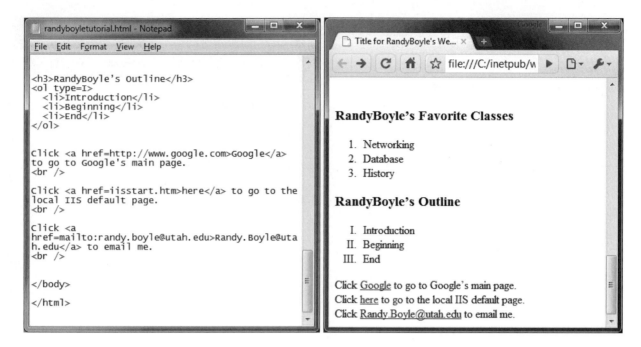

Figure 8-27: Link tags are added.

Figure 8-28: HTML page showing external, local, and email links.

42. Add the image tags shown below. (The welcome.png image is the same image shown in the IIS default page. See the note below. See Figure 8-29.)

```
<img src="welcome.png" width="30" height="30" />
<br />

<img src="welcome.png" width="60" height="60" />
<br />

<img src="welcome.png" width="60" height="60" align="right" />
<br />

<img src="http://www.google.com/intl/en_ALL/images/logo.gif"
width="60" height="60" />
<br />
```

Note: You can use any image you want for this part of the project. Just place a copy of your picture in the directory at C:\inetpub\wwwroot. The Google image (logo.gif) is linked from the www.Google.com main page. Right-click the Google logo and select Copy Image URL and paste it into the code above. You can also type the text manually.

43. Click File and Save. (You can also press Ctrl-S to save the file.)
44. Refresh your Web browser to display the changes. (You can also press F5 to refresh the screen.)
45. Take a screenshot. (See Figure 8-30.)

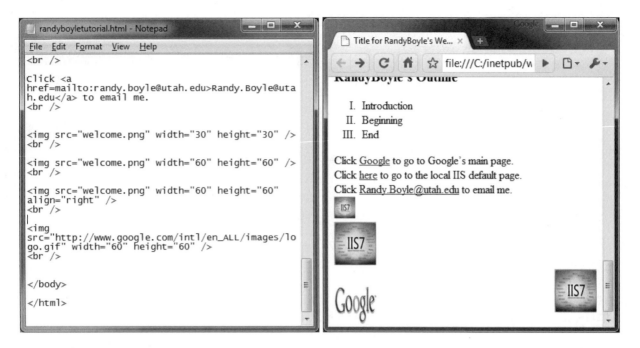

Figure 8-29: Image tags are added.   Figure 8-30: HTML page showing formatting changes to images.

46. Add the form tags shown below. (Copying and pasting some of the elements below will save you time. See Figure 8-31.)

```
<form>
Your Name: <input type="text" name="FirstName" id="Name"
value=YourName />
<br />
<input type="submit" id="Submit" />
</form>


<form>
Your Password: <input type="password" name="MyPassword" id="Password"
value=YourName />
<br />
<input type="submit" id="Submit" />
</form>


<form>
Foods I'm willing to eat: <br />
<input type="checkbox" name="Italian" id="IT" value="Yes" /> Italian
<br />
<input type="checkbox" name="Mexican" id="MX" value="Yes" /> Mexican
<br />
<input type="checkbox" name="Indian" id="IN" value="Yes" /> Indian
<br />
<input type="submit" id="Submit" />
</form>
```

47. Click File and Save. (You can also press Ctrl-S to save the file.)
48. Refresh your Web browser to display the changes. (You can also press F5 to refresh the screen.)
49. Take a screenshot. (See Figure 8-32.)

Figure 8-31: HTML code for three forms.   Figure 8-32: HTML page showing forms in a Web browser.

THOUGHT QUESTIONS

1. What tag would you use to create a comment that would not be seen when the user viewed the page?
2. What type of form would you use to create radio button options?
3. What tag would you use to show a © character?
4. What does the <blockquote> tag do?

8.3   CREATE SITE AND HOST PAGES

In this project you will create a simple Web site using a template in Microsoft Publisher®. Microsoft Publisher comes with the Microsoft Office Professional Suite. It is also widely available at most college campuses. If you are a student at a university that has access to an MSDNAA account you can get the Microsoft Expression Suite as a free download. Contact your professor or MSDNAA administrator to get access to this resource.

There are many other Web design tools like Dreamweaver, Microsoft Expression, etc. that can be used in place of Publisher. They have automated templates and are excellent tools. The instructions will be slightly different but the outcome will be the same. Pre-made Web sites will be available at http://www.pearsonhighered.com/boyle/ if you don't have access to Web design software.

Once you have created the Web pages you will add a new Web site to IIS. Then, you will configure this new Web site to serve your new Web pages. At the end of this project you will change the template and update your new Web site.

1. Click Start, All Programs, Microsoft Office, and Microsoft Publisher.
2. Click Web Sites. (See Figure 8-33.)
3. Select one of the templates. (In this case it was PhotoScope. See Figure 8-34.)

4. Click Create.

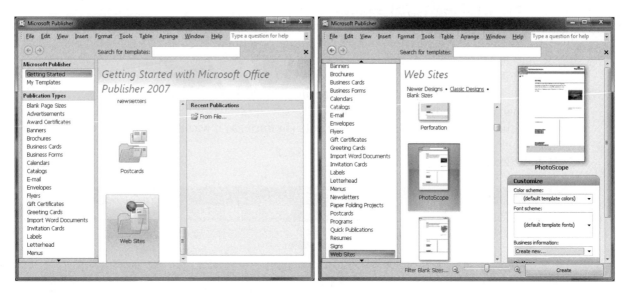

Figure 8-33: Selecting IIS components for installation. | Figure 8-34: IIS shortcut in the Control Panel.

5. Select all of the options on the Your Site Goals page. (See Figure 8-35.)
6. Click OK.
7. Click Edit and Business Information.
8. Enter your name in the Organization name and Individual name fields. (Your name must appear in the Organization name field. In this case it was Randy Boyle. See Figure 8-36.)
9. Complete the other fields with information if you choose to do so.
10. Click Save.
11. Click Update Publication.

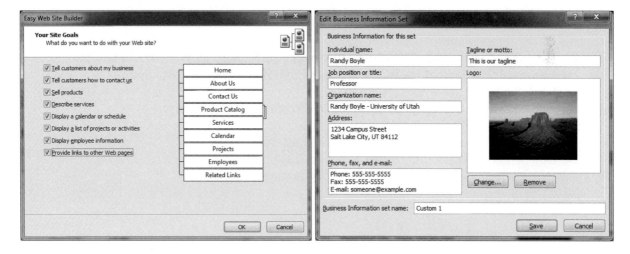

Figure 8-35: Selecting features to include in your Web site. | Figure 8-36: Business information that will be used in Microsoft Publisher templates.

12. Click Start, All Programs, Accessories, and Windows Explorer. (You can also open Windows Explorer by pressing ⊞+E.)
13. Browse to C:\networking\.
14. Create a folder labeled YourNameWebsites. (In this case it was RandyBoyleWebsites. Your new Web sites will be located in this directory.)

15. Browse to C:\networking\YourNameWebsites. (In this case it was C:\networking\RandyBoyleWebsites.)
16. Create a folder labeled YourNameHomeWebsite. (In this case it was RandyBoyleHomeWebsite. This will be the directory for your first Web site. See Figure 8-37.)
17. Return to Microsoft Publisher.
18. Click File and Save As.
19. Browse to C:\networking\YourNameWebsites. (In this case it was C:\networking\RandyBoyleWebsites.)
20. Name the file YourNameHomeWebsite.pub. (In this case it was RandyBoyleHomeWebsite.pub. See Figure 8-38.)
21. Click Save.

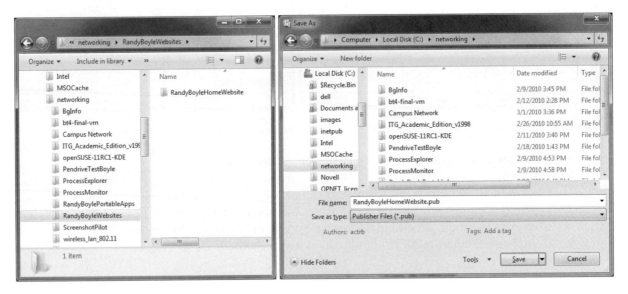

Figure 8-37: Creating directories to store your Web sites.   Figure 8-38: Saving your Publisher file.

22. Click File and Publish to the Web.
23. Browse to C:\networking\YourNameWebsites\YourNameHomeWebsite. (In this case it was C:\networking\RandyBoyleWebsites\RandyBoyleHomeWebsite. See Figure 8-39.)
24. Click Save.
25. Click OK if you see a popup about a filtered version of the Web pages.
26. Click Start and Control Panel.
27. Double-click System and Security and Administrative Tools.
28. Double-click Internet Information Services (IIS) Manager.
29. Expand the tree in the left-hand pane until you see the Sites icon.
30. Click on the Sites icon. (See Figure 8-40.)

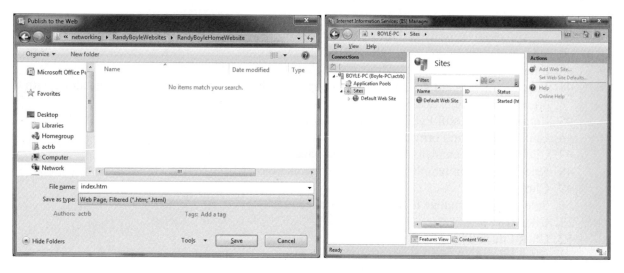

Figure 8-39: Saving your Web site.

Figure 8-40: IIS Manager.

31. Click Add Web Site in the right-hand pane.
32. Enter "YourNameHome" for the Site name. (In this case it was RandyBoyleHome.)
33. Click the "…" button.
34. Browse to C:\networking\YourNameWebsites. (In this case it was C:\networking\RandyBoyleWebsites.)
35. Select the folder labeled YourNameHomeWebsite. (In this case it was RandyBoyleHomeWebsite. You must make sure you select the correct folder. The YourNameHomeWebsite folder should have a file labeled index.htm and a folder labeled index_files inside it. See Figure 8-41.)
36. Click OK.
37. Click Yes when you see the popup. (This popup is saying that another Web site (the default Web site) is also configured to route all Web requests to it. You will only be able to run one Web site at a time until the next project.)
38. Click on the Default Web Site.
39. Click Stop in the right-hand pane.
40. Click on the Web site labeled YourNameHome. (In this case it was RandyBoyleHome.)
41. Click Start in the right-hand pane. (See Figure 8-42.)

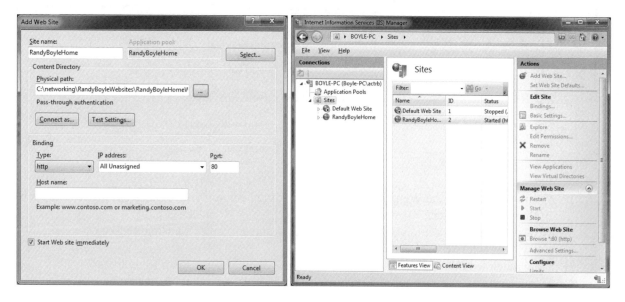

Figure 8-41: Adding a Web site to IIS.

Figure 8-42: Default Web site is stopped and YourNameHome Web site is started.

42. Open a Web browser.
43. Enter "localhost" into the address bar.
44. Take a screenshot of your Web site. (Your name should appear on the main page along with the organization name. See Figure 8-43.)
45. Return to Microsoft Publisher.
46. Click Format and Format Publication.
47. Click Change Template in the left-hand pane.
48. Select a different template. (In this case it was Marker.)
49. Click OK.
50. Select Apply template to the current publication.
51. Click OK.
52. Click File and Save.
53. Click File and Publish to the Web. (It should automatically save in the same YourNameHomeWebsite folder.)
54. Click Save and Yes.
55. Return to your Web browser.
56. Click refresh or press F5.
57. Take a screenshot of your Web site using the new template. (See Figure 8-44.)

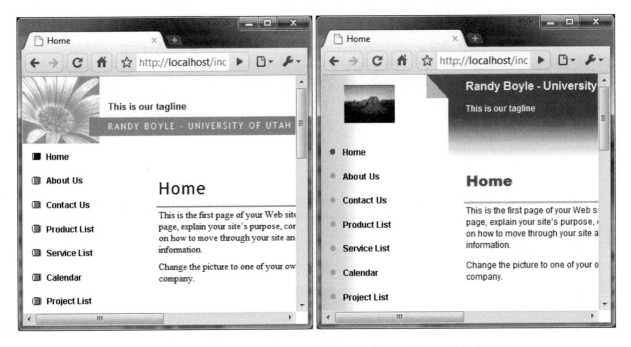

Figure 8-43: Web site shown in a Web browser.   Figure 8-44: New template applied to Web site.

THOUGHT QUESTIONS

1. Could someone on the Web see your Web site if they entered your IP address in the address bar of their Web browser?
2. How would people get to your Web site if they wanted to enter a hostname like www.YourName.com?
3. How much would a company charge to register a domain name to an IP address?
4. How could you check to see if someone already has reserved that host name?

In this project you are going to add two new Web sites to your instance of IIS. You will create one and copy one from this book's Web site. You will then edit the "hosts" file to manually resolve your hostnames into IP addresses. Changes to your hosts file will keep you from getting DNS errors because you haven't registered your hostnames to an IP address.

Manually editing your host file will not allow external clients to view your pages by entering in your hostnames. This is just a shortcut. If you want these Web sites to be available to external hosts you will have to go through the registration process to match your IP address to each hostname.

The goal of this project is to show you that a single Web server can host multiple Web sites. It will show you how your Web server will sort each Web request based on the hostname within the Web request. You will also get an error at the end of this project and fix it.

1. Click Start, All Programs, Accessories, and Windows Explorer.
2. Browse to C:\networking\YourNameWebsites. (In this case it was C:\networking\RandyBoyleWebsites.)
3. Create a folder labeled YourNameCarsWebsite. (In this case it was RandyBoyleCarsWebsite.)
4. Create a folder labeled YourNameBooksWebsite. (In this case it was RandyBoyleBooksWebsite.)
5. Browse to C:\networking\YourNameWebsites.
6. Double-click the Microsoft Publisher file labeled YourNameHomeWebsite.pub. (In this case it was RandyBoyleHomeWebsite.pub. See Figure 8-45.)
7. Click File and Save As.
8. Enter YourNameCarsWebsite.pub. (In this case it was RandyBoyleCarsWebsite.pub.)
9. Save the file in the directory labeled C:\networking\YourNameWebsites. (This is the same directory where the other Publisher file was saved. You should have two Publisher files after you save this file. See Figure 8-46.)
10. Click Save.

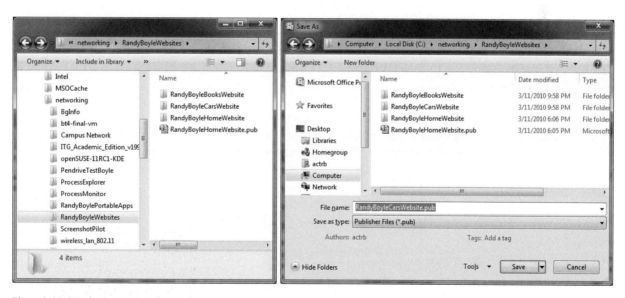

Figure 8-45: Opening your Prior Web site in Publisher.   Figure 8-46: Saving your new Web site in Publisher.

11. Click Format and Format Publication.
12. Click Change Template in the left-hand pane.
13. Select a different template. (In this case it was Even Break.)

14. Click OK.
15. Select Apply template to the current publication. (See Figure 8-47.)
16. Click OK.
17. Click File and Save.
18. Click File and Publish to the Web.
19. Save the file in the directory labeled C:\networking\YourNameWebsites\YourNameCarsWebsite. (In this case it was C:\networking\RandyBoyleWebsites\RandyBoyleCarsWebsite. See Figure 8-48.)
20. Click Save and Yes.

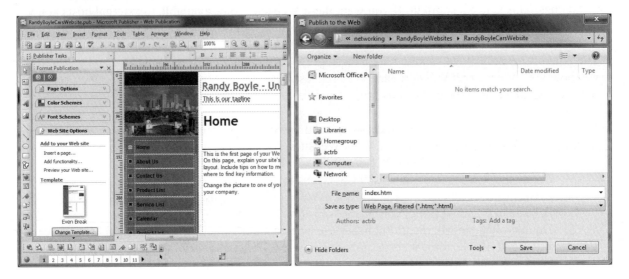

Figure 8-47: The Cars Web site.   Figure 8-48: Saving the Cars Web site.

21. Open a Web Browser. (Chrome, Internet Explorer, or Firefox will work.)
22. Browse to http://www.pearsonhighered.com/boyle/. (This is the Web site for this book.)
23. Click File and Save Page As. (See Figure 8-49.)
24. Select Complete Web Page as the type.
25. Save the file in the directory labeled C:\networking\YourNameWebsites\YourNameBooksWebsite. (In this case it was C:\networking\RandyBoyleWebsites\RandyBoyleBooksWebsite. See Figure 8-50.)
26. Click Save.

Note: The Web site you just saved had a main page with a long name (Pearson-Online…). This is not one of the default documents listed when you create a new Web site in IIS. This will cause an error later in the project and you will need to rename this file index.htm for the page to work correctly.

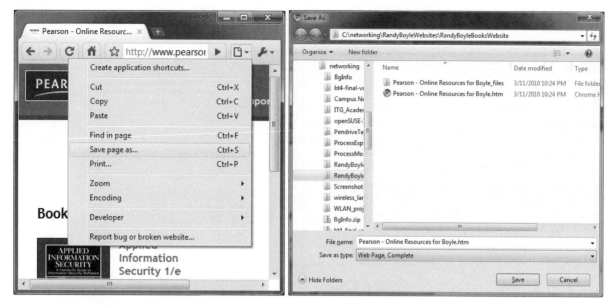

Figure 8-49: Saving a Web site from a Web browser.   Figure 8-50: Saving a Web site as the Books Web site.

27. Click Start and Control Panel.
28. Double-click System and Security and Administrative Tools.
29. Double-click Internet Information Services (IIS) Manager.
30. Expand the tree in the left-hand pane until you see the Sites icon.
31. Click on the Sites icon.
32. Click Add Web Site in the right-hand pane.
33. Enter "YourNameCars" for the Site name. (In this case it was RandyBoyleCars.)
34. Click the "…" button.
35. Browse to C:\networking\YourNameWebsites. (In this case it was C:\networking\RandyBoyleWebsites.)
36. Select the folder labeled YourNameCarsWebsite. (In this case it was RandyBoyleCarsWebsite. You must make sure you select the correct folder.)
37. Enter "www.YourNameCars.com" for the Host name. (In this case it was www.RandyBoyleCars.com. See Figure 8-51.)
38. Click OK.
39. Click Add Web Site in the right-hand pane.
40. Enter "YourNameBooks" for the Site name. (In this case it was RandyBoyleBooks.)
41. Click the "…" button.
42. Browse to C:\networking\YourNameWebsites. (In this case it was C:\networking\RandyBoyleWebsites.)
43. Select the folder labeled YourNameBooksWebsite. (In this case it was RandyBoyleBooksWebsite. You must make sure you select the correct folder.)
44. Enter "www.YourNameBooks.com" for the Host name. (In this case it was www.RandyBoyleBooks.com. See Figure 8-52.)
45. Click OK.

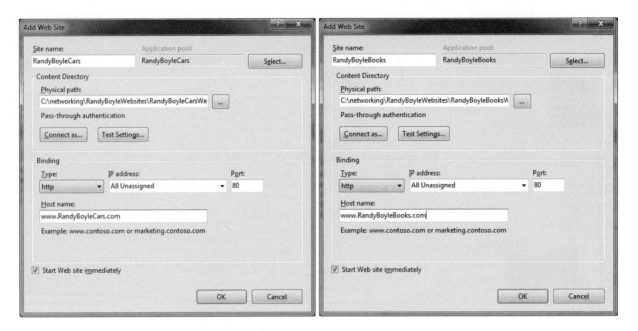

Figure 8-51: Adding the Cars Web site.　　　　　　　Figure 8-52: Adding the Books Web site.

46. Click on the site labeled YourNameHome. (In this case it was RandyBoyleHome.)
47. Click on Bindings in the right-hand pane.
48. Click Add.
49. Enter "www.YourNameHome.com" as the Host name. (In this case it was www.RandyBoyleHome.com. See Figure 8-53.)
50. Click OK.
51. Click on the empty row.
52. Click Remove.
53. Click Yes. (There should only be the new binding labeled www.YourNameHome.com in the window. See Figure 8-54.)
54. Click Close.

Figure 8-53: Adding a hostname to the Home Web site.　　　Figure 8-54: Site binding for the Home Web site.

Note: You should now have four Web sites (Default, Home, Cars, and Books) running on your Web Server. However, you have not registered your IP address and their associated host names (e.g. www.YourNameCars.com). We are going to trick your computer into thinking it resolved the hostnames by editing your "hosts" file.

Your computer will check this file before it makes a DNS request. After these changes are made you can enter a hostname like www.YourNameCars.com into your Web browser's address bar and your Web site will come up. This only works on your local computer. If you want these hostnames to work on other people's computers you will have to register your hostnames and IP address.

55. Open Notepad by clicking Start, All Programs, and Accessories.
56. Right-click Notepad.
57. Select Run as administrator. (If you don't start Notepad with administrator-level privileges you will not be able to save the changes you are going to make to this file. The rest of the project will not work if you don't save these changes.)
58. Click File and Open.
59. Browse to C:\Windows\System32\drivers\etc\.
60. Change the file type to All Files (*.*). (This will allow you to see the hosts file.)
61. Select the hosts file. (See Figure 8-55.)
62. Click Open.
63. Scroll to the bottom of the text file.
64. Add the following text to the bottom of the file. (Replace YourName with your first and last name so it matches the hostnames for your Web sites. You can add as many blank lines as you want. It won't affect how the hostnames are processed. Make sure these host names are EXACTLY the same as the bindings you entered when you set up the Web site. See Figure 8-56.)

```
127.0.0.1   www.YourNameHome.com
127.0.0.1   www.YourNameCars.com
127.0.0.1   www.YourNameBooks.com
```

65. Click File and Save.
66. Close the hosts file.

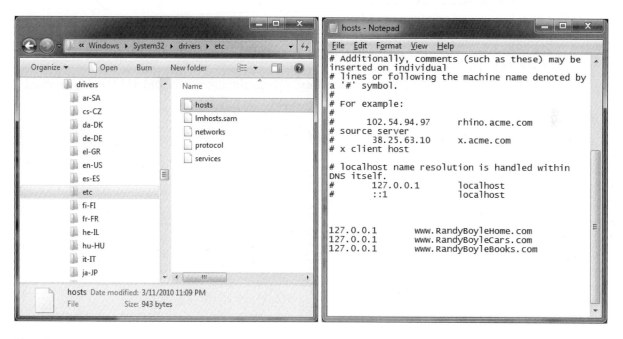

Figure 8-55: Opening the hosts file.   Figure 8-56: Changes made to the hosts file.

67. Open a Web browser.
68. Enter "www.YourNameHome.com" into the address bar.
69. Take a screenshot of your Web site with your name showing in the address bar. (See Figure 8-57.)
70. Enter "www.YourNameCars.com" into the address bar.

71. Take a screenshot of your Web site with your name showing in the address bar. (See Figure 8-58.)

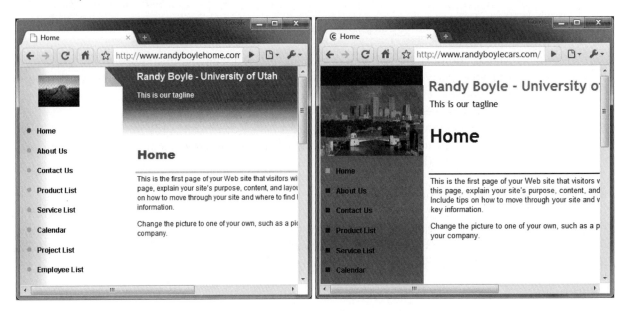

Figure 8-57: Your Home Web site.   Figure 8-58: Your Cars Web site.

72. Enter "www.YourNameBooks.com" into the address bar. (You should get an error message because the main page in the folder is not listed in the list of default pages for that Web site.)
73. Take a screenshot of the error message. (See Figure 8-59.)
74. Open Windows Explorer.
75. Browse to C:\networking\YourNameWebsites\YourNameBooksWebsite. (In this case it was C:\networking\RandyBoyleWebsites\RandyBoyleBooksWebsite. There should be one folder and one HTML page in that directory.)
76. Right-click the HTML page in that directory. (There should only be one HTML page named "Pearson-Online…")
77. Select Rename.
78. Name the file "index.htm". (See Figure 8-60.)
79. Press enter.
80. Click Yes.

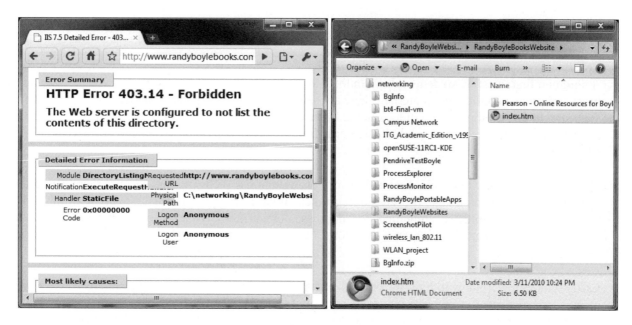

Figure 8-59: Error message for the Books Web site.

Figure 8-60: Renamed main page for the Books Web site.

81. Return to your Web browser.

82. Enter "www.YourNameBooks.com" into the address bar.

83. Take a screenshot of your Web site with your name showing in the address bar. (See Figure 8-61.)

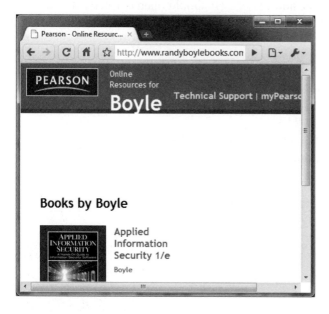

Figure 8-61: Books Web site with your name in the address bar.

THOUGHT QUESTIONS

1. Could you make changes to the HTML code for the Books Web page and have it display in the browser?

2. How does IIS know which Web site to serve if they are all on the same computer?

3. What would happen if you left off the "www" in front of your www.YourNameCars.com hostname when you entered it into a Web browser? Why did this happen?

4. Could you edit your hosts file to display Yahoo's main page when someone enters www.Google.com into a Web browser? How?

A common first question students ask when they are beginning to learn to host Web content is how to password protect confidential material. There are several different methods of authenticating users to a Web site. In this example you will look at the Basic Authentication option in IIS. This method of authentication uses the usernames and passwords from the local computer to authenticate access to a Web site.

You will also see how to enable/disable directory browsing on a Web site. Just because there isn't a link to a page (or document, image, file, etc.) doesn't mean it isn't available. There are many files on the Web that aren't linked to directly. Sometimes leaving these objects on the Web server can have negative consequences. You can also access pages before "official" links are created if you know how to browse the directory.

Lastly, you will learn how to limit the number of current connections. Limiting the number of connections to a specific Web site may keep your entire server from crashing. Denial of Service (DOS) attacks and/or dramatic increases in legitimate usage do occur. If you limit the number of connections or bandwidth to a given site you may prevent your other Web sites (on the same machine) from being affected by the increased traffic.

1. Open a Web browser.
2. Enter "www.YourNameHome.com" into the address bar. (It should open correctly if you completed the prior project. If you haven't completed the prior project you will need to complete it before continuing. See Figure 8-62.)
3. Click Start and Control Panel.
4. Double-click System and Security and Administrative Tools.
5. Double-click Internet Information Services (IIS) Manager.
6. Expand the tree in the left-hand pane until you see the Sites icon.
7. Click on the Sites icon.
8. Click on the Web site labeled YourNameHome. (In this case it was RandyBoyleHome.)
9. Double-click the icon labeled Authentication. (See Figure 8-63.)

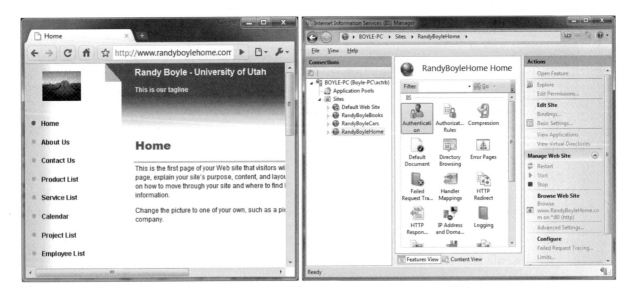

Figure 8-62: The Home Web site.

Figure 8-63: Authentication icon.

10. Select the row labeled Anonymous Authentication.
11. Click Disable in the right-hand pane.
12. Click on the row labeled Basic Authentication.
13. Click Enable. (Basic Authentication should be the only form of authentication enabled. See Figure 8-64.)
14. Click on the Web site labeled YourNameHome in the left-hand pane.
15. Click Restart in the right-hand pane.
16. Close your Web browser.
17. Reopen your Web browser.
18. Enter "www.YourNameHome.com" into the address bar. (In this case it was www.RandyBoyleHome.com. You should see a login screen. You might see your Web site opened in the background if your Web browser cached it. Without having it cached first you wouldn't be able to see it without authenticating first.)
19. Enter your username and password as if you were logging into your local computer. (In this case the user name was actrb. This is the same username and password you use to log into your computer on a daily basis.)
20. Take a screenshot. (See Figure 8-65.)
21. Click Log In.

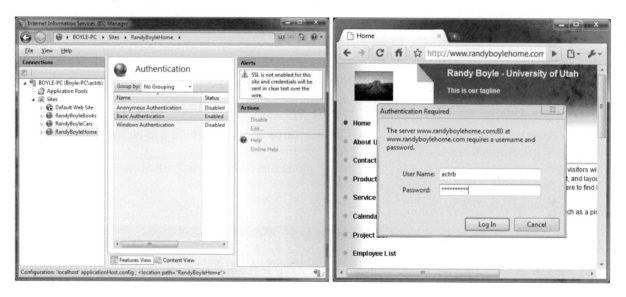

Figure 8-64: Changing authentication for the Web site.   Figure 8-65: Login screen for access to the Web site.

22. Click on one of the side links to access a sub page within the site. (In this case it was the About Us page. See Figure 8-66.)
23. Click on the address bar.
24. Edit the URL in the address bar by deleting the reference to the specific html page you are on so that you see just the hostname and subdirectory. (Note the examples below showing the modified URL. If you have done this correctly you should get a forbidden error message. See Figure 8-67.)

Before deleting the specific page reference:

`http://www.randyboylehome.com/index_files/`**`Page736.htm`**

After deleting the specific page reference:

`http://www.randyboylehome.com/index_files/`

25. Press Enter.

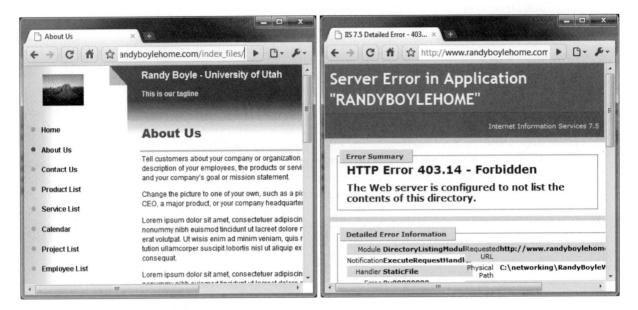

Figure 8-66: Modifying the URL to get a directory listing.   Figure 8-67: Forbidden error message.

26. Return to the IIS Manager.
27. Click on the Web site labeled YourNameHome. (In this case it was RandyBoyleHome.)
28. Double-Click the icon labeled Directory Browsing. (See Figure 8-68.)
29. Click Enable in the right-hand pane.
30. Return to your Web browser. (The forbidden error message should still be showing.)
31. Click Refresh or press F5.
32. Take a screenshot of the directory listing. (This should be a listing of all the files in the index_files directory. See Figure 8-69.)
33. Click Back in your Web browser.

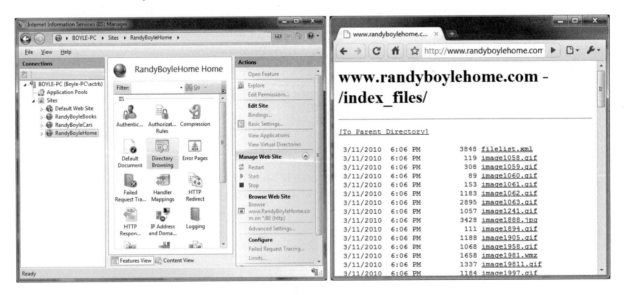

Figure 8-68: Modifying directory browsing.   Figure 8-69: Directory listing.

34. Return to the IIS Manager.

35. Click on the Web site labeled YourNameHome. (In this case it was RandyBoyleHome.)
36. Click Limits in the right-hand pane.
37. Select Limit number of connections.
38. Enter "2" for the number of connections. (See Figure 8-70.)
39. Click OK.
40. Return to your Web browser. (The main page or a sub page should be showing.)
41. Copy the URL in to the address bar. (You can copy it by pressing Ctrl-C.)
42. Press Ctrl-T three times to open three additional tabs.
43. Paste the copied URL from your Web page into each of the tabs.
44. Press enter on each of the tabs to start loading the page.
45. Keep refreshing each tab (F5) quickly until you start seeing parts of the page fail to load.
46. Take a screenshot of one of the tabs that failed to load properly. (See Figure 8-71.)
47. Return to the IIS Manager.
48. Change the limits back to unlimited connections.

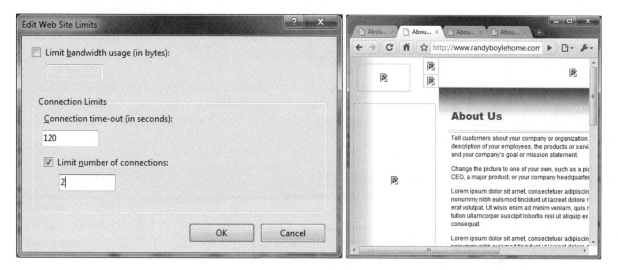

Figure 8-70: Limiting the number of connections.

Figure 8-71: Page elements failing to load correctly due to limitations on the number of connections.

THOUGHT QUESTIONS

1. Can IIS integrate authentication with Active Directory?
2. Why would you want to limit the bandwidth usage for a Web site?
3. Why did certain elements of the Web page fail to load when you limited the number of connections?
4. Why would you want to forbid directory browsing?

CHAPTER 9: APACHE

Apache is the leading Web server in the world. It's also completely free and used by some of the biggest Web sites in the world. Almost 50% of the top 100 most visited Web sites use Apache. In an earlier project (Netcraft.com) you saw that Apache has been around for many years. Based on its past performance and current market share it looks like it is here to stay.

This chapter is designed to give you a first experience with Apache. Most students in their first Networking/Telecommunications course have not used Apache before. After you complete these projects you won't be ready to start your own Web hosting company but you will know the basics.

These projects will walk you through the installation, configuration, and management of an Apache Web server. You will learn some basic commands to start/stop Apache through a DOS prompt. You will also Edit the httpd.conf file and do some basic performance testing.

Apache does not come with a GUI interface like IIS does. Apache is configured through text-based configuration files. The main file (httpd.conf) is the equivalent of the IIS Manager. Editing a text file can be a little more intimidating to beginning students. However, once you become familiar with it you may find it to be just as easy (or easier) to use.

9.1   INSTALLATION AND SETUP

In this project you will download and install Apache. You will shut down IIS from a prior project and view the default Web page that comes with Apache. You will then edit the HTML code for the default page by adding your name to it and serve the modified page.

Downloading and installing Apache is quick and easy. Configuring it is also straightforward when you become familiar with the layout of the configuration file. With practice you can download, install, and configure Apache in less than 3 minutes. Adding a full Web site may only take another 30 seconds for an experienced user.

Showing a potential employer that you can quickly and correctly get a Web server running may help you get a really good job. Practice and repetition is all you need. Apache is widely used and will likely be around for a long time. It's a good idea to know it well.

1. Download the Apache Web Server from http://httpd.apache.org/download.cgi.
2. Click on the link for the Win32 binary file without crypto (In this case it was httpd-2.2.15-win32-x86-no_ssl.msi. The link may be slightly different due to more current releases. Make sure it has the MSI extension.)
3. Click Save.
4. Select the C:\networking\ folder.
5. Click Run and OK.
6. If your download doesn't automatically run you can double-click the httpd-2.2.15-win32-x86-no_ssl.msi installer.
7. Click Run, Next, I Accept, Next, and Next.
8. Enter "YourName.com" for the network domain. (In this case it was RandyBoyle.com.)
9. Enter "www.YourName.com" for the server name. (In this case it was www.RandyBoyle.com.)

10. Enter an email address with your name in it. (In this case it was Randy.Boyle@utah.edu. It does not need to be a real email address but it does have to have your name in it. See Figure 9-1.)
11. Take a screenshot.
12. Click Next, Next, Next, Install, and Finish. (See Figure 9-2.)

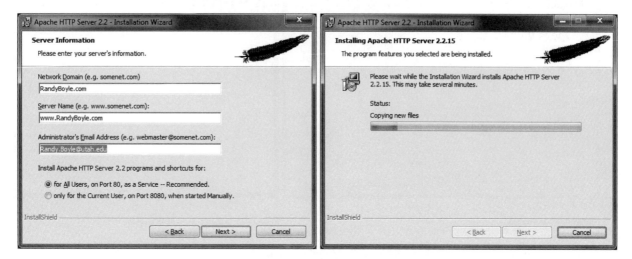

Figure 9-1: Apache configuration screen.   Figure 9-2: Installing Apache.

Note: IIS is still running and serving pages on port 80. You will need to shut it down (temporarily) before Apache can start. You can always shut down Apache and start IIS again.

13. Click Start and Control Panel.
14. Double-click System and Security and Administrative Tools.
15. Double-click Internet Information Services (IIS) Manager.
16. Click on your computer at the top of the tree. (In this case it was BOYLE-PC.)
17. Click Stop in the right-hand pane. (This should stop all of your Web sites. See Figure 9-3.)
18. Close the IIS Manager window.
19. Click Start, All Programs, Apache HTTP Server 2.2, Control Apache Server, and Start. (You may have to run this "as Administrator" if you are using Windows 7. Windows XP users will not see this pop-up.)
20. Open a Web browser.
21. Enter "127.0.0.1".
22. Press Enter.
23. Take a screenshot of the Web page saying "It works!" (See Figure 9-4.)

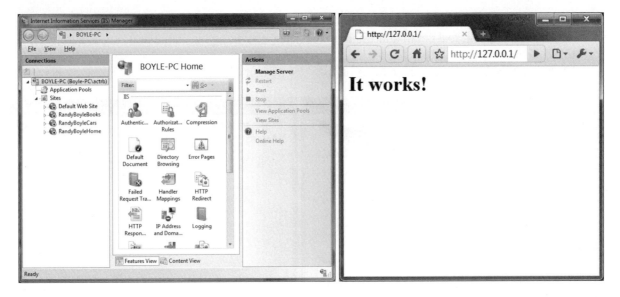

Figure 9-3: Shutting down IIS.

Figure 9-4: Apache default Web page.

24. Open Notepad by clicking Start, All Programs, and Accessories.
25. Right-click Notepad.
26. Select Run as administrator.
27. Click File and Open.
28. Browse to C:\Program Files\Apache Software Foundation\Apache2.2\htdocs.
29. Change the file type drop-down to All Files (*.*).
30. Select the file labeled index.html. (See Figure 9-5.)
31. Click Open.
32. Add the following HTML code between the `<body>` tag and the `<h1>It works!</h1>` tag.

```
<h1>Randy Boyle, Apache, Default Page</h1>
<br />
```

33. Click File, Save, and Save. (See Figure 9-6.)

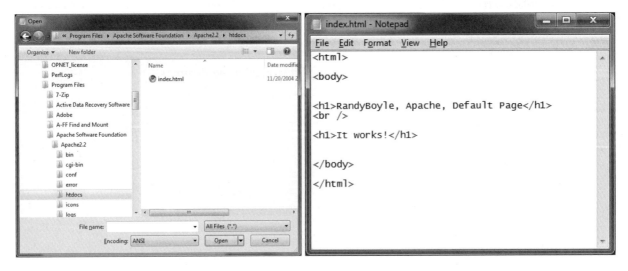

Figure 9-5: Location of the default Apache Web page (index.html).

Figure 9-6: Modified HTML code for the default Apache Web page.

34. Return to your Web browser.

35. Click Refresh or press F5.
36. Take a screenshot with your name showing in the Web browser. (See Figure 9-7.)

Figure 9-7: Modified default Web page.

THOUGHT QUESTIONS

1. Do large companies like CNN use Apache? Why?
2. Can you host multiple Web sites using Apache?
3. If the code for Apache is available to everyone isn't it less secure? Why not?
4. Can you run Apache exclusively through a command-line interface (i.e. without a GUI)?

9.2 APACHE COMMAND-LINE & BENCHMARKING

In this project you will learn some basic commands that are used to administer Apache through a command-line interface. These are just a few basic commands. There is a lot more to learn about Apache. There are some excellent online resources at http://httpd.apache.org/docs/.

Learning command line is important because more and more Web servers are being run without a GUI interface. Web servers that utilize a command-line interface use less resources, run faster, have fewer problems, and are easier to administer remotely.

You will also do some basic benchmarking against your Web server. You will see how your Web server responds to increases in the number of page requests and the number of concurrent users. You will look at statistics such as requests per second, transfer rate, time per request, etc.

1. Click Start, All Programs, and Accessories.
2. Right-click Command Prompt.
3. Select Run as administrator. (This isn't necessary if you are using Windows XP. The following commands will not work on Windows 7 if you don't start the command prompt with administrator-level privileges.)
4. Click Yes.

5. Type **cd ..**
6. Press Enter. (Repeat **cd ..** command multiple times until you get to C:\.)
7. Type **cd p**
8. Press Tab multiple times until you see "Program Files."
9. Press Enter.
10. Type **cd a**
11. Press Tab multiple times until you see "Apache Software Foundation."
12. Press Enter.
13. Type **cd a**
14. Press Tab multiple times until you see "Apache 2.2."
15. Press Enter.
16. Type **cd bin**
17. Press Enter. (See Figure 9-8.)
18. Type **dir**
19. Press Enter. (This will give you a listing of the applications and files in the bin directory.)

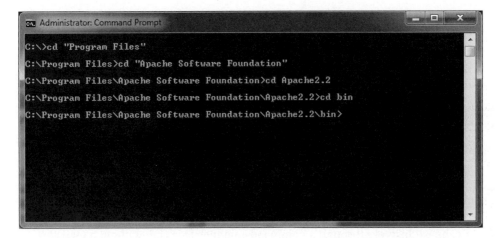

Figure 9-8: Traversing directories.

20. Type **httpd -v**
21. Press Enter. (This will display the version and build date of the current Apache installation.)
22. Type **httpd -t**
23. Press Enter. (This will run syntax tests for the Apache configuration files. This is a useful command to run after you have made changes to a configuration file. See Figure 9-9.)
24. Type **time**
25. Press Enter twice. (This adds a time stamp to your project.)
26. Take a screenshot.

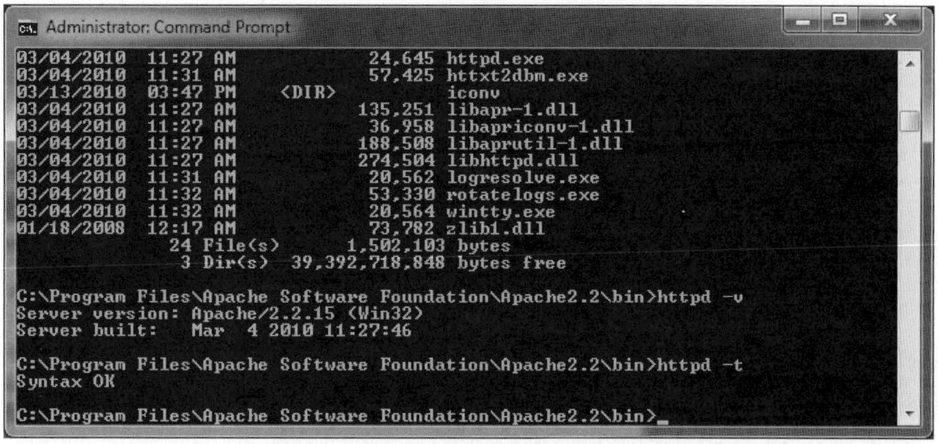

Figure 9-9: Apache -v and -t options.

27. Type **httpd -l**
28. Press Enter. (This will display a list of loaded modules.)
29. Type **httpd -S**
30. Press Enter. (This will display the settings from the config file for VirtualHost configuration. It should be empty. In the next project you will add a couple of virtual hosts. The next time you run this command you will see a different output.)
31. Type **time**
32. Press Enter twice.
33. Take a screenshot. (See Figure 9-10.)

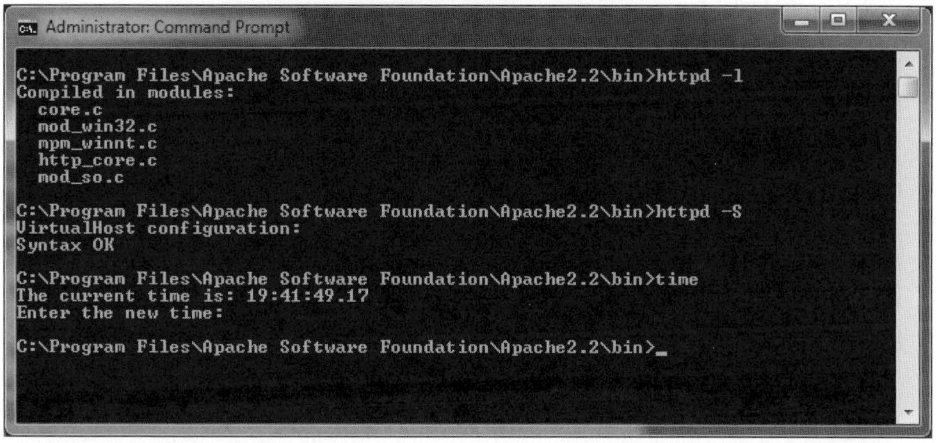

Figure 9-10: Apache -l and -S options.

34. Type **httpd -k stop**
35. Press Enter. (This will stop the Web server.)
36. Go back to your Web browser.
37. Click Refresh or F5. (You should get an error message because Apache was not serving pages.)
38. Type **httpd -k start**
39. Press Enter. (This will start the Web server.)
40. Go back to your Web browser.
41. Click Refresh or F5. (You should see the default page again.)
42. Type **httpd -k restart**

43. Press Enter. (This will restart the Web server. This command is useful if you make changes to a configuration file and then want to have the changes take effect.)
44. Type **time**
45. Press Enter twice.
46. Take a screenshot. (See Figure 9-11.)

Figure 9-11: Apache start, stop, and restart commands.

Note: Now you are going to do some benchmarking on your Apache Web server. Apache comes with an application (ab.exe) that will test your Apache Web server and give you statistics about its performance. Be careful not to use this tool inappropriately on other Web sites.

Hint: Pressing the up arrow key on your keyboard will display the previous command in the DOS prompt. Then you can make a small change to the command without retyping the entire command. This will also reduce errors.

47. Type **ab -n 10 http://www.cnn.com/**
48. Press Enter. (This will make 10 requests to www.CNN.com and provide you with statistics about those requests. Note that CNN is running an Apache Web server.)
49. Take a screenshot. (See Figure 9-12.)

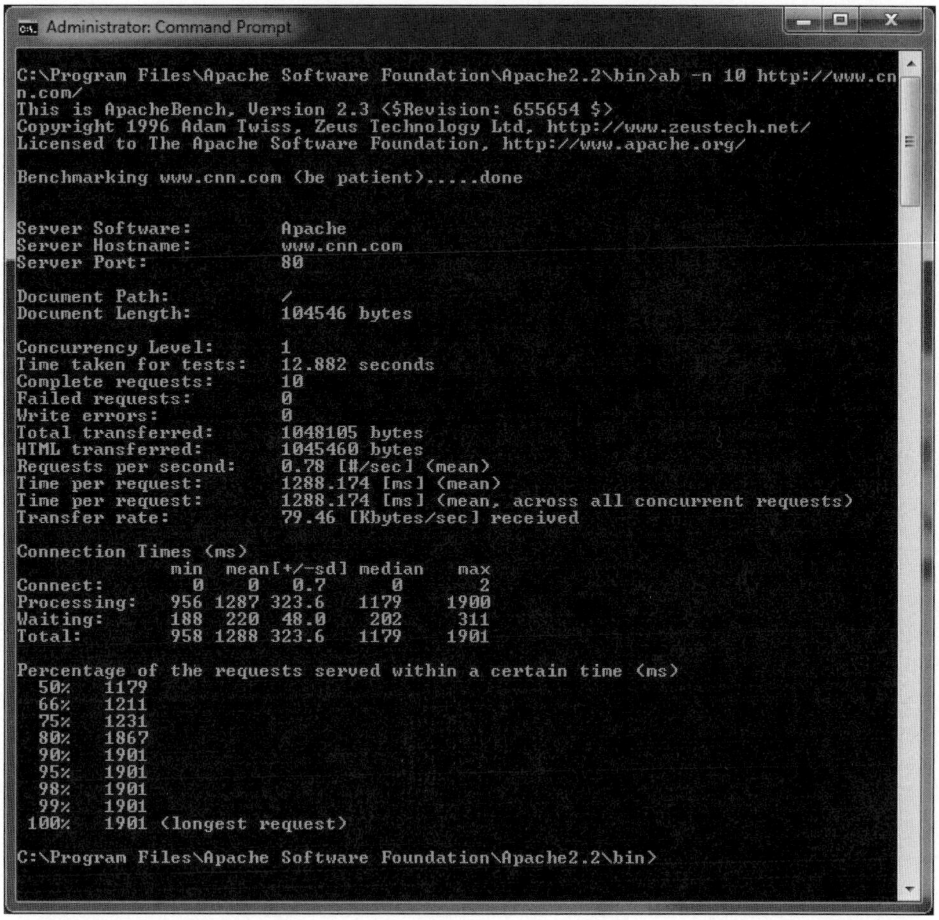

```
Administrator: Command Prompt

C:\Program Files\Apache Software Foundation\Apache2.2\bin>ab -n 10 http://www.cn
n.com/
This is ApacheBench, Version 2.3 <$Revision: 655654 $>
Copyright 1996 Adam Twiss, Zeus Technology Ltd, http://www.zeustech.net/
Licensed to The Apache Software Foundation, http://www.apache.org/

Benchmarking www.cnn.com (be patient).....done


Server Software:        Apache
Server Hostname:        www.cnn.com
Server Port:            80

Document Path:          /
Document Length:        104546 bytes

Concurrency Level:      1
Time taken for tests:   12.882 seconds
Complete requests:      10
Failed requests:        0
Write errors:           0
Total transferred:      1048105 bytes
HTML transferred:       1045460 bytes
Requests per second:    0.78 [#/sec] (mean)
Time per request:       1288.174 [ms] (mean)
Time per request:       1288.174 [ms] (mean, across all concurrent requests)
Transfer rate:          79.46 [Kbytes/sec] received

Connection Times (ms)
              min  mean[+/-sd] median   max
Connect:        0    0   0.7      0       2
Processing:   956 1287 323.6   1179    1900
Waiting:      188  220  48.0    202     311
Total:        958 1288 323.6   1179    1901

Percentage of the requests served within a certain time (ms)
  50%   1179
  66%   1211
  75%   1231
  80%   1867
  90%   1901
  95%   1901
  98%   1901
  99%   1901
 100%   1901 (longest request)

C:\Program Files\Apache Software Foundation\Apache2.2\bin>
```

Figure 9-12: Testing 10 requests on www.CNN.com.

50. Type **ab -n 10 http://127.0.0.1/**
51. Press Enter. (This will make 10 requests to your server. Compare the two screenshots to see the differences between Web requests and serving pages from your local machine. The server at www.CNN.com took about 1200 ms per request where your local machine should be less than 10 ms to send a request.)
52. Take a screenshot. (See Figure 9-13.)

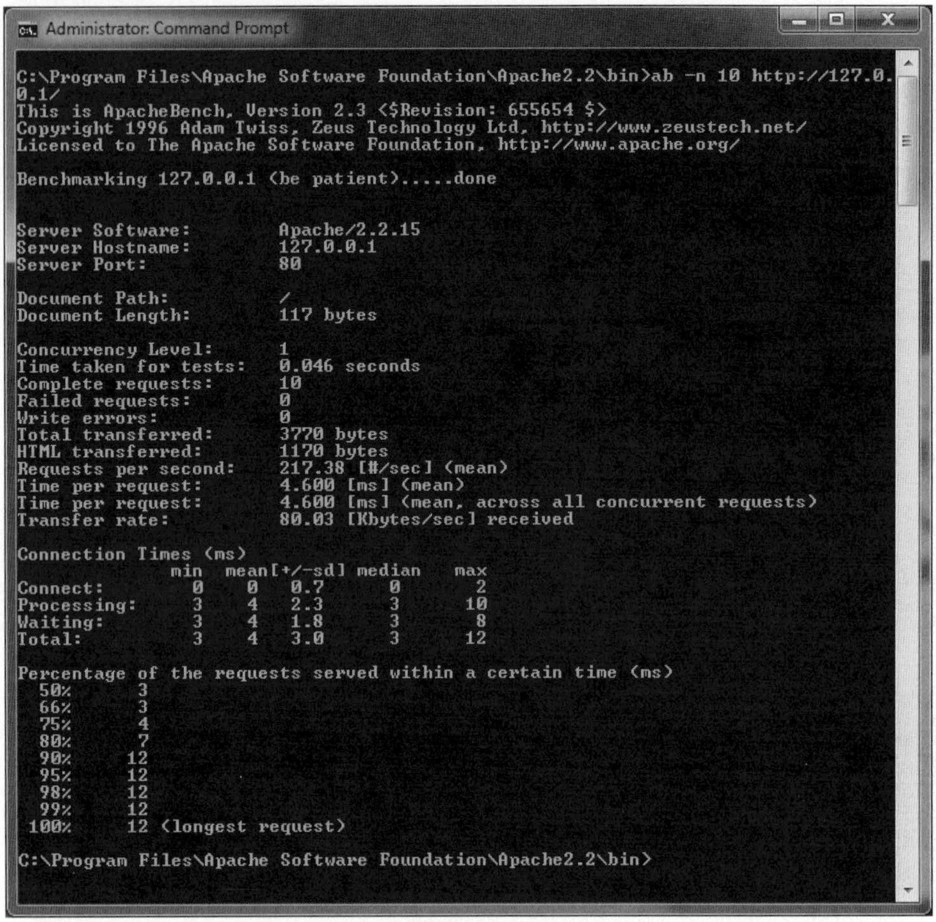

Figure 9-13: Testing 10 requests on your local Apache Web server.

53. Type **ab -n 1000 http://127.0.0.1/**

54. Press Enter. (This will make 1000 requests to your server. Compare the two screenshots to see the differences between this test and the prior test. Notice that Requests per second went up (not surprising). Transfer rate went from 75-90 KB/sec at 10 requests to 115-130 KB/sec at 1000 requests.)

55. Take a screenshot. (See Figure 9-14.)

Figure 9-14: Testing 1000 requests.

56. Type **ab –n 1000 –c 10 http://127.0.0.1/**
57. Press Enter. (This will make 1000 requests with 10 concurrent requests at a time. Compare the two screenshots to see the differences between this test and the prior test. Notice that Concurrency level went from 1 to 10. Requests per second almost doubled. Time per request went from about 3 ms at 1 concurrent connection to 20 ms at 10 concurrent connections.)
58. Take a screenshot. (See Figure 9-15.)

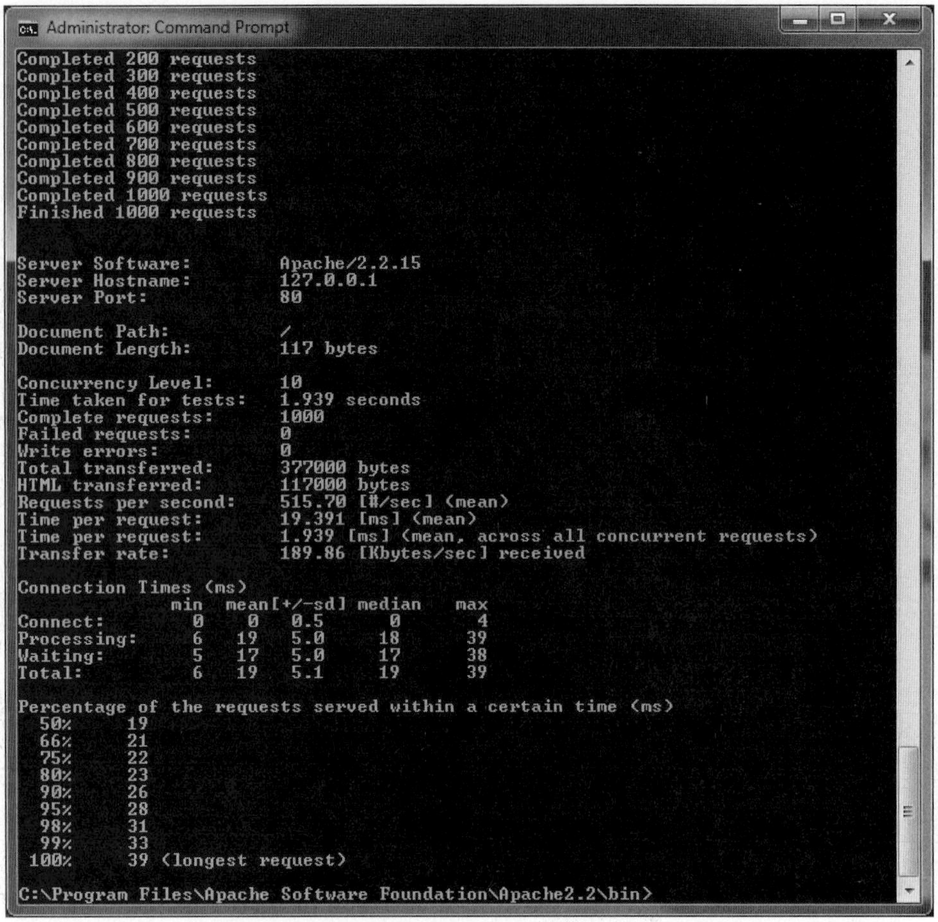

```
Administrator: Command Prompt

Completed 200 requests
Completed 300 requests
Completed 400 requests
Completed 500 requests
Completed 600 requests
Completed 700 requests
Completed 800 requests
Completed 900 requests
Completed 1000 requests
Finished 1000 requests


Server Software:        Apache/2.2.15
Server Hostname:        127.0.0.1
Server Port:            80

Document Path:          /
Document Length:        117 bytes

Concurrency Level:      10
Time taken for tests:   1.939 seconds
Complete requests:      1000
Failed requests:        0
Write errors:           0
Total transferred:      377000 bytes
HTML transferred:       117000 bytes
Requests per second:    515.70 [#/sec] (mean)
Time per request:       19.391 [ms] (mean)
Time per request:       1.939 [ms] (mean, across all concurrent requests)
Transfer rate:          189.86 [Kbytes/sec] received

Connection Times (ms)
              min  mean[+/-sd] median   max
Connect:        0    0   0.5      0       4
Processing:     6   19   5.0     18      39
Waiting:        5   17   5.0     17      38
Total:          6   19   5.1     19      39

Percentage of the requests served within a certain time (ms)
  50%     19
  66%     21
  75%     22
  80%     23
  90%     26
  95%     28
  98%     31
  99%     33
 100%     39 (longest request)

C:\Program Files\Apache Software Foundation\Apache2.2\bin>
```

Figure 9-15: Testing 10 concurrent connections.

59. Type **ab -n 1000 -c 200 http://127.0.0.1/**
60. Press Enter. (This will make 1000 requests with 200 concurrent requests at a time. Compare the two screenshots to see the differences between this test and the prior test. Notice that Concurrency level went from 10 to 200. Requests per second stayed about the same. Time per request went from about 20 ms at 10 concurrent connections to 433 ms at 200 concurrent connections.)
61. Take a screenshot.
62. Type **ab -n 1000 -c 500 http://127.0.0.1/**
63. Press Enter. (You should get an error.)
64. Take a screenshot. (See Figure 9-16.)

Figure 9-16: Testing 200 concurrent connections.

THOUGHT QUESTIONS

1. Why did you get an error when you tried 500 concurrent connections? (Hint: MaxClients is 256.)
2. Why doesn't Apache come with a GUI like IIS?
3. Does Apache have the ability to handle SSL connections?
4. What DOS command would you use to determine if IIS or Apache was using port 80?

9.3   CONFIGURATION FILE (HTTPD.CONF)

In this project you will edit the main configuration file (httpd.conf), restart your Web server, and see what effect those changes made on your Web site. The httpd.conf file is a large text file. Each line is processed in order by Apache. Lines with a pound sign (#) are not processed. These lines are used as comments or to prevent a given line from being processed.

In this project you will change the default port from 80 to 8080 and modify the URL to use this new port. You will change it back to port 80 to reduce confusion. You will then change the default directory from htdocs to the directory where your "Home" Web site is located. This was the Web site you created earlier. Finally, you will add index.htm to the list of default documents so you can view your main page.

After making changes you will save the httpd.conf file, restart the server, and then refresh the Web browser to see the effects of those changes. It's good to experiment with the httpd.conf file. It can be intimidating when you see it for the first time. Making a lot of changes and becoming familiar with the httpd.conf file will give you confidence in your ability to administer it properly.

1. Open Notepad by clicking Start, All Programs, and Accessories.
2. Right-click Notepad.
3. Select Run as administrator.
4. Click File and Open.
5. Browse to C:\Program Files\Apache Software Foundation\Apache2.2\conf.
6. Change the file type drop-down to All Files (*.*).
7. Select the file labeled httpd.conf. (See Figure 9-17.)
8. Click Open. (See Figure 9-18.)

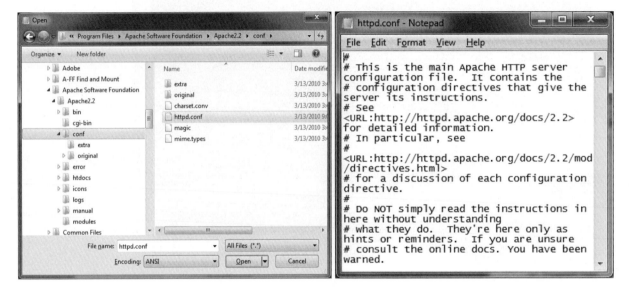

Figure 9-17: Location of the httpd.conf file.   Figure 9-18: Contents of the httpd.conf file.

9. Scroll down until you see a heading labeled "Listen 80." (This is the line that tells Apache which port to listen on. Typically Web requests go to port 80. However, you can run your Web server on any port you want to. See Figure 9-19.)

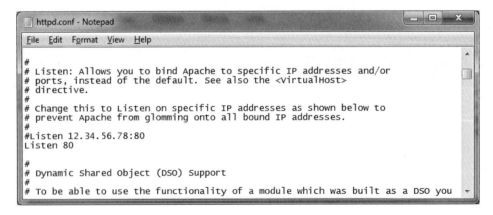

Figure 9-19: Default setting for Apache to listen on port 80.

10. Change the line from Listen 80 to **Listen 8080**. (Bold is added for emphasis; do not apply in the configuration file. See Figure 9-20.)
11. On the File menu click File and Save.

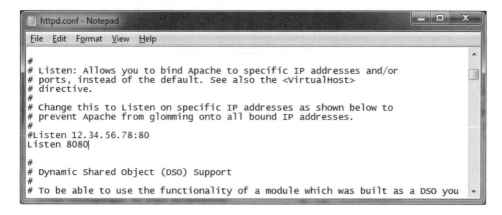

Figure 9-20: Changing the port from 80 to 8080.

12. Click Start, All Programs, and Accessories.
13. Right-click Command Prompt.
14. Select Run as administrator. (This isn't necessary if you are using Windows XP. The following commands will not work on Windows 7 if you don't start the command prompt with administrator-level privileges.)
15. Click Yes.
16. Type **cd C:\Program Files\Apache Software Foundation\Apache2.2\bin**
17. Press Enter.
18. Type **httpd -k restart**
19. Press Enter. (This restarted your Web server and put the changes you made to the httpd.conf file into effect. Apache will now serve pages over port 8080. See Figure 9-21.)

Note: Leave this command prompt and your Web browser open. You will be restarting your Web server and refreshing your Web browser several times in this project.

Figure 9-21: Restarting Apache after changes were made.

20. Open another Web browser.
21. Enter "**127.0.0.1**" into the address bar.
22. Press Enter. (This should give you an error because your Web browser is making a request at port 80. You configured Apache to serve pages on port 8080.)
23. Enter "**127.0.0.1:8080**" into the address bar. (It is important that you type the IP address and new port number correctly.)
24. Press Enter. (The default page should load correctly.)
25. Take a screenshot. (Your name should be displayed from a prior project. See Figure 9-22.)

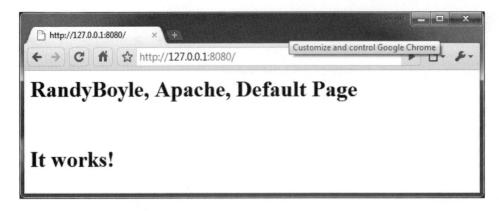

Figure 9-22: Viewing a page on port 8080.

26. Return to the httpd.conf file.
27. Scroll down until you see the heading labeled "Listen 80."
28. Change the line from Listen 8080 to **Listen 80**. (This changes it back to port 80. See Figure 9-23.)

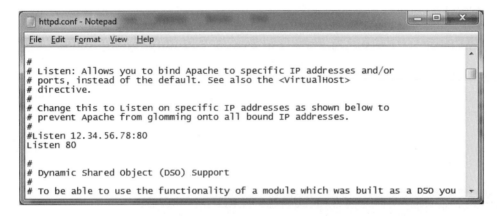

Figure 9-23: Changing the port back to 80.

29. Scroll down until you see a heading labeled "DocumentRoot."
30. Add a pound sign (#) in front of the following line.

```
DocumentRoot "C:/Program Files/Apache Software Foundation/Apache2.2/htdocs"
```

31. Add the following line below the line you just commented out. (This is the path to your "Home" Web site that you created in an earlier project. See Figure 9-24.)

```
DocumentRoot "C:/networking/YourNameWebsites/YourNameHomeWebsite"
```

Note: Remember to change YourName to your first and last name. In the example above the new path was C:/networking/RandyBoyleWebsites/RandyBoyleHomeWebsite. Make sure the syntax is correct and the forward slash (/) is used.

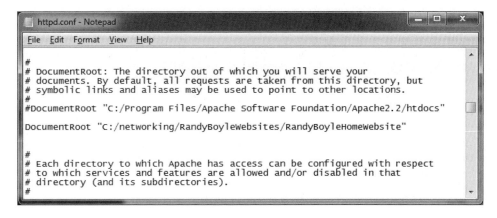

Figure 9-24: Changing the directory for your Web content.

32. Scroll down until you see a heading labeled "Directory."
33. Add a pound sign (#) in front of the following line.

```
<Directory "C:/Program Files/Apache Software Foundation/Apache2.2/htdocs">
```

34. Add the following line below the line you just commented out.

```
<Directory "C:/networking/YourNameWebsites/YourNameHomeWebsite">
```

35. Take a screenshot of the httpd.conf file with your name showing. (See Figure 9-25.)

Note: Remember to change YourName to your first and last name. In the example above the new path was C:/networking/RandyBoyleWebsites/RandyBoyleHomeWebsite. Make sure the syntax is correct and that you used both brackets (< >) and the forward slash (/) correctly.

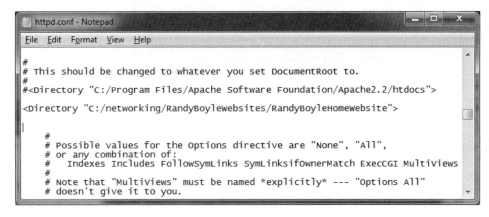

Figure 9-25: Changing the directory.

36. Scroll down until you see a heading labeled "DirectoryIndex."
37. Add "index.htm" to the following line.

```
DirectoryIndex index.html
```

38. Make sure the DirectoryIndex line looks like the following line. (This will tell Apache that index.htm is the main page for this Web site. This is the equivalent of the Default Document section in IIS. See Figure 9-26.)

```
DirectoryIndex index.html index.htm
```

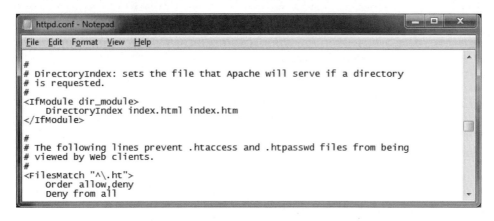

Figure 9-26: Adding index.htm to the directory index.

39. On the File menu click File and Save.
40. Return to the DOS prompt.
41. Type **httpd -k restart**
42. Press Enter. (This restarted your Web server and put the changes you made to the httpd.conf file into effect. You should see the main page for your Home Web site.)
43. Return to your Web browser.
44. Click Refresh.
45. Take a screenshot of your Home Web site with your name showing. (See Figure 9-27.)

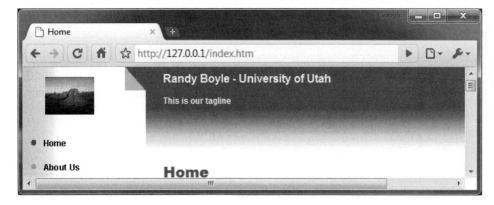

Figure 9-27: Web site served by Apache.

THOUGHT QUESTIONS

1. What line would you change to make a custom error message for a missing page?
2. Why did you have to add index.htm to the httpd.conf file?
3. Why is it better to comment out lines (using the # sign) in the httpd.conf file rather just deleting them?
4. Why would someone want to use a port other than port 80 to serve Web pages?

In this project you will configure Apache to host multiple sites. It will determine which site it should serve based on the header information (e.g. www.RandyBoyleCars.com) it receives. You can have many virtual hosts on a single machine.

Using name-based virtual hosts has several advantages. It conserves IP addresses, is simpler to configure, and easy to manage. You can host many sites that have fewer visitors rather than having a dedicated server for each host. This reduces server sprawl and hardware costs. However, virtual hosts cannot be used with SSL.

In this project you will enable a reference within the httpd.conf file that will call another configuration file called httpd-vhosts.conf. You will add the configuration lines for the virtual hosts (the three Web sites you created earlier) to the httpd-vhosts.conf file. You will also add permissions for these virtual hosts to the httpd.conf file. You will run the `httpd -S` command in a DOS prompt to see the configuration for the virtual hosts you will configure. In a prior project this command didn't return any results because there weren't any virtual hosts configured.

1. Open Notepad by clicking Start, All Programs, and Accessories.
2. Right-click Notepad.
3. Select Run as administrator.
4. Click File and Open.
5. Browse to C:\Program Files\Apache Software Foundation\Apache2.2\conf.
6. Change the file type drop-down to All Files (*.*).
7. Select the file labeled httpd.conf.
8. Click Open.
9. Scroll down to the line labeled "# Include conf/extra/httpd-vhosts.conf."
10. Remove the # from this line. (This will allow the configuration file labeled httpd-vhosts.conf to be processed. You are going to open this configuration file and add in the virtual host entries. See Figure 9-28.)

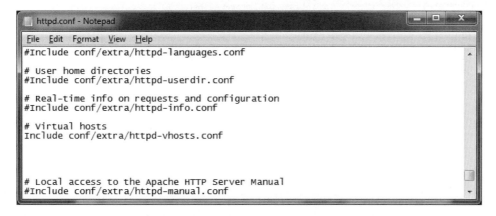

Figure 9-28: Enabling the httpd-vhosts.conf file to be included when Apache starts.

11. Add the following entry below the line labeled Include conf/extra/httpd-vhosts.conf. (These lines are for security purposes. They allow users (Web requests) to view files in this directory and all sub directories. Remember to replace YourName with your own first and last name. See Figure 9-29.)

```
<Directory "C:/networking/YourNameWebsites">
```

```
Order Deny,Allow
 Allow from all
</Directory>
```

12. On the File menu click File and Save. (You can leave this file open. You are now going to open the configuration file for your virtual hosts.)

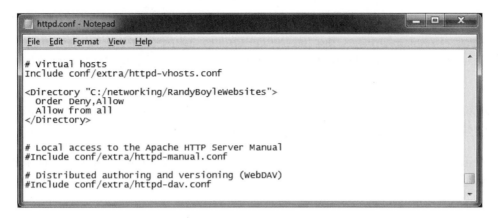

Figure 9-29: Adding permissions for the virtual hosts that are going to be added.

13. Open Notepad by clicking Start, All Programs, and Accessories.
14. Right-click Notepad.
15. Select Run as administrator.
16. Click File and Open.
17. Browse to C:\Program Files\Apache Software Foundation\Apache2.2\conf\etc.
18. Change the file type drop-down to All Files (*.*).
19. Select the file labeled httpd-vhosts.conf. (See Figure 9-30.)
20. Click Open. (See Figure 9-31.)

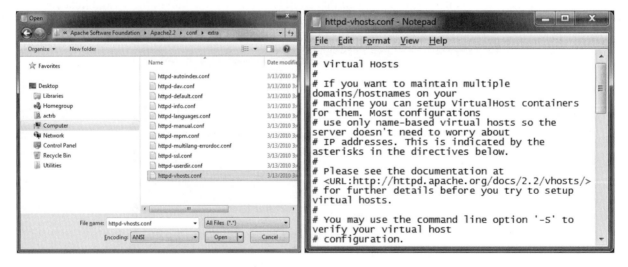

Figure 9-30: Location of the httpd-vhosts.conf file.   Figure 9-31: Contents of the httpd-vhosts.conf file.

Note: You are now going to have to comment out a couple of the "dummy" virtual hosts that are included by default in the httpd-vhost.conf file. You will add pound signs (#) at the start of each line of the dummy virtual hosts. This will prevent them from being included in the list of virtual hosts.

21. Comment out all of the "dummy" virtual hosts at the bottom of this file by adding the pound sign (#) to the beginning of each line. (This will prevent them from being loaded. See Figure 9-32.)

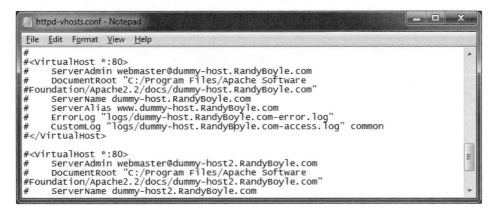

Figure 9-32: Commenting out the "dummy" virtual hosts.

22. Scroll to the line labeled NameVirtualHost *.80. (You are going to add your virtual hosts below this line. See Figure 9-33.)

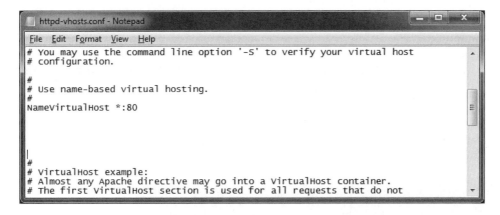

Figure 9-33: Location to add virtual host lines in the httpd-vhosts.conf file.

23. Add the following entry to the httpd-vhosts.conf file. (Remember to replace YourName with your own first and last name.)
24. Take a screenshot of the httpd-vhosts.conf file showing your virtual hosts. (Your name should be included as part of the server name and server alias. See Figure 9-34.)

```
<VirtualHost *:80>
ServerName www.YourNameHome.com
ServerAlias YourNameHome.com *.YourNameHome.com
DocumentRoot "C:/networking/YourNameWebsites/YourNameHomeWebsite"
</VirtualHost>

<VirtualHost *:80>
ServerName www.YourNameCars.com
ServerAlias YourNameCars.com *.YourNameCars.com
DocumentRoot "C:/networking/YourNameWebsites/YourNameCarsWebsite"
</VirtualHost>

<VirtualHost 127.0.0.1:80>
```

```
ServerName www.YourNameBooks.com
ServerAlias YourNameBooks.com *.YourNameBooks.com
DocumentRoot "C:/networking/YourNameWebsites/YourNameBooksWebsite"
</VirtualHost>
```

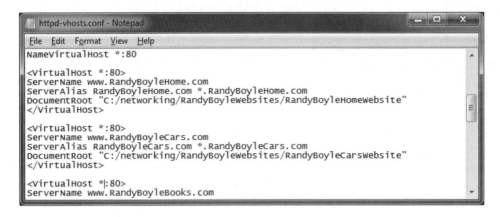

Figure 9-34: Virtual hosts added to the httpd-vhosts.conf file.

25. Click Start, All Programs, and Accessories.
26. Right-click Command Prompt.
27. Select Run as administrator.
28. Click Yes.
29. Type **cd C:\Program Files\Apache Software Foundation\Apache2.2\bin**
30. Press Enter.
31. Type **httpd -S**
32. Press Enter. (The -S above is capitalized. This will give a listing of all the virtual hosts. In a prior project you entered this command but it didn't return any results. Now you can see multiple virtual hosts listed. See Figure 9-35.)

Figure 9-35: Virtual hosts on this Web server.

33. Type **httpd -k restart**
34. Press Enter. (This restarted your Web server and put the changes you made to both the httpd.conf file and the httpd-vhosts.conf file into effect. See Figure 9-36.)

Figure 9-36: Restarting Apache after changes were made.

35. Open a Web browser.
36. Enter "www.YourNameHome.com" into the address bar.
37. Take a screenshot of your Home Web site with your name showing.
38. Enter "www.YourNameCars.com" into the address bar.
39. Take a screenshot of your Cars Web site with your name showing. (See Figure 9-37.)

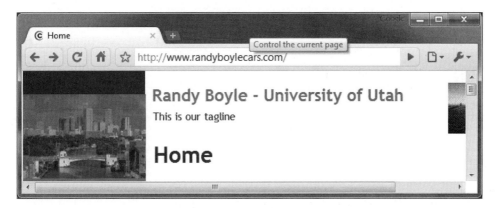

Figure 9-37: The Cars Web site served by Apache.

40. Enter "www.YourNameBooks.com" into the address bar.
41. Take a screenshot of your Books Web site with your name showing. (See Figure 9-38.)

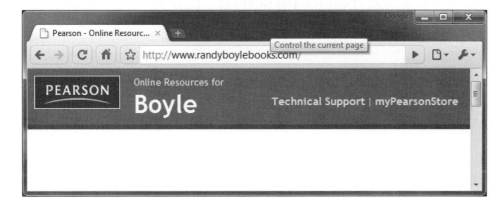

Figure 9-38: The Books Web site served by Apache.

THOUGHT QUESTIONS

1. Could you have added the lines for the virtual hosts directly to the httpd.conf file?
2. Can you assign a specific IP address to a specific virtual host? How?
3. Why did you have to give permission to the "websites" directory that had the other Web sites?
4. Could you configure one of the virtual Web sites to bind to port 8080 and the others to port 80? How?

CHAPTER 10: WINDOWS SERVER 2008

Windows Server 2008 is one of the dominant enterprise-level operating systems being used in corporate environments. It provides the ability to centrally manage large numbers of computers, users, printers, etc. It can also function as an application server (DNS, DHCP, Terminal Services, etc.), a Web server, file server, and/or print server. It is also easy to learn because it looks a lot like Windows XP, Windows Vista, and Windows 7.

In this project you are going to use the Windows Server 2008 virtual machine you created in the earlier chapter on virtualization. This is a free virtual machine provided by Microsoft for testing and training purposes. If you are a student at a university that has access to an MSDNAA account you can get a key to authenticate this copy of Server 2008. This will keep it from expiring. Ask your instructor about access to MSDNAA.

The following projects will include 1) installing roles and features 2) adding users, groups, and organizational units (OUs) through Active Directory, 3) enabling several group policies to manage your domain, 4) managing password and auditing policies, and 5) configuring and managing an FTP server.

There are many parts of Windows Server 2008 that are not covered in this chapter. Choosing which ones to cover was difficult because there are so many parts from which to choose. You can learn more about what Server 2008 can do by reading Microsoft's TechNet or by buying a more comprehensive book. It's a good idea to explore all of the different functionality contained in Server 2008.

10.1 SERVER MANANGER

Windows Server Manager is the main application that you will use to manage your Windows Server 2008 virtual machine. It acts like a central management console for all server activities. In this project you will perform several tasks through Server Manager.

You will add Active Directory Domain Services, IIS (to run an FTP site in a later project), Windows PowerShell, and Desktop Experience. These tasks will show you how to add roles and features to your server. These are just a fraction of the roles and features that you could add.

After you add Active Directory (AD) to your server you will configure your new domain. Due to space constraints you won't be able to experience all of the functionality available in Active Directory. If you are new to Windows Server 2008 you should push every button on every screen to see what they do. Many of Server 2008's functions are intuitive. Others will require more reading.

If your virtual machine is running slowly you may want to increase the amount of RAM allocated to this virtual machine. If you have 1.5 GB of memory to spare you should turn off your Server 2008 virtual machine and increase the memory settings. It will make the following projects go much faster.

1. Click Start, All Programs, Windows Virtual PC, and Windows Virtual PC.
2. Double-click the virtual machine labeled YourNameServer2008.vmcx. (In this case it was RandyBoyleServer2008. You should have created this virtual project earlier. If you haven't already created a Windows Server 2008 virtual machine you can return to project 4.5 for instructions on how to create one.)

3. Wait for the virtual machine to boot.
4. In the Windows Virtual PC menu click Tools and Install Integration Components (if you haven't done so already).
5. In the Windows Virtual PC menu click Ctrl-Alt-Del.
6. Click in the virtual machine. (To leave the virtual machine you can press Alt-Tab.)
7. Enter your password. (If you followed the instructions in the prior project then the password is Evaluation1.)
8. Press Enter. (This should log you onto your Server 2008 virtual machine.)
9. In your virtual machine click Start, All Programs, Accessories, and Windows Explorer. (See Figure 10-1.)
10. Click Computer and your DVD drive. (This is a virtual drive with an image containing the additions for Virtual PC. You are going to install them to allow sharing between your local computer and the virtual machine. This will also allow your cursor to move smoothly between your desktop and virtual machine.)
11. Double-click setup.exe on the DVD drive. (See Figure 10-2.)
12. Click Next, Finish, and Yes to restart your virtual machine. (Click Install/allow to any pop-ups you may see. Your virtual machine will restart after you click yes.)

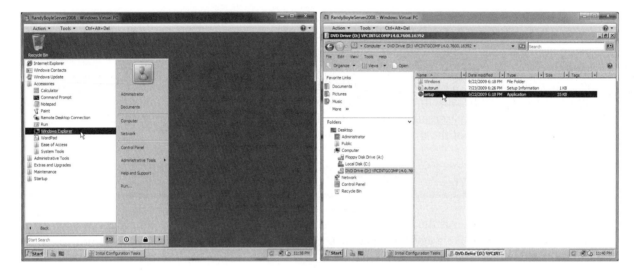

Figure 10-1: Server 2008 desktop.   Figure 10-2: Installing Virtual PC additions.

13. In the Windows Virtual PC menu click Ctrl-Alt-Del.
14. Click in the virtual machine. (Your cursor should be able to move in/out of your virtual machine without having to press Alt-Tab. You will also notice that you can share drives between your host and virtual machine.)
15. Enter your password. (If you followed the instructions in the prior project then the password is Evaluation1.)
16. Press Enter.
17. Click the Internet Explorer icon in the bottom left-hand of your virtual desktop.
18. Browse to www.Google.com. (This will make sure your Internet connection is working properly. Also note that Web sites are automatically blocked in new installs of Server 2008 until you add them. This is done to protect your server. You can turn it off.)
19. If your Internet connection is not working correctly you may have to adjust your networking settings for your virtual machine.
20. In the File menu for your virtual machine click Tools and Settings.
21. Click on the Networking setting.
22. Make sure Adapter 1 is set to Shared Networking (NAT). (See Figure 10-3.)
23. Click OK.

24. Click the Ctrl-Alt-Del button in the Virtual PC File menu.
25. Click Change Password.
26. Change your password to a password you can remember. (For simplicity purposes you can make it the same password that you used for all of your other virtual machines. You may have to have a change of case and make sure your password is long enough.)
27. Press Enter.
28. Click OK.
29. Close the Initial Configuration Tasks. (Windows Server Manager should automatically open. If it doesn't you can click Start and Server Manager. See Figure 10-4.)

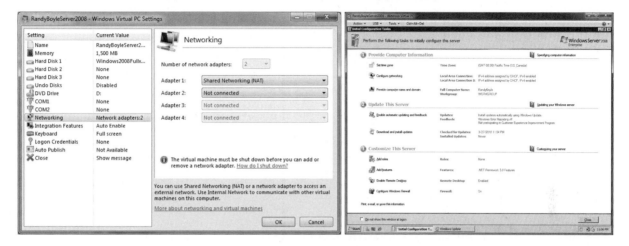

Figure 10-3: Network configuration for Windows Virtual PC.   Figure 10-4: Server 2008 Initial Configuration Tasks.

Note: You may see several windows about updating your server. It's a good idea to apply all of the updates and patches. It's a fairly simple task. You can also authenticate your copy of Windows Server 2008 if you have access to an MSDNAA account at your university. You can enter the key from the MSDNAA site to your virtual machine. This will keep your virtual machine from expiring.

30. Scroll down in Server Manager to the Roles Summary. (See Figure 10-5.)
31. Click Add Roles and Next.
32. Select Active Directory Domain Services.
33. Click Next, Next, Install, and Close. (See Figure 10-6.)

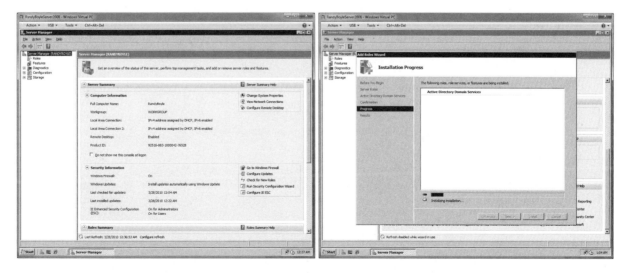

Figure 10-5: Windows Server 2008 Server Manager.   Figure 10-6: Installing Active Directory Domain Services.

34. Click on the link labeled Active Directory Domain Services.
35. Click on the link labeled Run the Active Directory Domain Services Installation Wizard. (See Figure 10-7.)
36. Click Next and Next.
37. Select "Create a new domain in a new forest."
38. Click Next. (See Figure 10-8.)

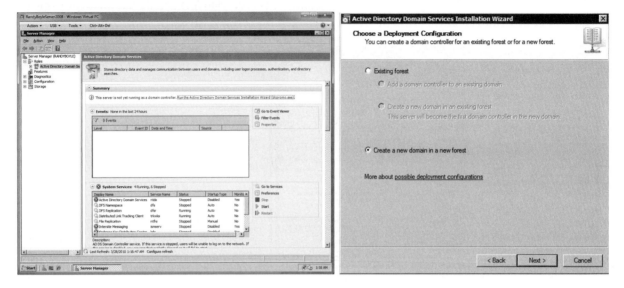

Figure 10-7: Active Directory Installation Wizard.   Figure 10-8: Creating a new domain.

39. Enter "YourName.com" as the FQDN. (In this case it was randyboyle.com. See Figure 10-9.)
40. Click Next. (If, for some reason, the name is already in use you can add "server2008" to the end of YourName.)
41. Click OK, Next, Next, Next, Next, Yes, Yes, and Next.
42. Enter your new administrator password (twice). (See Figure 10-10.)
43. Click Next and Next.
44. Wait. (This may take several minutes. When this finishes you will need to reboot your Server2008 virtual machine. It will also take several minutes to reboot and configure correctly.)
45. Click Finish and Restart Now.

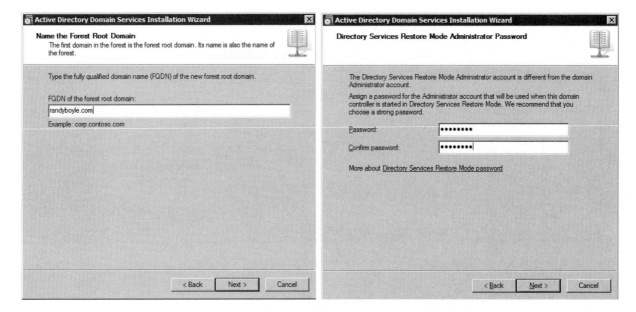

Figure 10-9: Naming a domain.

Figure 10-10: Restore Mode administrator password.

46. Log back into your Server 2008 virtual machine. (If you have problems logging in you may have to disable Integration Features in the Virtual PC File menu under Tools.)
47. In Server Manager click Add Roles and Next.
48. Select Web Server (IIS). (See Figure 10-11.)
49. Click Next, Add Required Features, Next, and Next.
50. Select all of the components for FTP Publishing Service in addition to the default settings. (See Figure 10-12.)
51. Click Add Required Role Services.
52. Click Next, Install, and Close.

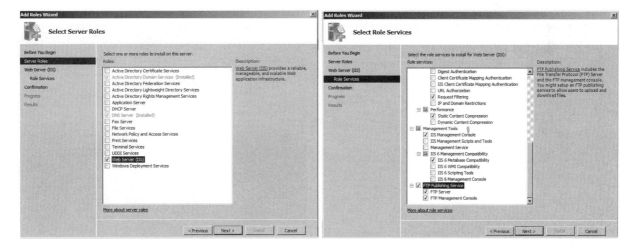

Figure 10-11: Adding the Web server role.

Figure 10-12: Including FTP Publishing Service.

53. In Server Manager click Features, Add Features, and Next. (See Figure 10-13.)
54. Select Desktop Experience and Windows PowerShell. (See Figure 10-14.)
55. Click Next, Install, Close, and Yes. (This will reboot your virtual machine.)
56. Click Close. (This will close the screen saying that Desktop Experience and Windows PowerShell were successfully installed.)

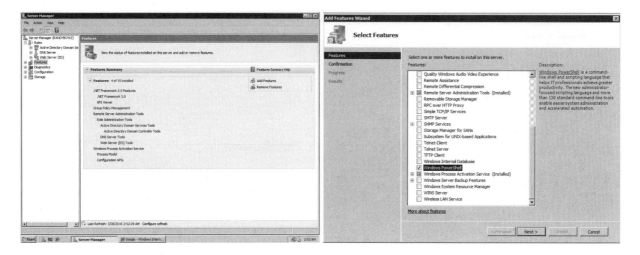

Figure 10-13: Summary of installed features.   Figure 10-14: Adding Windows PowerShell.

57. Return to Server Manager. (See Figure 10-15.)
58. Expand the trees below Roles and Features.
59. Click on Server Manager. (Your name should appear to the right.)
60. Take a screenshot.
61. Click Start, All Programs, Accessories, Windows PowerShell, and Windows PowerShell. (You can also press ⊞+r and enter "powershell.")
62. Type **whoami**
63. Press Enter.
64. Type **ping yourname.com**
65. Press Enter. (Replace yourname with your first and last name. In this case it was ping randyboyle.com. If you followed the directions correctly when setting up Active Directory you should see your local IP address listed.)
66. Take a screenshot. (See Figure 10-16.)

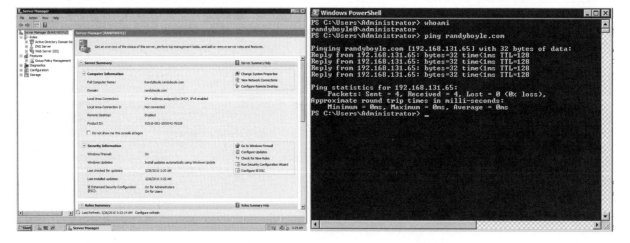

Figure 10-15: Summary of installed roles and functionality.   Figure 10-16: PowerShell terminal.

THOUGHT QUESTIONS

1. Why did the ping command work on yourname.com?
2. Does Active Directory manage more than just users?
3. What is the advantage of having Windows Server 2008 look so much like the traditional Windows desktop (i.e. Windows XP)?
4. Why doesn't Windows Server 2008 come with all roles and functions already installed, enabled, and turned on?

10.2 ACTIVE DIRECTORY

In this project you are going to perform some basic administrative tasks in Active Directory (AD). You are going to create 4 users, 2 groups, and 5 organizational units (OU). You will then add the users to groups and the groups to an OU. You will also put the OUs in a hierarchy. These are common tasks when setting up a domain. Systems administrators add new users and groups on a regular basis.

If this is the first time you are performing these tasks within Active Directory please feel free to create additional users, groups, and OUs. This additional practice will help you become familiar with Active Directory and reduce any anxiety you may have related to managing users or groups.

If you apply for a systems or network administrator job in the future it's highly likely they will ask you to perform some simple AD tasks. The following tasks are common tasks that you will be expected to perform with little effort or hesitation.

1. Click Start, All Programs, Windows Virtual PC, and Windows Virtual PC.
2. Double-click the virtual machine labeled YourNameServer2008.vmcx. (In this case it was RandyBoyleServer2008.)
3. Wait for the virtual machine to boot.
4. Logon.
5. Click Start, Administrative Tools, and Active Directory Users and Computers.
6. Expand the tree under your domain to show the Users folder. (In this case the domain was named randyboyle.com.)
7. Click on the Users folder. (See Figure 10-17.)
8. Click the Add User icon at the top of the screen. (You can also click Action, New, and User or right-click the right-hand pane and select New, and User. All methods yield the same result.)
9. Complete the information for a new user including your first name, last name, and a username.
10. Take a screenshot. (See Figure 10-18.)
11. Click Next.

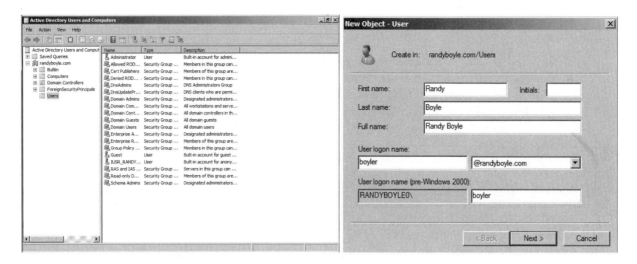

Figure 10-17: Active Directory Users and Computers.   Figure 10-18: Creating a new user.

12. Enter a password twice. (Make sure it is at least 8 characters, uses a number, and a change of case. See Figure 10-19.)
13. Deselect all other options.
14. Select User cannot change password and Password never expires.
15. Click Next and Finish.
16. Create four more users named Alpha, Bravo, Charlie, and Delta with YOUR same last name. (You can use the same password for all of the new accounts. You can make additional changes to these accounts later.)
17. Take a screenshot after you have created four additional users. (See Figure 10-20.)

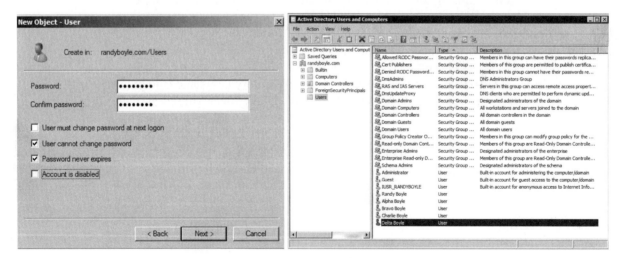

Figure 10-19: Setting a new user's password.   Figure 10-20: New users are created.

18. Click the Add Group icon at the top of the screen. (You can also click Action, New, and Group.)
19. Name the new group "Tax." (This will be a group of accountants that deal with preparing taxes. Make sure the group scope is set to Global and the group type is Security. See Figure 10-21.)
20. Click OK.
21. Add another group named "Audit." (This will be a group of accountants that deal with auditing.)
22. Click OK.
23. Double-click the group named Tax.
24. Click on the Members tab.
25. Click Add.

26. Enter "Delta" into the text box. (This was one of your new users.)
27. Click Check Names.
28. Enter your first name into the text box. (In this case it was "Randy.")
29. Click Check Names. (You should now see two users added to the Tax group. See Figure 10-22.)
30. Click OK and OK.

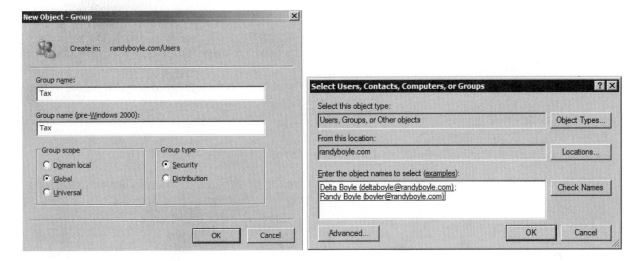

Figure 10-21: Creating the Tax group.   Figure 10-22: Adding members to the Tax group.

31. Click on the Built-in folder under your domain.
32. Double-click the Administrators group. (See Figure 10-23.)
33. Add yourself and the user named Alpha to this group. (This will give you and Alpha authority to administer the domain.)
34. Take a screenshot showing you and Alpha as members of the Administrators group. (See Figure 10-24.)

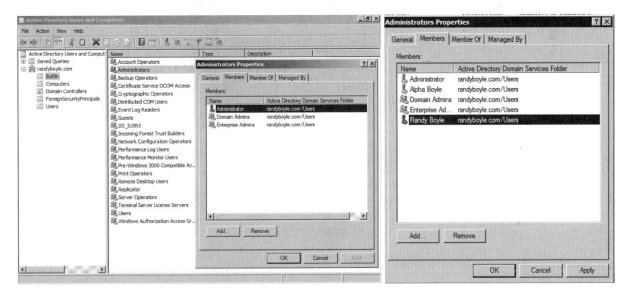

Figure 10-23: Properties for the Administrators group.   Figure 10-24: Users added to the Administrators group.

35. Click on your domain. (In this case it was randyboyle.com.)
36. Click on the icon to create a new Organizational Unit (OU). (You can also click Action, New, and Organizational Unit.

37. Name the Organizational Unit "Accountants." (See Figure 10-25.)
38. Deselect the option labeled Protect container from accidental deletion. (If you leave this selected you will not be able to delete these OUs if you make a mistake. If you want to delete an OU you will have to click View and Advanced Features. Then click the properties for each object, click the Object tab, and then deselect this option.)
39. Click OK.
40. Create another Organizational Unit named "Finance." (Remember to click on your domain before you create the OU.)
41. Create another Organizational Unit named "Financial Services." (Click on your domain before you create the OU.)
42. Create another Organizational Unit named "Marketing." (Click on your domain before you create the OU.)
43. Create another Organizational Unit named "Sales." (Click on your domain before you create the OU.)
44. Take a screenshot showing all of the newly created OUs. (See Figure 10-26.)

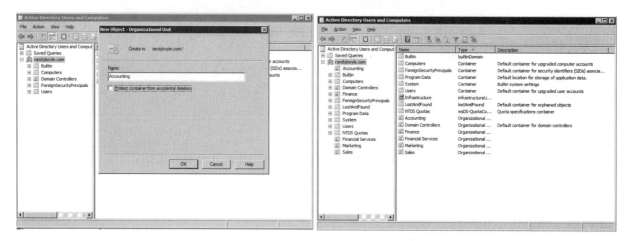

Figure 10-25: Creating the Accounting OU.   Figure 10-26: All of the new OUs created.

45. Click on the Users folder.
46. Drag-and-drop both the Tax and Audit groups into the Accounting OU.
47. Drag-and-drop the Accounting OU into the Financial Services OU.
48. Drag-and-drop the Finance OU into the Financial Services OU.
49. Right-click the Financial Services OU.
50. Select Delegate Control.
51. Click Next and Add.
52. Enter "Bravo".
53. Click Check Names, OK, and Next. (See Figure 10-27.)
54. Select all common tasks. (These are the tasks that this user will be able to do within his/her OU. See Figure 10-28.)
55. Click Next and Finish.

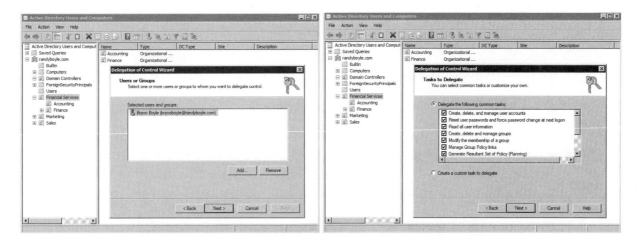

Figure 10-27: Selecting user to whom you will delegate control. Figure 10-28: Selecting tasks to delegate.

56. Click View and Advanced Features.
57. Right-click the Financial Services OU.
58. Select Properties.
59. Click on the Security tab.
60. Select the user named Bravo.
61. Scroll down to see his/her permissions. (They will be at the bottom of the list. This will confirm that Bravo is delegated control over this OU.)
62. Take a screenshot. (See Figure 10-29.)
63. Click OK to close the Financial Services Properties window.
64. Click on the folder labeled Users.
65. Double-click the user named Charlie.
66. Click on the Account tab.
67. Click End of. (This will set the account to expire.)
68. Set the date for one year from today. (See Figure 10-30.)

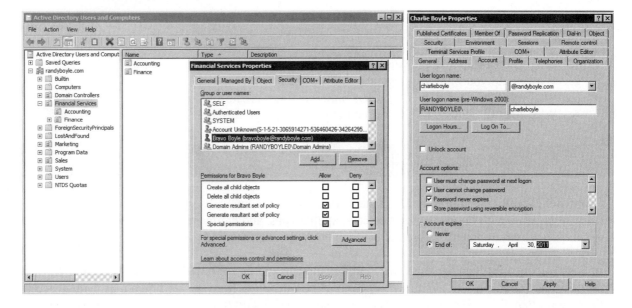

Figure 10-29: Confirming that Bravo has delegated control over the Financial Services OU. Figure 10-30: Setting account expiration date.

69. Click on the button labeled Logon Hours.

70. Set the logon days/times so Charlie can only logon M-F from 5:00AM-8:00PM.
71. Take a screenshot. (See Figure 10-31.)
72. Click OK.
73. Close the Active Directory window.

Note: You can leave your Windows Server 2008 virtual machine running and continue on to the next project.

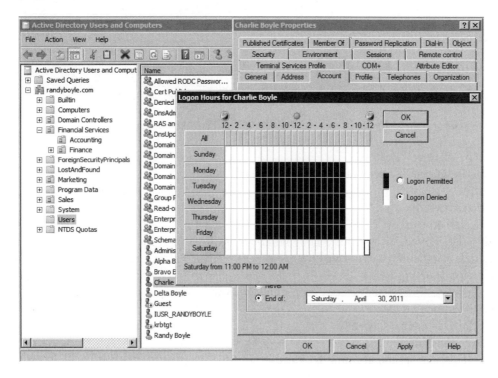

Figure 10-31: Restricting logon hours.

THOUGHT QUESTIONS

1. What is the difference between a Security group and a Distribution group?
2. Why would you want to delegate control over an OU?
3. Why would you want to "nest" OUs rather than just create another domain?
4. Why does Windows Server 2008 come with default groups and what do they do?

10.3 GROUP POLICIES

Group policies allow you to centrally manage all of your computers, users, applications, etc. You can set rules to govern a wide variety of tasks, access, applications, and hardware. Essentially, you can control the entire user environment. Group policies can be applied to OUs and domains.

In this project you will create three Group Policy Objects (GPOs). You will then apply them to the domain and a couple of OUs. You will 1) remove the run option from the start menu, 2) remove access to the Control Panel, and 3) restrict access to removable media. GPOs are typically created based on organization goals, security policies, or required standards (e.g. PCI-DSS, HIPAA, etc.).

1. Click Start, All Programs, Windows Virtual PC, and Windows Virtual PC.

2. Double-click the virtual machine labeled YourNameServer2008.vmcx. (In this case it was RandyBoyleServer2008.)
3. Wait for the virtual machine to boot.
4. Logon.
5. Click Start, Administrative Tools, and Group Policy Management.
6. Expand the directory tree to show your domain and all OUs.
7. Right-click on the Default Domain Policy for your domain. (See Figure 10-32.)
8. Select Edit.
9. Expand the tree under User Configuration, Policies, Administrative Templates, and Start Menu and Toolbar. (See Figure 10-33.)

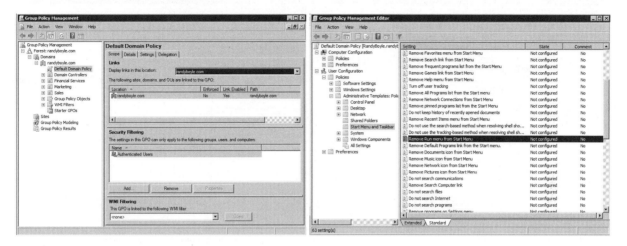

Figure 10-32: Default domain policy.   Figure 10-33: Policy to remove Run from the Start menu.

10. Click the Setting column to sort by the first letter in the Setting column.
11. Double-click the policy labeled Remove Run from Start Menu.
12. Click Enabled in the Settings tab. (See Figure 10-34.)
13. Click on the Explain tab to read about the effect this policy will have on your domain.
14. Click OK.
15. Take a screenshot. (See Figure 10-35.)
16. Close the Group Policy Management Editor. (Leave the Group Policy Management window open.)

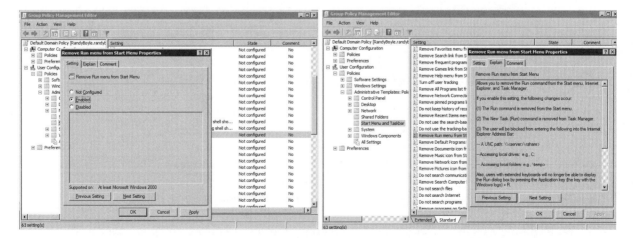

Figure 10-34: Enabling the policy.   Figure 10-35: Explanation of the policy.

17. Right-click on the Financial Services OU.
18. Select Create a GPO in this domain, and Link it here. (See Figure 10-36.)
19. Name the new GPO "No_Control_Panel".
20. Click OK.
21. Expand the tree under User Configuration, Policies, Administrative Templates, and Control Panel.
22. Click on the folder labeled Control Panel.
23. Double-click the policy labeled "Prohibit access to the Control Panel." (This is shown in the right-hand pane. See Figure 10-37.)

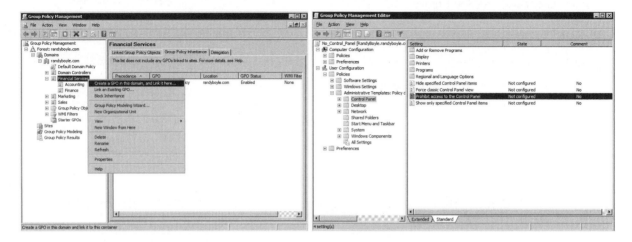

Figure 10-36: Creating a GPO in an OU.   Figure 10-37: Policy that prohibits access to the Control Panel.

24. Click Enabled in the Settings tab. (See Figure 10-38.)
25. Click on the Explain tab to read about the effect this policy will have.
26. Click OK.
27. Take a screenshot. (You should see the policy's state listed as enabled. See Figure 10-39.)
28. Close the Group Policy Management Editor. (Leave the Group Policy Management window open.)

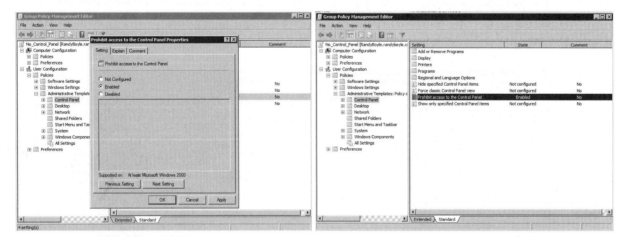

Figure 10-38: Enabling the policy.   Figure 10-39: Policy is listed as enabled.

29. Right-click on the folder labeled Group Policy Objects. (You are going to create a GPO here and then link it to the Accounting OU. You may also notice that the policy that you just created is listed in this folder.)
30. Select New. (See Figure 10-40.)

31. Name the new GPO "No_Removable_Media".
32. Click OK.
33. Right-click the policy labeled No_Removable_Media.
34. Select Edit.
35. Expand the tree under Computer Configuration, Policies, Administrative Templates, and System.
36. Click on the folder labeled Removable Storage Access.
37. Double-click the policy labeled "All Removable Storage classes: Deny all access." (This is shown in the right-hand pane. See Figure 10-41.)

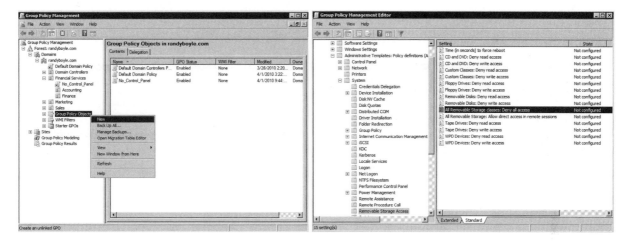

Figure 10-40: Creating a new GPO.   Figure 10-41: Policy that denies access to all removable media.

38. Click Enabled in the Settings tab. (See Figure 10-42.)
39. Click on the Explain tab to read about the effect this policy will have.
40. Click OK.
41. Take a screenshot. (You should see the policy's state listed as enabled. See Figure 10-43.)
42. Close the Group Policy Management Editor. (Leave the Group Policy Management window open.)

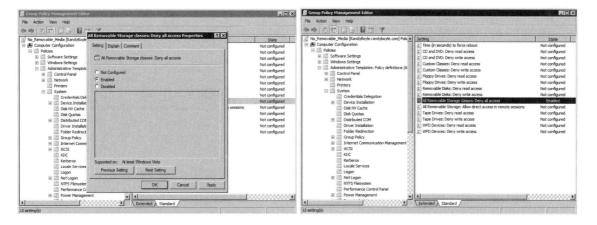

Figure 10-42: Enabling the policy.   Figure 10-43: Removable media policy is enabled.

43. Right-click on the folder labeled Group Policy Objects. (You are going to link the policy you just created to the Accounting OU.)
44. Drag-and-drop the policy labeled No_Removable_Media from the Group Policy Objects folder to the OU labeled Accounting. (The Accounting OU is located under the Financial Services OU.)
45. Click OK.

46. Click on the Accounting OU. (See Figure 10-44.)
47. Click on the tab labeled Linked Group Policy Objects. (Note that the No_Removable_Media is listed.)
48. Click on the tab labeled Delegation. (Note that the user Bravo is listed. You delegated control to Bravo in an earlier project.)
49. Click on the tab labeled Group Policy Inheritance.
50. Take a screenshot showing the list of all three of the policies you created. (See Figure 10-45.)
51. Close the Group Policy Management window.

Note: You can leave your Windows Server 2008 virtual machine running and continue on to the next project.

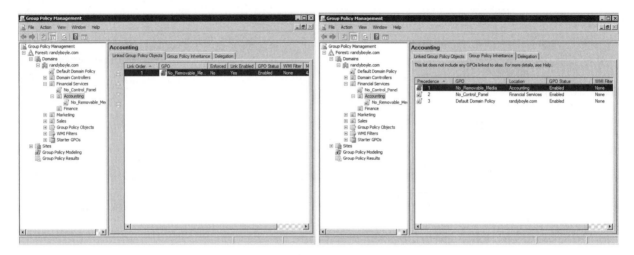

Figure 10-44: Linking a policy to an OU.   Figure 10-45: Listing of policies for the Accounting OU.

THOUGHT QUESTIONS

1. Could you keep users from accessing a command prompt? How?
2. What would you use Group Policy Results for?
3. Can you assign a user to manage all GPOs for an OU or domain? (Hint: Bravo.)
4. Could restrictive GPOs reduce end user productivity? How?

10.4 SECURITY POLICIES AND AUDITING

In this project you will change password policies, account lockout policies, and auditing for security related events. Stringent password policies can improve overall organizational security but can also negatively affect employee productivity. Users have a hard time remembering several different passwords. They have even more difficulty remembering passwords when they are changed every couple of months.

Lockout policies keep intruders from repeatedly trying passwords until they gain access to a system. After a few failed attempts the account is locked and must be unlocked by an administrator. However, a lockout policy does not replace the need for strong passwords. If an intruder gains access to your system through an exploit (weakness in an application, operating system, service, etc.) they can copy your password file and crack it later on his/her own machine. Both strong passwords and a reasonable lockout policy are needed.

Finally, you will enable auditing for security events. Failed and/or successful security events are logged. A network administrator can look at logs of these security events to identify unauthorized behavior. Repeated failed logon attempts may indicate an unauthorized user trying to access a system. You can also see when users are successfully logged into a system. If you see a pattern of successful logon events after normal business hours (let's say 3:00AM) it might indicate a potential security breach.

1. Click Start, All Programs, Windows Virtual PC, and Windows Virtual PC.
2. Double-click the virtual machine labeled YourNameServer2008.vmcx. (In this case it was RandyBoyleServer2008.)
3. Wait for the virtual machine to boot.
4. Logon.
5. Click Start, Administrative Tools, and Group Policy Management.
6. Expand the directory tree to show your domain and all OUs.
7. Right-click on the Default Domain Policy for your domain. (See Figure 10-46.)
8. Select Edit.
9. Expand the tree under Computer Configuration, Policies, Windows Settings, Security Settings, Account Policies, and Password Policy. (See Figure 10-47.)

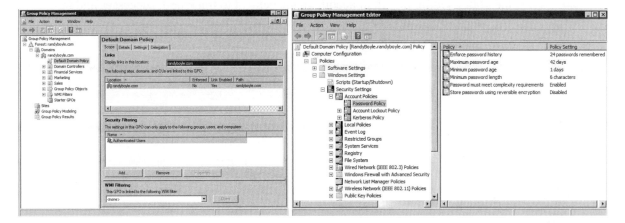

Figure 10-46: Default domain policy.   Figure 10-47: Default password policies.

10. Change the Enforce Password History policy to 10 passwords remembered.
11. Change the Maximum password age to 180 days.
12. Change the Minimum password length to 6 characters.
13. Take a screenshot. (See Figure 10-48.)
14. Click on Account Logout Policy.
15. Change the Account logout duration to 5 minutes.
16. Change the Account logout threshold to 3 invalid logon attempts.
17. Take a screenshot. (See Figure 10-49.)

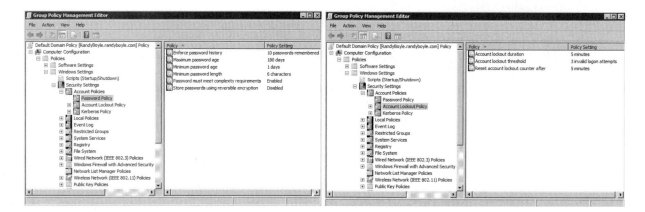

Figure 10-48: New password policies.   Figure 10-49: New account lockout policies.

18. Expand the tree under Computer Configuration, Policies, Windows Settings, Security Settings, Local Policies, and Audit Policy. (See Figure 10-50.)
19. Define the policy setting for Audit account logon events to track both successes and failures.
20. Define the policy setting for Audit account management to track both successes and failures.
21. Define the policy setting for Audit logon events to track both successes and failures.
22. Take a screenshot. (See Figure 10-51.)

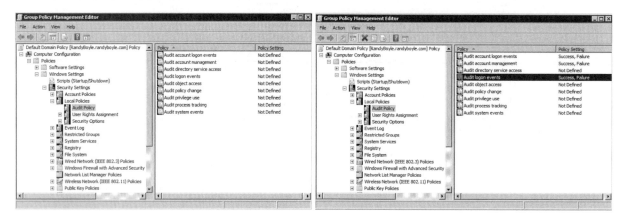

Figure 10-50: Default audit policies.   Figure 10-51: Auditing policies recording successes and failures.

23. Close the Group Policy Management Editor. (Leave the Group Policy Management window open.)
24. Right-click on the Default Domain Policy for your domain. (See Figure 10-52.)
25. Click on the Settings tab in the right-hand pane. (This is going to show you a summary of the current settings for your default domain policy.)
26. Click show for Security Settings.
27. Click show for Account Policies/Password Policy.
28. Click show for Account Policies/Account Lockout Policy.
29. Take a screenshot. (See Figure 10-53.)
30. Close the Group Policy Management window.

Note: You can leave your Windows Server 2008 virtual machine running and continue on to the next project.

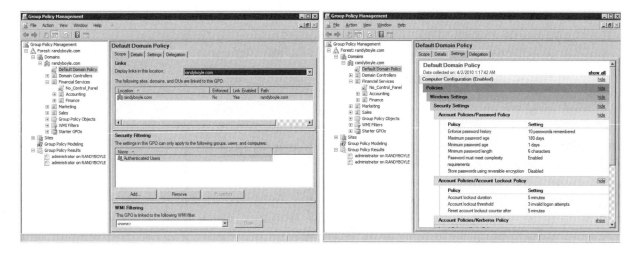

Figure 10-52: Default domain policy scope.   Figure 10-53: Default domain policy security settings.

THOUGHT QUESTIONS

1. Why enforce a minimum password length (e.g. seven characters) if accounts are locked after three attempts for five minutes anyway? Does automatic account lockout make password strength irrelevant?
2. Why force users to change their passwords every 2-6 months?
3. How could auditing logon failures improve security?
4. Why would a systems administrator want to track logon successes?

10.5 FTP SERVER

In this project you are going to configure an FTP (File Transfer Protocol) server. In a prior chapter you installed, configured, and managed a Web server (IIS). IIS includes an FTP server. Both FTP and Web servers have similar functions. One serves files and the other serves Web pages. You will see that there are many similarities between the two.

Web servers allow you to download large files but uploading large files is typically restricted. This keeps users from inadvertently bringing Web servers down. FTP can be used to upload large files. It is commonly used to upload files to a Web server. In fact, the book you are reading was uploaded to one of the editor's secured FTP sites. It was much too large to be emailed. FTP is still widely used.

1. Click Start, All Programs, Windows Virtual PC, and Windows Virtual PC.
2. Double-click the virtual machine labeled YourNameServer2008.vmcx. (In this case it was RandyBoyleServer2008.)
3. Wait for the virtual machine to boot.
4. Logon.
5. Click Start, Administrative Tools, and Internet Information Server (IIS) Manager.
6. Expand the tree under your server.
7. Click on FTP Sites. (See Figure 10-54.)
8. Click on the link to launch IIS 6.0 if necessary.

Note: If you have Windows Server 2008 then FTP functionality is passed off from IIS 7.0 to IIS 6.0. Windows Server 2008 R2 comes with IIS 7.5 that manages FTP without having to pass it off to IIS 6.0. The virtual machine used in the instructions for this book used Windows Server 2008.

9. Select the Default FTP Site. (See Figure 10-55.)
10. Click Action and Start. (You can also press the Play button.)

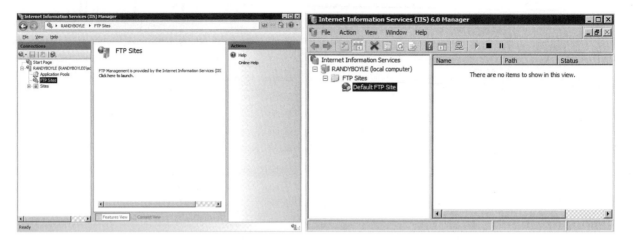

Figure 10-54: FTP sites within IIS.   Figure 10-55: Starting the default FTP site.

11. Click Action and Properties.
12. Click on the Messages tab.
13. Enter "Welcome to YourName's FTP Site!" into the Welcome text box. (Replace YourName with your first and last name. See Figure 10-56.)
14. Click OK.
15. Open Windows Explorer by clicking Start, All Programs, Accessories, and Windows Explorer.
16. Browse to C:\inetpub\ftproot. (This is where your FTP documents are going to be stored. Anything in this directory will be available on your FTP server. See Figure 10-57.)

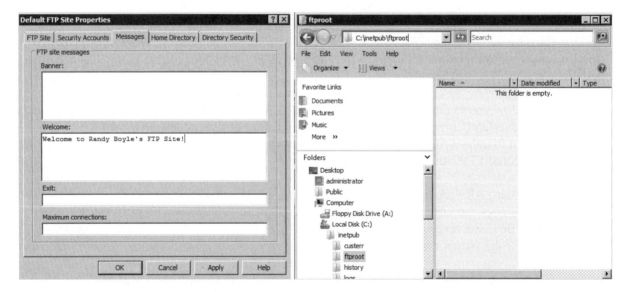

Figure 10-56: Setting a welcome message.   Figure 10-57: Browsing to the ftproot directory.

17. Right-click in the ftproot folder.
18. Select New and Text Document.
19. Name the new text file YourNameFTP_File. (In this case it was RandyBoyleFTP_File. See Figure 10-58.)
20. Open Internet Explorer by clicking Start, All Programs, and Internet Explorer.

21. Enter the following URL into the address bar: **ftp://127.0.0.1/**. (You can also try ftp://yourname.com.)
22. Take a screenshot of the Internet Explorer window showing your welcome message. (See Figure 10-59.)

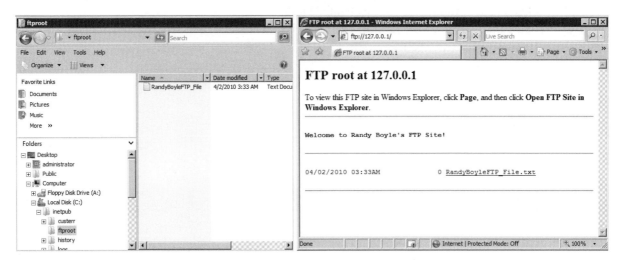

Figure 10-58: Created file in the ftproot directory.   Figure 10-59: FTP site hosted on a local machine.

23. Within Internet Explorer click Page and Open FTP Site in Windows Explorer. (See Figure 10-60.)
24. Drag-and-drop the text file from your FTP site to your desktop.
25. Return to IIS Manager.
26. Select your FTP site.
27. Click Action and Properties.
28. Click Current Sessions on the FTP Site tab.
29. Take a screenshot. (You should see at least one FTP user session. If you don't see any FTP user sessions listed you can refresh your Web browser or your Windows Explorer. This will reestablish the connection with your FTP server. See Figure 10-61.)

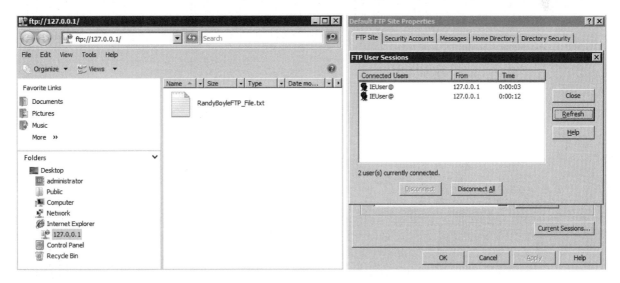

Figure 10-60: Viewing FTP site within Windows Explorer.   Figure 10-61: Viewing FTP user sessions.

THOUGHT QUESTIONS

1. How many seconds is the default "connection timeout" in IIS? What does this mean?
2. Can you block ranges of IP addresses from connecting to your FTP server? How?
3. Can you password protect your FTP site? How?
4. When would you use an FTP site? Isn't HTTP downloading and sending attachments via email sufficient?

CHAPTER 11: LINUX

This chapter is designed to be a basic Linux primer for the average Windows user. It is not intended to be an exhaustive survey of all the functionality contained in the Linux operating system. Each project will guide you through a few simple tasks. Many books have been written that explore the Linux operating system in greater detail.

Linux is a great operating system. It's free, extremely stable, highly customizable, remarkably secure, and runs on a wide variety of hardware (phones, mainframes, etc.). Many of the largest companies use the Linux operating system for their servers. It is also widely used internationally (e.g. India, China, Brazil, Europe, etc.) because of low adoption costs and customizability.

This chapter covers projects related to 1) installation and a tour of a Linux desktop, 2) a command-line primer, 3) methods of software installation, 4) basic networking tools and commands, 5) system tools and network configuration, and 6) user management.

In the prior chapter on virtualization you looked at three Linux distributions (OpenSUSE, Fedora, and Ubuntu). Ubuntu is currently the most popular "distro" followed by Fedora in the number two slot. Other popular distros include Mint, Debian, Mandriva, and Slackware, but there are many others. You can download each distro and see which one you like the best.

The projects in this chapter will use Fedora with a KDE desktop environment for the first two and then switch to Ubuntu with a Gnome desktop for the rest of the projects. This is done intentionally to give you experience with multiple distros and desktop environments. Each has its own advantages/disadvantages. That's the great thing about Linux. It's completely customizable.

11.1 INSTALLATION (FEDORA)

In this project you will install a flavor of Linux called Fedora. Fedora typically comes with the Gnome desktop environment. However, in this project you will install Fedora with the KDE desktop environment. Both Gnome and KDE are widely used. It's good to experience both desktop environments.

This project will walk you through a simple installation using Sun VirtualBox and then look at some features of the KDE desktop environment. You will look at a Web browser (Konqueror), a file manager (Dolphin), a command prompt (Konsole), the general desktop, system settings (like the Control Panel in Windows), and add a couple of widgets.

This project uses Fedora 12 (Constantine) but a later version will also work. The next release of Fedora (Goddard) should be available soon. Fedora releases a new version of their operating system about every six months. This means changes are made and adopted quickly. This has its advantages and disadvantages.

Note: You may have to press the right Ctrl key to exit the virtual machine and then use Screenshot Pilot or MWSnap to take screenshots in VirtualBox. If you didn't install Screenshot Pilot or MWSnap in an earlier project you can download them at the links below.

Screenshot Pilot: http://www.colorpilot.com/screenshot.html.
MWSnap: http://www.mirekw.com/winfreeware/mwsnap.html.

1. Download Fedora (KDE) from: http://fedoraproject.org/get-fedora-kde.
2. Click the link labeled "Download Now" for the installable live CD. (If you have a 64-bit architecture you can click on Other Download options. See Figure 11-1.)
3. Click Save.
4. Select the C:\networking\ folder. (This is a big download that will take a while unless you get it from your instructor or classmate. It should be about 688 MB. See Figure 11-2.)

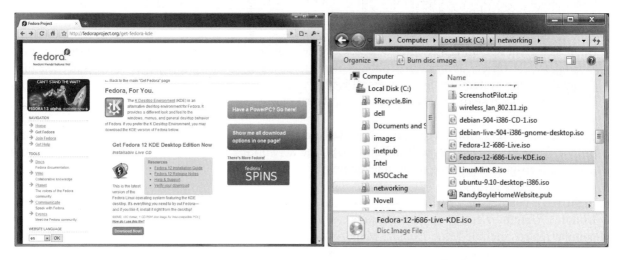

Figure 11-1: Fedora distribution page.   Figure 11-2: Fedora KDE image.

5. Open Sun VirtualBox by clicking Start, All Programs, Sun VirtualBox, and VirtualBox.
6. Click New and Next.
7. Enter "Fedora_YourName" for the Name. (In this case it was Fedora_RandyBoyle. See Figure 11-3.)
8. Select Linux for the Operating System.
9. Select Fedora for the Version.
10. Click Next.
11. Increase the amount of memory to 700 MB+. (See Figure 11-4.)

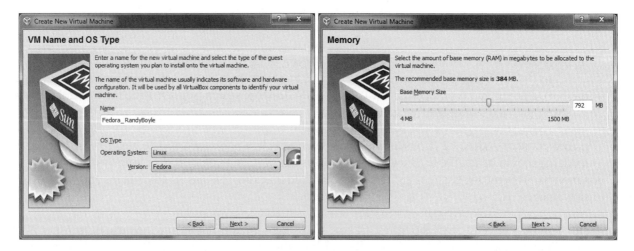

Figure 11-3: Naming the Fedora virtual machine.   Figure 11-4: Allocating RAM to the virtual machine.

12. Click Next, Next, Next, and Next.
13. Increase the hard drive space to 10GB (or more if you have the space). (See Figure 11-5.)

14. Click Next, Finish, and Finish.
15. Select the Virtual machine labeled Fedora_YourName. (See Figure 11-6.)

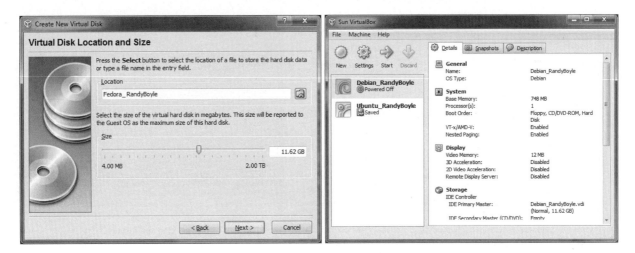

Figure 11-5: Setting the size of the virtual hard drive.   Figure 11-6: Fedora virtual machine created.

16. In the right-hand pane click Storage, IDE Controller, and Empty. (See Figure 11-7.)
17. Click the Browse button on the right-hand side of the screen.
18. Click Add.
19. Browse to C:\networking\.
20. Select the Fedora (KDE) image you downloaded. (In this case it was Fedora-12-i686-Live-KDE.iso.)
21. Click Open and Select. (See Figure 11-8.)
22. Click OK.

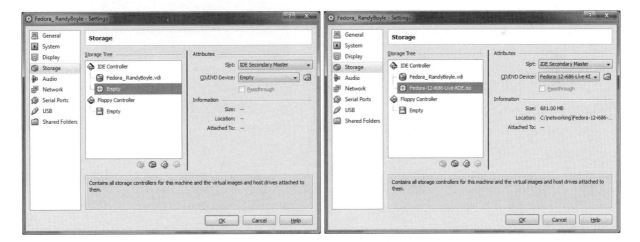

Figure 11-7: No CD/DVD image mounted.   Figure 11-8: Fedora ISO image mounted.

23. Take a screenshot showing the new virtual machine. (You may have to use Screenshot Pilot or MWSnap to take these screenshots. You can leave the virtual machine by holding down the right Ctrl key. To copy the screenshot from within Screenshot Pilot you click Image and Copy to Clipboard. See Figure 11-9.)
24. Click Start. (See Figure 11-10.)
25. Double-click the icon labeled Install to Hard Drive.

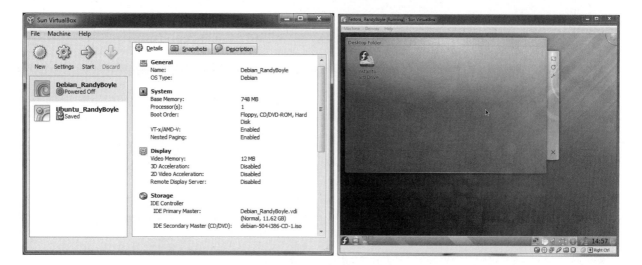

Figure 11-9: Fedora virtual machine ready to boot from the Fedora KDE image.

Figure 11-10: Fedora desktop and installer.

26. Click Next and Next.
27. Enter "YourNameFedora" for the Hostname. (In this case it was RandyBoyleFedora. See Figure 11-11.)
28. Click Next.
29. Select the closest city. (See Figure 11-12.)
30. Click Next.

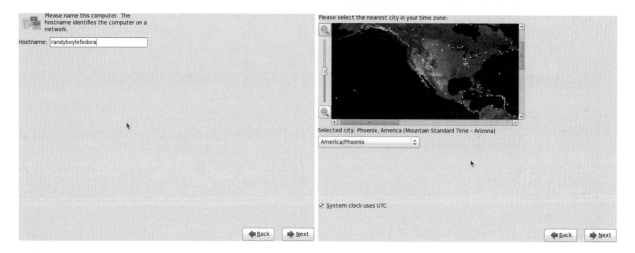

Figure 11-11: Entering a hostname.

Figure 11-12: Setting the time zone.

31. Enter a root password (twice). (It's a good idea to write down your root password if you have a bad memory. You will need to know this password for later projects. See Figure 11-13.)
32. Press Next, Next, Write changes to disk, and Close.

Note: You are now going to have to take the Fedora ISO image out of the virtual CD ROM so you don't have to go through the installation process again. If you don't take out the ISO image the installation process will start again when you reboot the virtual machine.

33. Press the right Ctrl key to exit the virtual machine.
34. In the VirtualBox menu for the virtual machine you are working on click Devices, CD-DVD ROM, Unmount CD/DVD Device. (This will unmount the Fedora ISO image. See Figure 11-14.)

35. In the VirtualBox menu click Machine and Reset. (This will reboot your virtual machine from the virtual hard drive.)

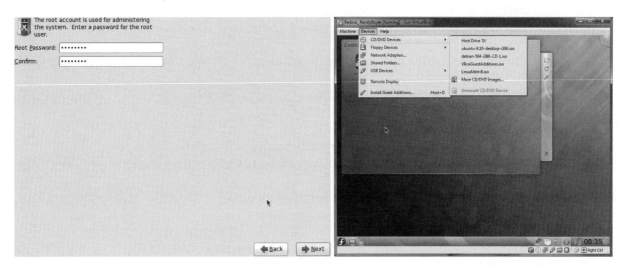

Figure 11-13: Entering a password for the root account.   Figure 11-14: Unmounting the Fedora installation image.

36. Click Forward and Forward. (See Figure 11-15.)
37. Enter your name as the username in lower-case and all one word. (In this case it was randyboyle.)
38. Enter your first and last name in the Full Name field.
39. Enter a password you can remember (twice). (It's a good idea to use the same password that you entered for the root account. In general this is not good practice. However, this is likely your first experience with Linux and this is only a virtual machine. You can change your password later. See Figure 11-16.)
40. Click Forward, Forward, Finish, No, do not send. (Your Fedora virtual machine should reboot at this time.)

Figure 11-15: Welcome screen.   Figure 11-16: Setting username and password.

41. Enter your username.
42. Take a screenshot of the login screen. (See Figure 11-17.)
43. Enter your password.
44. Click Log In.

Note: A few students have mentioned that they had screen resolution issues with their virtual machines. The virtual machine resolution was either too small or too large. Below are the steps to fix this issue. If you aren't experiencing any resolution issues please continue on at Step 45.

1. From the VirtualBox File menu for the virtual machine you are working on click Devices and Install Guest Additions.
2. Log into your Fedora virtual machine.
3. Click Applications, Accessories, and Terminal.
4. Type **cd /media/cdrom0**
5. Type **sudo sh ./VBoxLinuxAdditions-x86.run**
6. Restart your virtual machine. (You can also press Ctrl-Alt-Backspace.)
7. Log back into your virtual machine.
8. Click System, Preferences, and Screen resolution.
9. Adjust your screen resolution and you are done.

45. Click on the Fedora menu icon on the bottom left-hand of the screen. (This is similar to the Start button in Windows.)
46. Click Applications, Internet, and Web browser. (This will open the default Web browser called Konqueror.)
47. Browse to www.Google.com.
48. Enter your name into the search box.
49. Take a screenshot of your virtual desktop showing your name in the Google search box. (See Figure 11-18.)

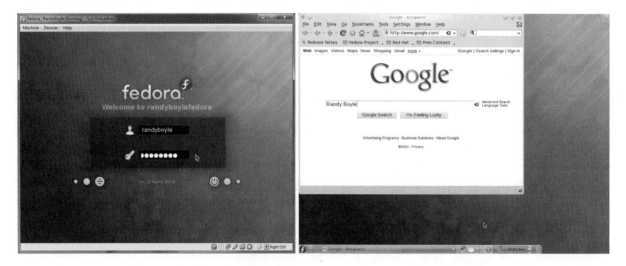

Figure 11-17: Fedora login screen.   Figure 11-18: Konqueror Web browser in Fedora.

50. Click on the Fedora menu icon on the bottom left-hand of the screen.
51. Click Applications, System, and File Browser. (This will open the default File browser called Dolphin. You will see your home directory. This is similar to the "My Documents" folder in Windows.)
52. Click on the red folder in the left-hand pane labeled root. (This will show a listing of all the directories under root. This is similar in many ways to the C: drive in Windows. Your personal home directory, along with all other user directories, is located in the home directory. See Figure 11-19.)
53. Click on the directory labeled home.
54. Click on the directory with your name on it.

55. Take a screenshot of the contents of your home directory. (See Figure 11-20.)

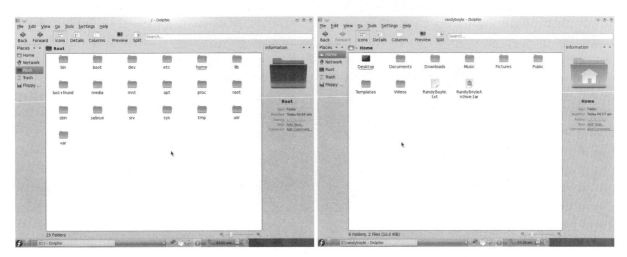

Figure 11-19: The root directory.   Figure 11-20: A user's home directory.

56. Click on the Fedora menu icon on the bottom left-hand of the screen. (This is similar to the Start button in Windows.)
57. Click Applications and System. (You are going to create a shortcut to the Terminal application (Konsole) from this menu.)
58. Right-click Terminal.
59. Select Add to Desktop. (This will add a shortcut to your desktop that will open a command-line terminal.)
60. Click the Konsole icon on your desktop. (This should open the Konsole terminal. See Figure 11-21.)
61. Type **ls**
62. Press Enter. (This will display the contents of your home directory.)
63. Type **cd Desktop**
64. Press Enter. (This will move you to the subdirectory that contains files, folders, links, etc. that are displayed in the Desktop Folder. You are going to create a text document and have it display on your desktop.)
65. Type **touch YourName.txt**
66. Press Enter. (This will create a simple text file. In this case it was RandyBoyle.txt.)
67. Type **ls**
68. Press Enter. (This will verify that you created the text file. You should see the new text file with your name on it. It should also appear in the Desktop Folder.)
69. Take a screenshot of your virtual machine desktop showing the Konsole terminal and the new text file in the Desktop folder. (See Figure 11-22.)

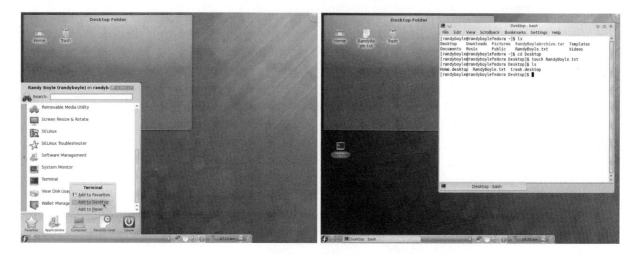

Figure 11-21: Opening a terminal.   Figure 11-22: New text file added to the Desktop Folder.

70. Click on the Fedora menu icon on the bottom left-hand of the screen.
71. Click Applications, Settings, and System Settings. (This will open an application similar to the Control Panel in Windows. See Figure 11-23.)
72. Close the System Settings window.
73. Click the Tool Box icon in the upper right-hand corner of your desktop.
74. Click Add Widgets. (See Figure 11-24.)

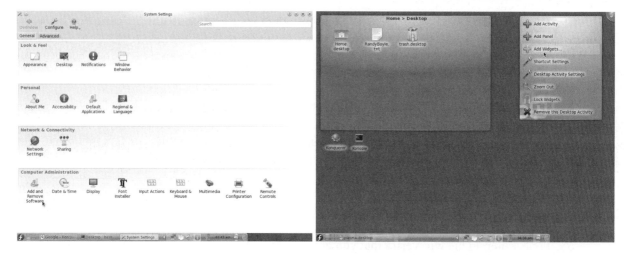

Figure 11-23: System Settings.   Figure 11-24: Adding widgets from the Tool Box.

75. Scroll to the right until you see the system monitor that looks like a graph. (See Figure 11-25.)
76. Drag-and-drop the System Monitor icon onto your desktop.
77. Click on each of the grayed-out icons to display the graphs below. (See Figure 11-26.)
78. Close the Add Widgets toolbar.

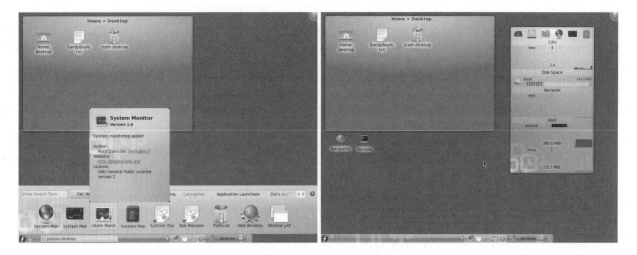

Figure 11-25: Adding the System Monitor widget.　　　　　　Figure 11-26: System Monitor widget.

79. Right-click the taskbar along the bottom of your screen.
80. Click Panel Options and Add Widgets.
81. Double-click the icon labeled Lock/Logout. (It's a red square icon. This will add it to your taskbar on the bottom of your screen. See Figure 11-27.)
82. Take a screenshot of your modified desktop. (See Figure 11-28.)

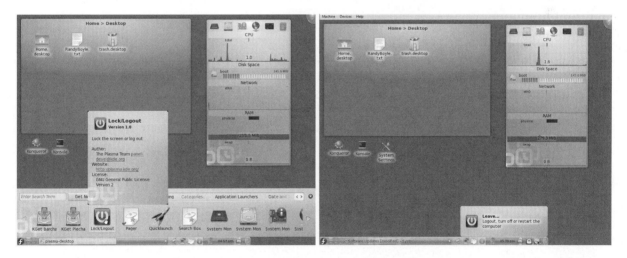

Figure 11-27: Adding the Lock/Logout widget.　　　　　　Figure 11-28: Lock/Logout widget now on taskbar.

THOUGHT QUESTIONS

1. Approximately how many software packages could be installed and used with Fedora?
2. What is in the /media directory?
3. Can you download additional widgets other than the ones shown?
4. Is KDE the default desktop environment for Fedora?

11.2 COMMAND-LINE PRIMER

This project will go through some basic command-line exercises. These few commands are intended to be a short primer NOT an exhaustive dissertation. These are just some of the more commonly used commands. There are additional online tutorials that provide much better coverage of the functionality of command-line tools.

You will need to practice these commands many times to become even moderately proficient. Only after entering them many hundreds of times will they become second nature to you. You can complete equivalent tasks using command-line in a fraction of the time it would take you to complete them using a GUI interface in Windows.

Taking screenshots using the Alt-PrntScrn key sequence does not always work with virtual machines. It's better to use Ctrl-PrntScrn or download Screenshot Pilot (http://www.colorpilot.com/screenshot.html). In this project you are going to press Enter after typing each command unless otherwise directed.

1. Open Sun VirtualBox by clicking Start, All Programs, Sun VirtualBox, and VirtualBox.
2. Select your Fedora virtual machine.
3. Click Start.
4. Login if you are not already logged in. (Your username should be "yourname" in all lower-case. In this case it was randyboyle.)
5. Click the Fedora icon, Applications, System, and Terminal. (See Figure 11-29.)
6. Type **ls**
7. Press Enter. (This displays a listing of the files in the current directory.)
8. Type **ls -l**
9. Press Enter. (This displays the listing in long format.)
10. Type **ls -al**
11. Press Enter. (This displays a listing of files including hidden files. There are many hidden files in your home directory.)
12. Take a screenshot. (See Figure 11-30.)

Figure 11-29: Starting a terminal.   Figure 11-30: Results from the ls command.

13. Type **man ls**
14. Press Enter. (This displays the manual page for the ls command.)
15. Type **q**
16. Press Enter. (This will exit the man page.)
17. Type **man man**
18. Press Enter. (This displays the manual page for the man command. See Figure 11-31.)
19. Take a screenshot.
20. Type **q**
21. Press Enter. (This will exit the man page.)
22. Type **date**
23. Press Enter. (This will display the current time and date.)
24. Type **cal**
25. Press Enter. (This will display the current month's calendar.)
26. Type **uptime**
27. Press Enter. (This will display how long the system has been up and running.)
28. Type **w**
29. Press Enter. (This will display who is logged on to the system.)
30. Type **whoami**
31. Press Enter. (This will display who you are logged on as.)
32. Type **finger yourname**
33. Press Enter. (This will display who "randyboyle" is. See Figure 11-32.)
34. Take a screenshot.
35. Type **clear**
36. Press Enter. (This will clear the screen.)

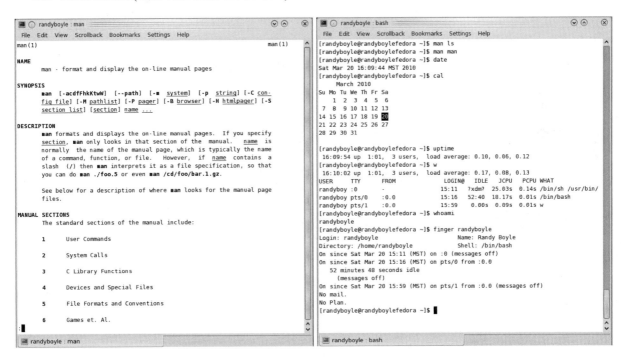

Figure 11-31: MAN page.

Figure 11-32: Results from the w, whoami, and finger commands.

37. Type **df**
38. Press Enter. (This will display how much of your hard disk you have used.)
39. Type **touch YourName.txt**
40. Press Enter. (This will create a simple text file. In this case it was RandyBoyle.txt.)

41. Type **ls**
42. Press Enter. (This will verify that you created the text file. You should see the new text file with your name on it.)
43. Type **vi YourName.txt**
44. Press Enter. (This will start the vi editor and enter text into the new file you created. You are now in the vi editor. You are not at the command prompt.)
45. Press **i**. (This will put you in "insert" mode and allow you to enter text into the document. It will say insert at the bottom of the screen.)
46. Enter your name three times.
47. Press the ESC key.
48. Press **ZZ**. (This will save the text file and exit the vi editor. Note, it is case-sensitive and those are capital Z's.)
49. Type **vi YourName.txt**
50. Press Enter. (This will open the vi editor and verify that you correctly saved the text document.)
51. Take a screenshot. (See Figure 11-33.)
52. Press **ZZ.** (This will save and exit the vi editor.)
53. Type **mkdir YourNameFolder**
54. Press Enter. (This will create a folder in your home directory.)
55. Type **ls**
56. Press Enter. (This will display the current directory and verify that you did create the new folder (directory). See Figure 11-34.)

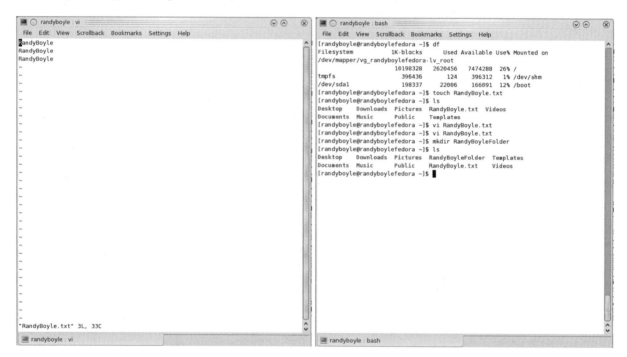

Figure 11-33: Editing a text file in vi.   Figure 11-34: Making a directory.

57. Type **cd YourN**
58. DO NOT PRESS THE ENTER KEY, instead press the Tab key to finish the name of the directory. (In this case the command was cd RandyB. Using the tab key can save you a lot of time and prevent errors. You need to be careful because commands are case-sensitive. A lower-case "r" and an upper-case "R" are not the same thing.)
59. Press Enter.
60. Type **pwd**

61. Press Enter. (This will display the full path. It stands for "print working directory.")
62. Type **cd ..**
63. Press Enter. (This will move back one level in the directory structure to your home directory.)
64. Type **ls**
65. Press Enter. (This will verify you are back in your home directory. See Figure 11-35.)
66. Type **cp YourName.txt YourNameCopy.txt**
67. Press Enter. (This will create a copy of your text file. In this case YourName will be RandyBoyle for the remainder of this project).
68. Type **ls**
69. Press Enter. (This will display the contents of the current directory and verify the copy was made correctly.)
70. Type the following command to make a copy of the copy, move it into the directory you just created, and give it a new name (case-sensitive).

cp YourNameCopy.txt /home/yourname/YourNameFolder/YourNameCopy2.txt

71. Type **cd YourNameFolder**
72. Press Enter. (This will enter your subdirectory.)
73. Type **ls**
74. Press Enter. (This will view the new file you just copied over.)
75. Take a screenshot. (See Figure 11-36.)

Figure 11-35: Making a copy of a file.   Figure 11-36: Copying a file from one directory to another.

76. Type **cd ..**
77. Press Enter. (This will move you back to your home directory.)
78. Type **ls**
79. Press Enter. (This will display the contents of your home directory.)
80. Type **rm YourNameCopy.txt**
81. Press Enter. (This will delete the copied file in your home directory.)
82. Type **ls**

83. Press Enter. (This will confirm the deletion of the YourNameCopy.txt file.)
84. Type **rm -r YourNameFolder**
85. Press Enter. (This will remove the directory and its contents.)
86. Type **ls**
87. Press Enter. (This will confirm the deletion of the directory. See Figure 11-37.)
88. Type **!!**
89. Press Enter. (This will repeat the last command.)
90. Type **cd ..**
91. Press Enter. (This will move you to the home directory. Directories for all users are located here.)
92. Type **cd ..**
93. Press Enter. (This will move you to the root directory. This is roughly the equivalent to the C: drive on your Windows computer.)
94. Type **ls**
95. Press Enter. (This will display a listing of all of the directories in root.)
96. Type **find -name YourName.txt**
97. Press Enter. (This will find the text file you created. It will take about a minute to find your file. You will also get several "permission denied" responses but you should see your file listed near the top.)
98. Take a screenshot. (See Figure 11-38.)

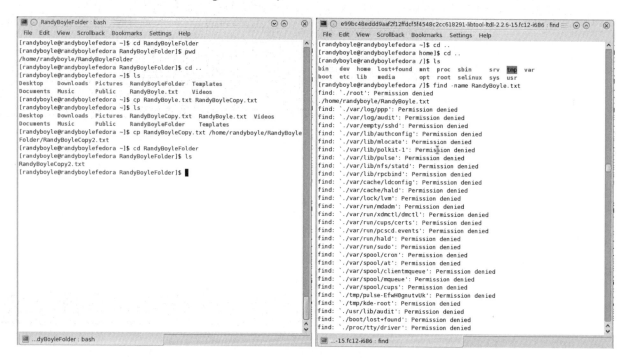

Figure 11-37: Deleting files and directories.   Figure 11-38: Results from the find command.

99. Type **su root**
100. Press Enter. (This will switch to the administrator account. In Linux the administrator account is called root.)
101. Enter the password you set when you installed Fedora. (Don't worry if you can't see the characters being entered. Linux doesn't display asterisks for password characters like Windows does.)
102. Press Enter.
103. Type **find -name YourName.txt**

104. Press Enter. (This will find your text file. You won't see all of the "permission denied" errors. In this case the command was `find -name RandyBoyle.txt`.)

105. Take a screenshot. (See Figure 11-39.)

106. Type **exit**

107. Press Enter. (This will exit the root account and lower your privileges. It's better to only run as root only when necessary. It will keep you from inadvertently damaging your system.)

108. Type **cd home**

109. Press Enter. (This will move you into the home directory.)

110. Type **cd yourname**

111. Press Enter. (In this case it was `cd randyboyle`. This will move you into your directory.)

112. Type **ls**

113. Press Enter. (This will confirm you are back in your directory.)

114. Type **grep lastname YourName.txt**

115. Press Enter. (This will search for instances where "lastname" appears in the YourName.txt file. In this case the command was `grep boyle RandyBoyle.txt`. It will return every line of text where your lastname appears.)

116. Type **grep Lastname YourName.txt**

117. Press Enter. (This is the same as above except for the change in capitalization. You will see if capitalization makes a difference when using the grep command.)

118. Take a screenshot. (See Figure 11-40.)

Figure 11-39: Results from the find command as root.　　Figure 11-40: Results from the grep command.

119. Type **tar cf YourNameArchive.tar YourName.txt**

120. Press Enter. (This will create a compressed archive of your text file similar to a zip file. Remember to replace YourName with your first and last name. In this case the file was named RandyBoyleArchive.tar.)

121. Type **ls**

122. Press Enter. (This will confirm the creation of the tar file.)

123. Type **rm YourName.txt**

124. Press Enter. (This will delete the text file. In this case it was RandyBoyle.txt.)

125. Type **ls**
126. Press Enter. (This will confirm the deletion of the text file.)
127. Type **tar xf YourNameArchive.tar**
128. Press Enter. (This will extract the file from the archive into your directory. In this case the file was named RandyBoyleArchive.tar.)
129. Type **ls**
130. Press Enter. (This will confirm that the archive did extract the text file into your home directory.)
131. Take a screenshot. (See Figure 11-41.)
132. Type **top**
133. Press Enter. (This will display a listing of the processes currently running on your virtual machine. You are now in interactive mode. See Figure 11-42.)
134. Press q. (This will quit interactive mode and return you to the command prompt.)
135. Click on the Fedora menu icon (like the Start menu in Windows), Applications, Office, and Spreadsheets (Kspread). Enter a couple of random values in a few of the cells.

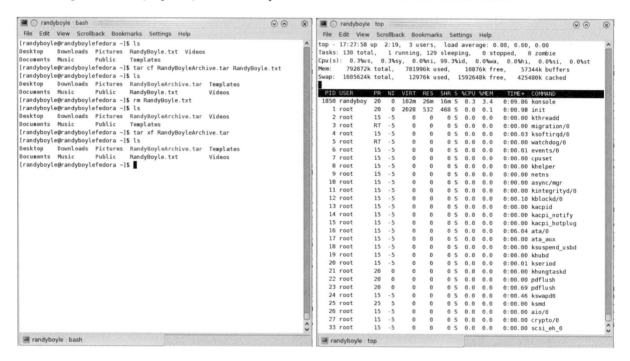

Figure 11-41: Archiving a file with the tar command.   Figure 11-42: Listing processes with the top command.

136. Return to the command prompt.
137. Type **top -u yourname**
138. Press Enter. (This will display only the processes you are running. You are now in interactive mode.)
139. Press M. (This is case-sensitive. This will sort the processes by the amount of memory they are using. The kspread process should be listed near the top.)
140. Write down the process ID for kspread. (In this case the PID was 4231. Your process ID (PID) will be different. You will have to correctly identify the PID for kspread on your machine.)
141. Press k.
142. Press Enter. (This is will now allow you to enter the PID you want to kill.)
143. Type the Kspread pin.
144. Press Enter twice. (It is very unlikely that your PID was 4231. You need to enter your PID. You should see the process disappear and the spreadsheet window close. See Figure 11-43.)
145. Press q.
146. Press Enter. (This will quit the interactive mode and return you to the command prompt.)

147. Type **ping www.google.com**

148. Press Enter. (This will ping one of Google's Web servers. You will stop this command by pressing Ctrl-C.)

149. Press Ctrl-C to cancel the ping command after about four responses.

150. Press the up arrow key to scroll through prior commands until you get to the ping www.Google.com command.

151. Press Enter.

152. Press Ctrl-C to cancel the ping command after about four responses.

153. Type **su root**

154. Press Enter. (This will switch to the root account.)

155. Enter the password you set when you installed Fedora.

156. Press Enter.

157. Type **ifconfig lo**

158. Press Enter. (This will display information about the loopback adapter.)

159. Type **ifconfig eth0**

160. Press Enter. (That is a zero not the letter "O." This will display information about your network card.)

161. Type **dig www.google.com**

162. Press Enter. (This will display detailed information about some of Google's Web servers.)

163. Take a screenshot. (See Figure 11-44.)

164. Type **exit**

165. Press Enter. (This will close the command prompt.)

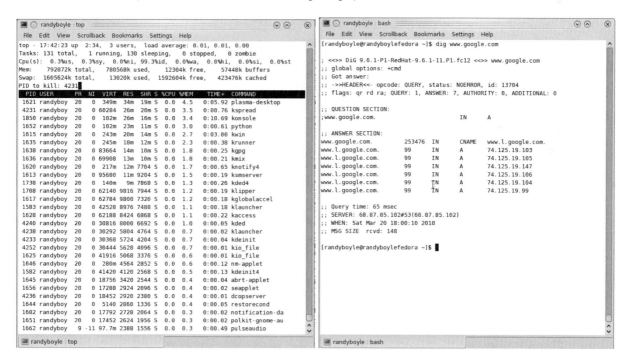

Figure 11-43: Killing a process.   Figure 11-44: Results from the dig command.

THOUGHT QUESTIONS

1. Do these commands work on a MAC? Why or why not?
2. Are there study sheets available as a reference?
3. How can knowing command-line Linux save you time?
4. Which of the commands in this project was a compression utility?

In this project you will install software using 1) the Ubuntu Software Center, 2) the Synaptic Package Manager, and 3) using the command line. You will also configure the settings for a third-party software repository (Google) and download an application (Google Chrome). There are a large number of excellent pieces of software available for the Linux operating system.

There are many thousands of pieces of software available for Linux that provide the same functionality you will find on Windows or MAC. In fact, many cutting-edge applications are developed initially for the Linux platform. There are new applications being developed every day by the opensource community and being made available to everyone for free.

This project will use the Ubuntu distribution that you installed in Chapter 4. Not only is this a different flavor of Linux but this also uses the Gnome desktop environment. This is a good chance to compare and contrast the differences between KDE and Gnome. You can get both KDE and Gnome on either Fedora or Ubuntu. You can also run applications made for KDE in Gnome and vice versa. It's all a matter of personal preference.

1. Open Sun VirtualBox by clicking Start, All Programs, Sun VirtualBox, and VirtualBox.
2. Select your Ubuntu virtual machine.
3. Click Start.
4. Login if you are not already logged in.
5. Click Applications and Ubuntu Software Center. (See Figure 11-45.)
6. Click on Sound & Video in the left-hand pane.
7. Scroll down until you see gtkpod.
8. Double-click gtkpod. (This is an application that allows you to manage an IPod when it is connected to a Linux machine. See Figure 11-46.)
9. Click Install.
10. Enter your root password when prompted.

Note: If you get an error stating that the software packages could not be updated you might have an issue with your virtual machine correctly accessing the Internet. Open a Web browser within your virtual machine and make sure you have Internet access.

Figure 11-45: Menu for Add/Remove Applications.   Figure 11-46: Selecting gtkpod to be installed.

11. Click on Get Free Software at the top of the Window.
12. Click on System Tools.

13. Scroll down until you see EtherApe. (This is a network monitoring tool that provides a graphical representation of network traffic.)
14. Double-click EtherApe.
15. Click Install.
16. Enter your root password when prompted.
17. Click on Get Free Software at the top of the Window.
18. Click on Internet.
19. Scroll down until you see Wireshark. (This is the same program you used in earlier projects. You are installing it here to show you that the same software used in earlier projects can run on Linux.)
20. Double-click Wireshark. (See Figure 11-47.)
21. Click Install.
22. Enter your root password when prompted.
23. Click on Get Free Software at the top of the Window.
24. Click on Internet.
25. Scroll down until you see Zenmap. (This is a GUI frontend to Nmap. Nmap is a powerful network mapping, scanning, and host identification tool.)
26. Double-click Zenmap. (See Figure 11-48.)
27. Click Install.
28. Enter your root password when prompted.

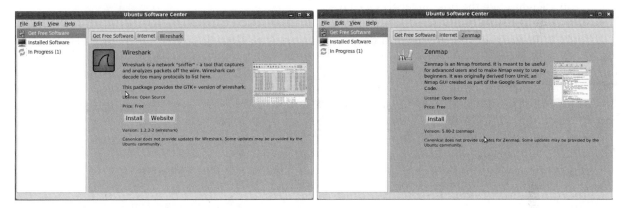

Figure 11-47: Selecting Wireshark to be installed.   Figure 11-48: Selecting Zenmap to be installed.

29. Click Applications, Sound and Video, and gtkpod.
30. Take a screenshot.
31. Click Applications, Internet, and EtherApe (as root).
32. Enter your root password when prompted.
33. Open the Firefox Web browser by clicking on the icon at the top of the screen.
34. Go to www.yahoo.com.
35. Return to EtherApe. (You should see EtherApe changing.)
36. Take a screenshot. (See Figure 11-49.)
37. Click Applications, Internet, and Zenmap.
38. Enter your root password when prompted.
39. Enter "127.0.0.1" as the target.
40. Click Scan.
41. Take a screenshot after the scan completes. (See Figure 11-50.)
42. Close all applications.

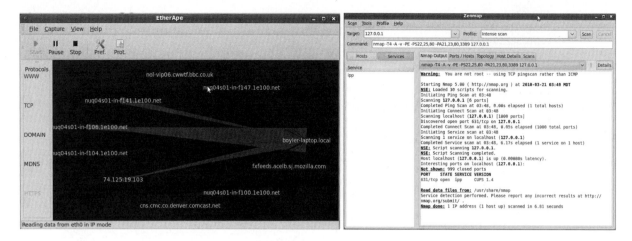

Figure 11-49: EtherApe displaying a graphical representation of network traffic from this host.

Figure 11-50: Zenmap installed and running.

43. Click Applications, Internet, and Firefox Web Browser.
44. Enter the following URL: http://www.google.com/linuxrepositories/ubuntu704.html. (This will take you to the instructions about how to add Google's software repository.)
45. Click on the link labeled "Google Linux Package Signing Key." (See Figure 11-51.)
46. Right-click the link under Key Details.
47. Select Save Link As.
48. Change the Save in Folder to your folder. (In this case it was boyler. See Figure 11-52.)
49. Click Save.
50. Minimize the Web browser.

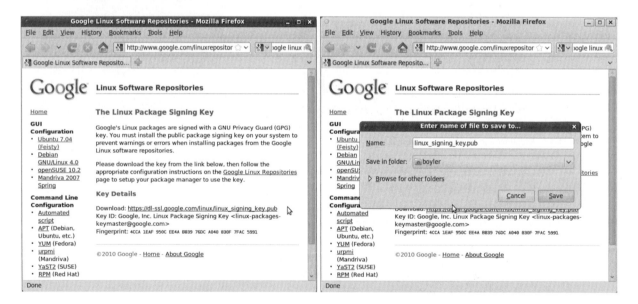

Figure 11-51: Saving the Linux signing key.

Figure 11-52: Saved Linux signing key in your directory.

51. Click System, Administration, and Synaptic Package Manager.
52. Enter your root password if prompted.
53. In the File menu within Synaptic Package Manager click Settings and Repositories. (See Figure 11-53.)
54. Click on the Authentication tab.
55. Click Import Key File.

56. Select the key you saved in the folder labeled yourname. (In this case it was the file labeled linux_signing_key.pub in the folder labeled boyler.)
57. Click OK. (You should now see Google in the list of trusted software providers. See Figure 11-54.)

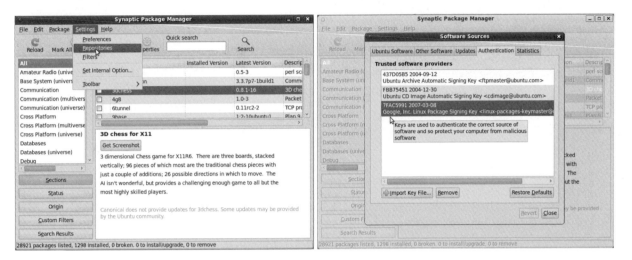

Figure 11-53: Synaptic Package Manager.   Figure 11-54: Google is listed as a trusted software source.

58. Click on the Other Software tab. (You may not see all of the repositories shown below.)
59. Click Add. (See Figure 11-55.)
60. Enter the following for the APT line:

deb http://dl.google.com/linux/deb/ stable non-free main

61. Click Add Source. (See Figure 11-56.)
62. Click Close and Close.

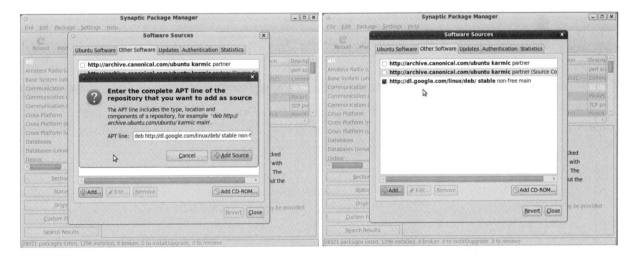

Figure 11-55: Adding the APT line for Google's repository.   Figure 11-56: Added an additional software repository.

63. In the File menu for Synaptic Package Manager click Edit and Reload Package Information. (You can also press Ctrl-R. This may take a couple of minutes. See Figure 11-57.)
64. Click on the Origin button in the left-hand pane.
65. Click on dl.google.com/main.
66. Double-click google-chrome-beta in the right-hand pane. (See Figure 11-58.)

67. Click Apply and Apply.

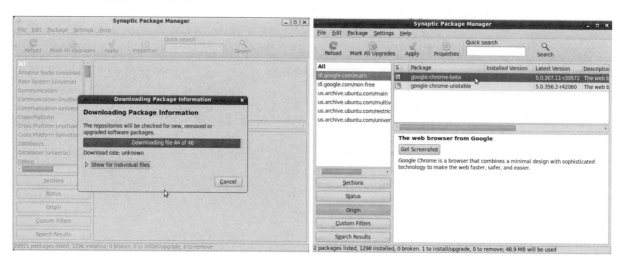

Figure 11-57: Reloading package information.

Figure 11-58: Selecting Google Chrome to be installed.

68. Click Close when you see the notification that the installation was successful.
69. Close the Synaptic Package Manager.
70. Close any Web browsers that may be open.
71. Click Applications, Internet, and Google Chrome.
72. Browse to www.Google.com.
73. Enter your name into the search box.
74. Take a screenshot showing Google Chrome running within your virtual machine. (See Figure 11-59.)
75. Click Applications, Accessories, and Terminal.
76. Type **su root**
77. Press Enter.
78. Enter the root password you set during the installation process.
79. Press Enter.
80. Type **sudo apt-get install apache2**
81. Press Enter. (See Figure 11-60.)

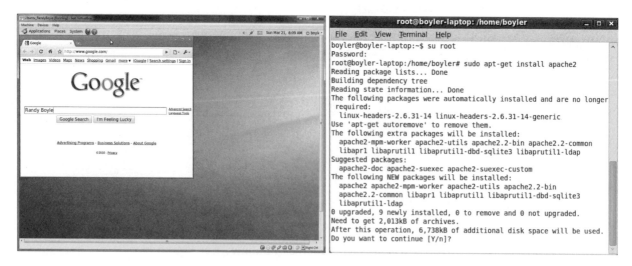

Figure 11-59: Google Chrome successfully installed.

Figure 11-60: Installing Apache via a command prompt.

82. Press Y.

83. Press Enter.
84. Type **/etc/init.d/apache2 start**
85. Press Enter. (This will make sure Apache is running. See Figure 11-61.)
86. Open the Chrome Web browser.
87. Enter "127.0.0.1" into the address bar. (This is the loopback adapter. This will direct your Web browser to request the default page on your locally installed Apache Web server.)
88. Take a screenshot. (See Figure 11-62.)

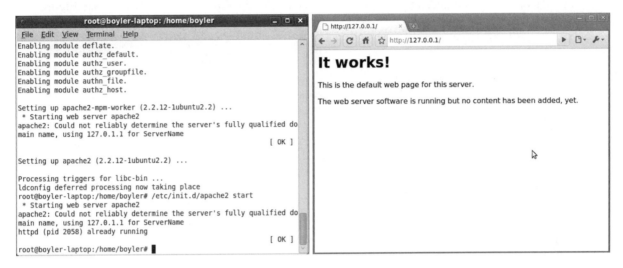

Figure 11-61: Starting Apache.　　　　　　　　Figure 11-62: Apache Web server running in Linux.

THOUGHT QUESTIONS

1. Can you install Sun VirtualBox on Linux and run a Windows virtual machine?
2. Why are there different repositories and who manages them?
3. Was it faster to install software on Linux from the command-line or through the GUI interface?
4. Can you install KDE applications in a Gnome desktop environment?

11.4 NET-TOOLS AND NETWORKING COMMANDS

In this project you will look at some of the basic networking tools that come loaded with Linux. In the first part of the project you will use an application that has several commonly used networking utilities. In the second half of this project you will use command-line tools to produce the same results. You will see that some of the command-line tools are similar to the tools you used in the DOS prompt.

You will also use the tcpdump command to capture packets, write them to a log file, and then read the log file. This is the command-line equivalent of the packet capturing software you used in earlier projects (Wireshark). Many of the same options you used in the Wireshark projects are also available in tcpdump.

Knowing how to use the command-line tools is important because they are available on almost every computer by default. Experienced network administrators use them every day. This project is a very basic primer.

1. Open Sun VirtualBox by clicking Start, All Programs, Sun VirtualBox, and VirtualBox.
2. Select your Ubuntu virtual machine.
3. Click Start.
4. Login if you are not already logged in.

5. Click System, Administration, and Network Tools.
6. Change the Network device from the loopback adapter to your network card.
7. Click Applications, Internet, and Firefox.
8. Resize the Web browser so it is next to the Network Tools screen.
9. Go to www.Google.com and search for YourName. (Watch the Interface Statistics change.)
10. Leave the virtual machine and click on your desktop. (You may have to press the right Ctrl key to leave the virtual machine.)
11. Take a screenshot. (Your name should be visible in the Google search results. See Figure 11-63.)

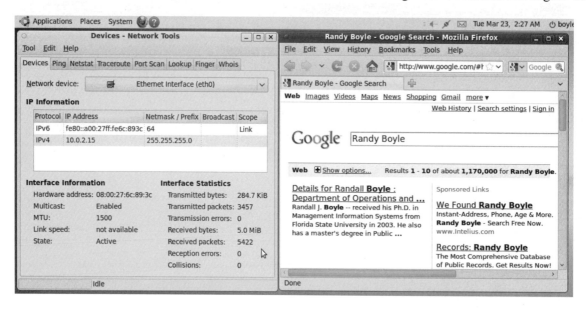

Figure 11-63: Network interface information and statistics.

5. Return to the Ubunutu virtual machine.
6. Click on the Ping tab in the Network tools menu.
7. Enter "www.Google.com" for the Network address.
8. Click Ping.
9. Minimize the Web browser.
10. Open another Network Tools window and position it next to the first Network Tools window.
11. Click on the Netstat tab.
12. Select Routing Table Information.
13. Click Netstat.
14. Take a screenshot showing the results in the Ping and Netstat tabs. (Press the right Ctrl key to leave the virtual machine. See Figure 11-64.)

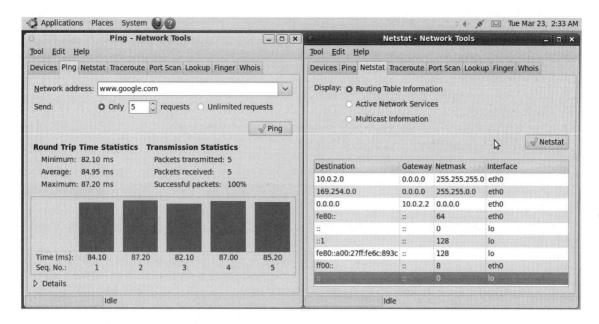

Figure 11-64: Results displayed for the Ping and Netstat tabs.

15. Return to the Ubuntu virtual machine.
16. Click on the Portscan tab.
17. Enter "127.0.0.1" for the Network address. (This is going to port scan your own virtual machine.)
18. Click Scan.
19. Click on Active Network Services in the Netstat tab.
20. Click Netstat.
21. Click on the other Network Tools window.
22. Take a screenshot showing the results for the Port Scan and Active Network Services. (Press the right Ctrl key to leave the virtual machine. See Figure 11-65.)

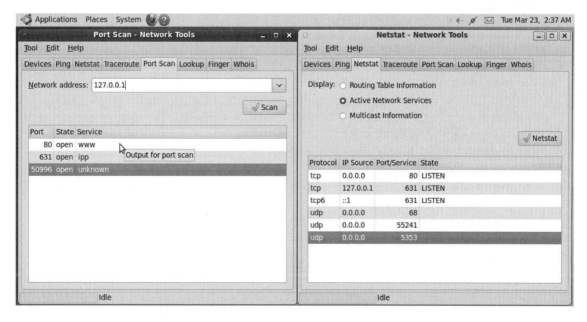

Figure 11-65: Results displayed for Active Network Services (Netstat) and Port Scan tabs.

23. Return to the Ubuntu virtual machine.
24. Click on the Lookup tab in the Network tools menu.

25. Enter "www.Google.com" for the Network address.
26. Click Lookup.
27. Click on the other Network Tools window.
28. Click on the Whois tab.
29. Enter "www.Google.com" for the Network address.
30. Click Whois.
31. Take a screenshot showing the results in the Lookup and Whois tabs. (Press the right Ctrl key to leave the virtual machine. See Figure 11-66.)

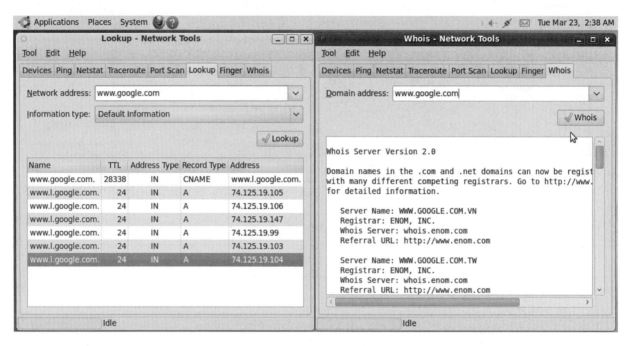

Figure 11-66: Results displayed for the Lookup and Whois tabs.

32. Click Applications, Accessories, and Terminal.
33. Type **netstat --route**
34. Press Enter. (This will display the routing table.)
35. Type **netstat -r**
36. Press Enter. (This will also display the routing table. All of the commands below can be shortened to use just the first letter. For added clarity this project will use more explicit options.)
37. Type **netstat --interfaces**
38. Press Enter. (This will display all current network interfaces on your virtual machine.)
39. Take a screenshot. (See Figure 11-67.)
40. Type **netstat --statistics --tcp**
41. Press Enter. (This will display TCP statistics.)
42. Type **netstat --statistics --udp**
43. Press Enter. (This will display UDP statistics.)
44. Take a screenshot. (See Figure 11-68.)

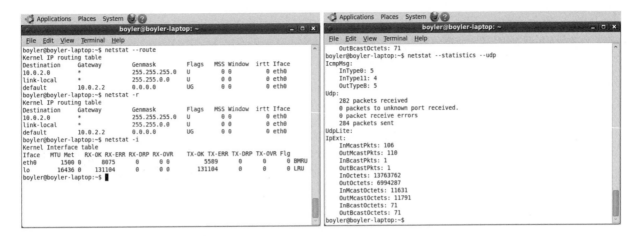

Figure 11-67: Routing table produced using the netstat command.

Figure 11-68: UDP statistics.

45. Type **ping www.google.com -c 3**
46. Press Enter. (This will display information about the ping responses. See Figure 11-69.)
47. Type **tracepath www.google.com**
48. Press Enter. (This will display information about the route from your virtual machine to one of Google's servers.)
49. Take a screenshot.
50. Type **host www.google.com**
51. Press Enter. (This will resolve www.Google.com into multiple IP addresses.)
52. Type **dig www.google.com**
53. Press Enter. (This will display the information provided by the host command plus additional information from DNS.)
54. Type **whois www.google.com**
55. Press Enter. (This will display the whois entry for www.Google.com. Scroll up so the command you typed and the first entry are showing in the terminal before you take the screenshot.)
56. Take a screenshot. (See Figure 11-70.)

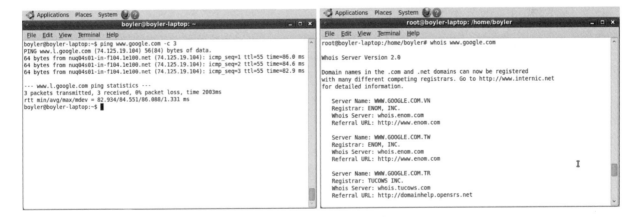

Figure 11-69: Ping results from www.Google.com.

Figure 11-70: Results from a whois lookup.

Note: The following command (tcpdump) can capture filtered packets in a similar way Wireshark captures packets. This is the command-line equivalent. After entering each command you will need to refresh your Web browser to produce packets. You can press the up/down arrow keys to scroll through prior commands and edit them. This can save you time and reduce syntax errors.

57. Type **su root**

58. Press Enter. (This command requires root-level permission to run.)
59. Enter your root password.
60. Type **tcpdump -c 5**
61. Press Enter. (This will capture the first five packets going through your network card. See Figure 11-71.)
62. Refresh your Web browser. (This will push packets through your network card.)

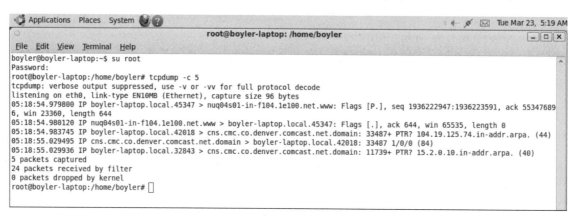

Figure 11-71: Capturing packets using the tcpdump command.

63. Type **tcpdump -c 5 -n**
64. Press Enter. (This will display the five packets showing unresolved IP addresses.)
65. Refresh your Web browser.
66. Type **tcpdump -c 5 -n port 80**
67. Press Enter. (This will display only those five packets going over port 80. This will only capture Web traffic.)
68. Refresh your Web browser.
69. Type **tcpdump -c 5 -n port 80 -w YourNameCapture.log**
70. Press Enter. (This will write the packets you capture to a log file. In this case the log file was RandyBoyleCapture.log. See Figure 11-72.)
71. Refresh your Web browser.

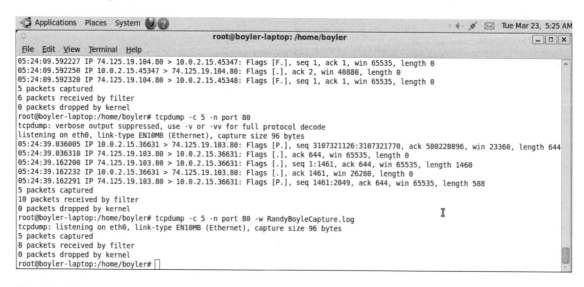

Figure 11-72: Capturing packets and writing them to a log file.

72. Type **ls**

73. Press Enter. (This will give a listing of the files in the current directory. You should see the log file listed that was just created.)
74. Type **tcpdump -r YourNameCapture.log**
75. Press Enter. (This will display the packets you captured.)
76. Take a screenshot. (See Figure 11-73.)

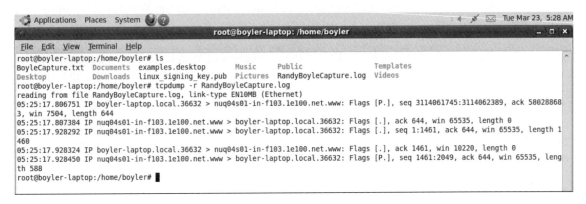

Figure 11-73: Results from the packet capture log file.

77. Type **ifconfig**
78. Press Enter. (This is similar to the ipconfig command you used in the DOS prompt.)
79. Take a screenshot. (See Figure 11-74.)

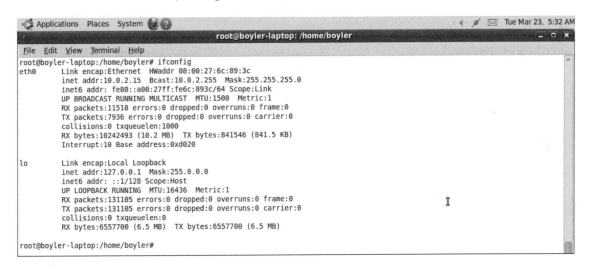

Figure 11-74: Results from the ifconfig command.

THOUGHT QUESTIONS

1. Could you use tcpdump to capture packets for a specific IP address?
2. Why did some commands (like tcpdump and ifconfig) require root-level permission to run?
3. If you hadn't set a limit (-c 3) when you used the ping command what would have happened?
4. Are there command-line tools that produce the same (or better) results that GUI tools do? What would be the advantage of a GUI tool over a command-line tool?

11.5 SYSTEM TOOLS AND CONFIGURATION

This project will look at some basic system tools that network administrators use often. Some of these tools may look familiar. These are the Linux equivalent to the Windows tools you used in earlier projects. You will see that you can accomplish the same tasks in Linux that you can in Windows. In some instances it can be done much more quickly and efficiently in Linux.

First, you will explore the System Monitor. This is the equivalent of Windows Task Manager. You will identify a process and kill it. You will also look at some basic system monitors. These are the same tasks you performed with Windows Task Manager.

Next, you will change your network settings. You will change the default DHCP IP address and settings to a manually configured static IP address. You will get the necessary information to set the static IP address from a few simple commands.

Finally, you will look at a disk usage analyzer and use a terminal server client to access a Windows machine. These basic tasks will help familiarize you with the Linux operating system and help you understand how Linux can make your job as a network administrator much easier.

1. Open Sun VirtualBox by clicking Start, All Programs, Sun VirtualBox, and VirtualBox.
2. Select your Ubuntu virtual machine.
3. Click Start.
4. Login if you are not already logged in.
5. Click System, Administration, and System Monitor.
6. Click on the Processes tab.
7. Click on the Memory column heading (twice) to sort by memory usage in descending order.
8. Click the Firefox icon at the top of your desktop. (You should see the Firefox process show up in the list and the Firefox Web browser open. See Figure 11-75.)
9. Return to the System Monitor.
10. Right-click the row for the Firefox process.
11. Take a screenshot. (See Figure 11-76.)
12. Select end process. (This is similar to the task you did in Windows Task Manager.)

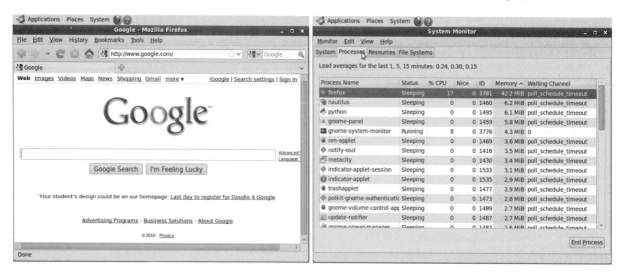

Figure 11-75: Started a Web browser.   Figure 11-76: List of processes.

13. Click on the Resources tab. (This will start the graphing functions for these resource meters.)

14. Return to your Firefox Web browser.
15. Click refresh (or press F5) 5-10 times. (This will put a load on the resource meters and make changes in the graphs.)
16. Return to the System Monitor.
17. Take a screenshot showing the changes in the resource meters. (See Figure 11-77.)
18. Click on the System tab.
19. Take a screenshot. (Your name should be showing in the computer name. See Figure 11-78.)

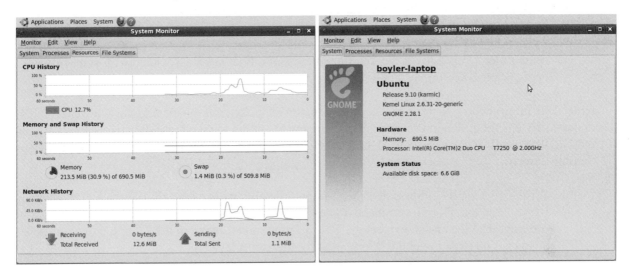

Figure 11-77: System monitors for CPU, memory, and bandwidth usage.

Figure 11-78: System information.

20. Click System, Preferences, and Network connections.
21. Select your wired network card. (In this case it was labeled Auto eth0. See Figure 11-79.)
22. Click Edit.
23. Take a screenshot showing the Wired tab and the MAC address of your virtual machine. (See Figure 11-80.)

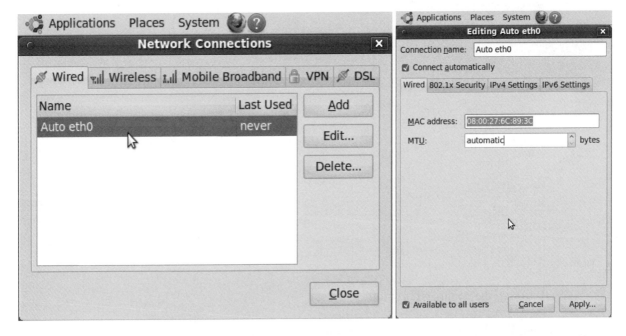

Figure 11-79: Network Connection settings per network card.

Figure 11-80: Network settings and MAC address.

24. Click on the IPv4 Settings tab.
25. Change the Method drop-down to Manual. (This will allow you to manually set your IP address, gateway, and subnet mask. You would do this if you had a static IP address that you didn't want to change.)
26. Click Applications, Accessories, and Terminal.
27. Type **su root**
28. Press Enter. (The ifconfig command requires root-level permission.)
29. Enter your root password.
30. Type **ifconfig**
31. Press Enter. (This will display the IP address and subnet mask associated with your virtual network card. See Figure 11-81.)

Note: This information was provided to your virtual machine by your host computer via DHCP. This is a dynamically changing IP address. For this project you are going to take these dynamic settings and use them to set your IP address as static (non-changing). You will enter this information into the IPv4 Settings screen.

32. Write down the IP addresses you see for the following parts of the eth0 settings displayed when you entered the ifconfig command. (The IP address assigned to your virtual machine might be different than the one shown below. This information is shown in the 2nd line down for each adapter. You want to get the information for the eth0 adapter.)

Inet addr: ____.____.____.____   (In this case it was 10.0.2.15.)
Mask: ____.____.____.____   (In this case it was 255.255.255.0.)

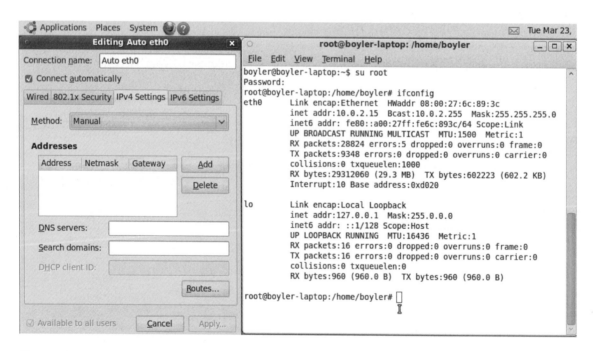

Figure 11-81: Results from the ifconfig command.

33. Return to the command prompt.
34. Type **route**
35. Press Enter. (The last line of your routing table (the default row) will display your gateway address. In this case it was 10.0.2.2.)

36. Type **cat /etc/resolv.conf**
37. Press Enter. (This will give a listing of the DNS servers your computer uses to resolve hostnames into IP addresses. In this case it was 68.87.85.102.)
38. Write down the correct IP addresses for your gateway and DNS.

Gateway: ____.____.____.____ (In this case it was 10.0.2.2.)
DNS: ____.____.____.____ (In this case it was 68.87.85.102.)

39. Enter the IP addresses for your computer, network mask, gateway, and DNS server.
40. Take a screenshot. (See Figure 11-82.)
41. Click Apply.
42. Enter your root password when prompted.

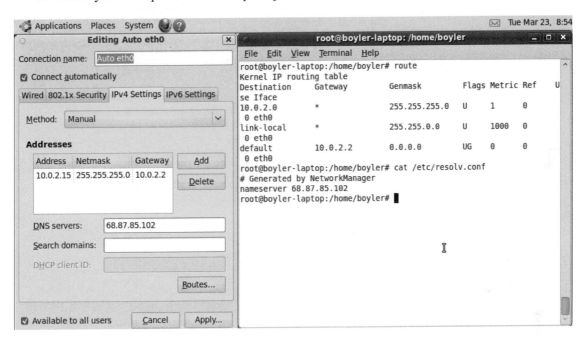

Figure 11-82: Showing the default gateway and DNS server from the route command and resolv.conf file.

43. Return to the command prompt.
44. Type **ifconfig eth0 down**
45. Press Enter. (This will disable the network interface. The number zero, not the letter "O," is used at the end of eth0.)
46. Type **ifconfig eth0 up**
47. Press Enter. (This will enable the network interface.)
48. Type **ifconfig**
49. Press Enter. (This will display the interface configuration information. See Figure 11-83.)

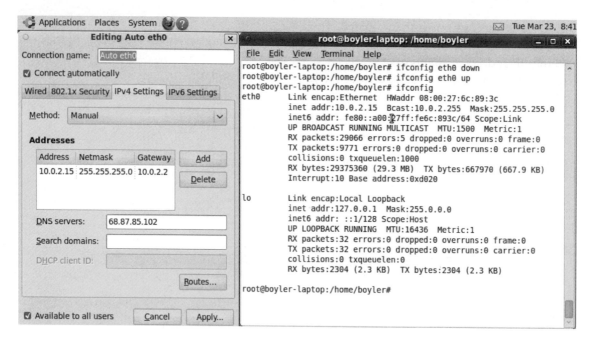

Figure 11-83: Static IP address is configured.

Note: The IP address for your computer is still the same one issued by the internal DHCP managed by VirtualBox. We can change the host IP address to confirm that it is a static IP address.

50. Return to the configuration screen for eth0.
51. Change your IP address by adding two to the fourth octet. (In this case it was changed from 10.0.2.15 to 10.0.2.17.)
52. Click Apply.
53. Enter your root password when prompted to do so.
54. Return to the command prompt.
55. Type **ifconfig eth0 down**
56. Press Enter. (This will disable the network interface.)
57. Type **ifconfig eth0 up**
58. Press Enter. (This will enable the network interface.)
59. Type **ifconfig**
60. Press Enter. (This will display the interface configuration information.)
61. Take a screenshot showing the changed IP address. (See Figure 11-84.)

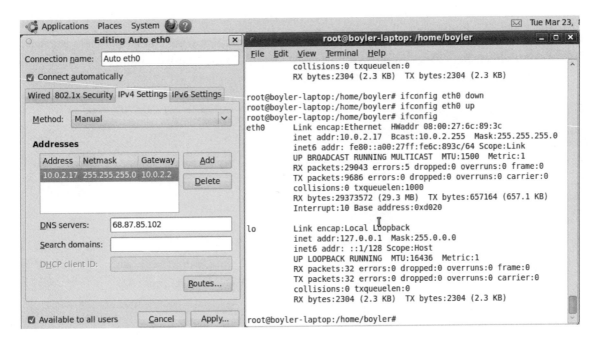

Figure 11-84: Results showing a changed static IP address.

62. Click Applications, Accessories, and Disk Usage Analyzer.
63. Click Analyzer and Scan Filesystem. (You can also press Ctrl-F. See Figure 11-85.)
64. Expand the tree under Home.
65. Click on your username. (In this case it was boyler.)
66. Take a screenshot. (You should see a graphical representation of which directories and/or files are using the most storage capacity on your virtual hard drive. See Figure 11-86.)
67. Close the Disk Usage Analyzer.

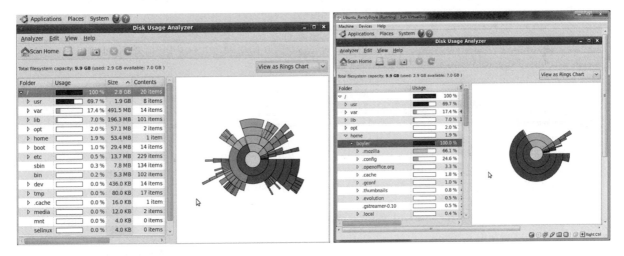

Figure 11-85: Disk usage for entire hard drive.

Figure 11-86: Disk usage for a specific user.

68. Click Applications, Internet, and Terminal Server Client.
69. Enter in the IP address of a remote Windows computer that you can access. (You must have a valid username and password to log in. You can use a classmate's computer, a computer set up by your instructor, or any other Windows computer to complete this project. See Figure 11-87.)
70. Enter your username and password for the remote Windows computer.
71. Click Connect.
72. Open a Web browser within the remote Windows computer.

73. Browse to www.Google.com.
74. Enter your name into the search box.
75. Take a screenshot of the remote Windows desktop within the Linux desktop. (Your name should appear in the search box. See Figure 11-88.)

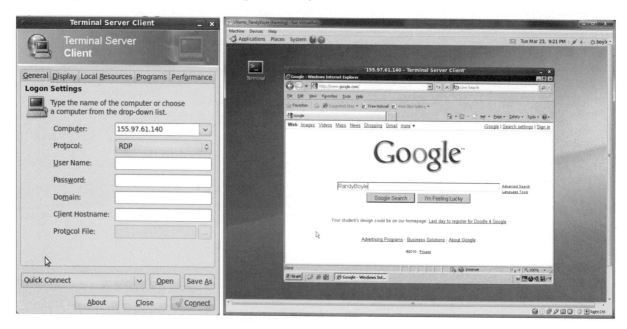

Figure 11-87: Terminal Server Client in Linux.   Figure 11-88: Remote desktop from Linux to Windows.

THOUGHT QUESTIONS

1. Is it easier to administer a network using DHCP or setting all IP addresses manually? Why?
2. Do certain computers need a static IP address? Why?
3. When will IPv6 be implemented (i.e. widely used)?
4. Can you have multiple concurrent users logged on to a Linux computer at the same time? Does this work in Windows?

11.6 USER AND GROUP MANAGEMENT

In this project you will add/remove users and groups using both graphical (GUI) and command-line (CLI) interfaces. You will add users to groups, learn how to reset a password, and lock/unlock an account. These are all common tasks performed by systems administrators.

Using the graphical interface to add/remove users is fairly intuitive. However, managing users via the command line is not. Repeated practice using the command line will make it second nature to you. This is also a good opportunity to compare the differences between GUI and CLI administration.

1. Open Sun VirtualBox by clicking Start, All Programs, Sun VirtualBox, and VirtualBox.
2. Select your Ubuntu virtual machine.
3. Click Start.
4. Login if you are not already logged in.
5. Click System, Administration, and Users and Groups.
6. Click the keys icon at the bottom of the screen so you can make changes.
7. Enter your root password.

8. Click Authenticate. (See Figure 11-89.)
9. Click Add User.
10. Enter a username. (This can be any username. Make sure it is lower-case with no spaces. In this case it was noah.)
11. Enter the user's real name. (In this case it was Noah Boyle.)
12. Set a password. (See Figure 11-90.)

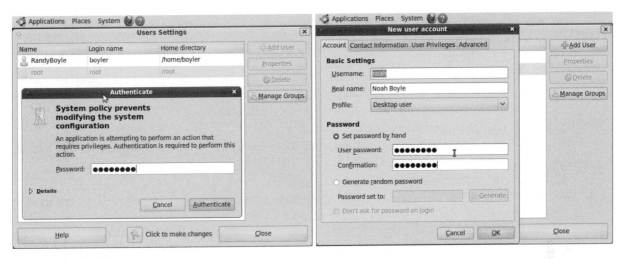

Figure 11-89: Entering the root password.

Figure 11-90: Adding a user.

13. Click on the User Privileges tab.
14. Click on the Administrator's group. (See Figure 11-91.)
15. Click OK.
16. Click Manage Groups.
17. Scroll down until you see a group labeled admin.
18. Select the admin group.
19. Click Properties.
20. Take a screenshot showing you and the new user as members of the admin group. (See Figure 11-92.)
21. Click OK.

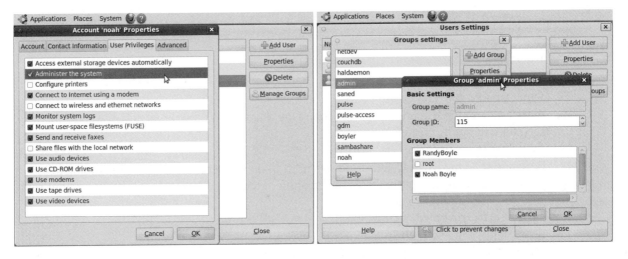

Figure 11-91: Adding a user to a group.

Figure 11-92: Verifying that the user was added to the group.

22. Click Add Group.

23. Enter "sales" for the group name. (Make sure the group name is lower-case.)
24. Select yourself and the new user to be members of this group.
25. Take a screenshot. (See Figure 11-93.)
26. Click OK.
27. Click Close and Close.
28. Click Applications, Accessories, and Terminal.
29. Type **users**
30. Press Enter. (This will give a listing of all users currently logged in. Since you are likely the only user logged in, you should only see yourself listed.)
31. Type **ls /home**
32. Press Enter. (This will display a listing of all the user directories. This gives you an idea of the users on this system as long as their accounts were created with the default values. To get a full listing of all accounts you can use `cat /etc/passwd`.)
33. Type **finger yournewuser**
34. Press Enter. (This will display information about the new user you just created. In this case the command was `finger noah`.)
35. Type **id yournewuser**
36. Press Enter. (This will display group membership for the new user you created. In this case the command was `id noah`. See Figure 11-94.)

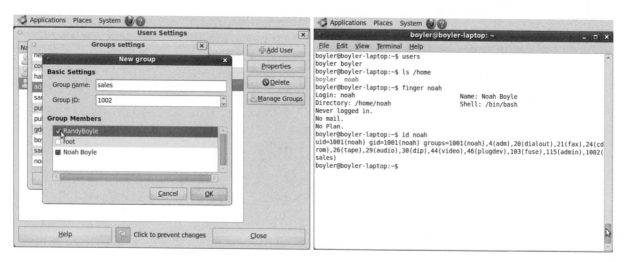

Figure 11-93: Creating a new group.　　　　　　Figure 11-94: Identifying users.

37. Type **clear**
38. Press Enter. (This will clear the screen.)
39. Type **useradd –m john**
40. Press Enter. (This will attempt to add John Doe as a user. You will get an error and John's account will not be created.)
41. Type **sudo useradd –m john**
42. Press Enter. (This will add John Doe as a user. Sudo runs the command with administrator privileges and the -m option forces the creation of the user's home directory. Enter your root password if prompted to do so.)
43. Type **sudo passwd john**
44. Press Enter. (This will set John Doe's password.)
45. Enter "john1234" as the password. (You will have to enter it twice.)
46. Type **ls /home**
47. Press Enter. (This will display a listing of all the user directories. You should see the new "john" directory.)

48. Take a screenshot. (See Figure 11-95.)

Note: It is good practice to use "sudo" to perform administrative tasks rather than being logged in as root. This helps prevent errors and system damage. There is also a log made each time sudo is used. You could complete the rest of this tutorial by logging in as root (su root). However, this project will use sudo.

49. Type **sudo useradd -c "Jane Doe" -m jane**
50. Press Enter. (This will add Jane Doe as a user and create her home directory. It will also enter her full name as a comment.)
51. Type **sudo passwd jane**
52. Press Enter. (This will set Jane Doe's password.)
53. Enter "jane4444" as the password. This is not a typo. You are intentionally entering Jane's password this way. You will reset it to jane1234 in the next step.
54. Type **sudo passwd jane**
55. Press Enter. (This will reset Jane's password. Resetting user passwords can be a common occurrence.)
56. Enter "jane1234" as the password.
57. Type **ls /home**
58. Press Enter. (This will provide a listing of all users and confirm that Jane Doe's account was created.)
59. Type **finger jane**
60. Press Enter. (Note that Jane Doe's full name is displayed. When you created John Doe's account you did NOT use the comment option (-c) and enter his full name. His full name will not be displayed.)
61. Take a screenshot. (See Figure 11-96.)

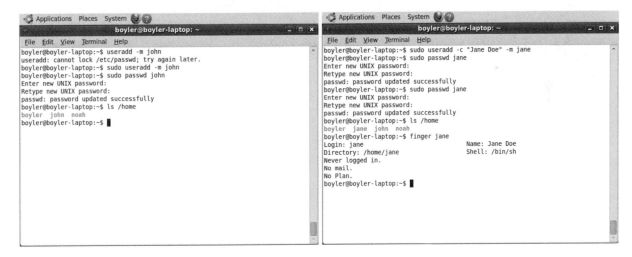

Figure 11-95: Adding a user.　　　　　　　　Figure 11-96: Adding a user and resetting the password.

62. Type **sudo usermod -L jane**
63. Press Enter. (This will lock Jane's account. This is useful if someone goes on vacation or needs to have their access disabled temporarily.)
64. Type **sudo passwd -S jane**
65. Press Enter. (This will provide the status of Jane's password. You will see an "L" for locked.)
66. Type **sudo usermod -U jane**
67. Press Enter. (This will unlock Jane's account.)
68. Type **sudo passwd -S jane**

69. Press Enter. (This will provide the status of Jane's password. You will see a "P" for passworded. This account is unlocked and Jane has access.)
70. Type `sudo userdel -r john`
71. Press Enter. (This will force the removal of John Doe's account and his home directory. This is useful if someone is permanently leaving the organization.)
72. Type `id john`
73. Press Enter. (You shouldn't see John listed.)
74. Type `ls /home`
75. Press Enter. (This will confirm that John Doe's account was deleted.)
76. Take a screenshot. (See Figure 11-97.)
77. Type `sudo groupadd nerds`
78. Press Enter. (This will add a group called nerds.)
79. Type `cat /etc/group`
80. Press Enter. (This will list all groups. Your new group should show up near the bottom of the list.)
81. Type `sudo groupmod -n techies nerds`
82. Press Enter. (This will change the group name from nerds to techies.)
83. Type `cat /etc/group`
84. Press Enter. (You should see the new group name.)
85. Type `sudo usermod -a -G techies jane`
86. Press Enter. (This will add Jane Doe to the techies group.)
87. Type `cat /etc/group`
88. Press Enter. (You should see Jane listed as a group member.)
89. Take a screenshot. (See Figure 11-98.)

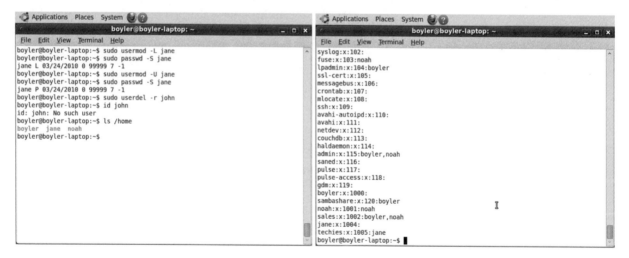

Figure 11-97: Locking/unlocking an account and deleting a user.　　Figure 11-98: Creating a group and adding a user to that group.

90. Type `sudo groupdel techies`
91. Press Enter. (This will delete the group called techies.)
92. Type `cat /etc/group`
93. Press Enter. (You shouldn't see the techies group anymore.)
94. Take a screenshot. (See Figure 11-99.)

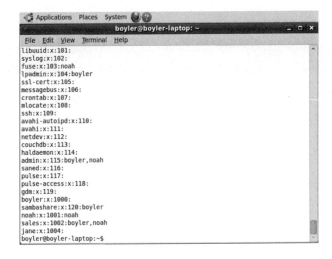

Figure 11-99: Deleting a group.

THOUGHT QUESTIONS

1. Was it faster to add a user using the GUI or CLI?
2. Can you set a user account to expire at a specific time?
3. Why are there default groups that are already created?
4. Can all users use the sudo command?

CHAPTER 12: CAREERS IN NETWORKING

Many people complete years of higher education without thinking about their future job prospects. They will spend hours studying for an exam but fail to spend 5 minutes looking up the average salary for their chosen vocation. They will spend many thousands of dollars investing in their education without considering how much, if any, payback they will get from their education. This is mind boggling.

This chapter will show you how to look up occupational statistics for your chosen career. If you haven't chosen a career, or are undecided, this is the perfect opportunity to do some research. You can get unbiased and independent information about job demand, job growth, and expected salaries per occupation.

This chapter will also explore IT certifications related to networking. Certifications are a good way to show that you have a minimum level of knowledge certified by an independent third-party. They also tell potential employers that you are a self-starter, motivated, ambitious, and can learn on your own. These are all critical attributes in the fast-changing IT landscape.

Finally, you will search Monster.com to look at actual job listings and salary figures. You will search for keywords and terms you learned in earlier projects. You will see the value prior projects have added to your future earnings potential. You will also see what skill sets, applications, and job requirements employers are looking for.

12.1 OCCUPATIONAL STATISTICS

In this project you will look at statistics related to networking jobs. For several years the demand for IT workers has been increasing. So have average annual wages for IT workers. Projects about future job demand and salary growth are also well above average. There will be more high-paying jobs for IT workers in the future.

The following sites allow you to search by a job code (e.g. 15-1071) or by job title. The data is aggregated by state but you can look up statistics for your individual city through the Department of Labor (http://www.dol.gov/dol/location.htm). The Department of Labor links to your local state government's Web page.

This project will give you an idea of what you can realistically expect to make on your future job. This project looks specifically at statistics for network administrators. However, you can also look at wage data for other occupations too.

1. Go to O*NET at http://online.onetcenter.org/. (See Figure 12-1.)
2. Enter "network administrator" into the Occupation Quick Search in the top right-hand of the screen.
3. Press Enter. (See Figure 12-2.)
4. Click on the first link. (In this case it was Network and Computer Systems Administrators.)

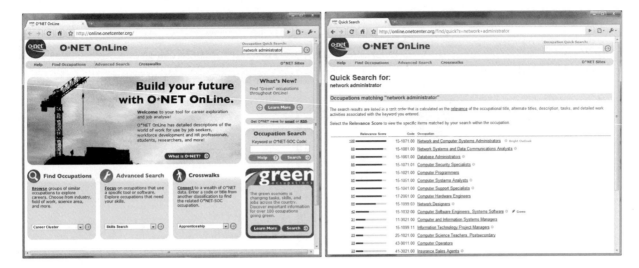

Figure 12-1: O*NET OnLine.

Figure 12-2: Search results for "network administrator."

5. Click on Wages & Employment Trends.
6. Take a screenshot. (See Figure 12-3.)
7. Select your state from the drop-down box. (In this case it was Utah.)
8. Click Go.
9. Scroll down to the State and National Wages section.
10. Click on the Yearly Wage Chart.
11. Take a screenshot. (See Figure 12-4.)

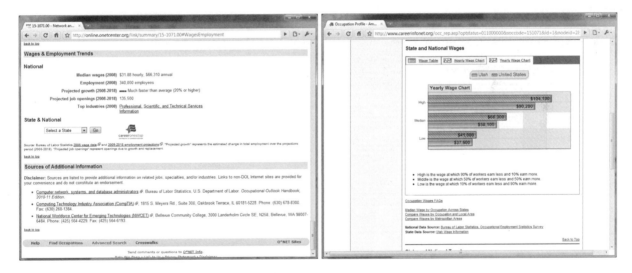

Figure 12-3: Wages and employment trends.

Figure 12-4: State and national wages.

12. Go to the U.S. Bureau of Labor Statistics at http://www.bls.gov/OES/. (See Figure 12-5.)
13. Click on Pay & Benefits.
14. Click Wages by Area and Occupation. (See Figure 12-6.)
15. Click the link labeled "By State" under the State Wage Data section.
16. Click on your state. (In this case it was Utah.)

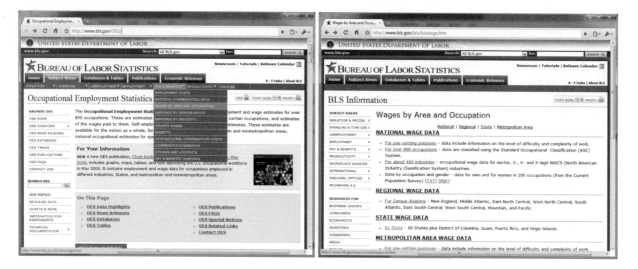

Figure 12-5: Bureau of Labor Statistics.

Figure 12-6: Wages by area and occupation.

17. Click on the link labeled "15-0000 Computer and Mathematical Science Occupations."
18. Take a screenshot. (See Figure 12-7.)
19. Click on the link labeled "Network Systems and Data Communications Analysts." (Note the mean annual wage.)
20. Click on the link labeled "State profile for this occupation."
21. Take a screenshot. (This will show you the states with the highest concentration of workers in this job category. It will also show you the states that have the highest annual salaries for this job category. See Figure 12-8.)

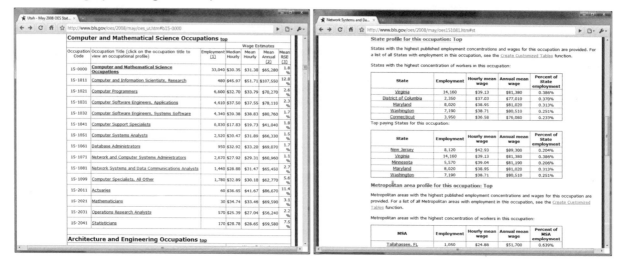

Figure 12-7: Wage estimates for computer and mathematical science occupations.

Figure 12-8: State profile for network systems and data communications analysts.

THOUGHT QUESTIONS

1. Could you find statistics for employment by city within your state? (Hint: U.S. Department of Labor at http://www.dol.gov/dol/location.htm.)
2. Is the demand for IT jobs (networking administrators) projected to increase more than the national average? Why?
3. Is the average salary for IT workers (networking administrators) projected to increase more than the national average? Why?
4. Why do you think the projections for job demand and salary increase for IT workers are so high?

12.2 IT CERTIFICATIONS

In this project you are going to look at three companies offering networking certifications. You will look at certifications from MCSE (Microsoft), CCIE (Cisco), and Network+ (CompTIA). There are other networking certifications available. These are just a sampling of the networking certifications available. There are also certifications in other areas including database, programming, project management, Linux, etc.

You will also look up the median salary per certification at PayScale.com. Not all certifications add the same amount of value to your annual salary. Certifications can vary in value from year to year depending on supply and demand. It is a good idea to look up the added value for a certification before you get it. In general, more certifications will yield a higher annual salary.

1. Go to Microsoft Learning at http://www.microsoft.com/learning/. (See Figure 12-9.)
2. Point to the Certification tab, point to By Name, and then click MCSE.
3. Take a screenshot. (See Figure 12-10.)

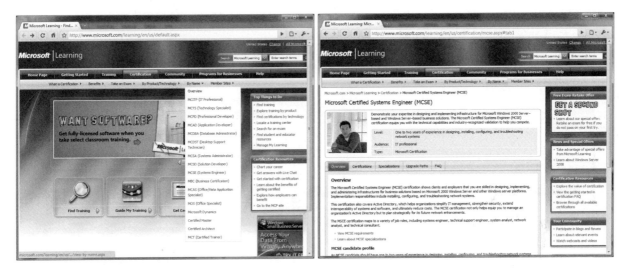

Figure 12-9: Microsoft Learning.   Figure 12-10: Microsoft Certified Systems Engineer (MCSE) overview.

4. Go to Cisco's Training and Events page at http://www.cisco.com/web/learning/. (See Figure 12-11.)
5. Click on the link labeled CCIE under the Certifications section.
6. Click on the link labeled Track Comparison under the Select a Track section.
7. Take a screenshot. (You should see a comparison of the CCIE tracks. See Figure 12-12.)

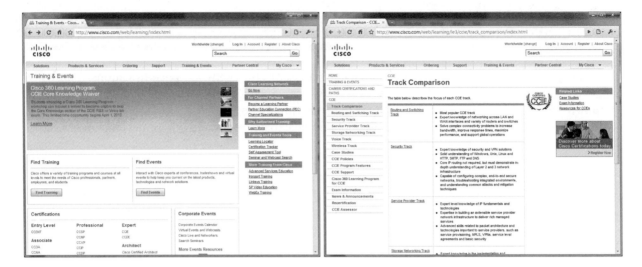

Figure 12-11: Cisco training and events.

Figure 12-12: Cisco Certified Internetwork Expert (CCIE) track comparison.

8. Go to CompTIA at http://www.comptia.org. (See Figure 12-13.)
9. Click on the Certifications and Exams tab.
10. Click on CompTIA Certifications and then Network+ in the left-hand navigation pane.
11. Take a screenshot. (You should see detailed information about the Network+ exam. See Figure 12-14.)

Figure 12-13: CompTIA certifications.

Figure 12-14: CompTIA Network+.

12. Go to PayScale's Certification Index at http://www.payscale.com/index/US/Certification .
13. Scroll down until you see Cisco Certified Internetwork Expert (CCIE).
14. Click on the link labeled Cisco Certified Internetwork Expert (CCIE). (See Figure 12-15.)
15. Click on the link labeled By Years Experience. (See Figure 12-16.)
16. Take a screenshot.

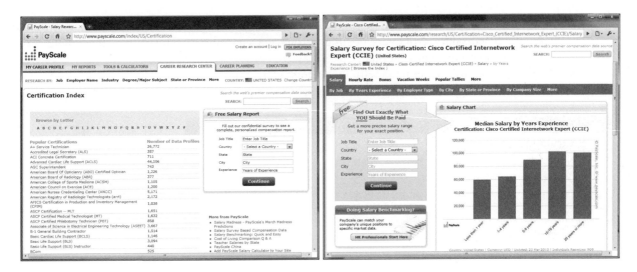

Figure 12-15: PayScale certification index.

Figure 12-16: CCIE median salary by years of experience.

THOUGHT QUESTIONS

1. If you were CCIE certified would you get paid more by a hospital or a school?
2. Do larger cities pay larger salaries? Why?
3. How many exams do you have to pass to be MCSE certified?
4. Where can you go to take a certification exam?

12.3 JOB SEARCH

In this project you are going to search Monster.com for several applications, operating systems, and keywords. You will then look at three to four salary listings and estimate an average salary for each keyword. Include these tables with the screenshots for this chapter.

1. Go to www.Monster.com.
2. Search for each of the keywords listed in Table 12-1 below.
3. Write down an estimated average salary for the first 3-4 jobs listed. (Click on the Salary link to view the listed salary. Not every posting will have a salary listed. This is just an estimate. You don't have to do any calculations.)
4. Reproduce the following table with the estimated average salary column completed.
5. Include this completed table with your screenshots.

	Application/OS	Estimated Average Salary
1	OPNET IT Guru	$
2	Apache	$
3	IIS	$
4	Windows Server 2003	$
5	Windows Server 2008	$
6	Windows Active Directory	$
7	Debian, Fedora, Ubuntu	$

Table 12-1: Estimated average salary by application or operating system.

6. Search for each of the keywords listed in Table 12-2 below.

7. Write down an estimated average salary for the first 3-4 jobs listed. (Click on the Salary link to view the listed salary. Not every posting will have a salary listed. This is just an estimate. You don't have to do any calculations.)
8. Reproduce the following table with the estimated average salary column completed.
9. Include this completed table with your screenshots.

	Keyword	Average Listed Salary
1	Virtualization	$
2	Network administrator	$
3	Linux	$
4	TCP/IP	$
5	DNS	$
6	Firewall	$

Table 12-2: Estimated average salary by keyword.

THOUGHT QUESTIONS

1. What was the highest salary listed for "network administrator" in your search results?
2. Were there more jobs listed for IIS or Apache? Why?
3. What would an average listed salary be if you searched for "CCIE"?
4. If you restricted the search to only show jobs in your state do you think the average salary would be higher or lower?

APPENDIX

A.1   LINKS TO SOFTWARE

Below is a listing of the software, and accompanying URLs, used in this book. Web links don't last forever and it's likely by the time you pick up this book at least one of the links listed below is out of date. There will also be newer versions of the software.

If a link below is broken, chances are you will be able to find the software listed somewhere on the main page of the listed domain. You can also search for the name of the software through www.Google.com or www.Yahoo.com. Download the latest version of each piece of software.

Name	Size	Link
OpenOffice	150 MB	http://www.openoffice.org/
Microsoft PowerShell	6 MB	http://www.microsoft.com/powershell
VMware Player	92 MB	http://www.vmware.com/download/player/download.html
BgInfo	400 KB	http://technet.microsoft.com/en-us/sysinternals/bb897557.aspx
Process Explorer	1 MB	http://technet.microsoft.com/en-us/sysinternals/bb896653.aspx
Process Monitor	1 MB	http://technet.microsoft.com/en-us/sysinternals/bb896645.aspx
7-Zip	1 MB	http://www.7-zip.org/download.html
MWSnap	600 KB	http://www.mirekw.com/winfreeware/mwsnap.html
BackTrack	2.1 GB	http://www.backtrack-linux.org/downloads/
Ubuntu	706 MB	http://www.ubuntu.com/
VirtualBox	72 MB	http://www.virtualbox.org/wiki/Downloads
Windows XP Mode and Virtual PC	481 MB	http://www.microsoft.com/windows/virtual-pc/download.aspx
Virtual PC	30 MB	http://www.microsoft.com/downloads/details.aspx?FamilyId=04D26402-3199-48A3-AFA2-2DC0B40A73B6&displaylang=en
Windows XP virtual machine	846 MB	http://www.microsoft.com/downloads/details.aspx?FamilyId=21EABB90-958F-4B64-B5F1-73D0A413C8EF&displaylang=en
Windows Server 2003 virtual machine	2 GB	http://www.microsoft.com/DOWNLOADS/details.aspx?familyid=77F24C9D-B4B8-4F73-99E3-C66F80E415B6&displaylang=en
Windows Server 2008 virtual machine	2 GB	http://www.microsoft.com/downloads/details.aspx?FamilyID=764b531e-4526-4329-80b5-921fd3297883&displaylang=en
Pendrivelinux	536 MB	http://www.pendrivelinux.com/
Pendriveapps	-	http://www.pendriveapps.com/

LiveUSB Creator	8 MB	https://fedorahosted.org/liveusb-creator/
Wireshark	18 MB	http://www.wireshark.org/download.html
OPNET IT Guru	48 MB	http://www.opnet.com/university_program/index.html
InSSIDer	2 MB	http://www.metageek.net/products/inssider
Ekahau HeatMapper	52 MB	http://www.ekahau.com/products/heatmapper/overview.html
Apache Web server	5 MB	http://httpd.apache.org/download.cgi
Screenshot Pilot	3 MB	http://www.colorpilot.com/screenshot.html
Fedora KDE	697 MB	http://fedoraproject.org/get-fedora-kde